TOKYO MEW MEW

MIA IKUMI & REIKO YOSHIDA

VOLUME ONE

TOKYOPOP®

HAMBURG // LONDON // LOS ANGELES // TOKYO

Tokyo Mew Mew Vol. 1
Created by Mia Ikumi and Reiko Yoshida

Translation - Ikoi Hiroe
English Adaptation - Stuart Hazleton
Editors - Amy Court Kaemon and Jodi Bryson
Retouch and Lettering - Anna Kernbaum
Production Artist - Monalisa de Asis
Cover Design - Patrick Hook

Senior Editor - Julie Taylor
Digital Imaging Manager - Chris Buford
Pre-Press Manager - Antonio DePietro
Production Managers - Jennifer Miller and Mutsumi Miyazaki
Art Director - Matt Alford
Managing Editor - Jill Freshney
VP of Production - Ron Klamert
Editor-in-Chief - Mike Kiley
President and C.O.O. - John Parker
Publisher and C.E.O. - Stuart Levy

A  Manga

TOKYOPOP Inc.
5900 Wilshire Blvd. Suite 2000
Los Angeles, CA 90036

E-mail: info@TOKYOPOP.com
Come visit us online at www.TOKYOPOP.com

ISBN: 1-59182-236-X

First TOKYOPOP printing: April 2003
14 13 12 11 10 9 8 7 6
Printed in the USA

東京(とうきょう)ミュウミュウ

TOKYO MEW MEW

1

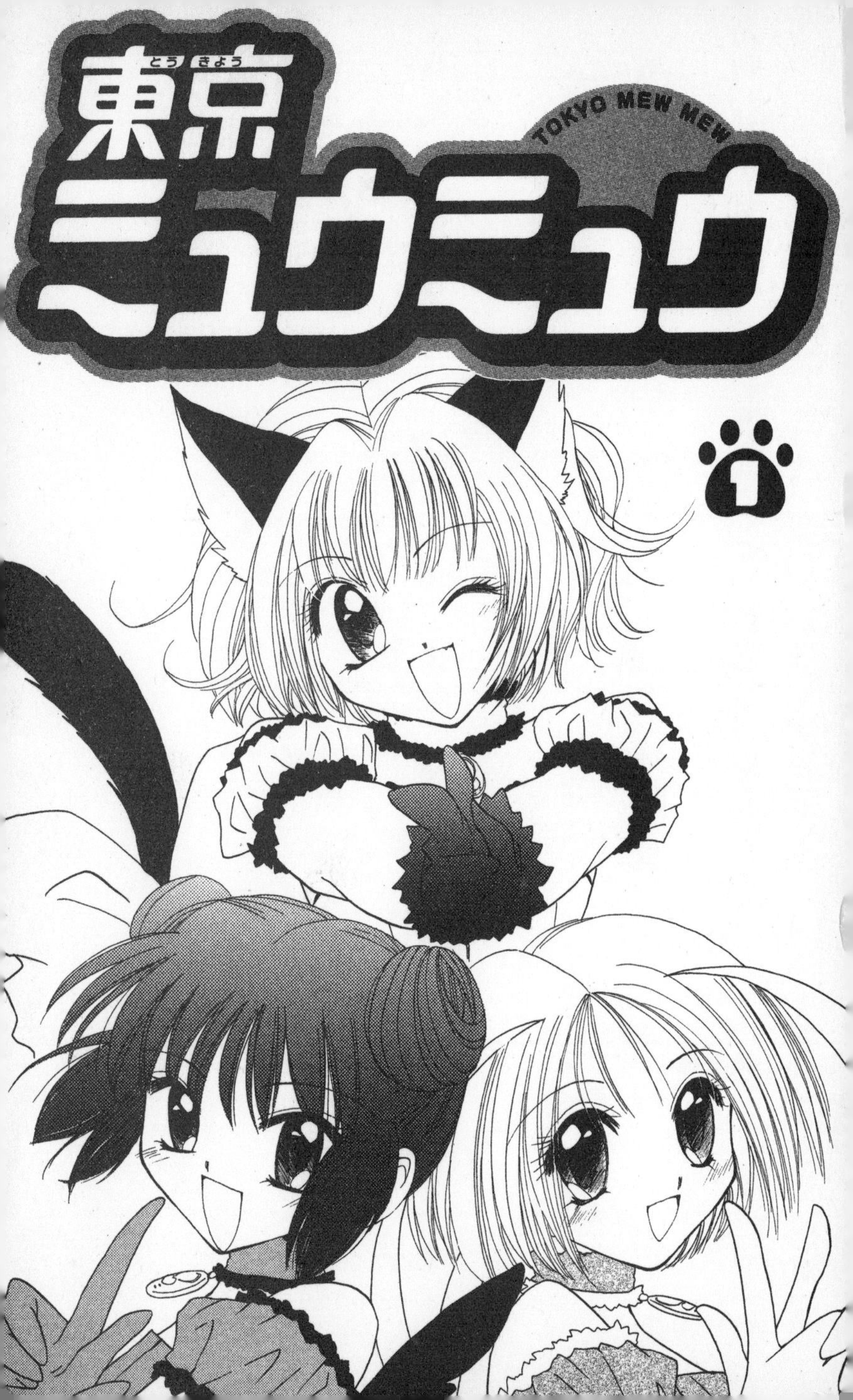

ALSO AVAILABLE FROM ⊙TOKYOPOP®

MANGA

ANGELIC LAYER*
BABY BIRTH* (September 2003)
BATTLE ROYALE*
BRAIN POWERED* (June 2003)
BRIGADOON* (August 2003)
CARDCAPTOR SAKURA
CARDCAPTOR SAKURA: MASTER OF THE CLOW*
CLAMP SCHOOL DETECTIVES*
CHOBITS*
CHRONICLES OF THE CURSED SWORD (July 2003)
CLOVER
CONFIDENTIAL CONFESSIONS* (July 2003)
CORRECTOR YUI
COWBOY BEBOP*
COWBOY BEBOP: SHOOTING STAR* (June 2003)
DEMON DIARY (May 2003)
DIGIMON
DRAGON HUNTER (June 2003)
DRAGON KNIGHTS*
DUKLYON: CLAMP SCHOOL DEFENDERS* (September 2003)
ERICA SAKURAZAWA* (May 2003)
ESCAFLOWNE* (July 2003)
FAKE*(May 2003)
FLCL* (September 2003)
FORBIDDEN DANCE* (August 2003)
GATE KEEPERS*
G-GUNDAM* (June 2003)
GRAVITATION* (June 2003)
GTO*
GUNDAM WING
GUNDAM WING: ENDLESS WALTZ*
GUNDAM: THE LAST OUTPOST*
HAPPY MANIA*
HARLEM BEAT
INITIAL D*
I.N.V.U.
ISLAND
JING: KING OF BANDITS* (June 2003)
JULINE
KARE KANO*
KINDAICHI CASE FILES* (June 2003)
KING OF HELL (June 2003)

KODOCHA*
LOVE HINA*
LUPIN III*
MAGIC KNIGHT RAYEARTH* (August 2003)
MAN OF MANY FACES* (May 2003)
MARMALADE BOY*
MARS*
MIRACLE GIRLS
MIYUKI-CHAN IN WONDERLAND* (October 2003)
MONSTERS, INC.
NIEA_7* (August 2003)
PARADISE KISS*
PARASYTE
PEACH GIRL
PEACH GIRL: CHANGE OF HEART*
PET SHOP OF HORRORS* (June 2003)
PLANET LADDER
PLANETS* (October 2003)
PRIEST
RAGNAROK
RAVE*
REAL BOUT HIGH SCHOOL*
REALITY CHECK
REBIRTH
REBOUND*
SABER MARIONETTE J* (July 2003)
SAILOR MOON
SAINT TAIL
SAMURAI DEEPER KYO* (June 2003)
SCRYED*
SHAOLIN SISTERS*
SHIRAHIME-SYO* (December 2003)
THE SKULL MAN*
SORCERER HUNTERS
TOKYO MEW MEW*
UNDER A GLASS MOON (June 2003)
VAMPIRE GAME* (June 2003)
WILD ACT* (July 2003)
WISH*
X-DAY* (August 2003)
ZODIAC P.I.* (July 2003)

CINE-MANGA™

AKIRA*
CARDCAPTORS
JIMMY NEUTRON (COMING SOON)
KIM POSSIBLE
LIZZIE McGUIRE
SPONGEBOB SQUAREPANTS (COMING SOON)
SPY KIDS 2

NOVELS

SAILOR MOON
KARMA CLUB (COMING SOON)

TOKYOPOP KIDS

STRAY SHEEP (September 2003)

ART BOOKS

CARDCAPTOR SAKURA*
MAGIC KNIGHT RAYEARTH*

ANIME GUIDES

GUNDAM TECHNICAL MANUALS
COWBOY BEBOP
SAILOR MOON SCOUT GUIDES

TABLE OF CONTENTS

IN THE BEGINNING...6

BONUS QUIZ...170

BEFORE TOKYO MEW MEW WAS CREATED...171

WHO IS THIS CHARACTER?....................172

PHOTO SHOOT REPORT.........................174

AFTERWARD..177

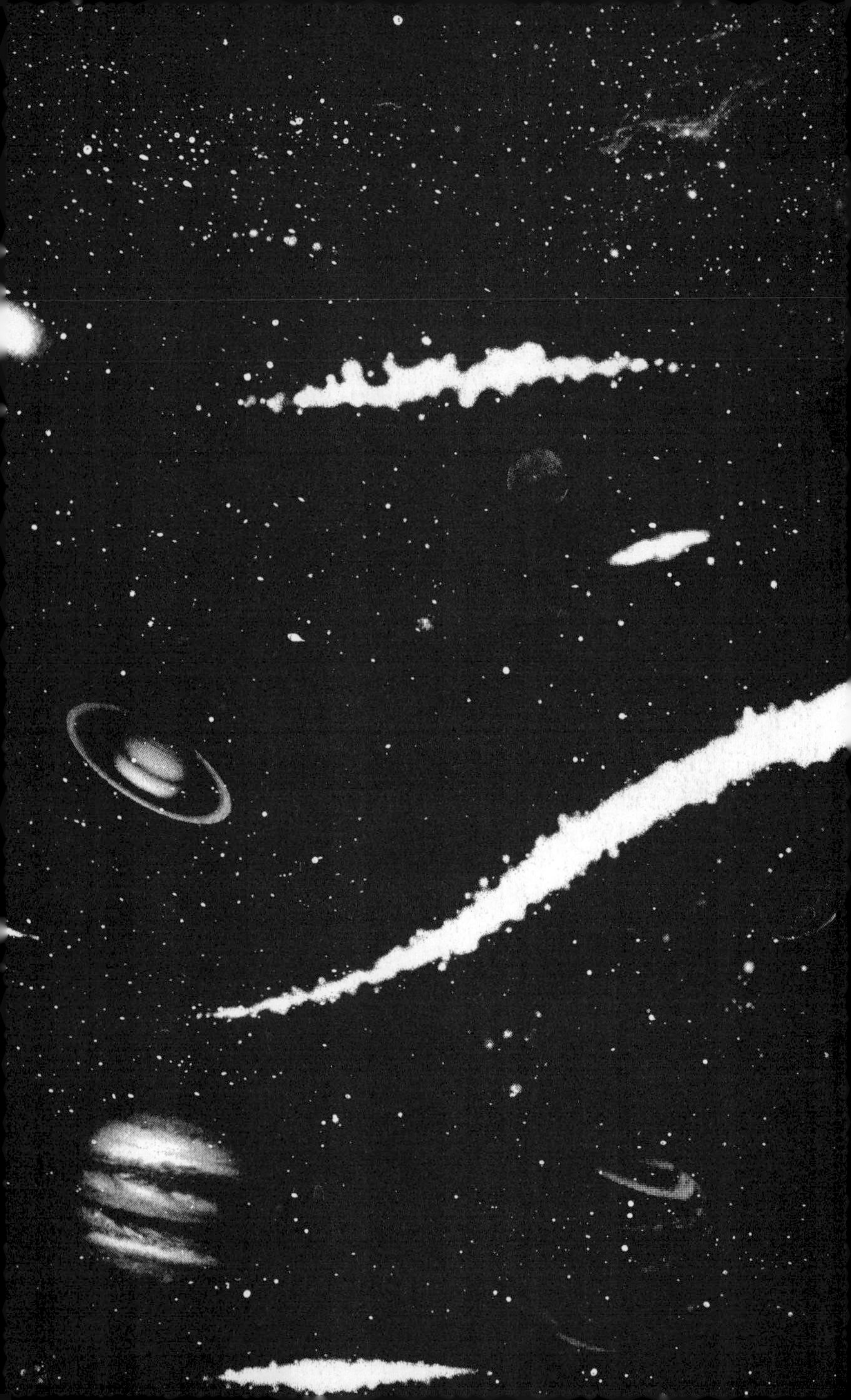

EARTH... A BEAUTIFUL, BLUE PLANET FILLED WITH MILLIONS OF LIFE FORMS.
EARTH
TODAY, HOWEVER, THERE ARE AROUND 2,580 SPECIES OF ANIMALS FACING EXTINCTION ON THIS PLANET.
IT IS TIME TO STAND UP AGAINST THIS DESTRUCTION...
...NOW.

東京ミュウミュウ

TOKYO MEW MEW

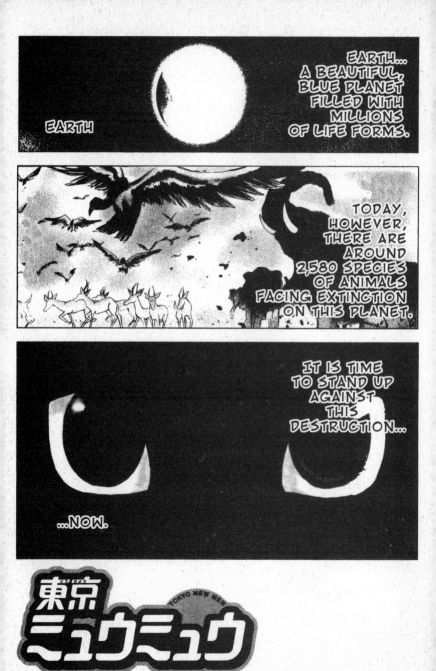

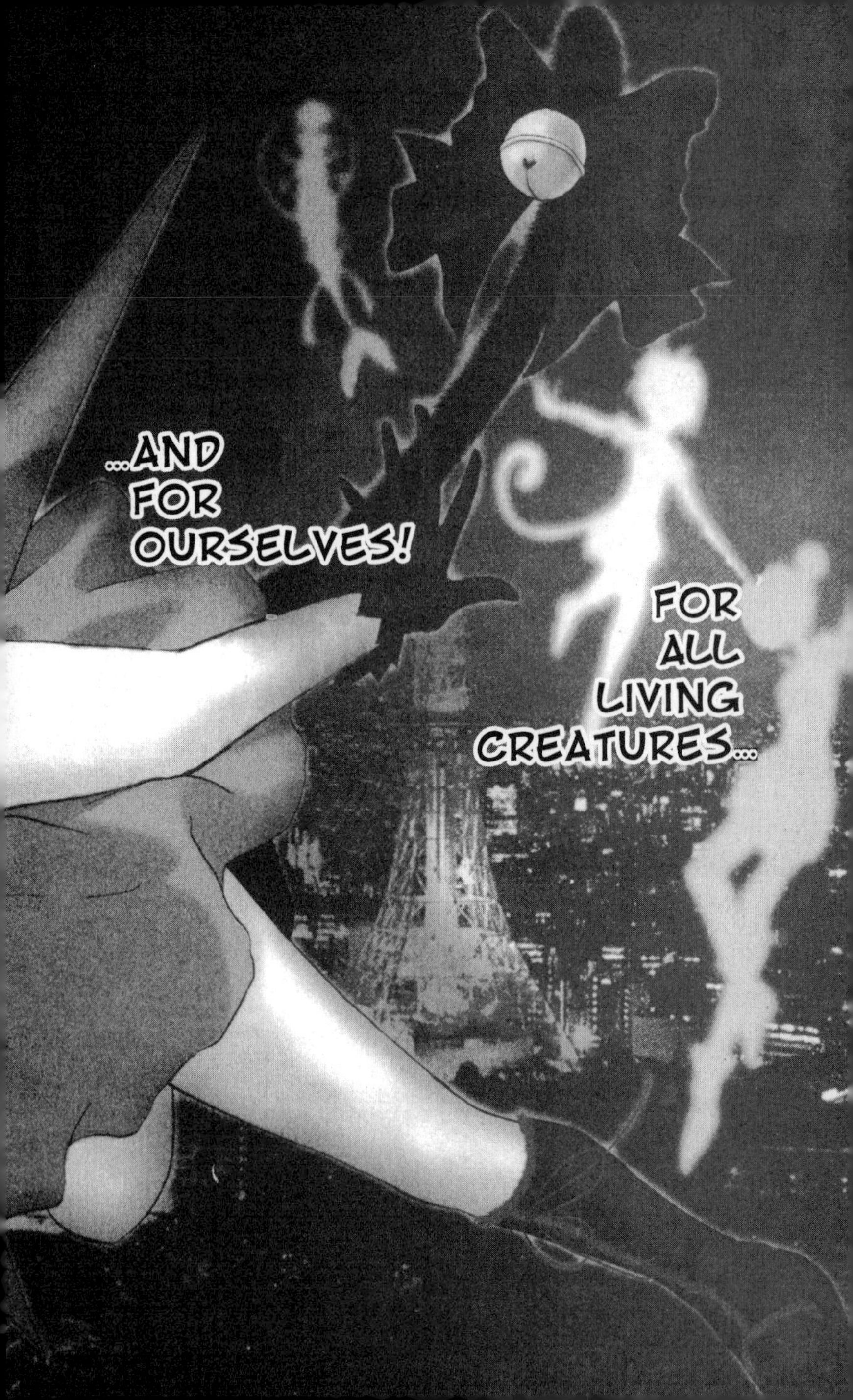
FOR ALL LIVING CREATURES...
...AND FOR OURSELVES!

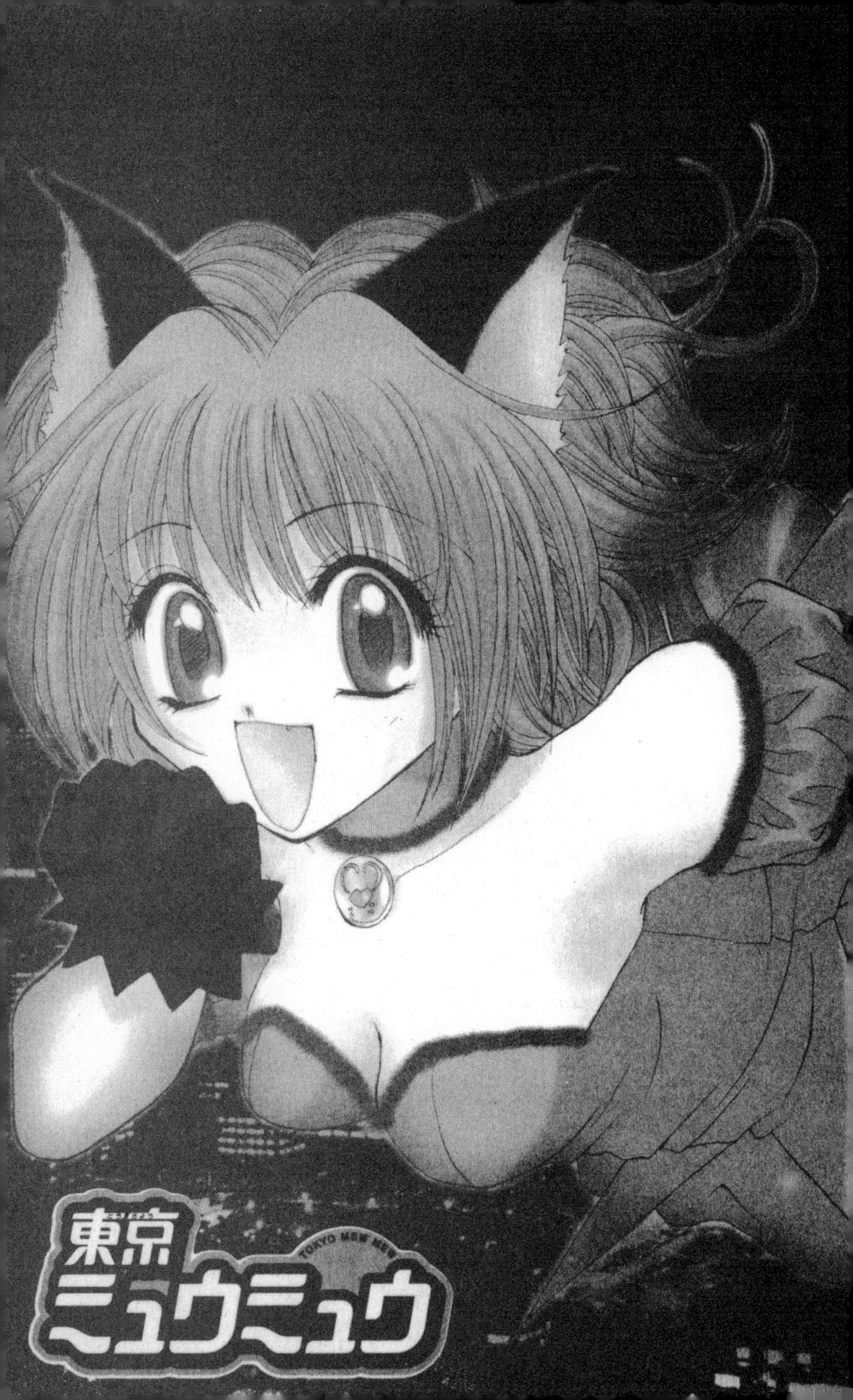
東京ミュウミュウ
TOKYO MEW MEW

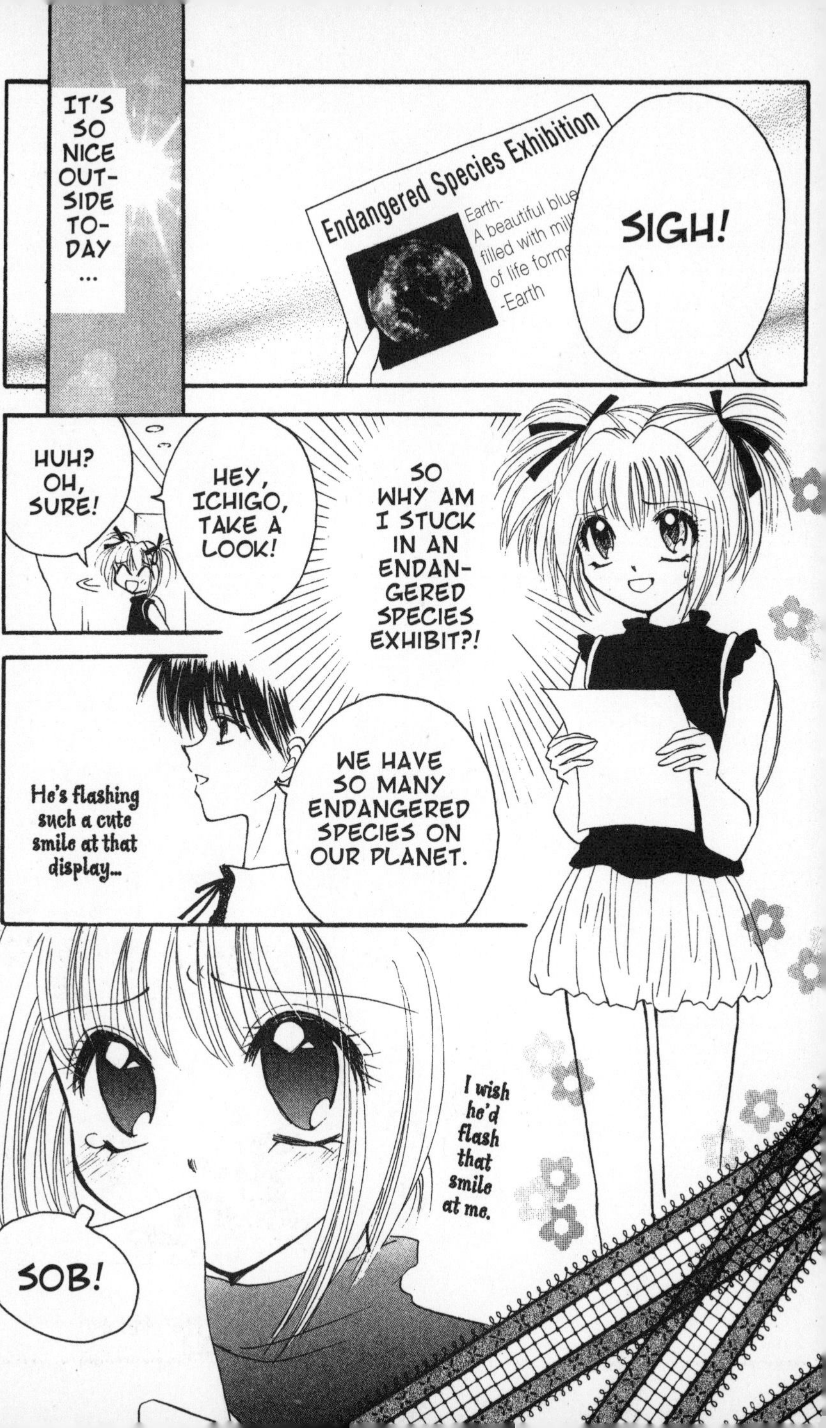
IT'S SO NICE OUT-SIDE TO-DAY...
Endangered Species Exhibition
Earth- A beautiful blue filled with mil of life forms -Earth
SIGH!
HEY, ICHIGO, TAKE A LOOK!
HUH? OH, SURE!
SO WHY AM I STUCK IN AN ENDAN-GERED SPECIES EXHIBIT?!
WE HAVE SO MANY ENDANGERED SPECIES ON OUR PLANET.
He's flashing such a cute smile at that display...
I wish he'd flash that smile at me.
SOB!

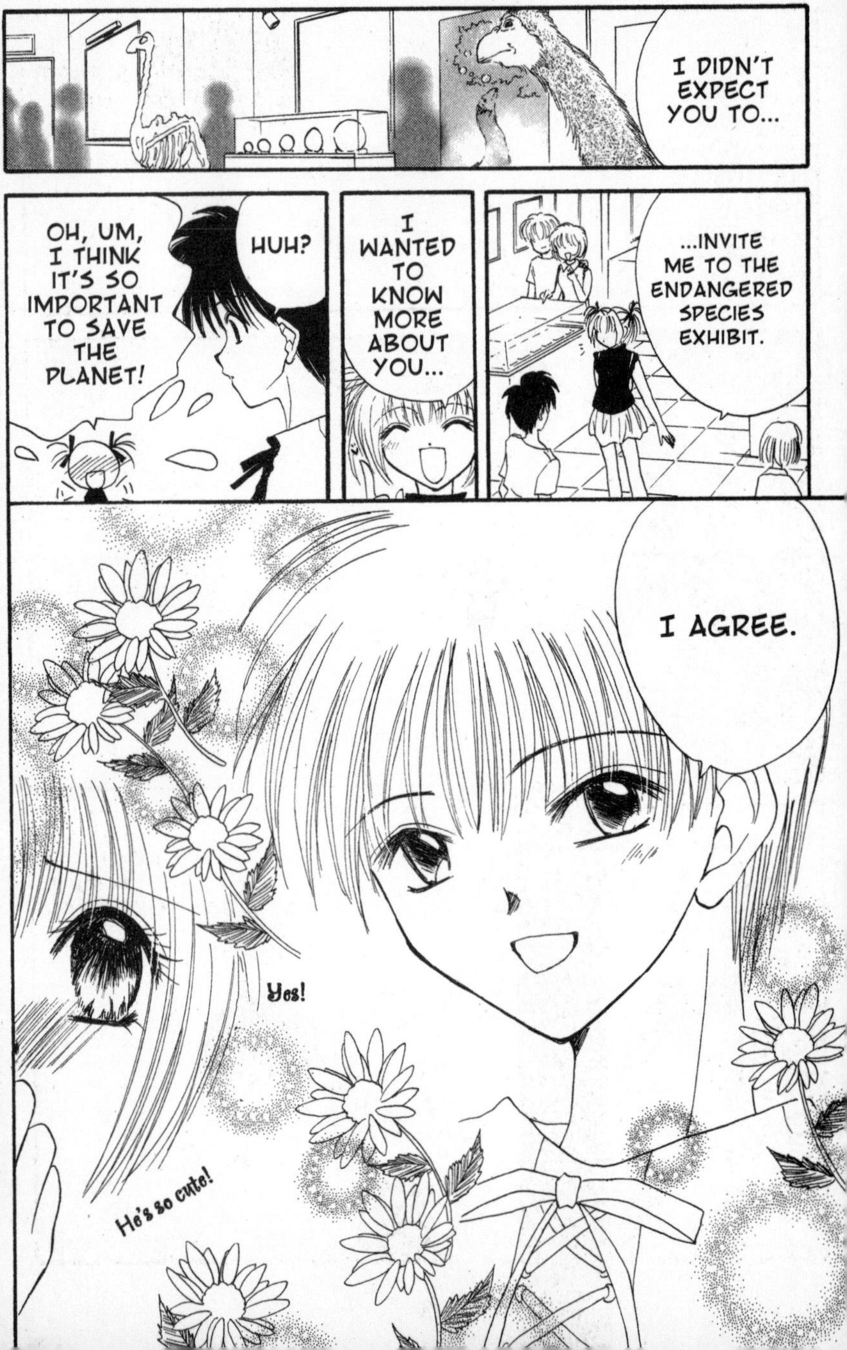
I DIDN'T EXPECT YOU TO...
...INVITE ME TO THE ENDANGERED SPECIES EXHIBIT.
I WANTED TO KNOW MORE ABOUT YOU...
HUH?
OH, UM, I THINK IT'S SO IMPORTANT TO SAVE THE PLANET!
I AGREE.
Yes!
He's so cute!

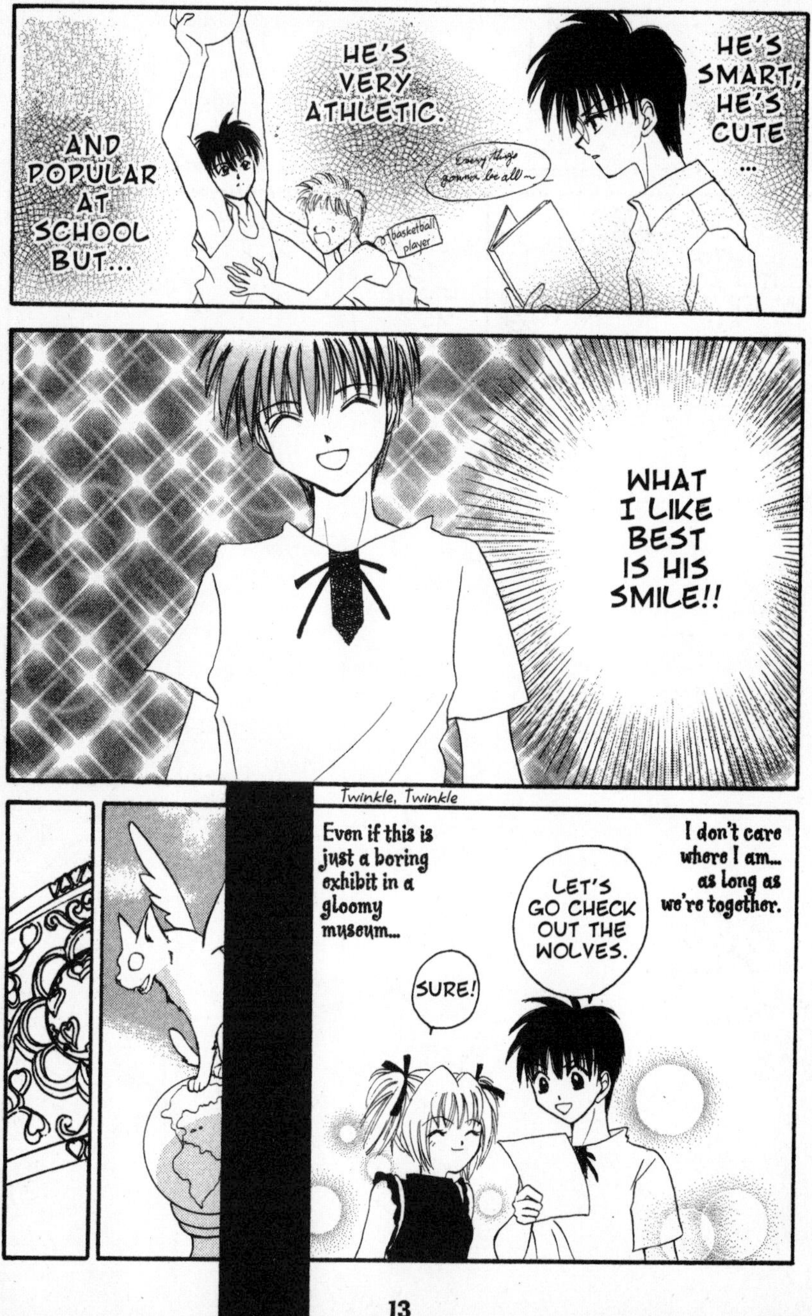
HE'S SMART, HE'S CUTE ...
HE'S VERY ATHLETIC.
Everything's gonna be all ~
basketball player
AND POPULAR AT SCHOOL BUT...
WHAT I LIKE BEST IS HIS SMILE!!
Twinkle, Twinkle
I don't care where I am... as long as we're together.
LET'S GO CHECK OUT THE WOLVES.
Even if this is just a boring exhibit in a gloomy museum...
SURE!

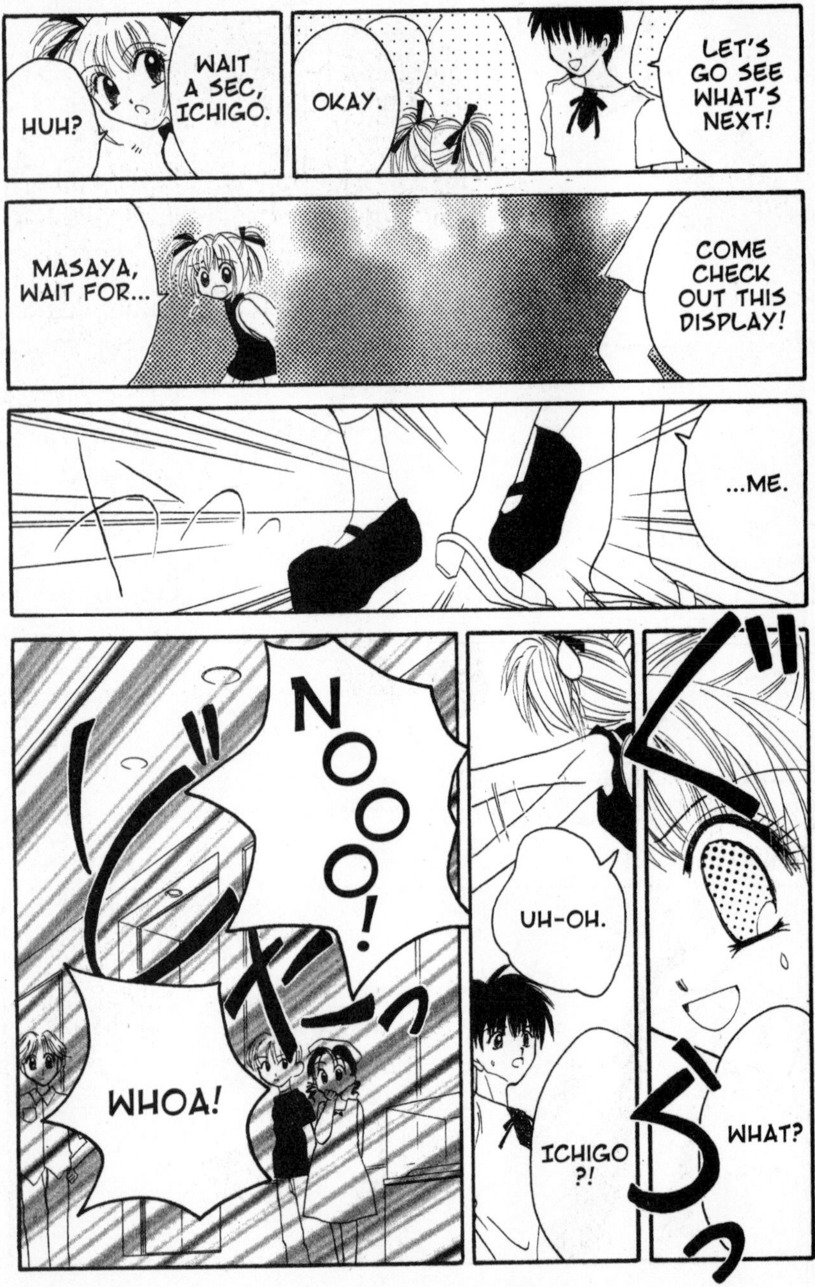
LET'S GO SEE WHAT'S NEXT!
OKAY.
WAIT A SEC, ICHIGO.
HUH?
COME CHECK OUT THIS DISPLAY!
MASAYA, WAIT FOR...
...ME.
WHAT?
UH-OH.
ICHIGO ?!
NOOOO!
WHOA!

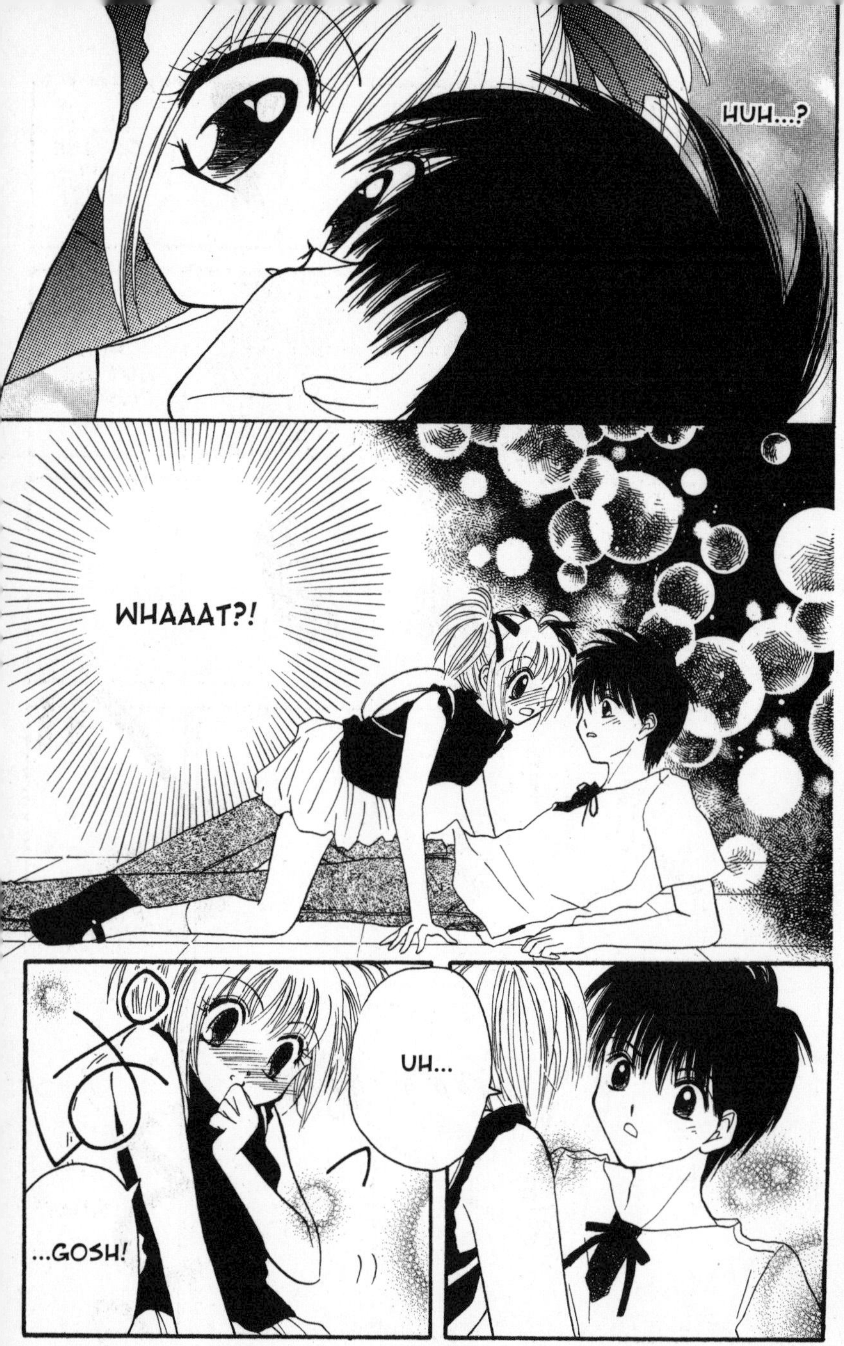
HUH...?
WHAAAT?!
UH...
...GOSH!

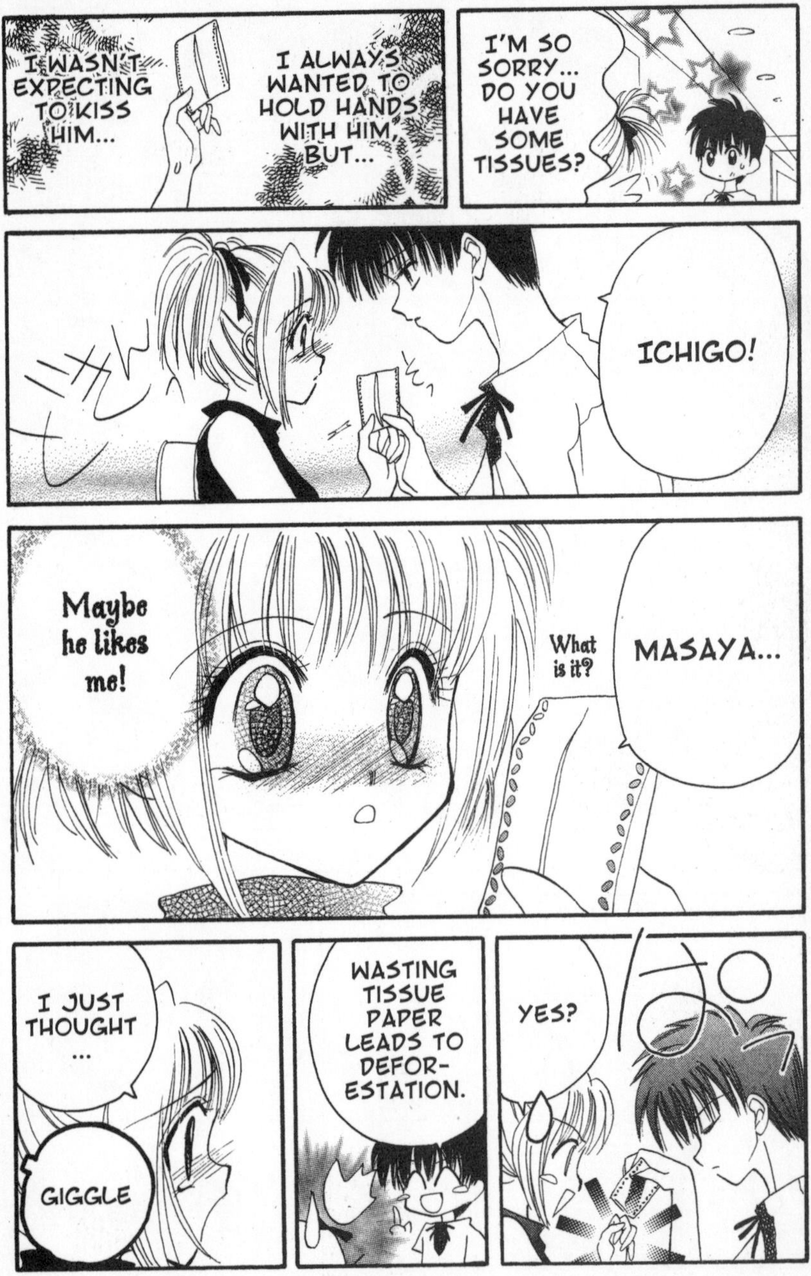
I'M SO SORRY... DO YOU HAVE SOME TISSUES?
I ALWAYS WANTED TO HOLD HANDS WITH HIM, BUT...
I WASN'T EXPECTING TO KISS HIM...
ICHIGO!
MASAYA...
What is it?
Maybe he likes me!
YES?
WASTING TISSUE PAPER LEADS TO DEFOR-ESTATION.
I JUST THOUGHT ...
GIGGLE

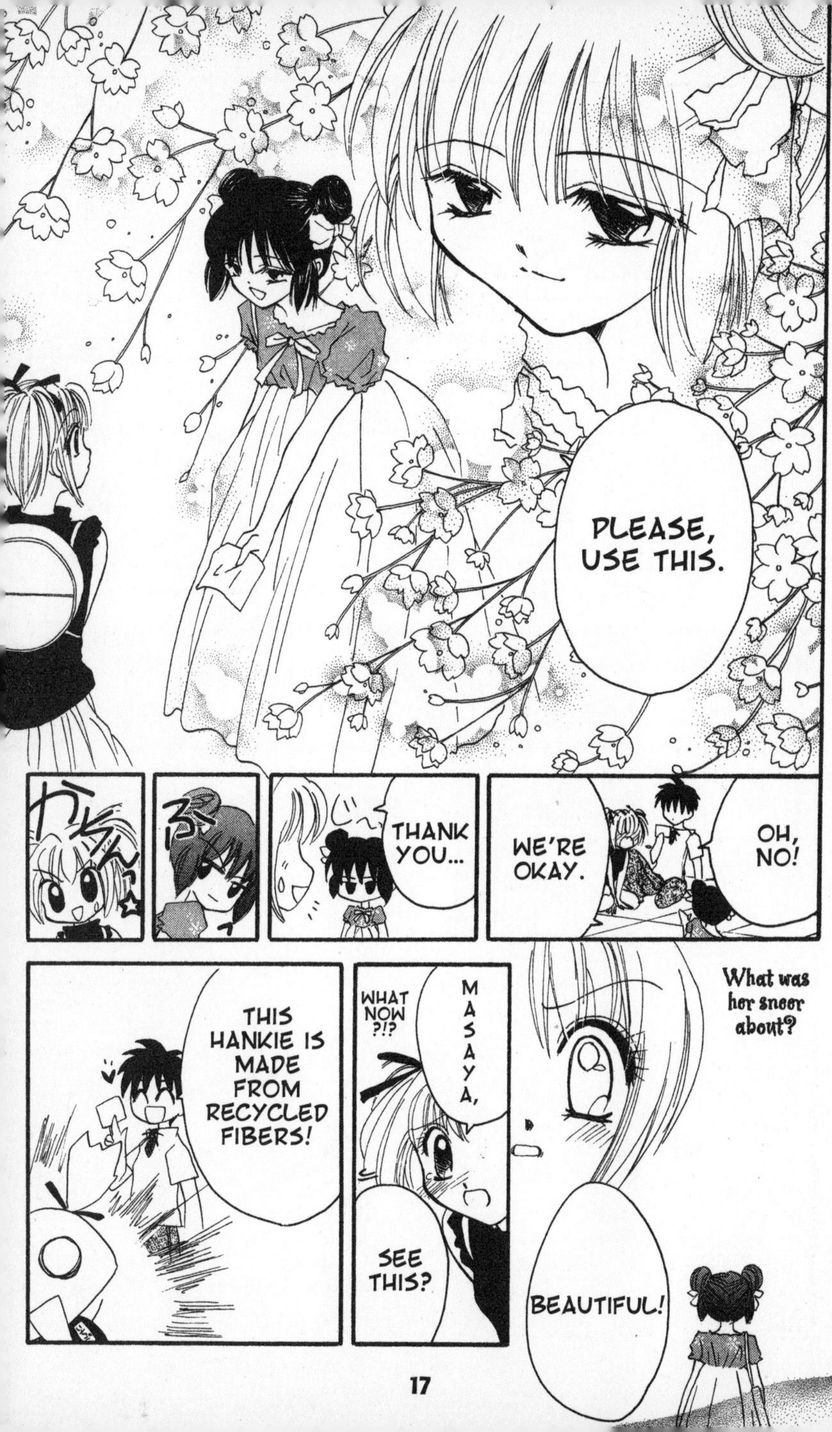
PLEASE, USE THIS.
OH, NO!
WE'RE OKAY.
THANK YOU...
What was her sneer about?
BEAUTIFUL!
MASAYA,
SEE THIS?
WHAT NOW ?!?
THIS HANKIE IS MADE FROM RECYCLED FIBERS!

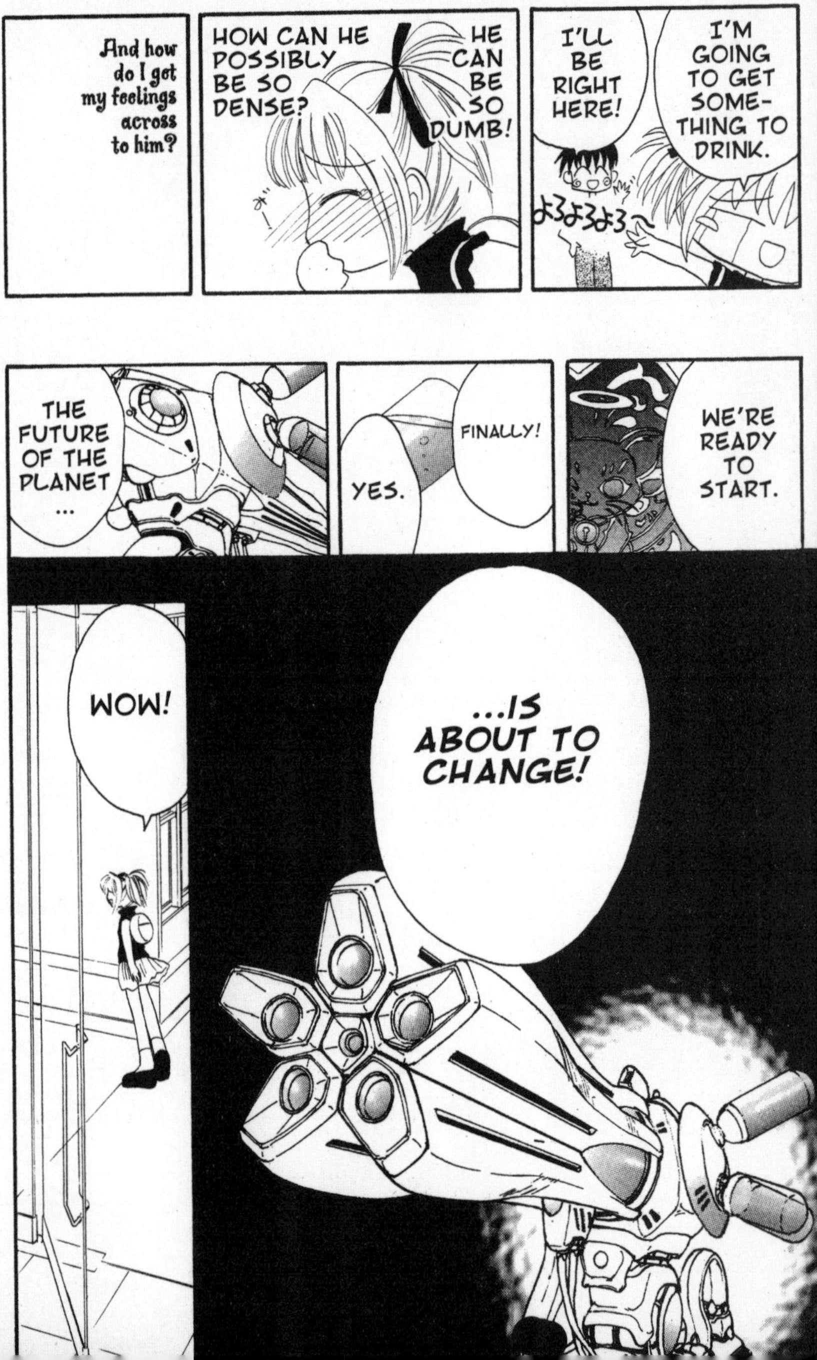
I'M GOING TO GET SOME-THING TO DRINK.
I'LL BE RIGHT HERE!
よろよろよろ〜
HE CAN BE SO DUMB!
HOW CAN HE POSSIBLY BE SO DENSE?
And how do I get my feelings across to him?
WE'RE READY TO START.
FINALLY!
YES.
THE FUTURE OF THE PLANET ...
...IS ABOUT TO CHANGE!
WOW!

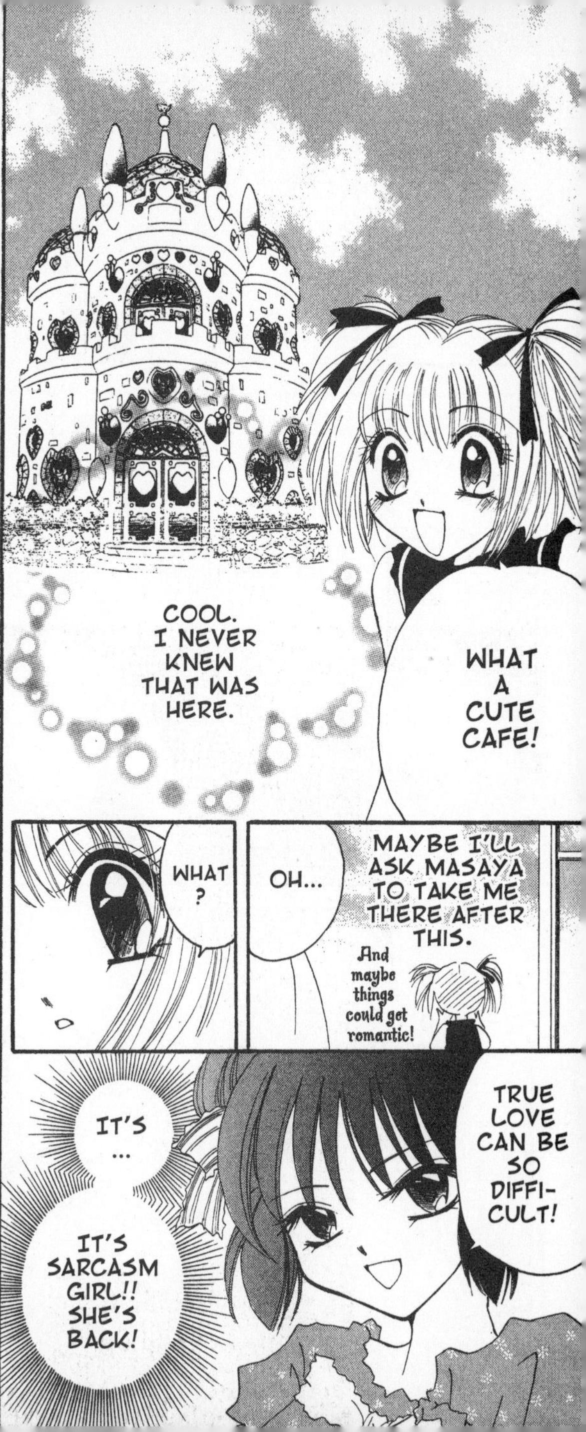
WHAT A CUTE CAFE!
COOL. I NEVER KNEW THAT WAS HERE.
MAYBE I'LL ASK MASAYA TO TAKE ME THERE AFTER THIS.
And maybe things could get romantic!
OH...
WHAT?
TRUE LOVE CAN BE SO DIFFI-CULT!
IT'S ...
IT'S SARCASM GIRL!! SHE'S BACK!

Project Meeting 2

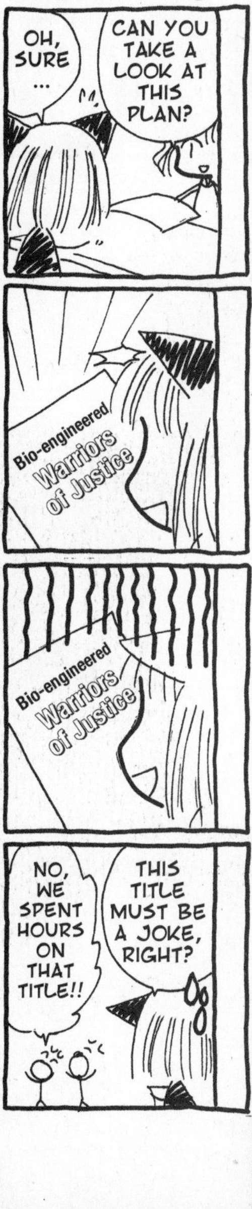
CAN YOU TAKE A LOOK AT THIS PLAN?
OH, SURE ...
Bio-engineered Warriors of Justice
Bio-engineered Warriors of Justice
THIS TITLE MUST BE A JOKE, RIGHT?
NO, WE SPENT HOURS ON THAT TITLE!!

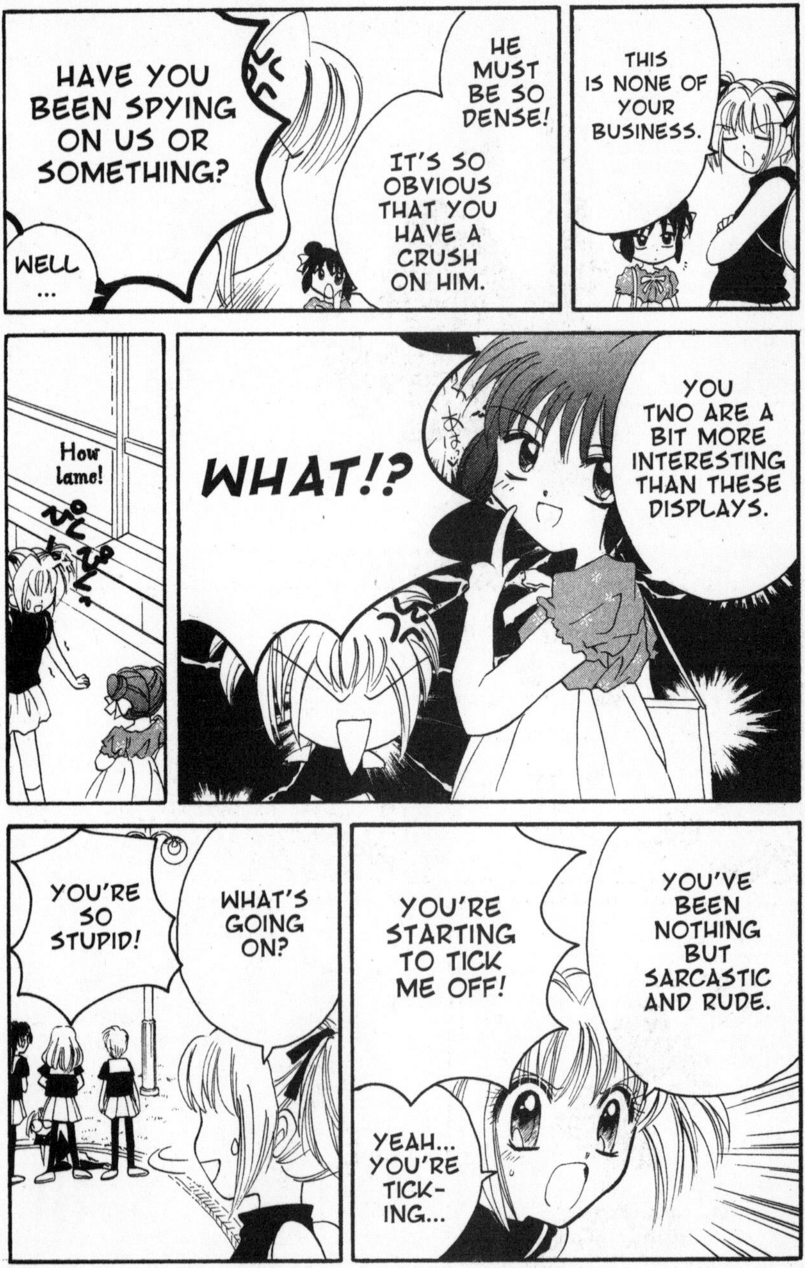
THIS IS NONE OF YOUR BUSINESS.
HE MUST BE SO DENSE!
IT'S SO OBVIOUS THAT YOU HAVE A CRUSH ON HIM.
HAVE YOU BEEN SPYING ON US OR SOMETHING?
WELL ...
YOU TWO ARE A BIT MORE INTERESTING THAN THESE DISPLAYS.
WHAT!?
How lame!
YOU'VE BEEN NOTHING BUT SARCASTIC AND RUDE.
YOU'RE STARTING TO TICK ME OFF!
YEAH... YOU'RE TICK-ING...
WHAT'S GOING ON?
YOU'RE SO STUPID!

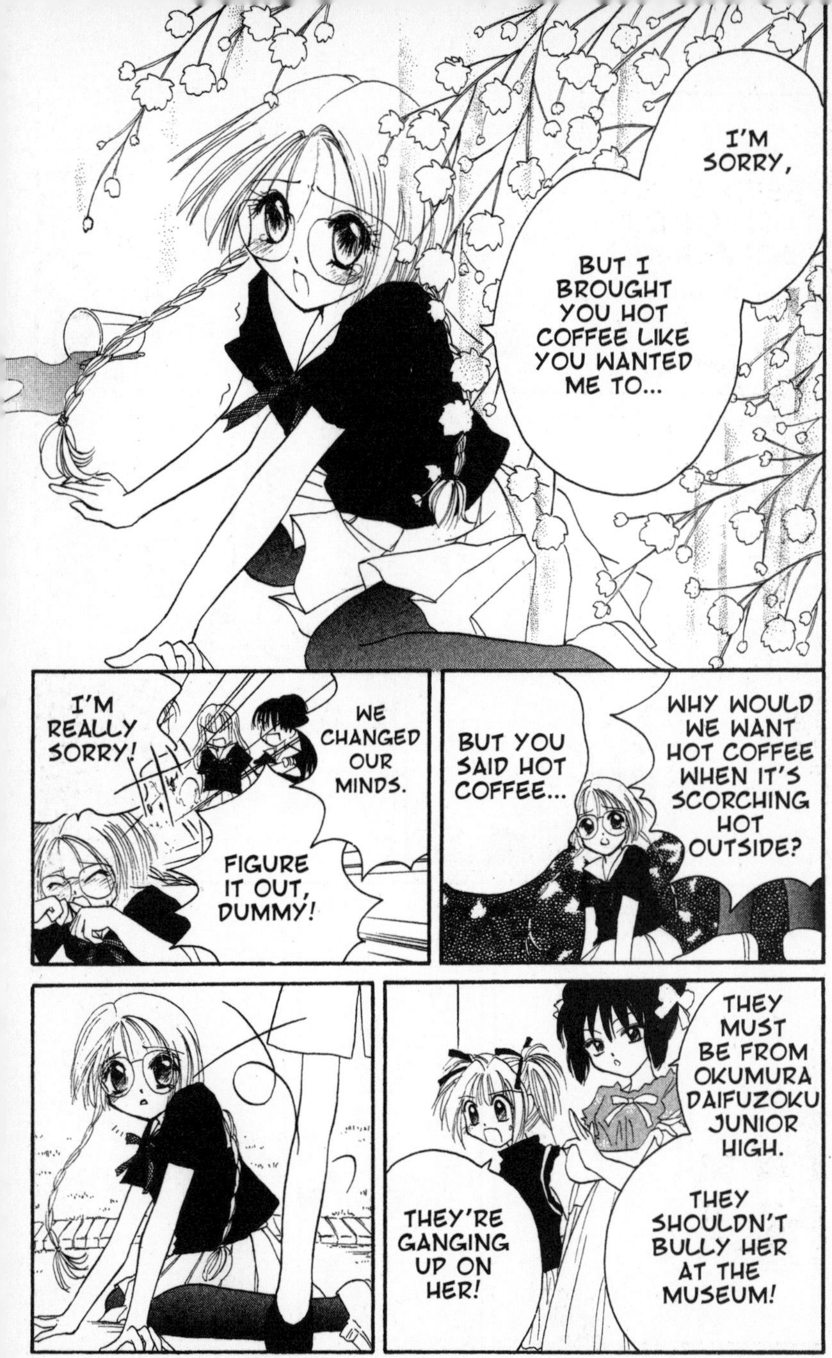

I'M SORRY,
BUT I BROUGHT YOU HOT COFFEE LIKE YOU WANTED ME TO...
WHY WOULD WE WANT HOT COFFEE WHEN IT'S SCORCHING HOT OUTSIDE?
BUT YOU SAID HOT COFFEE...
WE CHANGED OUR MINDS.
FIGURE IT OUT, DUMMY!
I'M REALLY SORRY!
THEY MUST BE FROM OKUMURA DAIFUZOKU JUNIOR HIGH.
THEY SHOULDN'T BULLY HER AT THE MUSEUM!
THEY'RE GANGING UP ON HER!

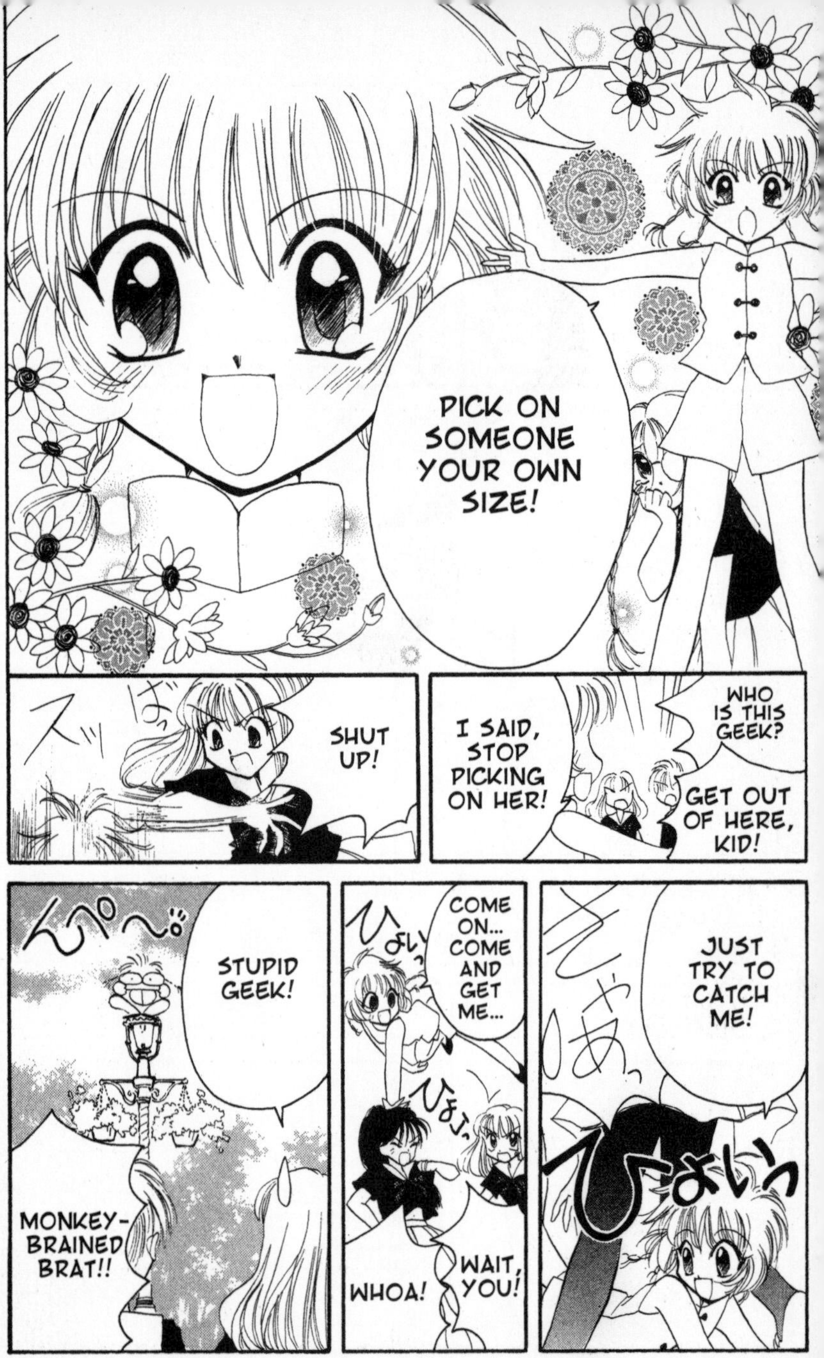
PICK ON SOMEONE YOUR OWN SIZE!
WHO IS THIS GEEK?
GET OUT OF HERE, KID!
I SAID, STOP PICKING ON HER!
SHUT UP!
JUST TRY TO CATCH ME!
COME ON... COME AND GET ME...
WAIT, YOU!
WHOA!
STUPID GEEK!
MONKEY-BRAINED BRAT!!

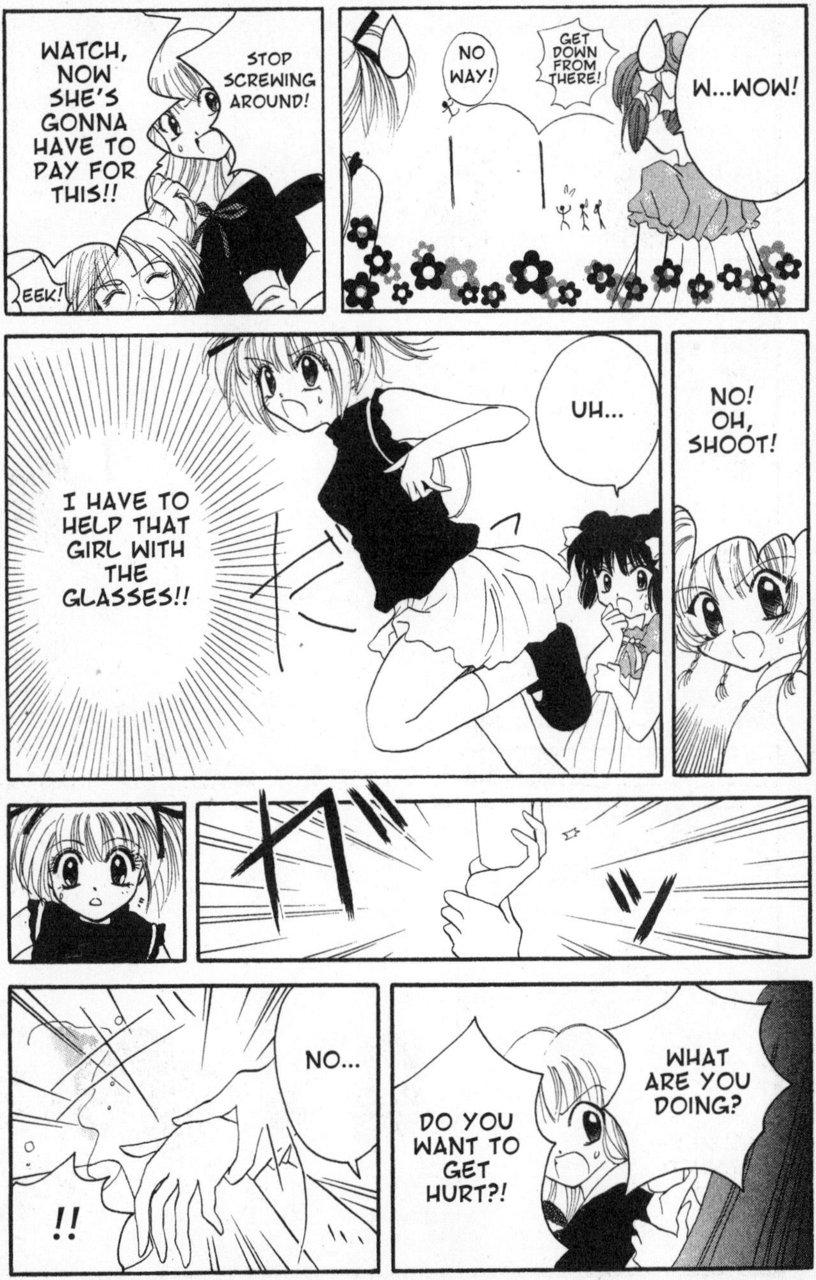
W...WOW!
GET DOWN FROM THERE!
NO WAY!
STOP SCREWING AROUND!
WATCH, NOW SHE'S GONNA HAVE TO PAY FOR THIS!!
EEK!
NO! OH, SHOOT!
UH...
I HAVE TO HELP THAT GIRL WITH THE GLASSES!!
WHAT ARE YOU DOING?
DO YOU WANT TO GET HURT?!
NO...
!!

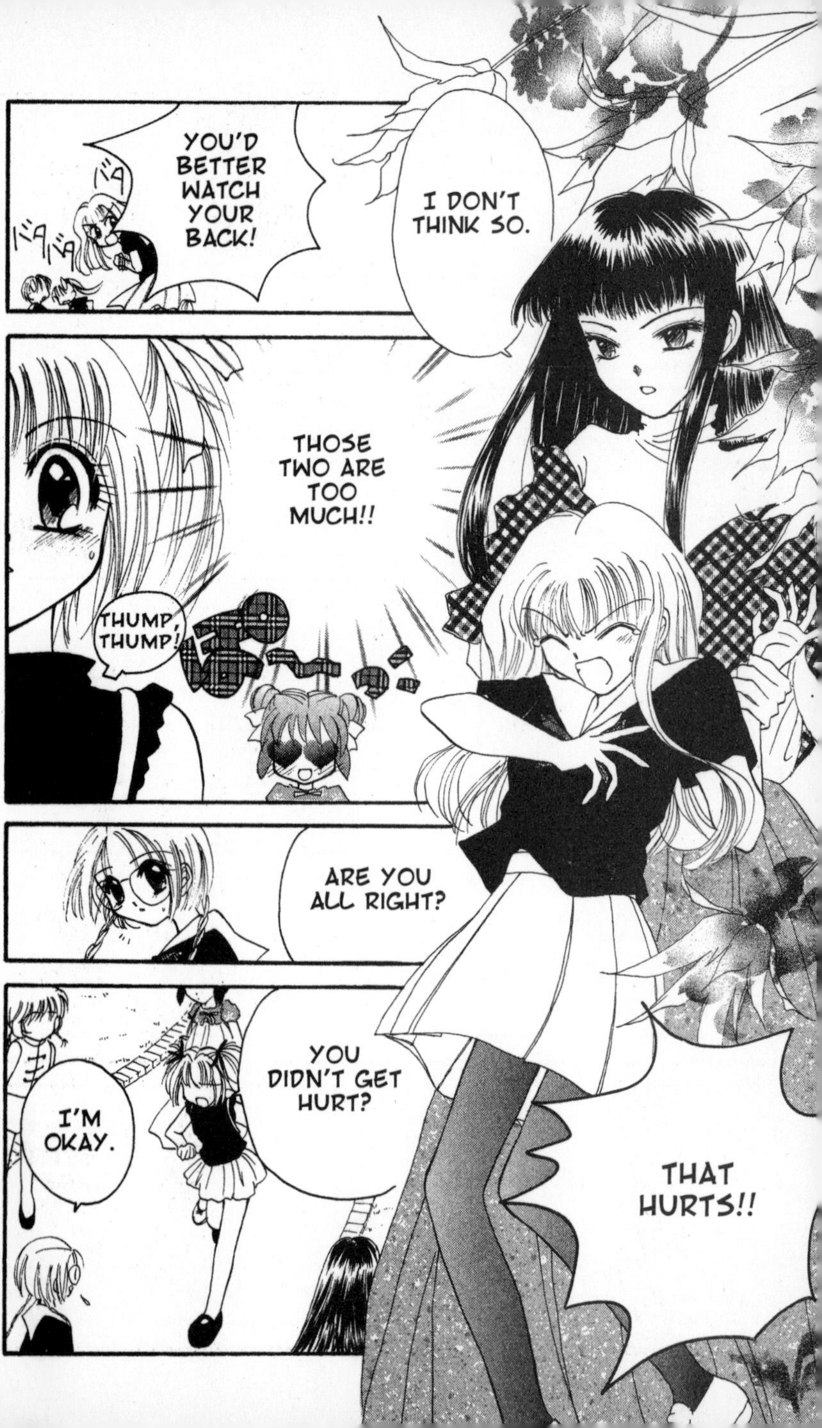
I DON'T THINK SO.
THAT HURTS!!
YOU'D BETTER WATCH YOUR BACK!
バタ
バタバタ
THOSE TWO ARE TOO MUCH!!
THUMP, THUMP!
ARE YOU ALL RIGHT?
YOU DIDN'T GET HURT?
I'M OKAY.

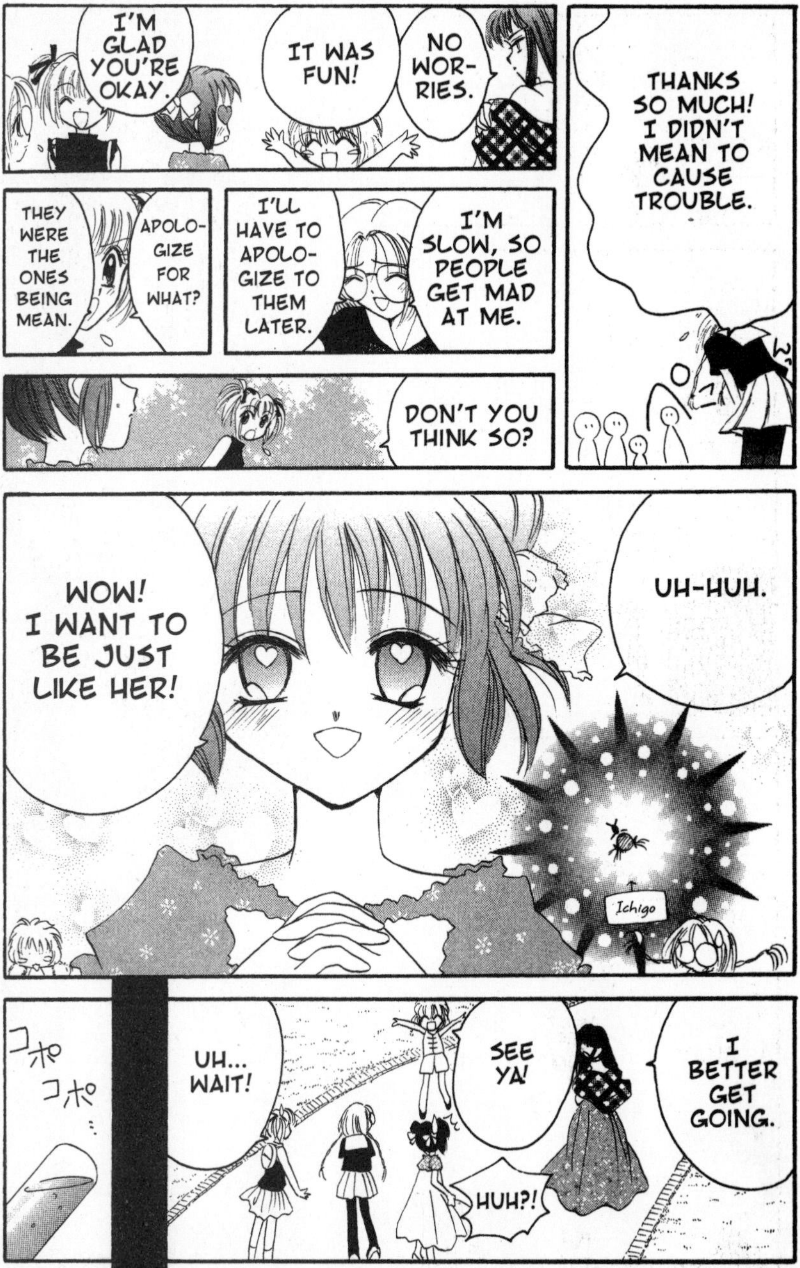
THANKS SO MUCH! I DIDN'T MEAN TO CAUSE TROUBLE.
NO WORRIES.
IT WAS FUN!
I'M GLAD YOU'RE OKAY.
I'M SLOW, SO PEOPLE GET MAD AT ME.
I'LL HAVE TO APOLOGIZE TO THEM LATER.
APOLOGIZE FOR WHAT?
THEY WERE THE ONES BEING MEAN.
DON'T YOU THINK SO?
UH-HUH.
WOW! I WANT TO BE JUST LIKE HER!
Ichigo
I BETTER GET GOING.
SEE YA!
HUH?!
UH... WAIT!
コポ
コポ

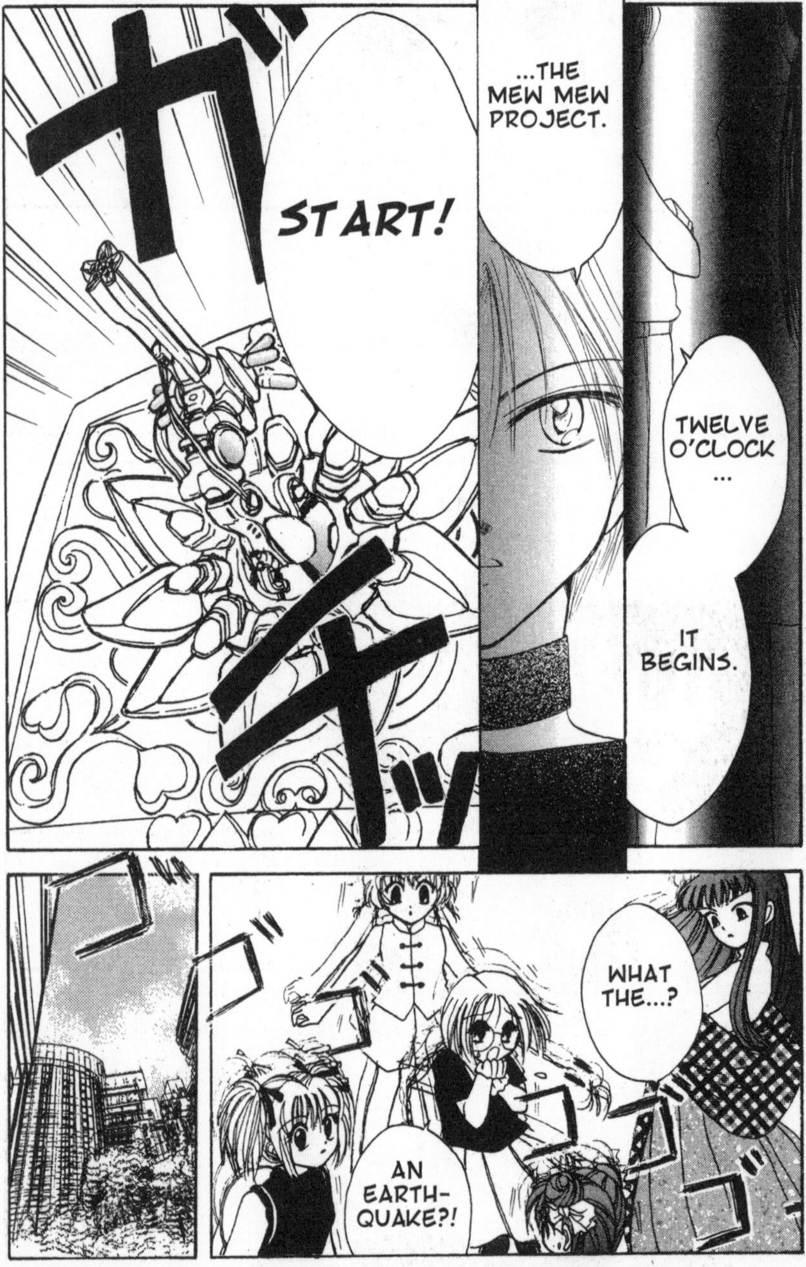
TWELVE O'CLOCK ...
IT BEGINS.
...THE MEW MEW PROJECT.
START!
WHAT THE...?
AN EARTH-QUAKE?!

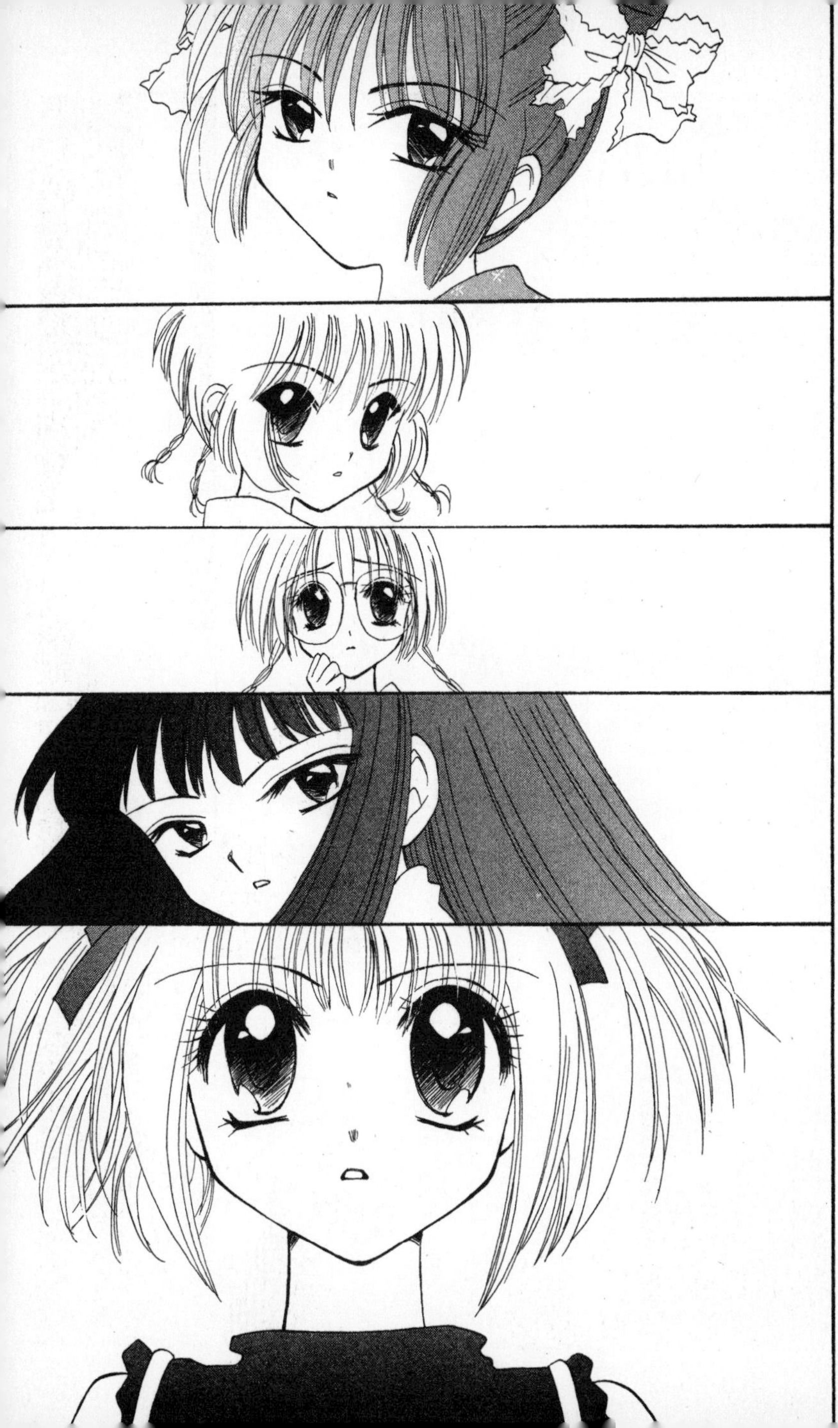

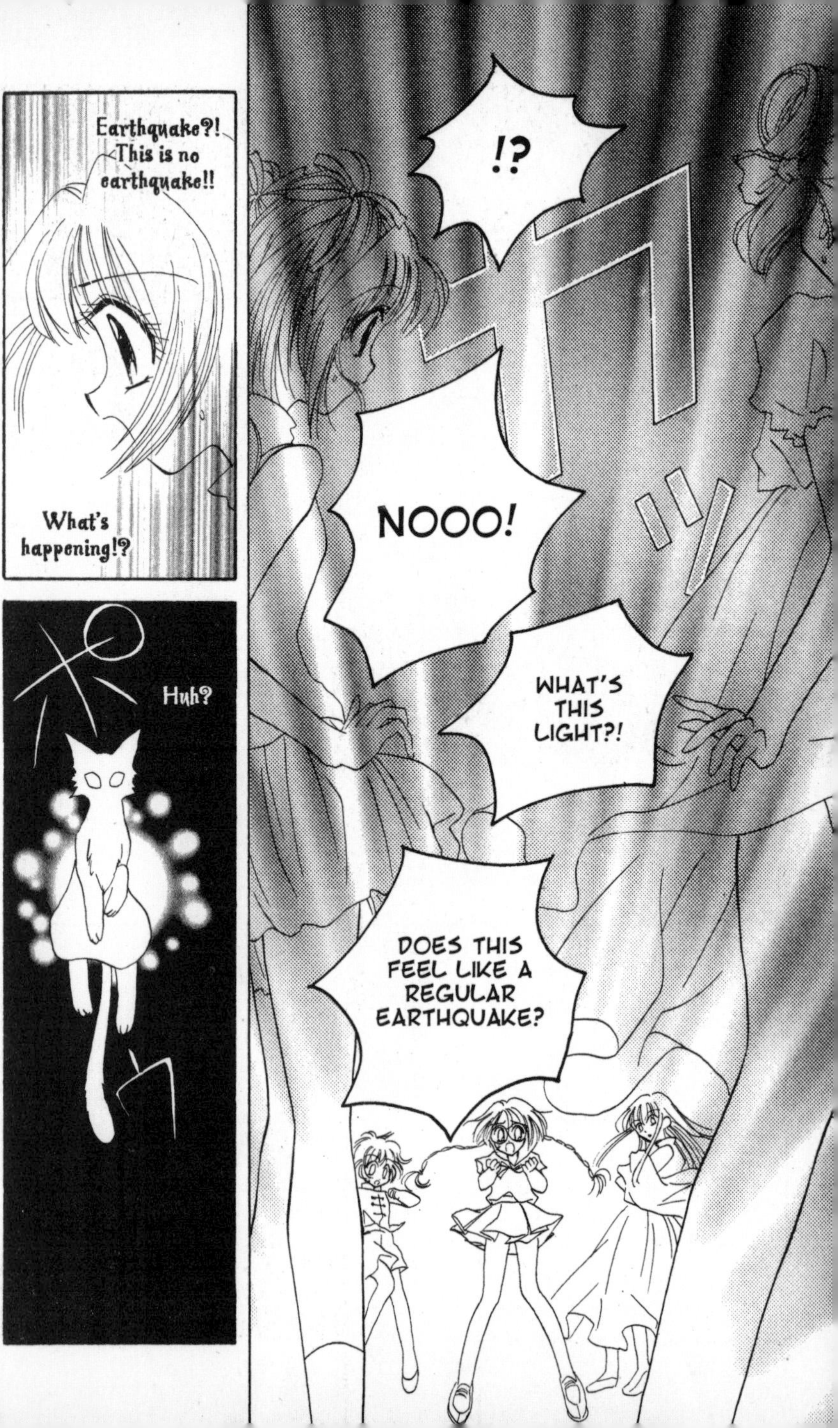
!?
NOOO!
WHAT'S THIS LIGHT?!
DOES THIS FEEL LIKE A REGULAR EARTHQUAKE?
Earthquake?! This is no earthquake!!
What's happening!?
Huh?

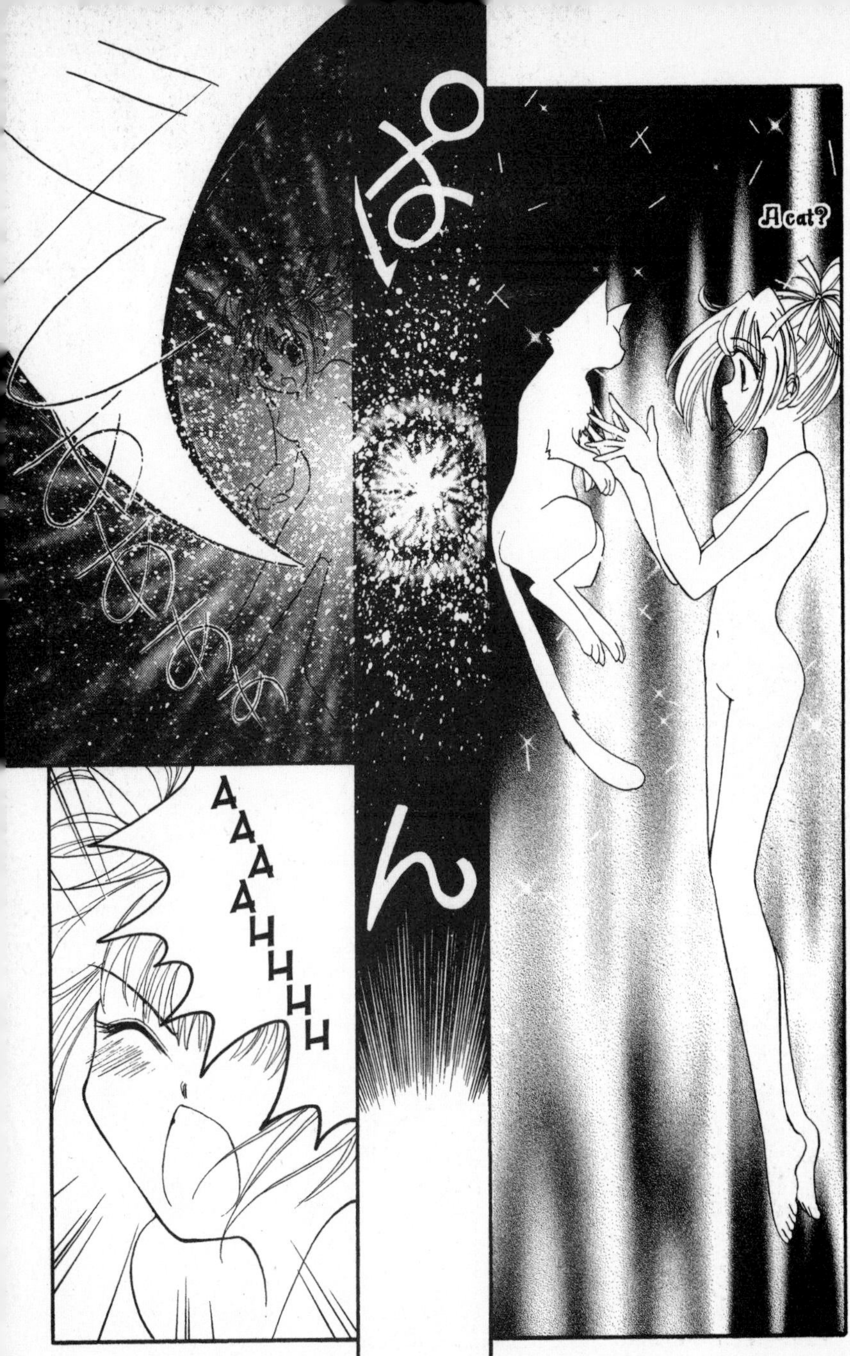

A cat?
ぽ
ん
AAAAHHHHH

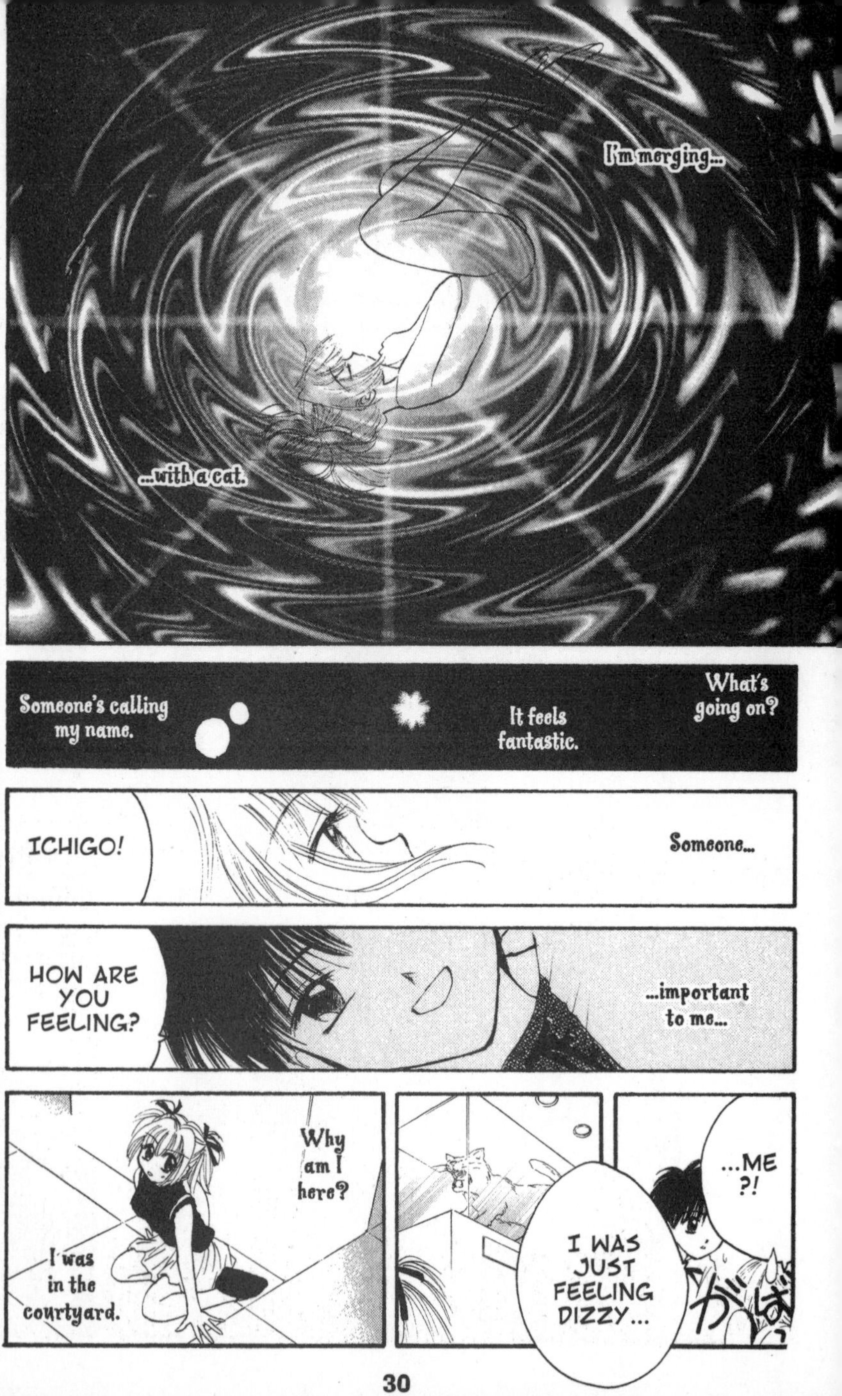
I'm merging...
...with a cat.
What's going on?
It feels fantastic.
Someone's calling my name.
Someone...
ICHIGO!
...important to me...
HOW ARE YOU FEELING?
...ME ?!
I WAS JUST FEELING DIZZY...
Why am I here?
I was in the courtyard.

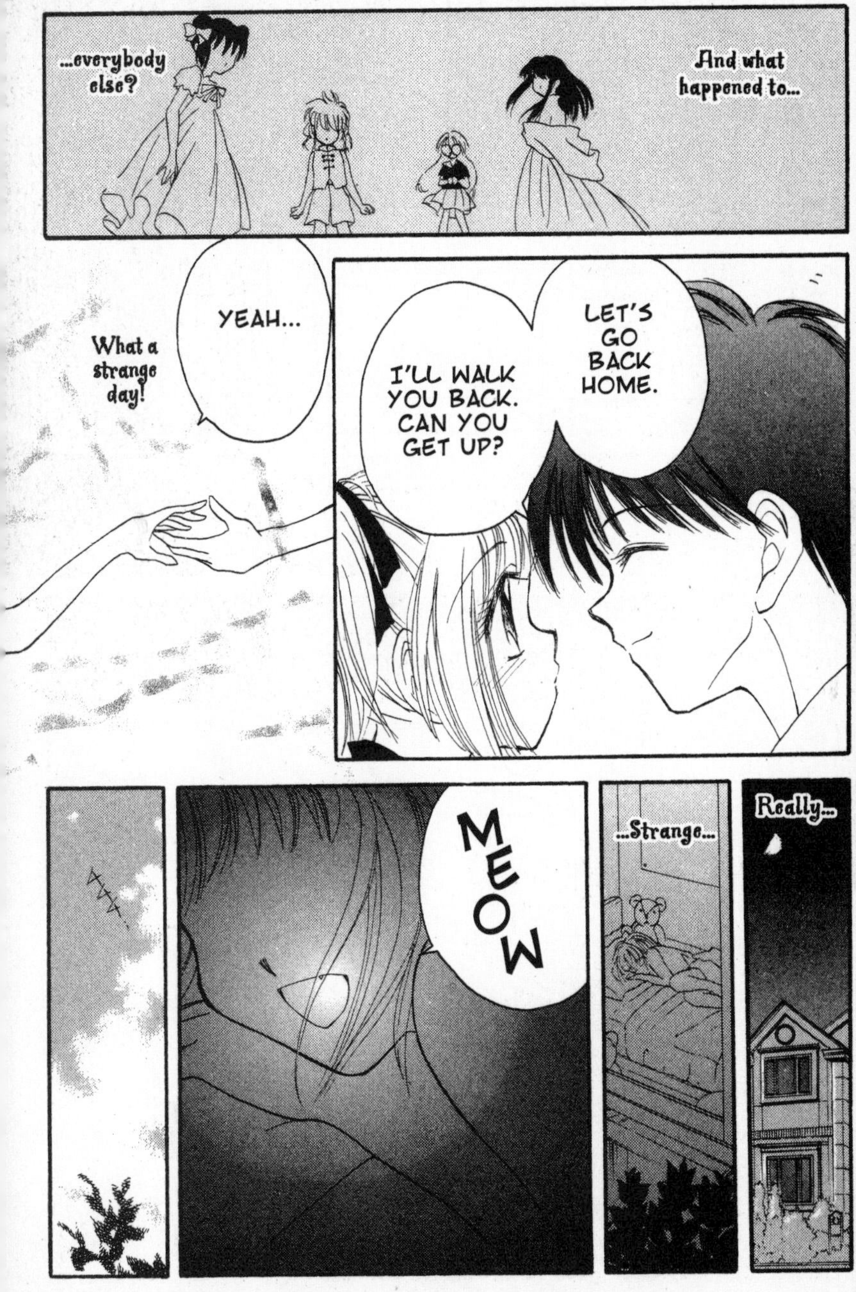
And what happened to...
...everybody else?
LET'S GO BACK HOME.
I'LL WALK YOU BACK. CAN YOU GET UP?
YEAH...
What a strange day!
Really...
...Strange...
MEOW

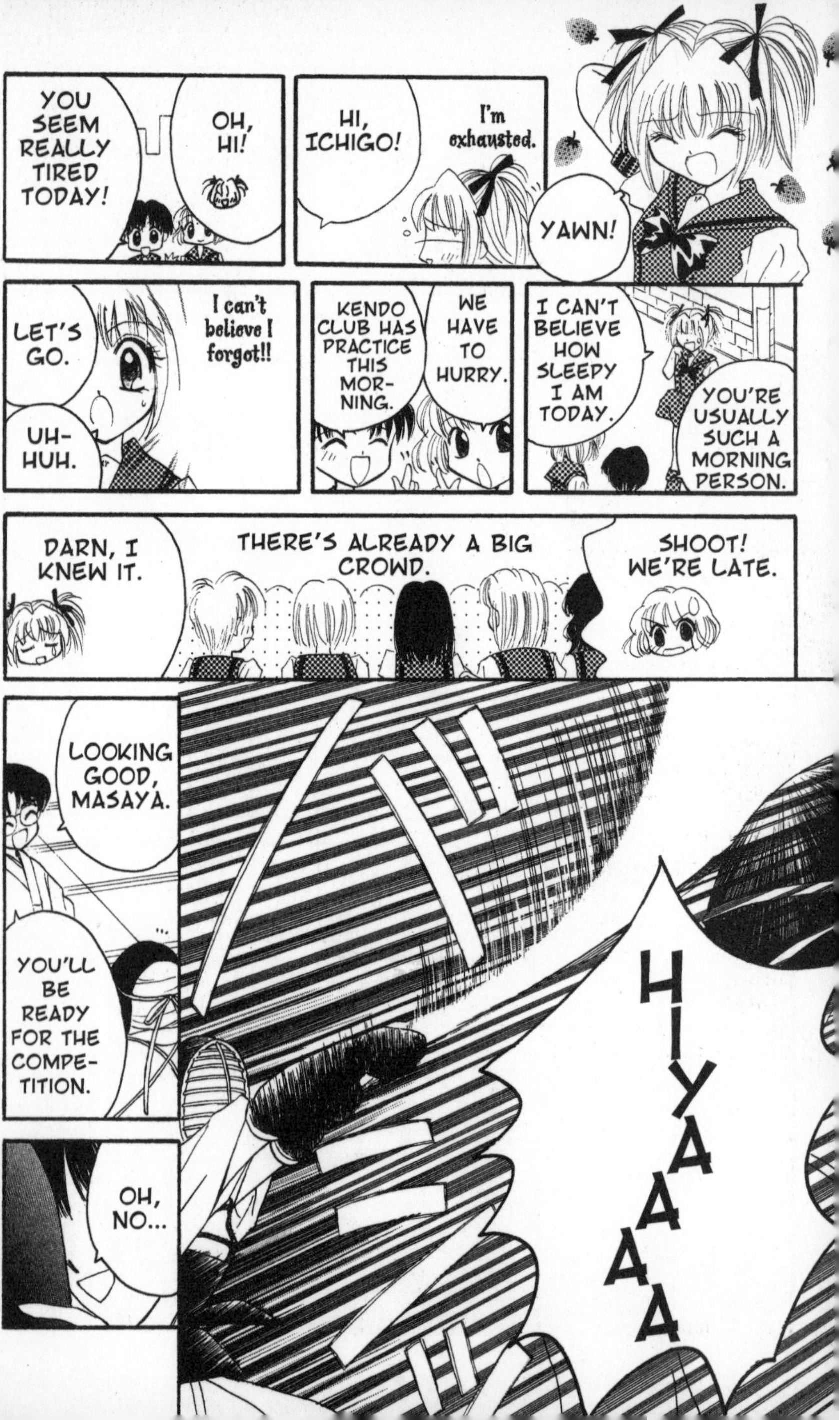
YAWN!
I'm exhausted.
HI, ICHIGO!
OH, HI!
YOU SEEM REALLY TIRED TODAY!
I CAN'T BELIEVE HOW SLEEPY I AM TODAY.
YOU'RE USUALLY SUCH A MORNING PERSON.
WE HAVE TO HURRY.
KENDO CLUB HAS PRACTICE THIS MORNING.
I can't believe I forgot!!
LET'S GO.
UH-HUH.
SHOOT! WE'RE LATE.
THERE'S ALREADY A BIG CROWD.
DARN, I KNEW IT.
HIYAAAAA
LOOKING GOOD, MASAYA.
YOU'LL BE READY FOR THE COMPETITION.
OH, NO...

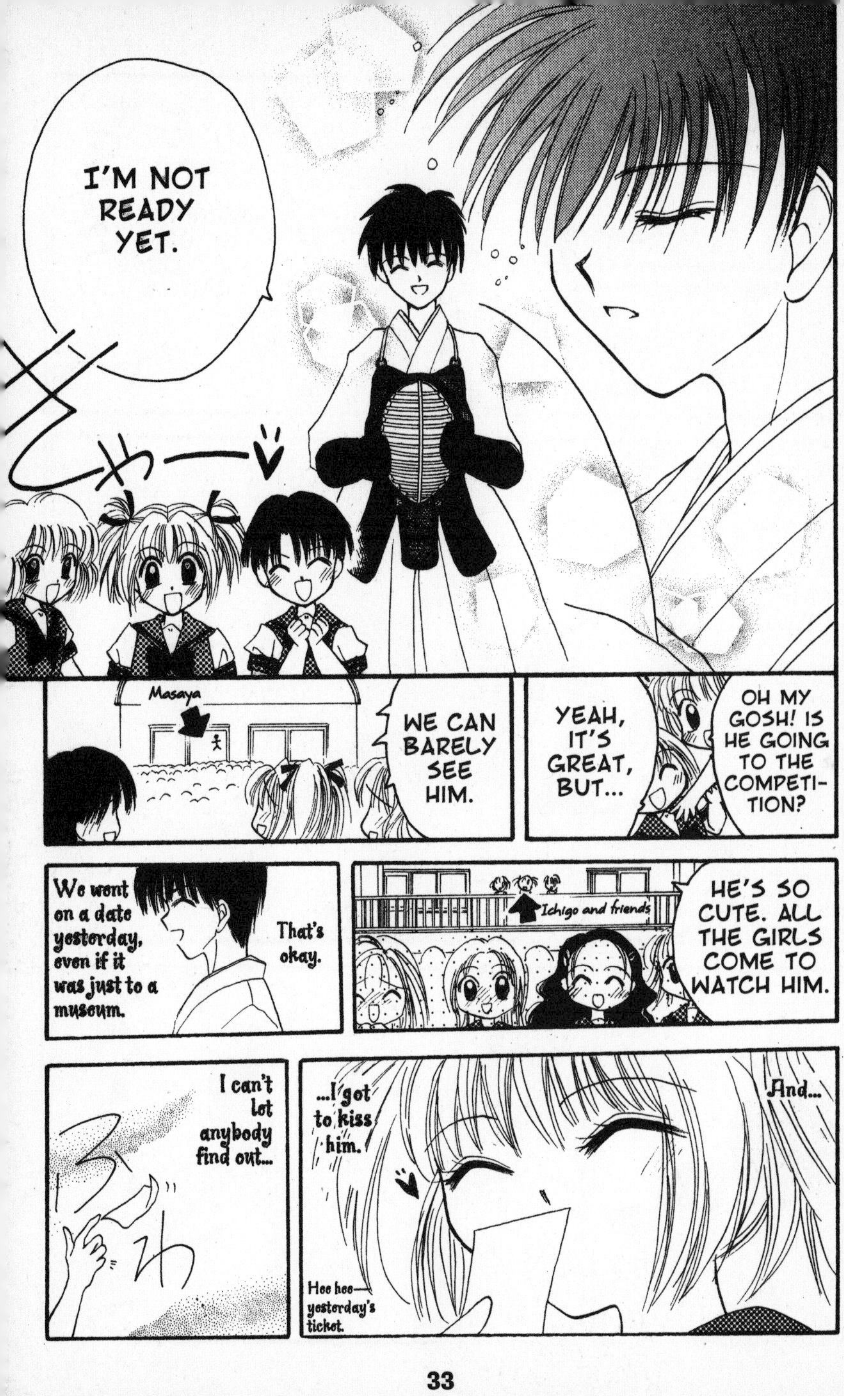
I'M NOT READY YET.
きゃー
OH MY GOSH! IS HE GOING TO THE COMPETITION?
YEAH, IT'S GREAT, BUT...
WE CAN BARELY SEE HIM.
Masaya
HE'S SO CUTE. ALL THE GIRLS COME TO WATCH HIM.
Ichigo and friends
That's okay.
We went on a date yesterday, even if it was just to a museum.
And...
...I got to kiss him.
Hee hee— yesterday's ticket.
I can't let anybody find out...

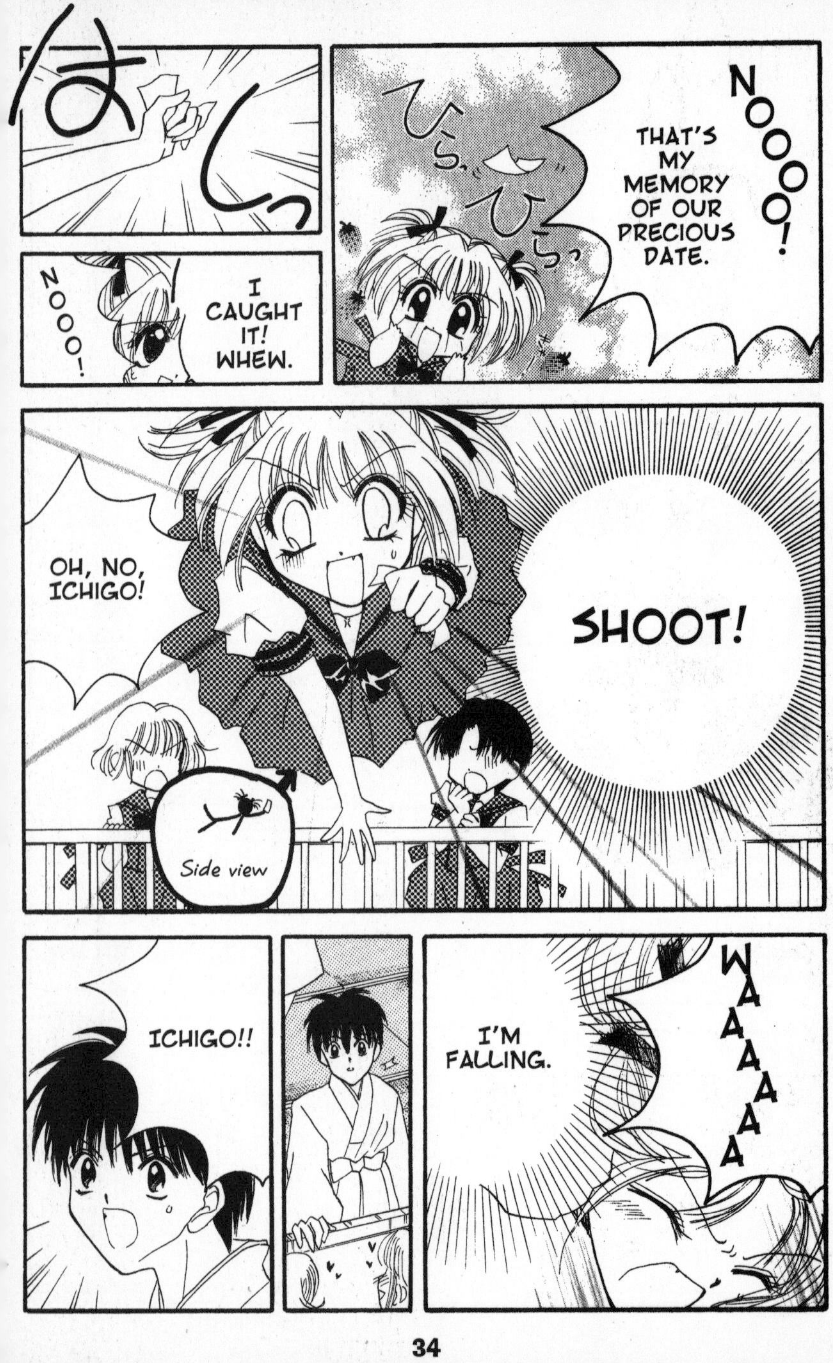
NOOOOO!
THAT'S MY MEMORY OF OUR PRECIOUS DATE.
ひらひらっ
はしっ
I CAUGHT IT! WHEW.
NOOO!
SHOOT!
OH, NO, ICHIGO!
Side view
WAAAAA
I'M FALLING.
ICHIGO!!

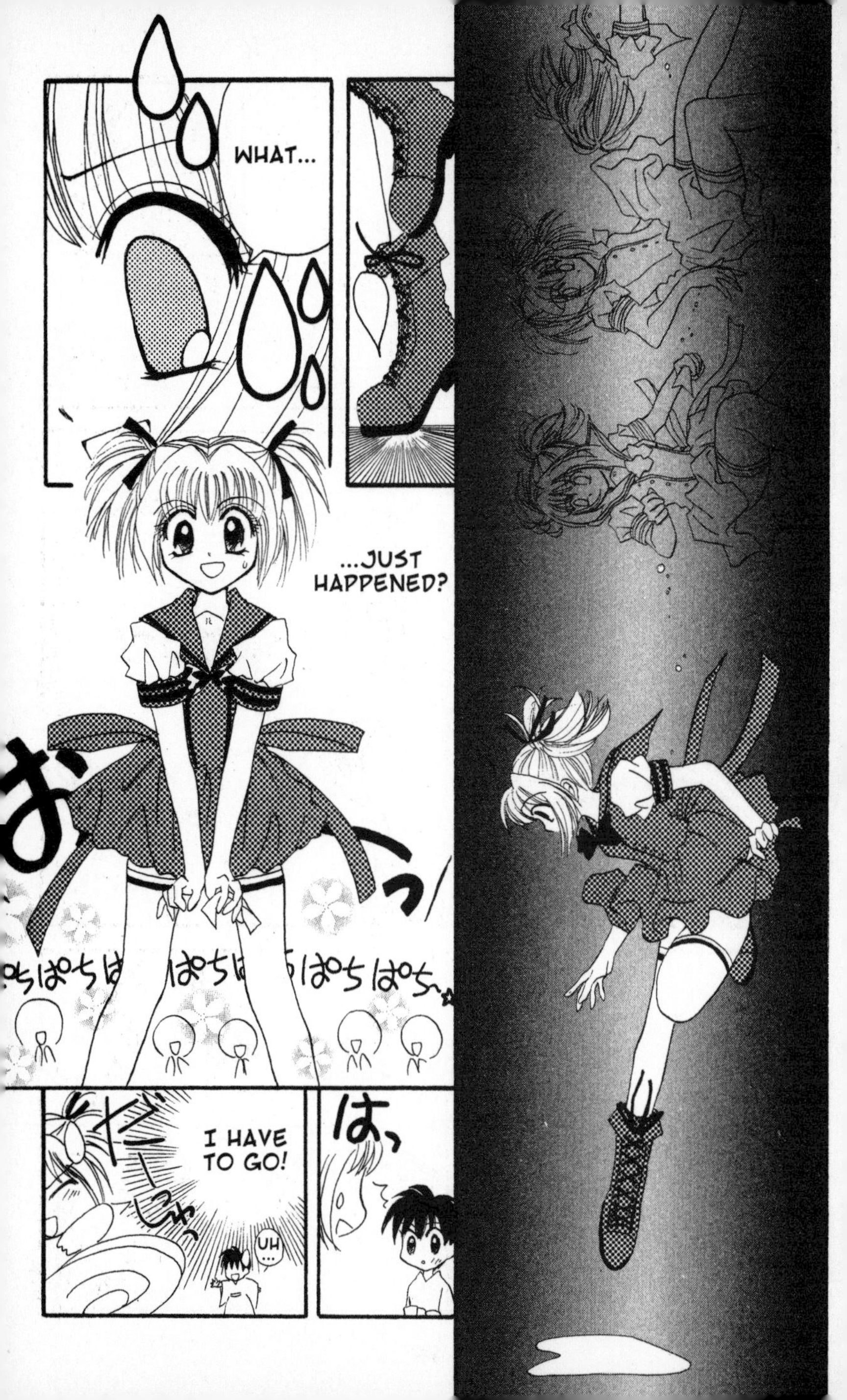
WHAT...
...JUST HAPPENED?
は、
I HAVE TO GO!
UH...

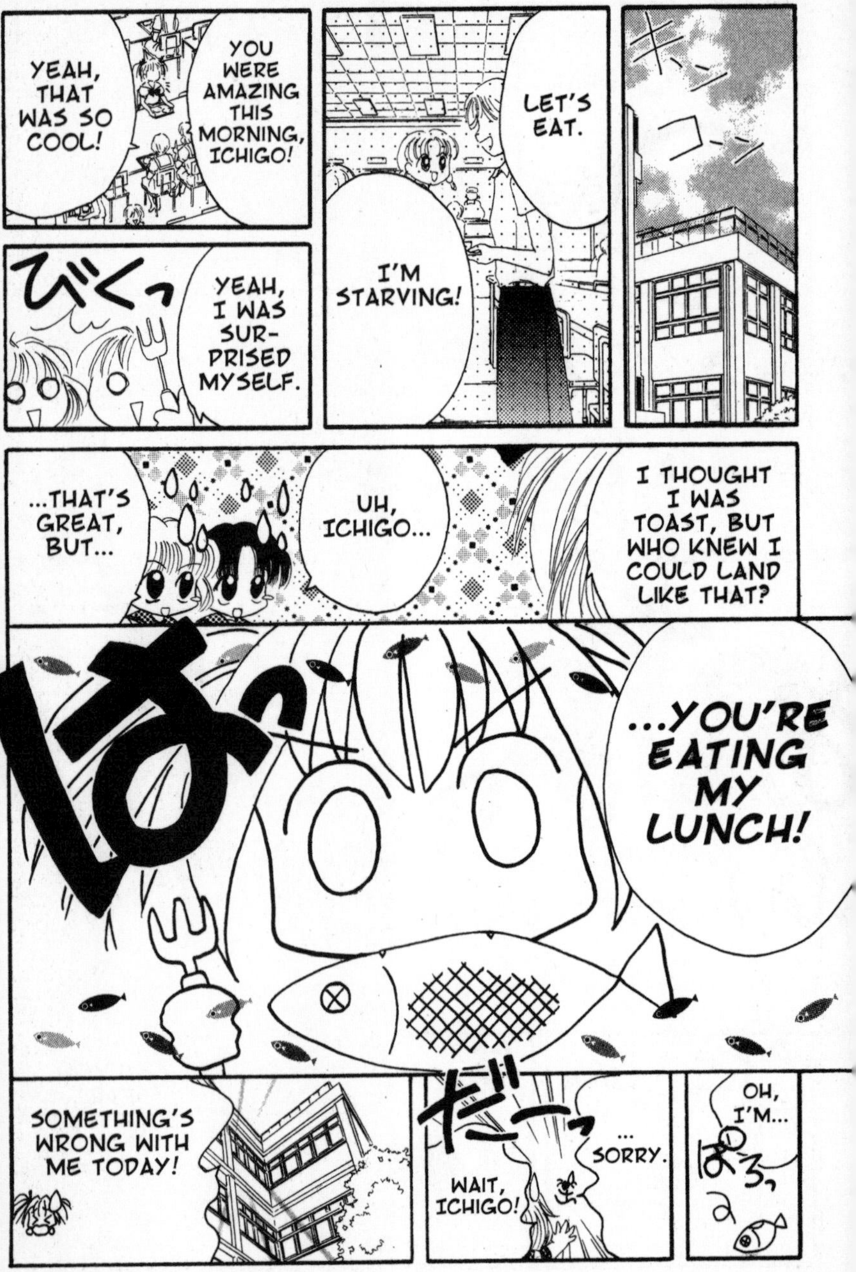
LET'S EAT.
I'M STARVING!
YOU WERE AMAZING THIS MORNING, ICHIGO!
YEAH, THAT WAS SO COOL!
YEAH, I WAS SUR-PRISED MYSELF.
びくっ
I THOUGHT I WAS TOAST, BUT WHO KNEW I COULD LAND LIKE THAT?
UH, ICHIGO...
...THAT'S GREAT, BUT...
...YOU'RE EATING MY LUNCH!
ばっ
OH, I'M...
ぽろっ
だーっ
... SORRY.
WAIT, ICHIGO!
SOMETHING'S WRONG WITH ME TODAY!

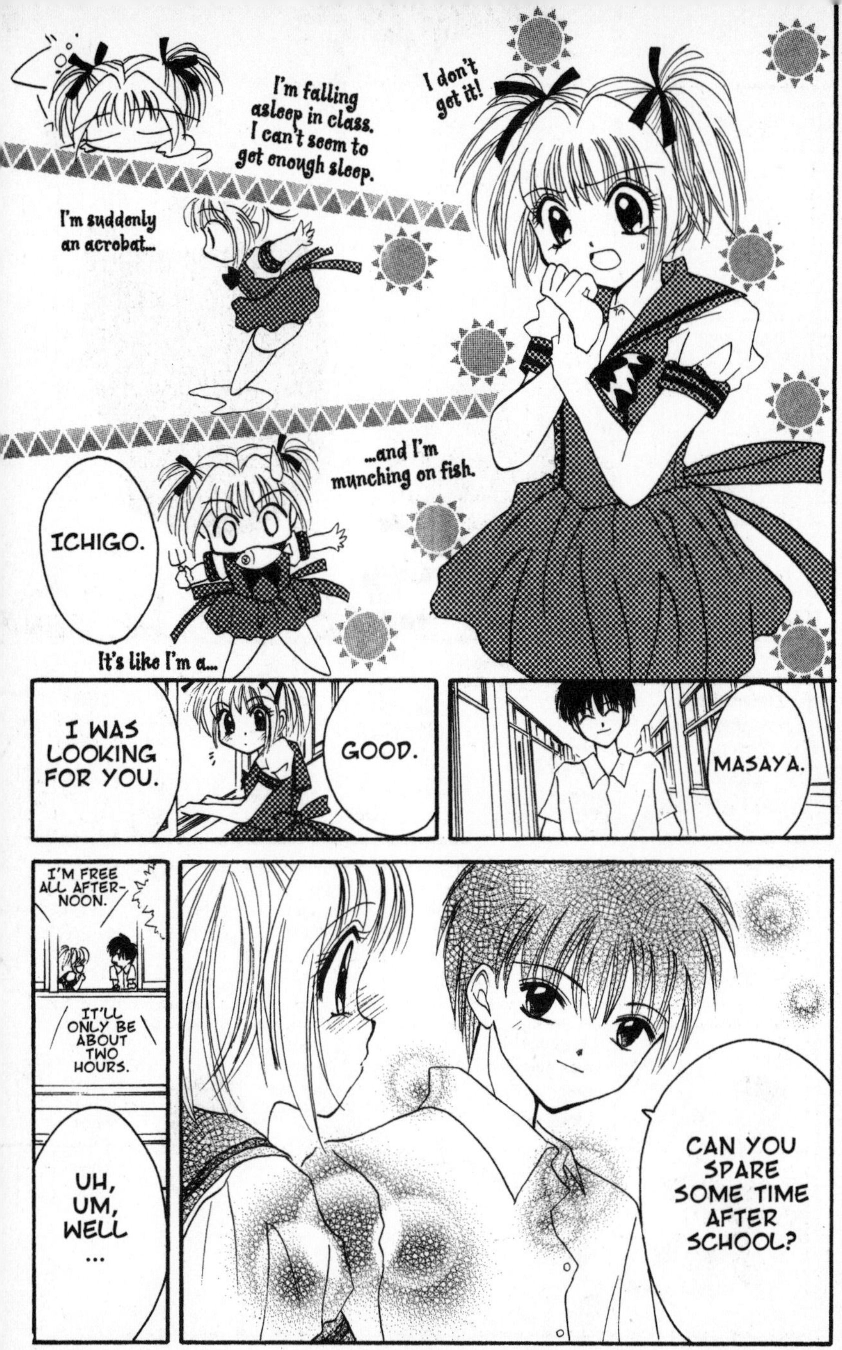
I don't get it!
I'm falling asleep in class. I can't seem to get enough sleep.
I'm suddenly an acrobat...
...and I'm munching on fish.
ICHIGO.
It's like I'm a...
MASAYA.
GOOD.
I WAS LOOKING FOR YOU.
CAN YOU SPARE SOME TIME AFTER SCHOOL?
I'M FREE ALL AFTERNOON.
IT'LL ONLY BE ABOUT TWO HOURS.
UH, UM, WELL ...

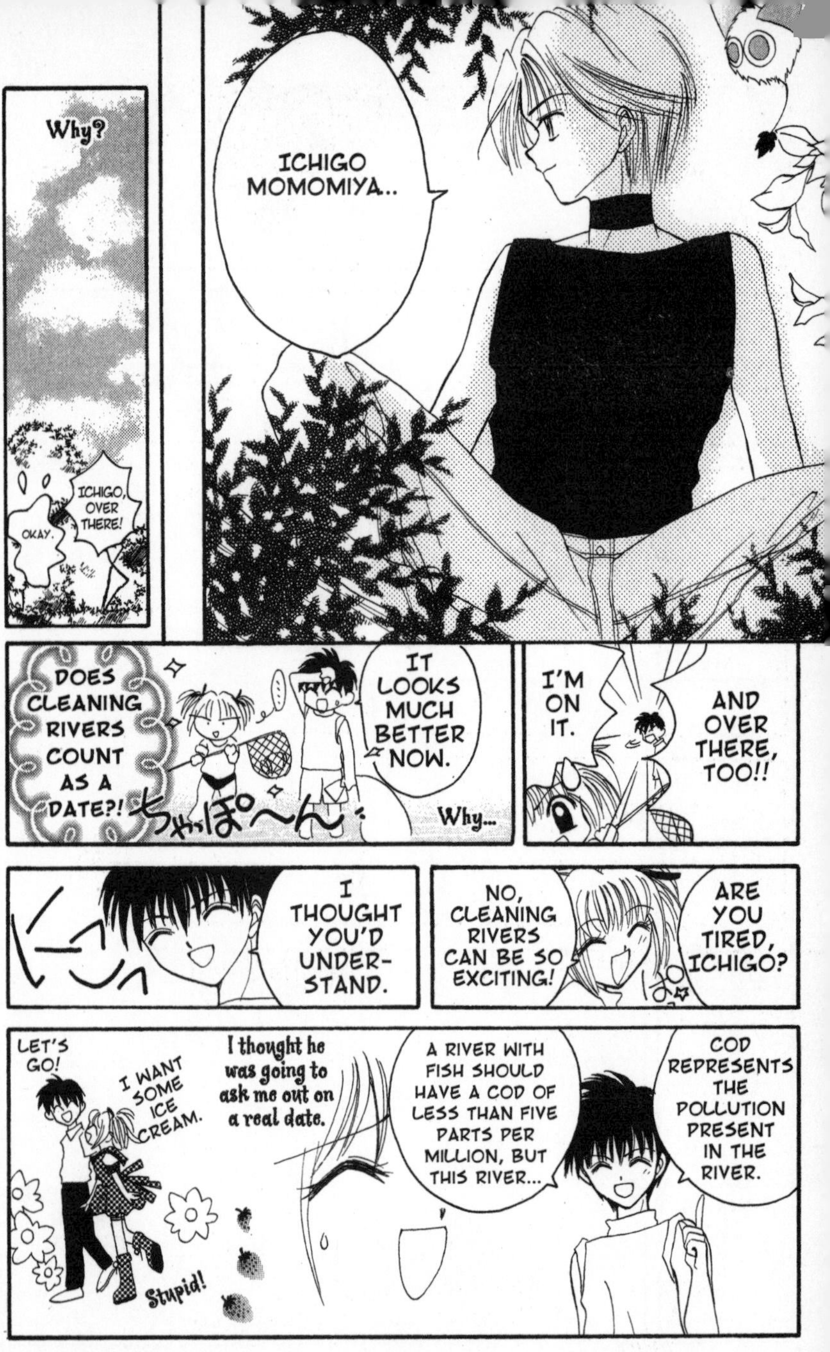
ICHIGO MOMOMIYA...
Why?
ICHIGO, OVER THERE!
OKAY.
AND OVER THERE, TOO!!
I'M ON IT.
IT LOOKS MUCH BETTER NOW.
DOES CLEANING RIVERS COUNT AS A DATE?!
ちゃぽ〜ん
Why...
ARE YOU TIRED, ICHIGO?
NO, CLEANING RIVERS CAN BE SO EXCITING!
I THOUGHT YOU'D UNDERSTAND.
COD REPRESENTS THE POLLUTION PRESENT IN THE RIVER.
A RIVER WITH FISH SHOULD HAVE A COD OF LESS THAN FIVE PARTS PER MILLION, BUT THIS RIVER...
I thought he was going to ask me out on a real date.
I WANT SOME ICE CREAM.
LET'S GO!
Stupid!

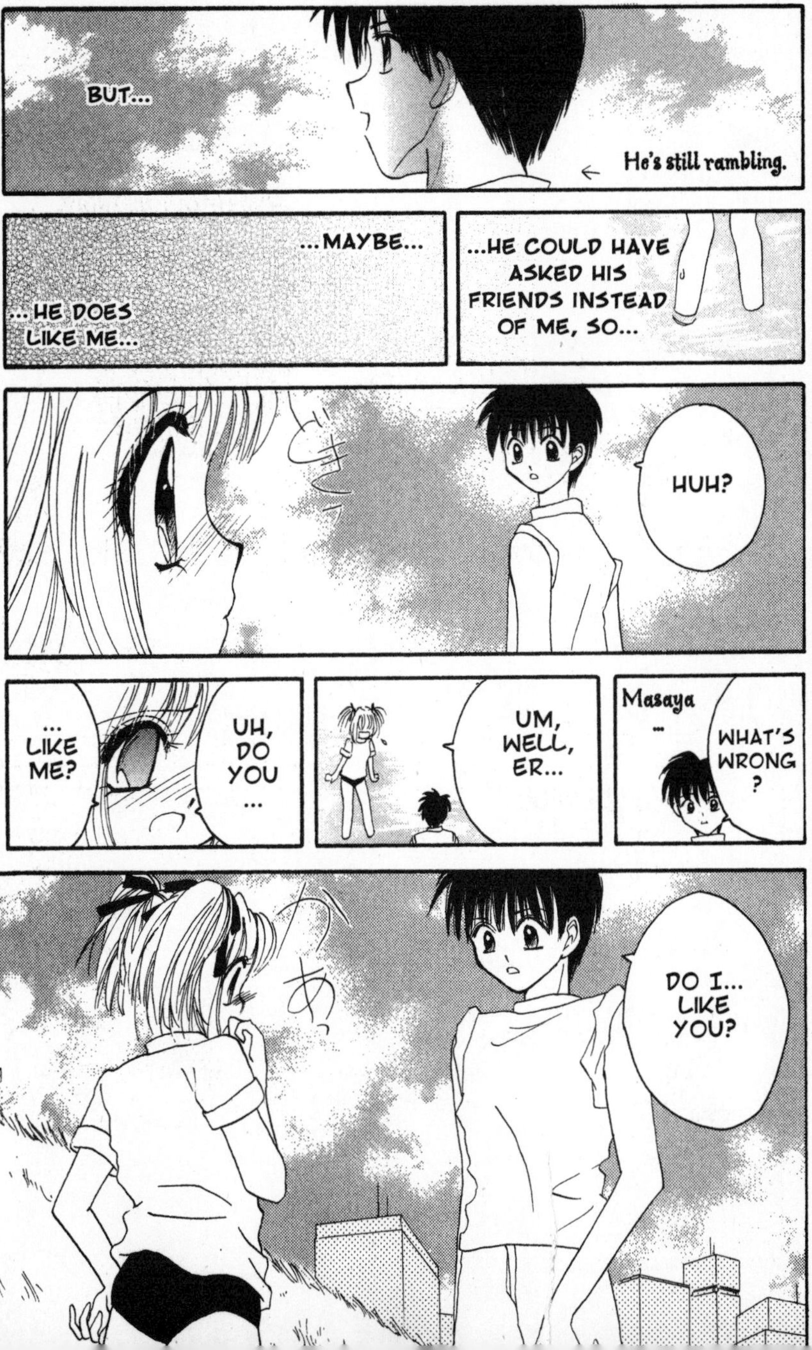
BUT...
He's still rambling.
...HE COULD HAVE ASKED HIS FRIENDS INSTEAD OF ME, SO...
...MAYBE...
...HE DOES LIKE ME...
HUH?
Masaya...
WHAT'S WRONG?
UM, WELL, ER...
UH, DO YOU...
...LIKE ME?
DO I... LIKE YOU?

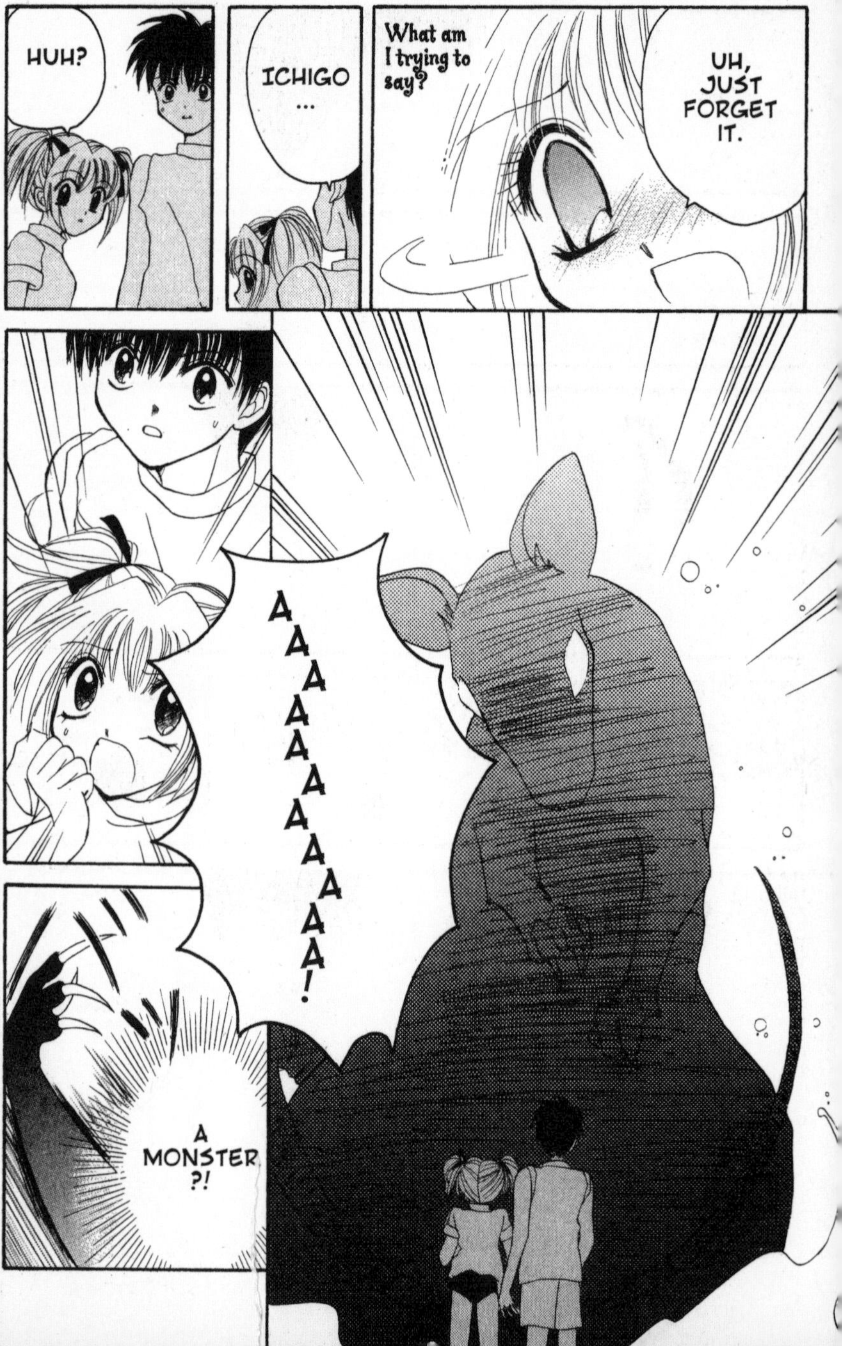
UH, JUST FORGET IT.
What am I trying to say?
ICHIGO ...
HUH?
AAAAAAAAAAAAA!
A MONSTER ?!

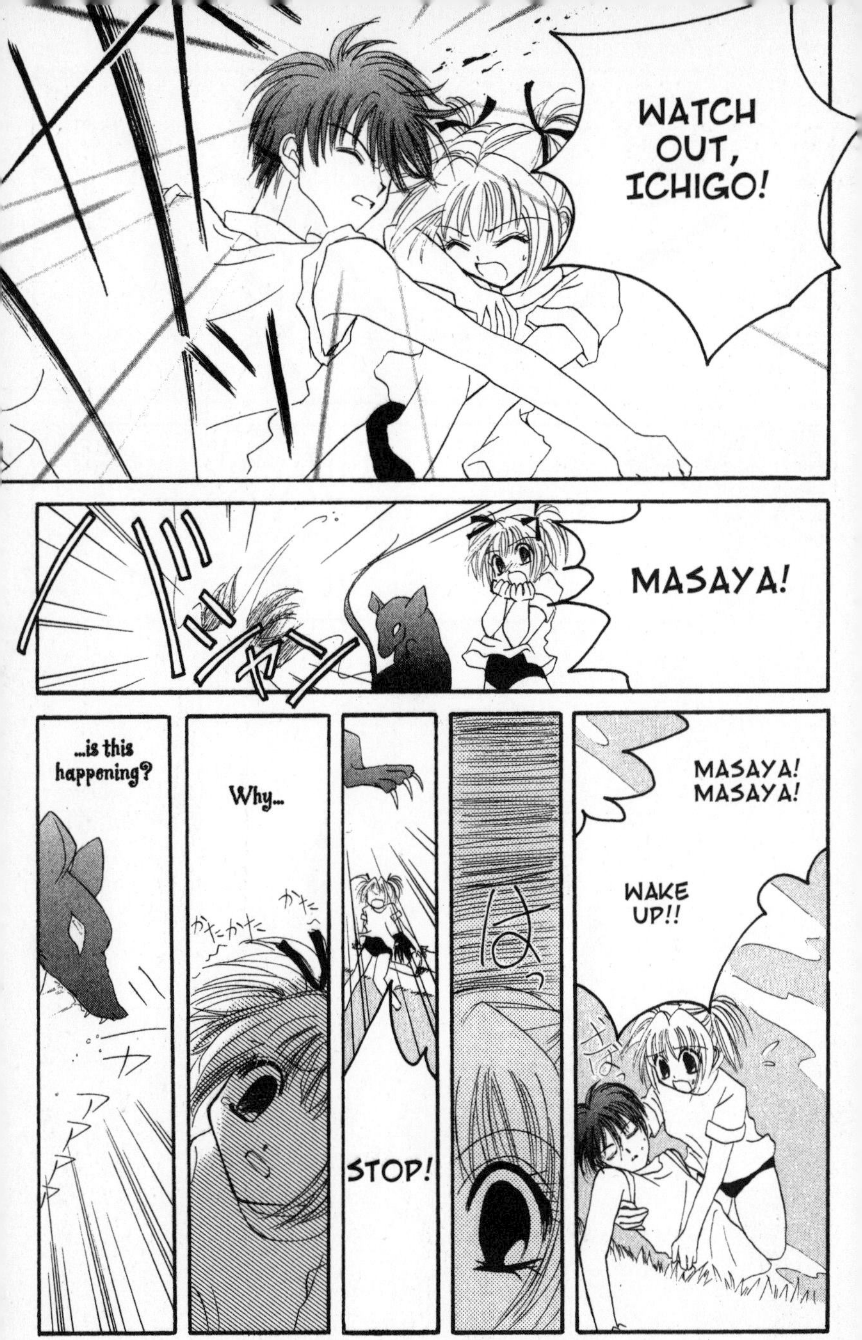
WATCH OUT, ICHIGO!
MASAYA!
MASAYA! MASAYA!
WAKE UP!!
はっ
STOP!
Why...
...is this happening?

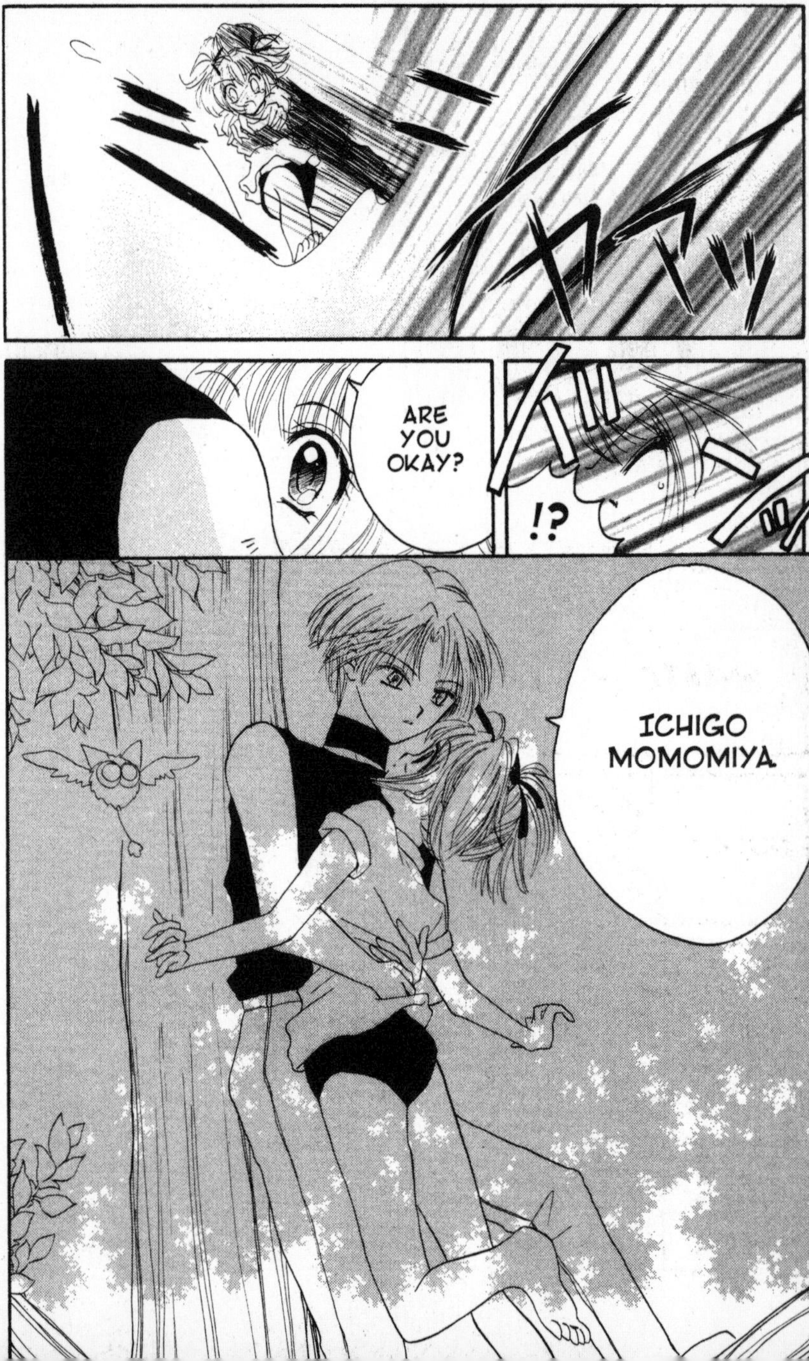
!?
ARE YOU OKAY?
ICHIGO MOMOMIYA.

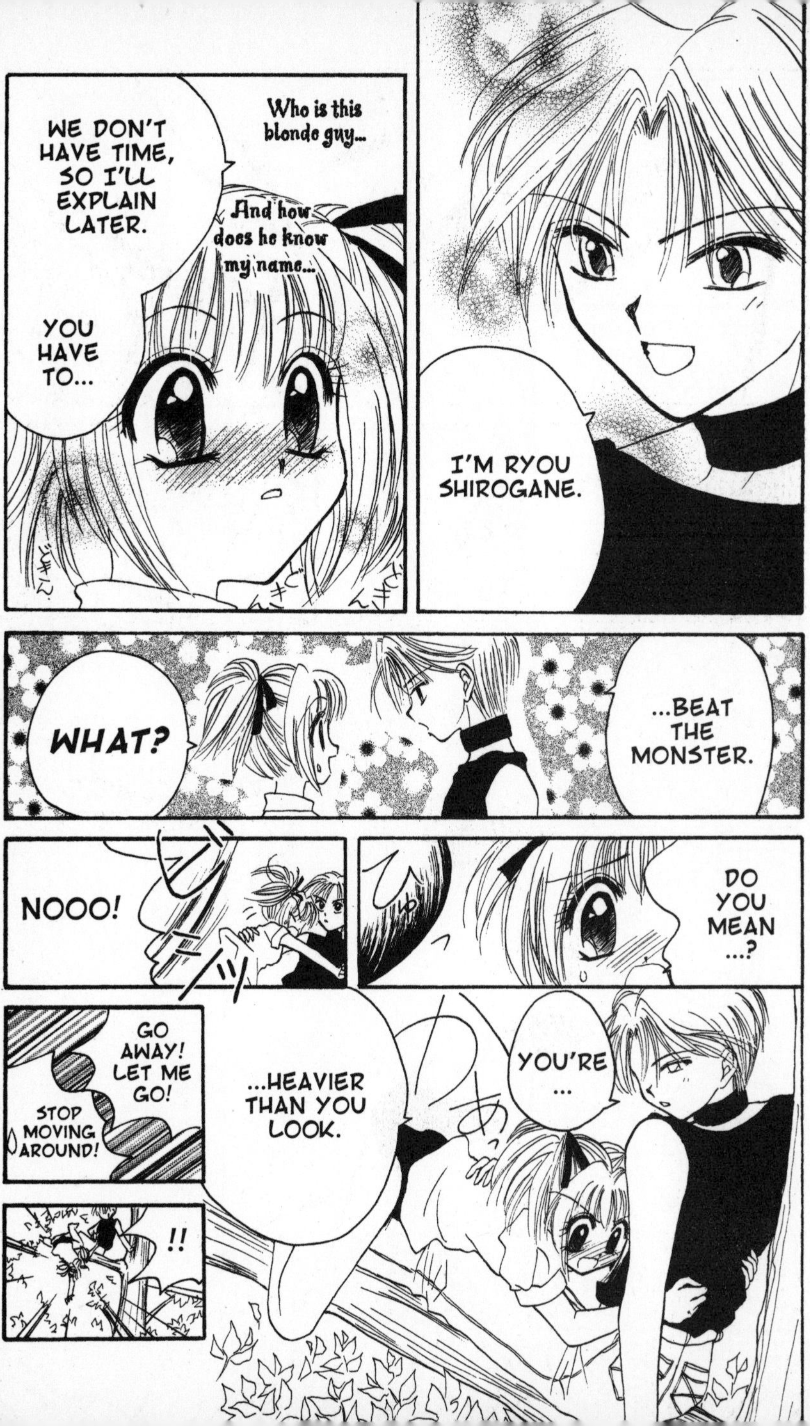
I'M RYOU SHIROGANE.
Who is this blonde guy...
And how does he know my name...
WE DON'T HAVE TIME, SO I'LL EXPLAIN LATER.
YOU HAVE TO...
...BEAT THE MONSTER.
WHAT?
DO YOU MEAN ...?
NOOO!
YOU'RE ...
...HEAVIER THAN YOU LOOK.
GO AWAY! LET ME GO!
STOP MOVING AROUND!
!!

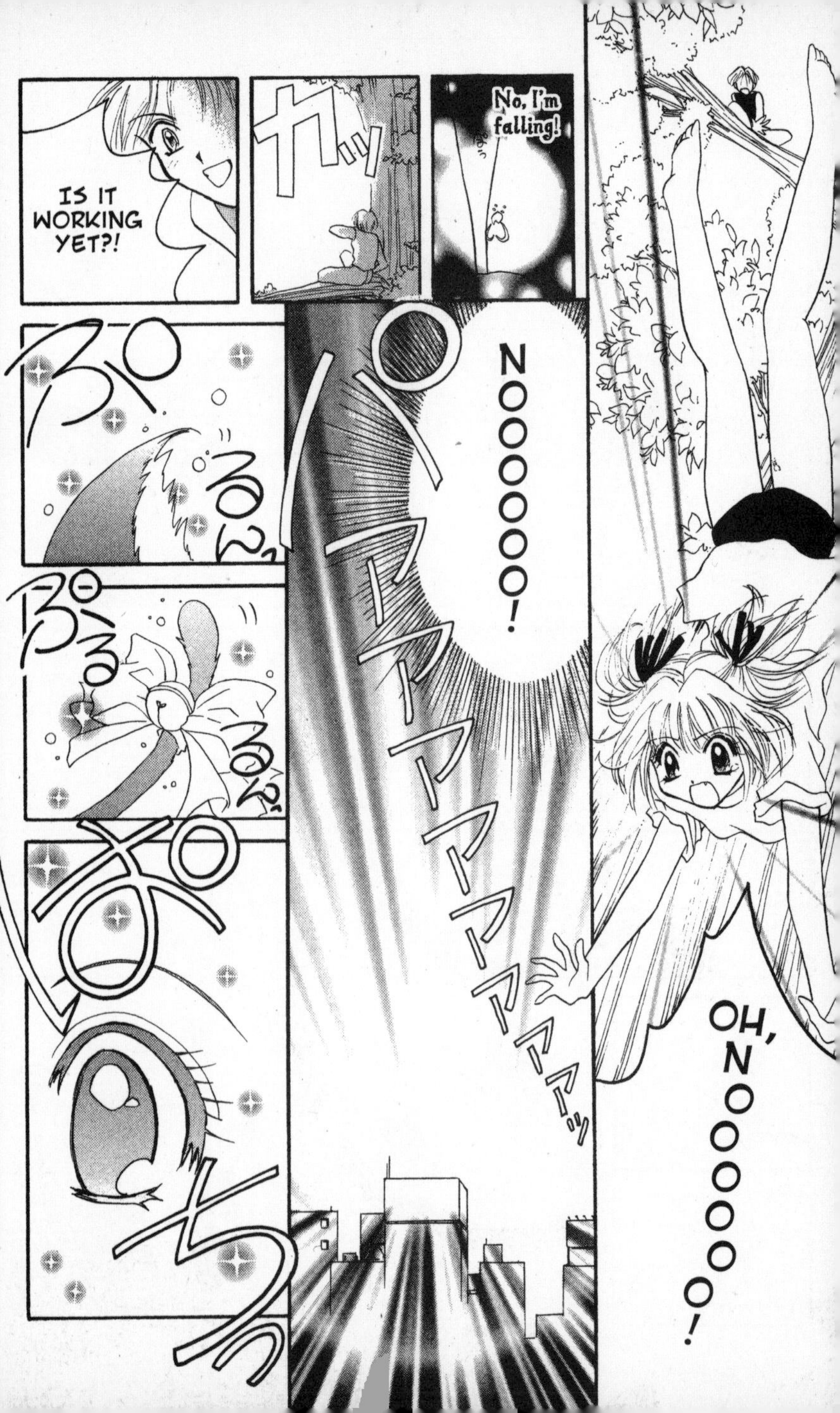
OH, NOOOOOOOO!
No, I'm falling!
IS IT WORKING YET?!
NOOOOOOO!

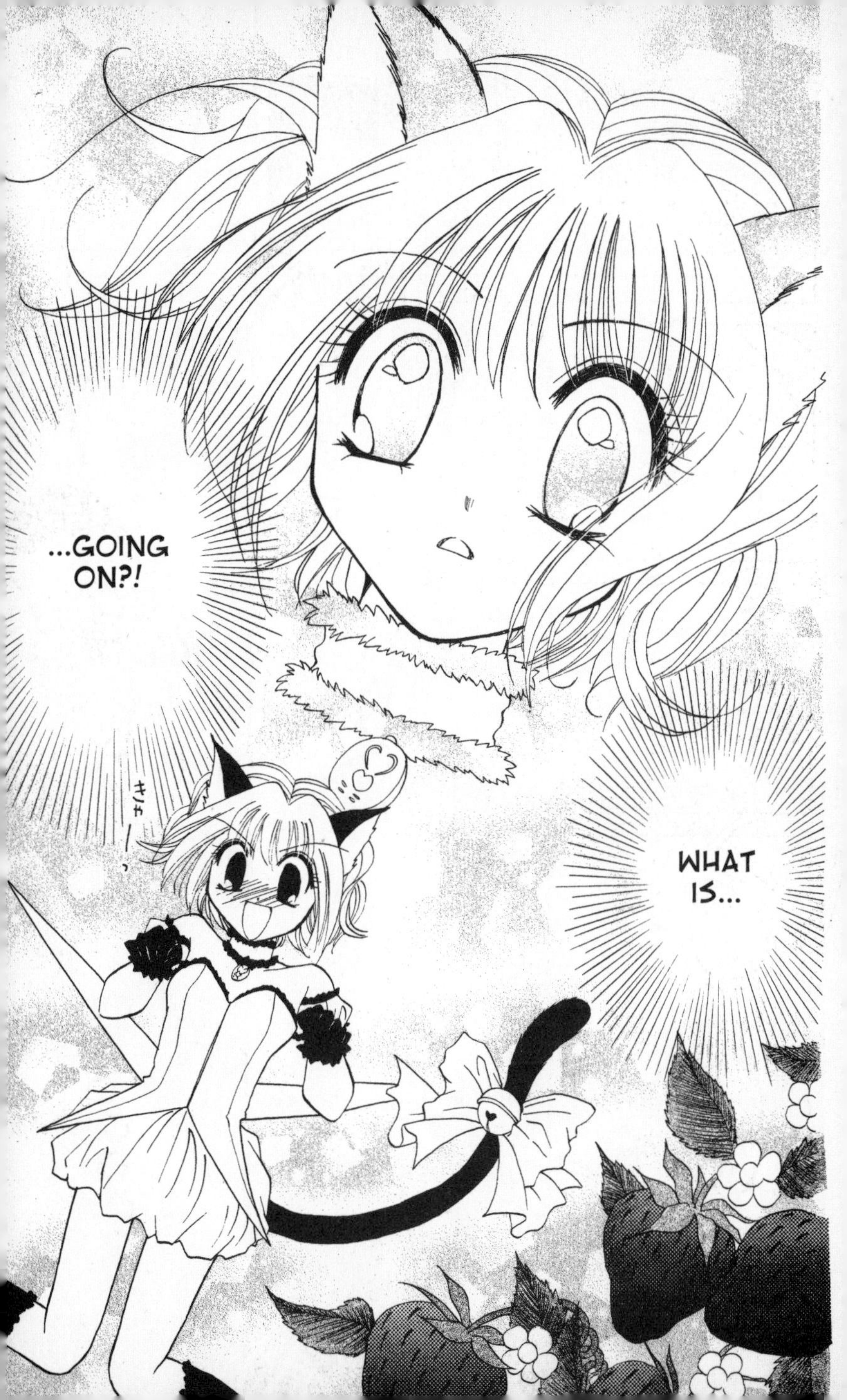
WHAT IS...
...GOING ON?!
キャー

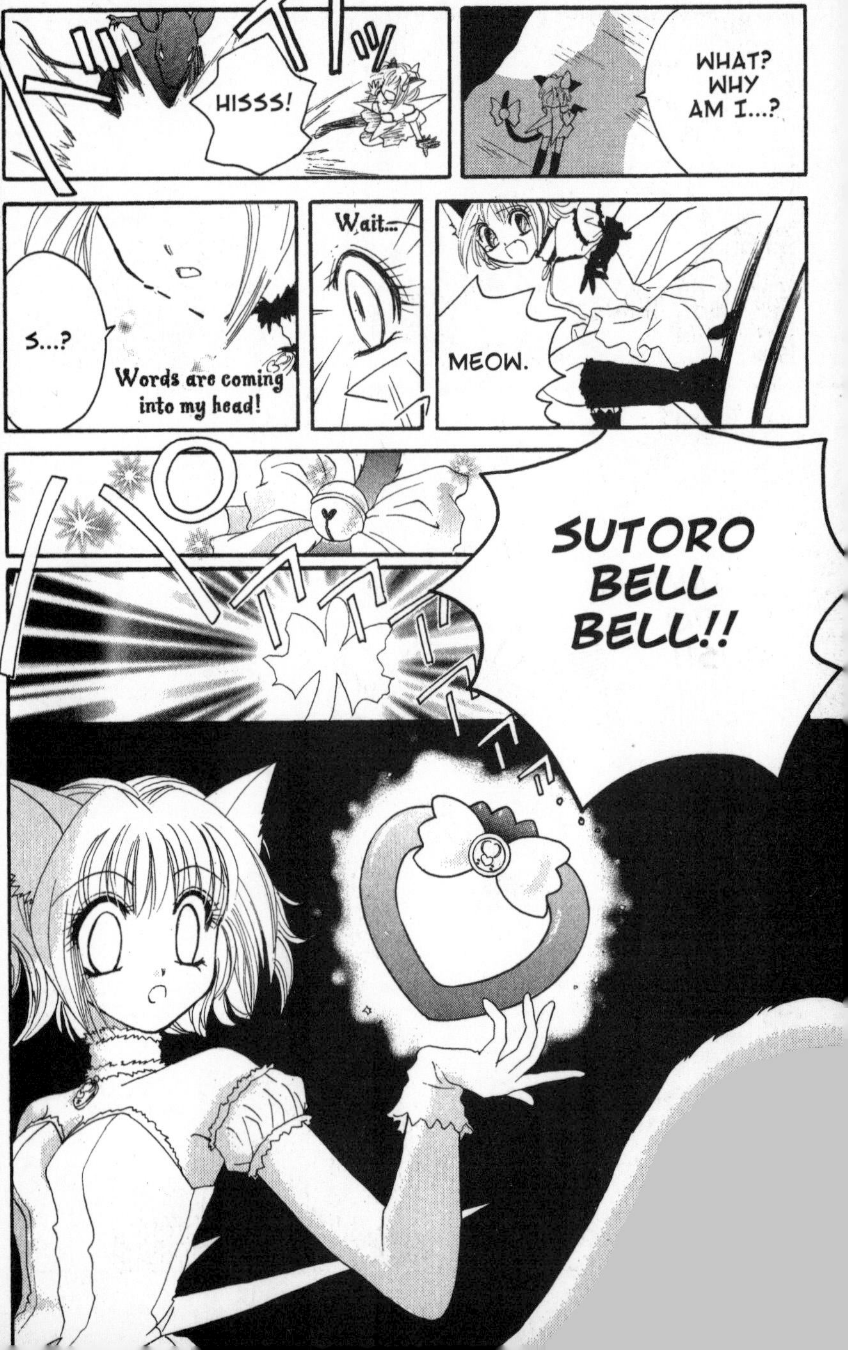
WHAT? WHY AM I...?
HISSS!
MEOW.
Wait...
S...?
Words are coming into my head!
SUTORO BELL BELL!!

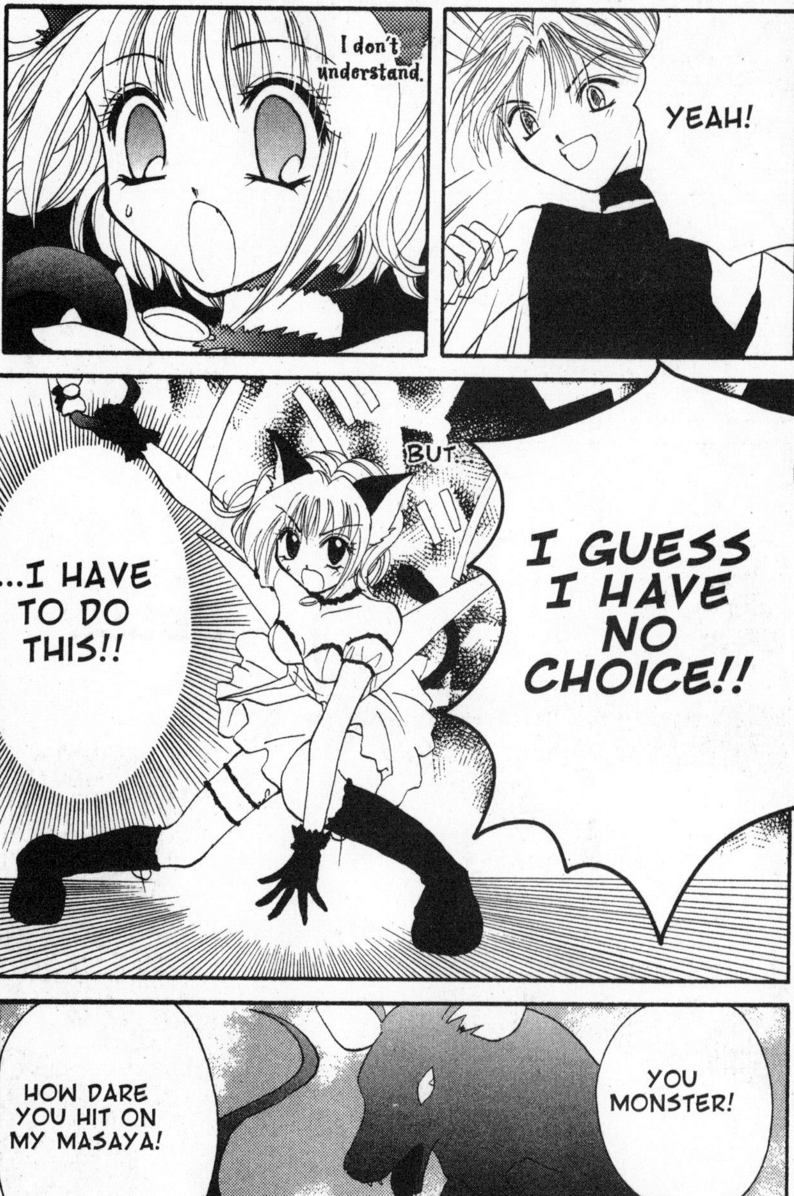

YEAH!
I don't understand.
BUT...
I GUESS I HAVE NO CHOICE!!
...I HAVE TO DO THIS!!
YOU MONSTER!
HOW DARE YOU HIT ON MY MASAYA!

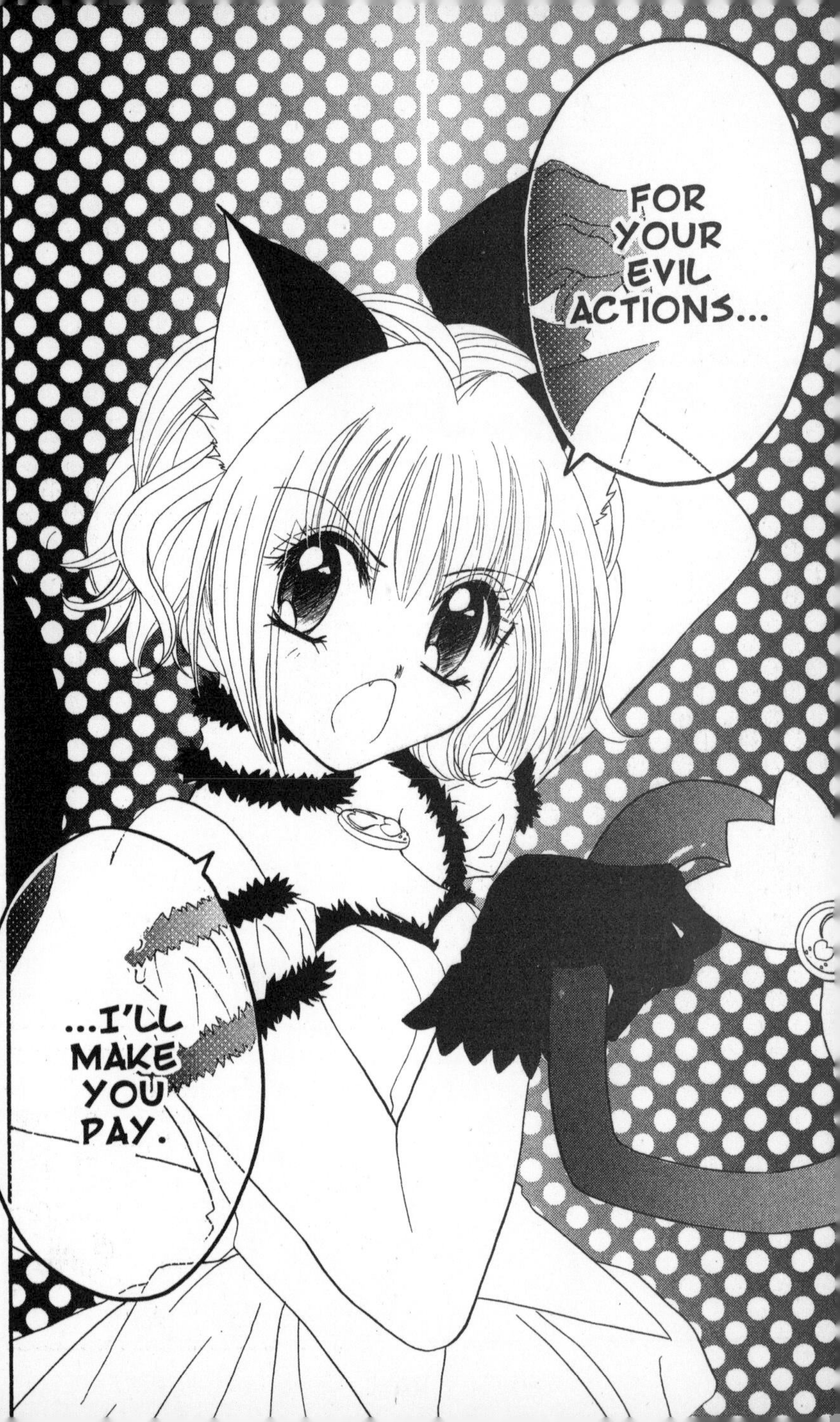
FOR YOUR EVIL ACTIONS...
...I'LL MAKE YOU PAY.

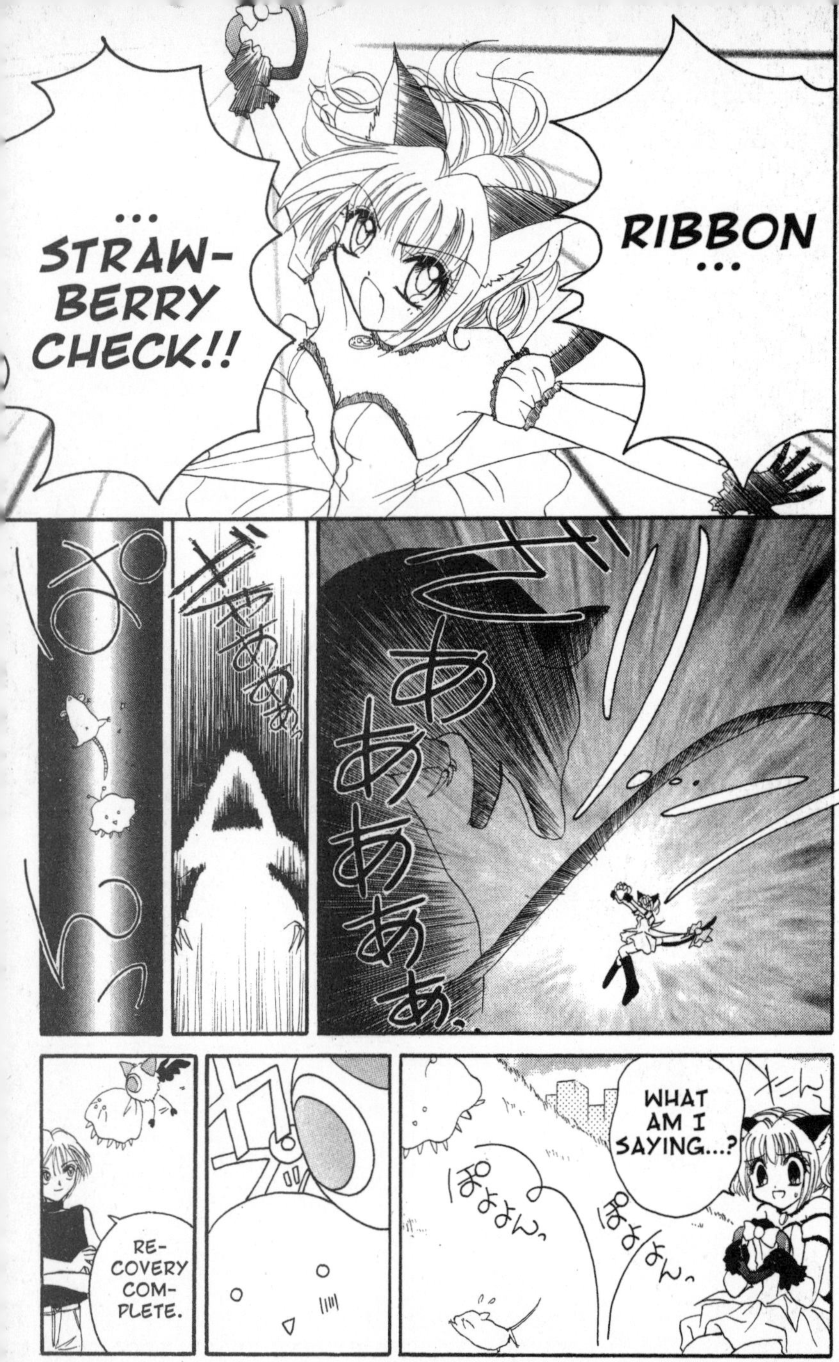
RIBBON ...
... STRAW-BERRY CHECK!!
ああああああ
ぎゃあああ
WHAT AM I SAYING...?
ぽよよん
ぽよよん
RE-COVERY COM-PLETE.

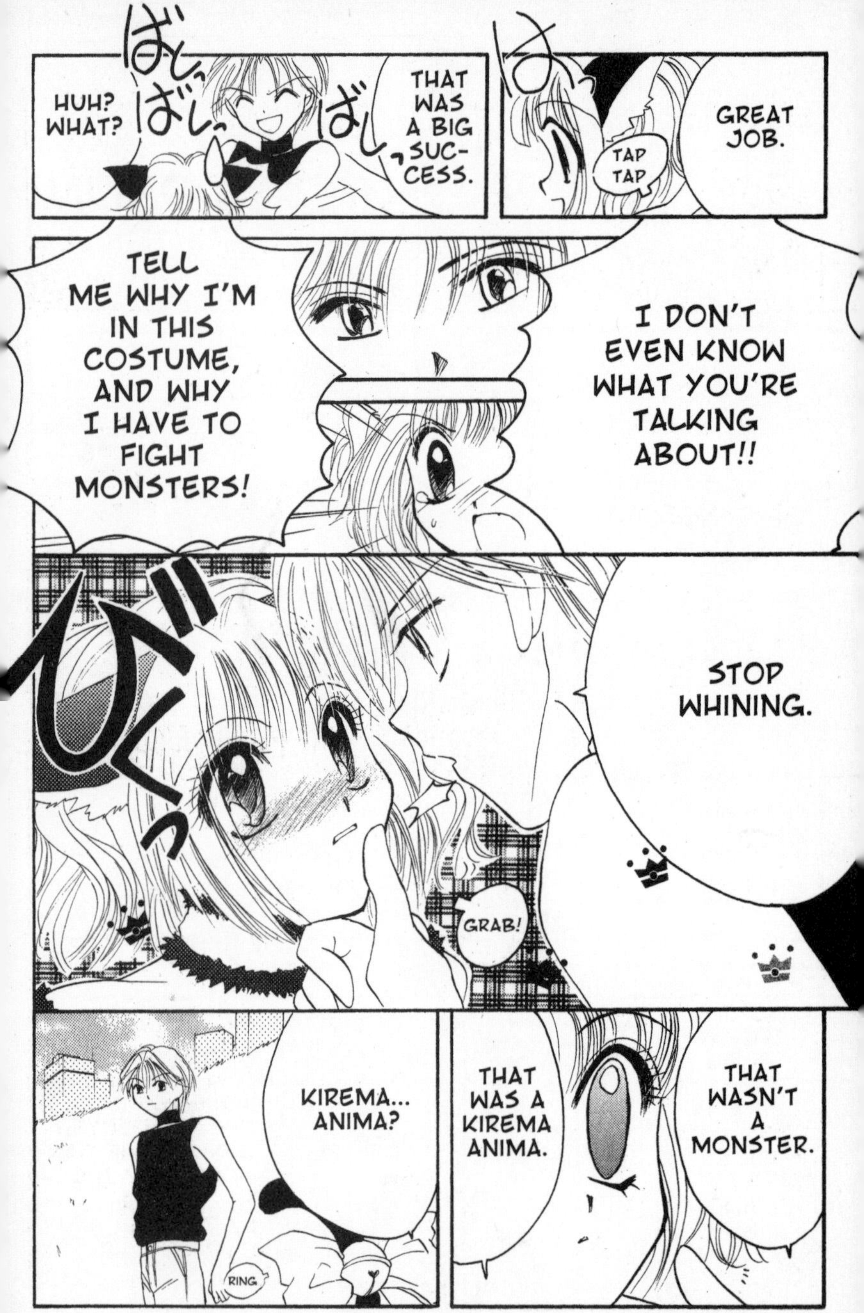
はっ
GREAT JOB.
TAP TAP
THAT WAS A BIG SUC-CESS.
ばしっ ばしっ ばしっ
HUH? WHAT?
I DON'T EVEN KNOW WHAT YOU'RE TALKING ABOUT!!
TELL ME WHY I'M IN THIS COSTUME, AND WHY I HAVE TO FIGHT MONSTERS!
STOP WHINING.
GRAB!
びくっ
THAT WASN'T A MONSTER.
THAT WAS A KIREMA ANIMA.
KIREMA... ANIMA?
RING

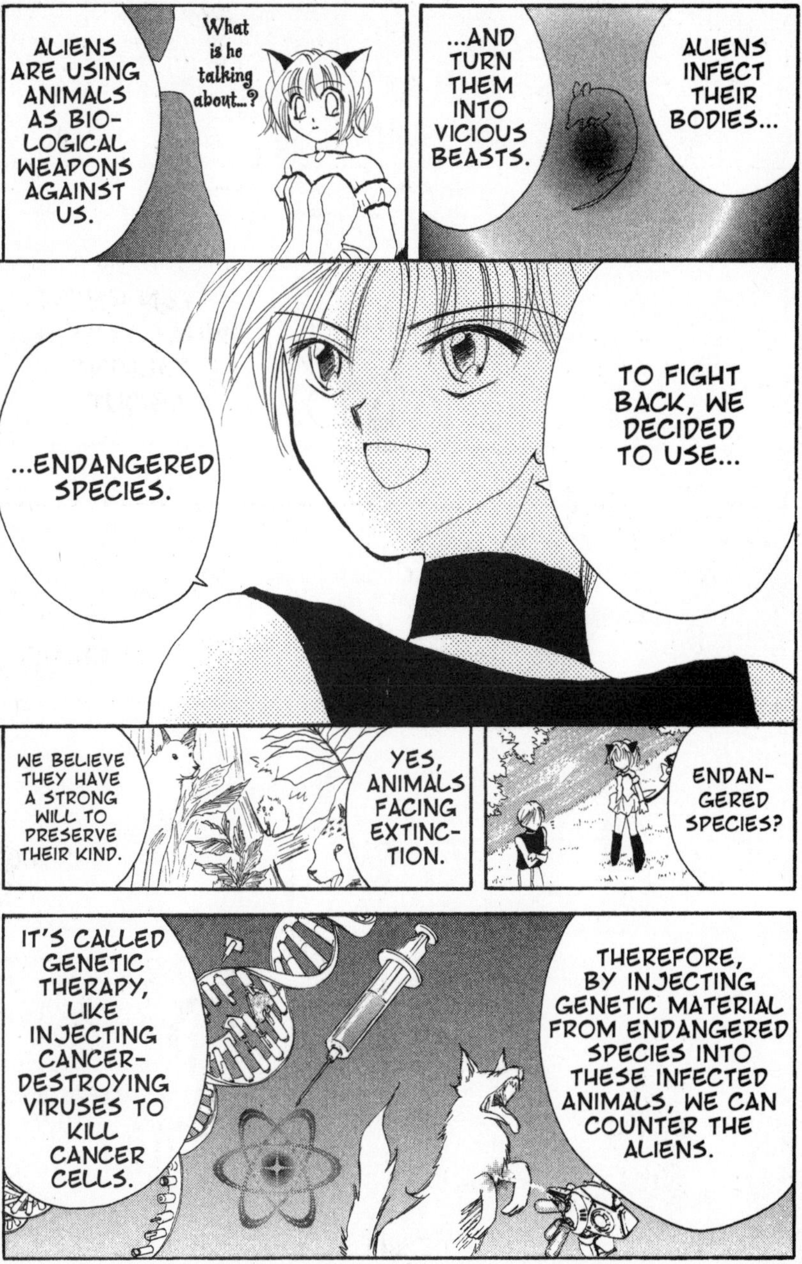
ALIENS INFECT THEIR BODIES...
...AND TURN THEM INTO VICIOUS BEASTS.
What is he talking about...?
ALIENS ARE USING ANIMALS AS BIOLOGICAL WEAPONS AGAINST US.
TO FIGHT BACK, WE DECIDED TO USE...
...ENDANGERED SPECIES.
ENDANGERED SPECIES?
YES, ANIMALS FACING EXTINCTION.
WE BELIEVE THEY HAVE A STRONG WILL TO PRESERVE THEIR KIND.
THEREFORE, BY INJECTING GENETIC MATERIAL FROM ENDANGERED SPECIES INTO THESE INFECTED ANIMALS, WE CAN COUNTER THE ALIENS.
IT'S CALLED GENETIC THERAPY, LIKE INJECTING CANCER-DESTROYING VIRUSES TO KILL CANCER CELLS.

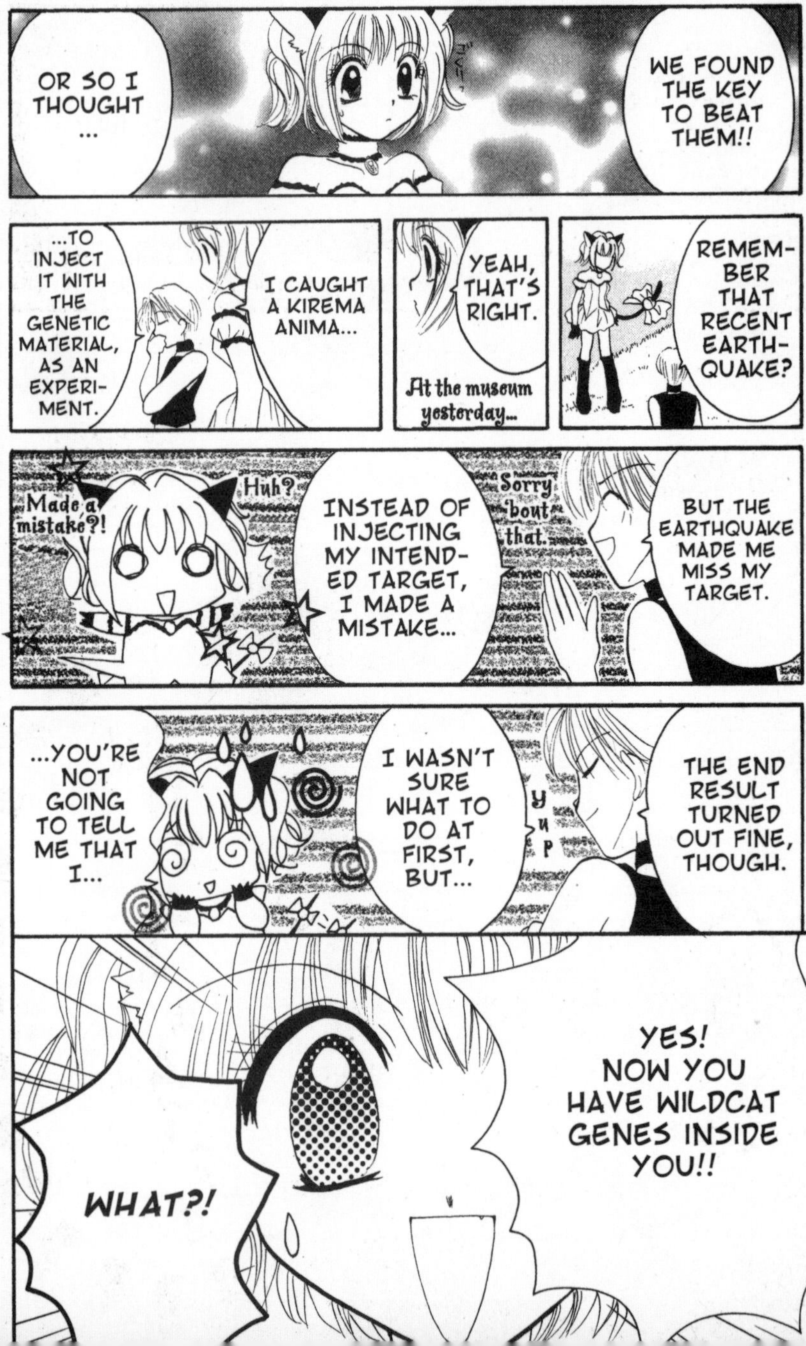
WE FOUND THE KEY TO BEAT THEM!!
OR SO I THOUGHT ...
REMEMBER THAT RECENT EARTHQUAKE?
YEAH, THAT'S RIGHT.
At the museum yesterday...
I CAUGHT A KIREMA ANIMA...
...TO INJECT IT WITH THE GENETIC MATERIAL, AS AN EXPERIMENT.
BUT THE EARTHQUAKE MADE ME MISS MY TARGET.
Sorry 'bout that.
INSTEAD OF INJECTING MY INTENDED TARGET, I MADE A MISTAKE...
Huh?
Made a mistake?!
THE END RESULT TURNED OUT FINE, THOUGH.
yup
I WASN'T SURE WHAT TO DO AT FIRST, BUT...
...YOU'RE NOT GOING TO TELL ME THAT I...
YES! NOW YOU HAVE WILDCAT GENES INSIDE YOU!!
WHAT?!

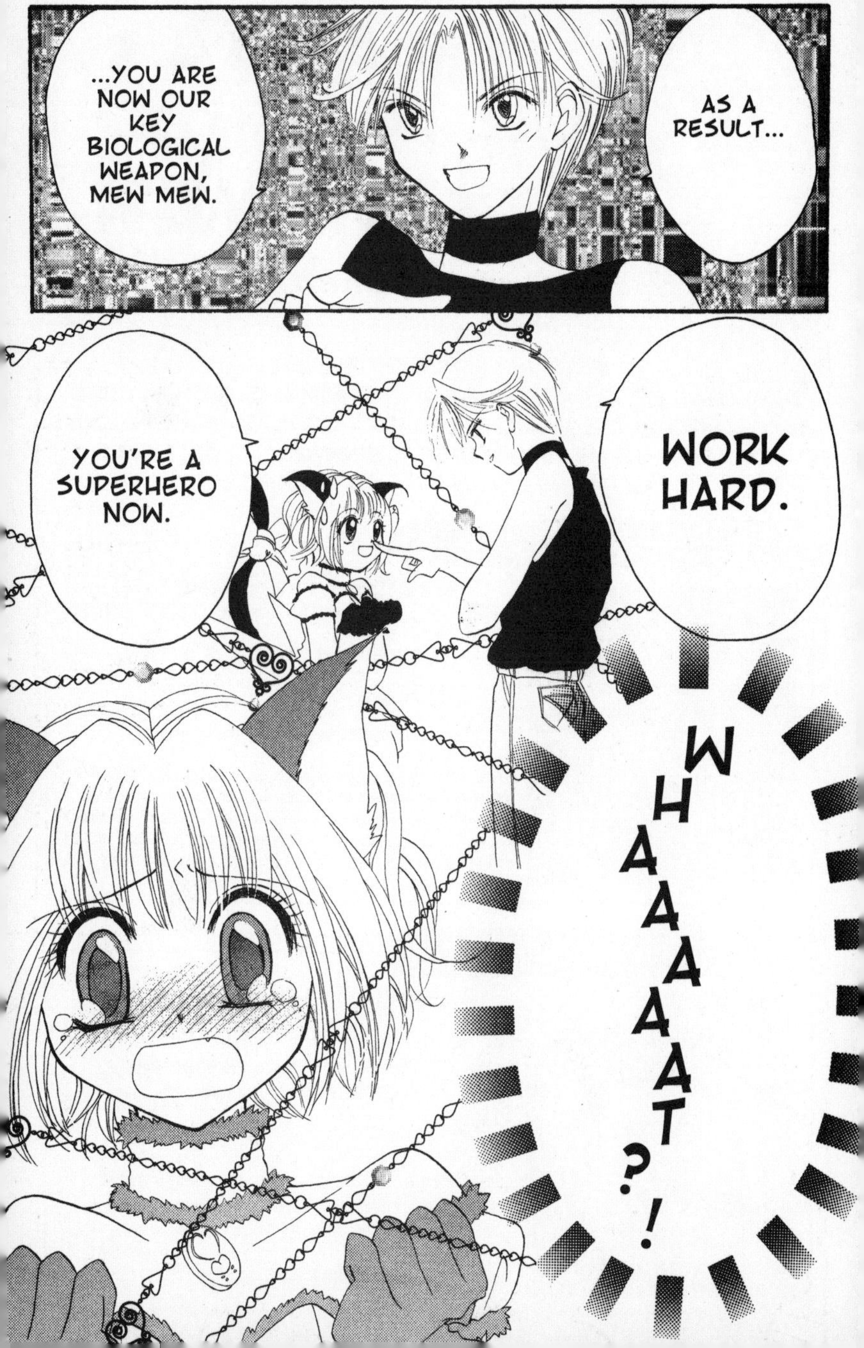
AS A RESULT...
...YOU ARE NOW OUR KEY BIOLOGICAL WEAPON, MEW MEW.
WORK HARD.
YOU'RE A SUPERHERO NOW.
WHAAAAAT?!

MASHA'S TOKYO MEW MEW

ENDANGERED SPECIES FILE

WHAT ARE ENDANGERED SPECIES?

ENDANGERED SPECIES ARE ANIMALS ON THE BRINK OF EXTINCTION. THERE ARE CURRENTLY 2,580 ENDANGERED SPECIES. THEIR NUMBERS ARE DECLINING FROM POACHING AND LOSS OF HABITAT. EVERYONE, LET'S ALL WORK TOGETHER TO SAVE ANIMALS FROM EXTINCTION!

FILE 1

IRIOMOTE YAMANEKO (IRIOMOTE CAT)
PRIONAILURUS BENGALENSIS IRIOMOTENSIS

SIZE: AVERAGE FEMALE BODY SIZE IS 1'7", WITH THE TAIL BEING NEARLY AN ADDITIONAL FOOT. MALES ARE SLIGHTLY LARGER IN SIZE.

HABITAT: IRIOMOTE ISLAND (OKINAWA PREFECTURE)

SINCE A NEW FELINE SPECIES HAD NOT BEEN DISCOVERED IN 72 YEARS, ITS DISCOVERY ATTRACTED WORLDWIDE ATTENTION. IN 1967, JAPAN DESIGNATED THE SPECIES AS A NATIONAL NATURAL MONUMENT. THEY ARE MAINLY TERRESTRIAL, BUT ARE ALSO ADEPT AT CLIMBING TREES. WITH LESS THAN A HUNDRED THOUGHT TO STILL EXIST IN THE WILD, ACTION HAS BEEN TAKEN TO PROTECT THEM FROM EXTINCTION.

FILE 2

IDOJIRORU INCO (ULTRAMARINE LORIKEET)
VINI ULTRAMARINA

SIZE: AVERAGE BODY SIZE IS 18 CENTIMETERS; WINGSPAN IS ABOUT 11 CENTIMETERS.

HABITAT: TAHITI

SIMILAR TO THE LORIKEETS FOUND IN PET STORES, THERE ARE ONLY ABOUT 1,500-2,000 LEFT IN THEIR WILD HABITAT. THEY HAVE WHITE THROATS. ON THEIR NATIVE ISLAND, IMPORTED FOREIGN SPECIES AND DISEASES HAVE BROUGHT THIS SPECIES TO THE BRINK OF EXTINCTION.

HI, IT'S ME, IKUMI !

Hello, there. It's been a while. Let me introduce myself. My name is Mia Ikumi. It's been a while since my last comic book. Thank you to everyone who has patiently waited for me. Since the preparation took so long, it seemed like a short time for the first book to come out. In reality, it's been over a year since my last book. Maybe some of you were wondering if I had retired as a manga artist, but not to worry. I plan on sticking to my career for a while. Now you can get back to enjoying "Tokyo Mew Mew."

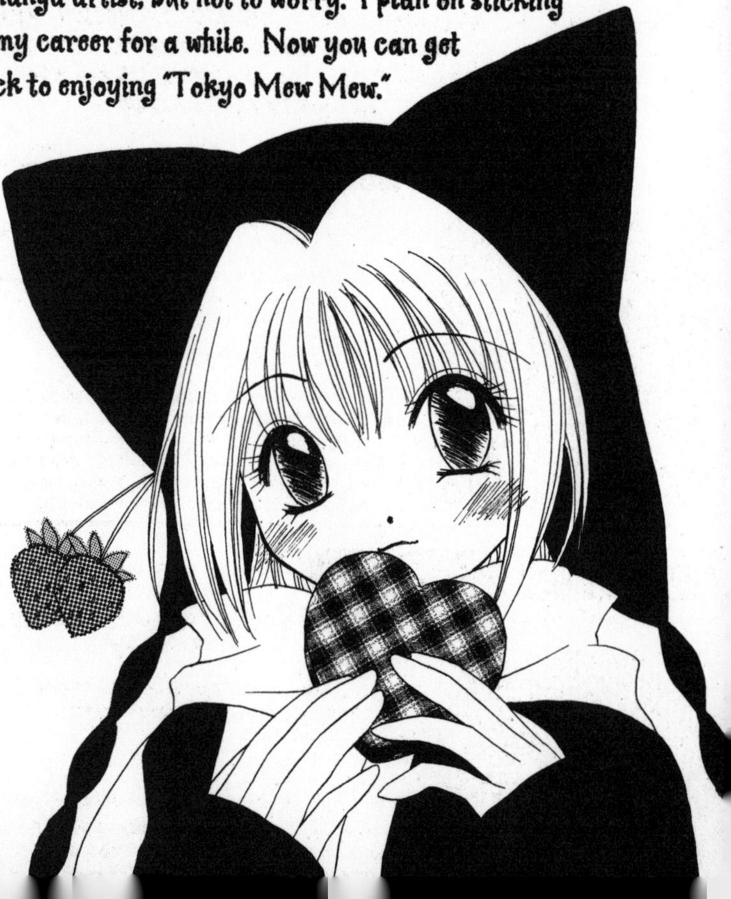

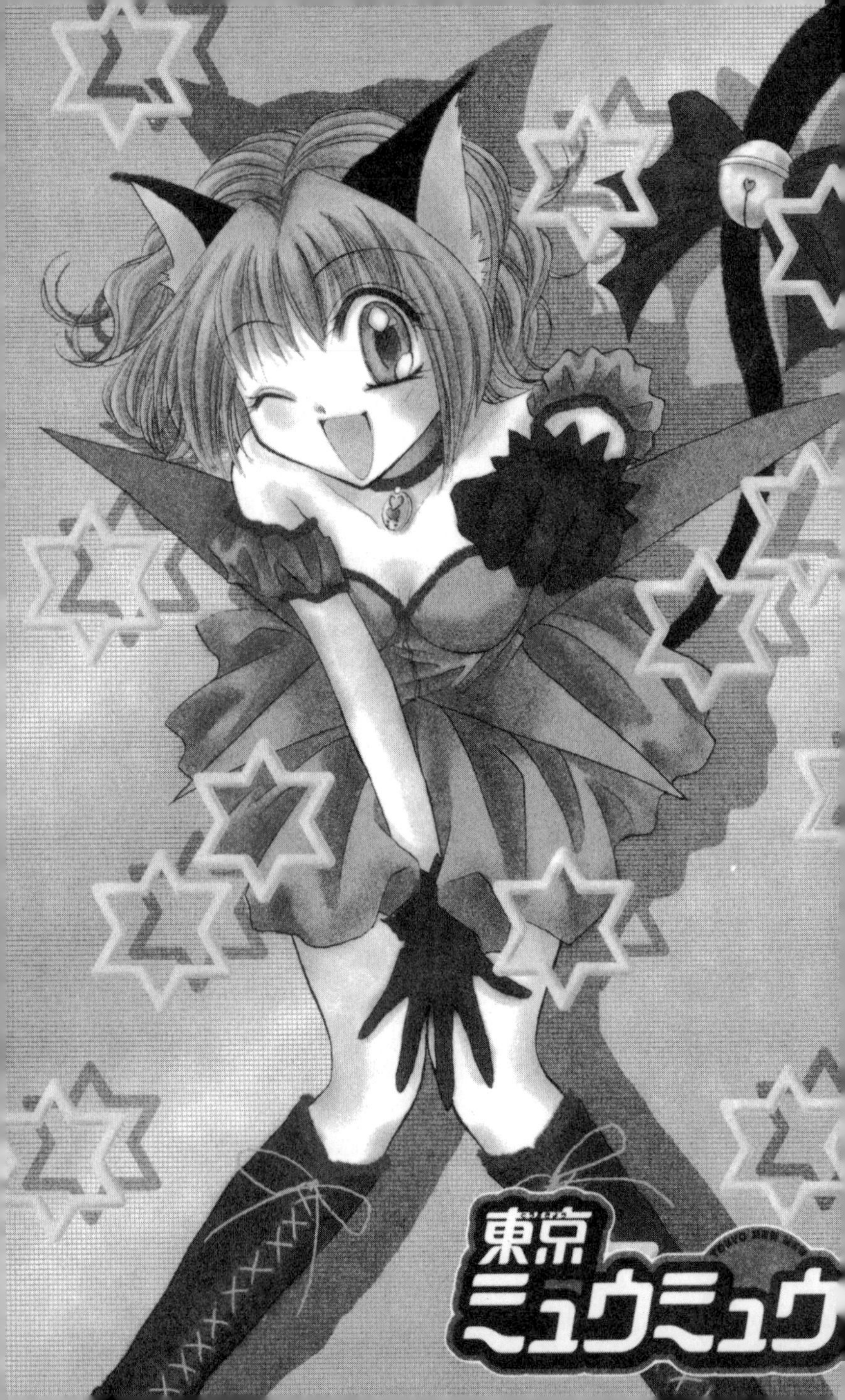
東京
ミュウミュウ

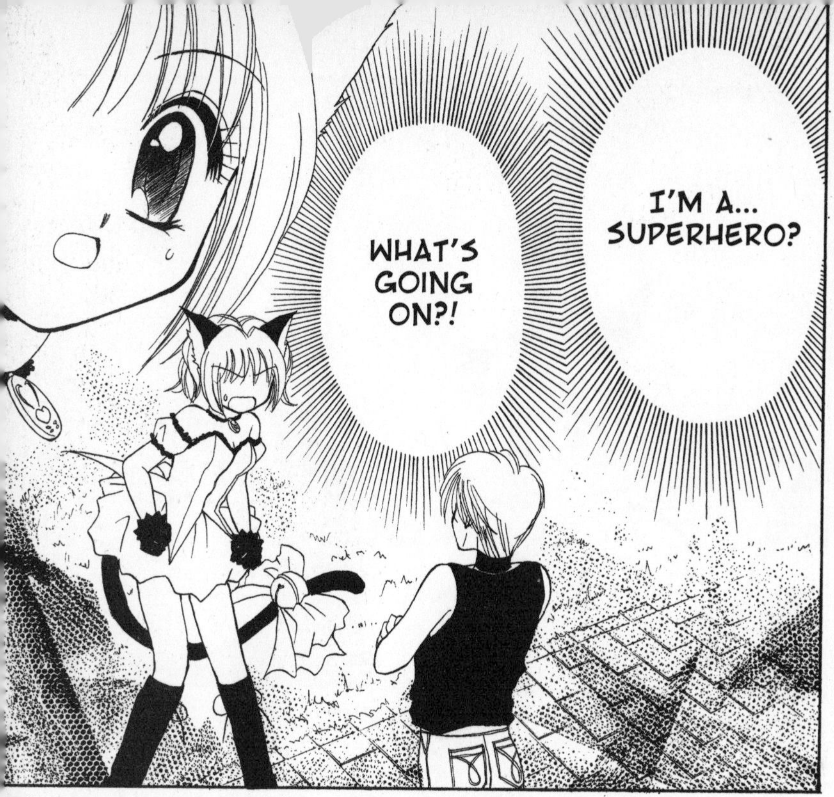
I'M A... SUPERHERO?
WHAT'S GOING ON?!

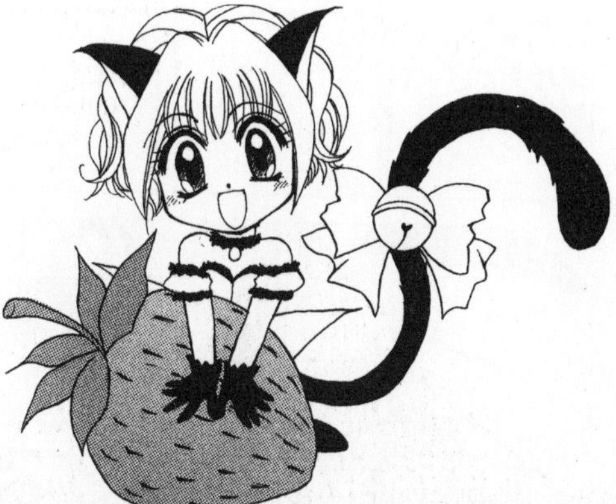

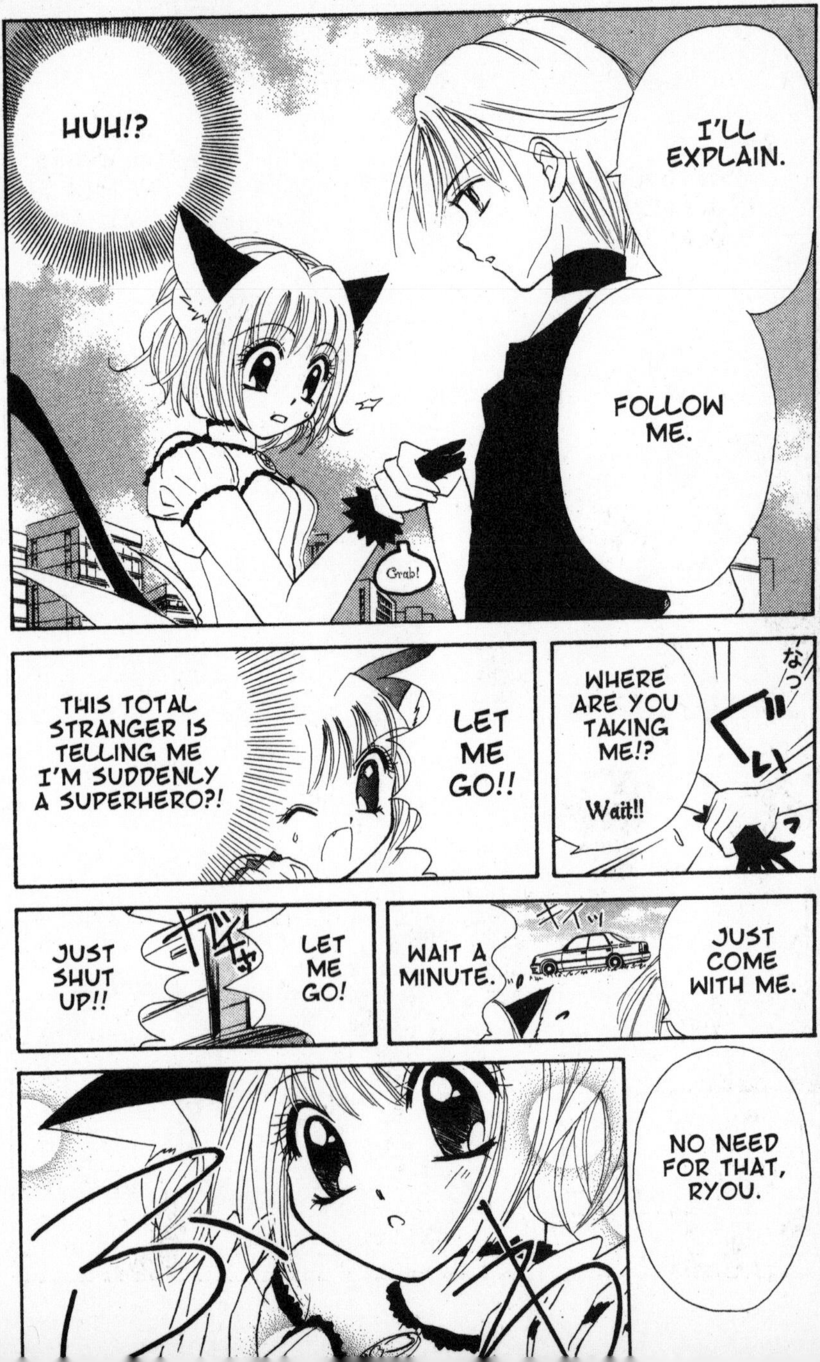
I'LL EXPLAIN.
FOLLOW ME.
HUH!?
Grab!
なっ
WHERE ARE YOU TAKING ME!?
Wait!!
LET ME GO!!
THIS TOTAL STRANGER IS TELLING ME I'M SUDDENLY A SUPERHERO?!
JUST COME WITH ME.
キイッ
WAIT A MINUTE.
LET ME GO!
JUST SHUT UP!!
NO NEED FOR THAT, RYOU.

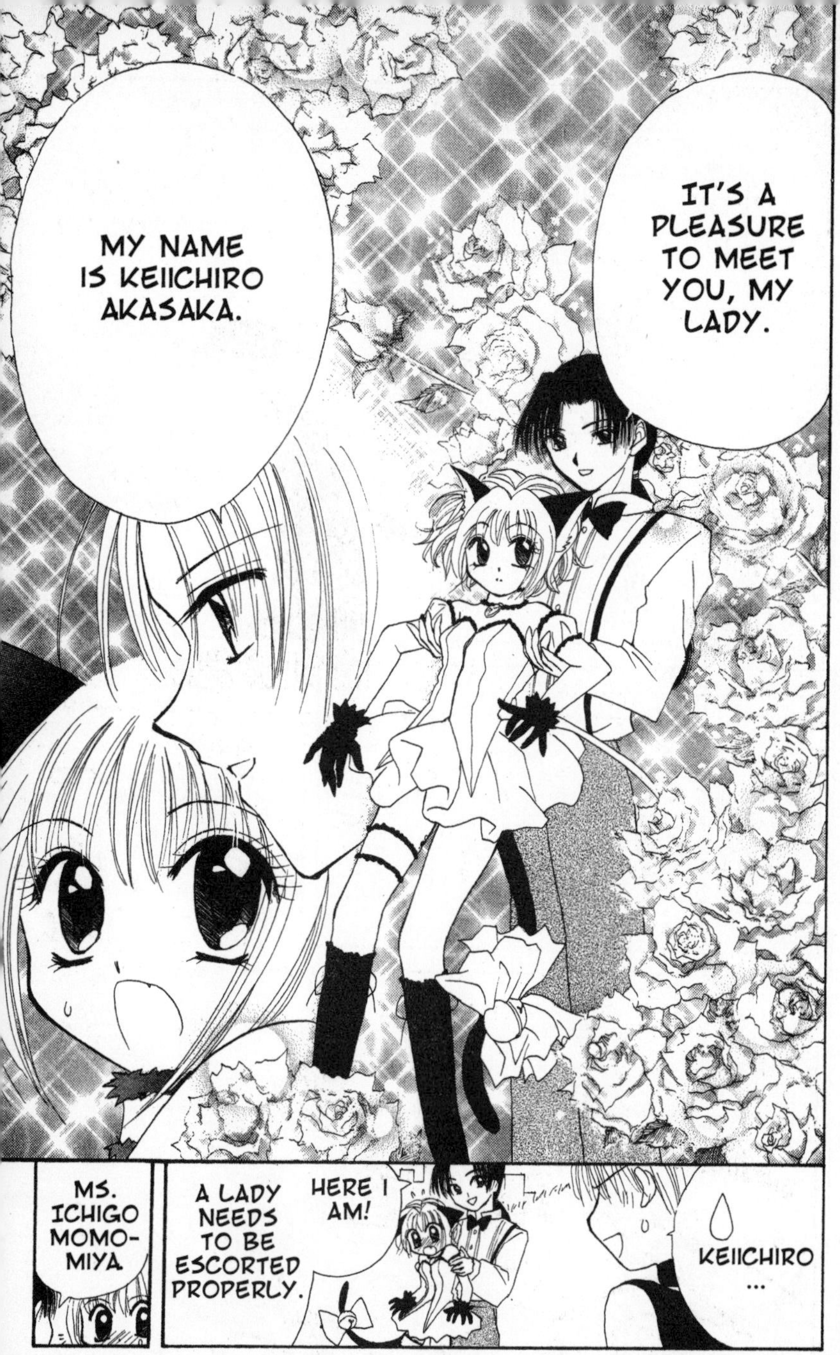
IT'S A PLEASURE TO MEET YOU, MY LADY.
MY NAME IS KEIICHIRO AKASAKA.
KEIICHIRO ...
HERE I AM!
A LADY NEEDS TO BE ESCORTED PROPERLY.
MS. ICHIGO MOMOMIYA.

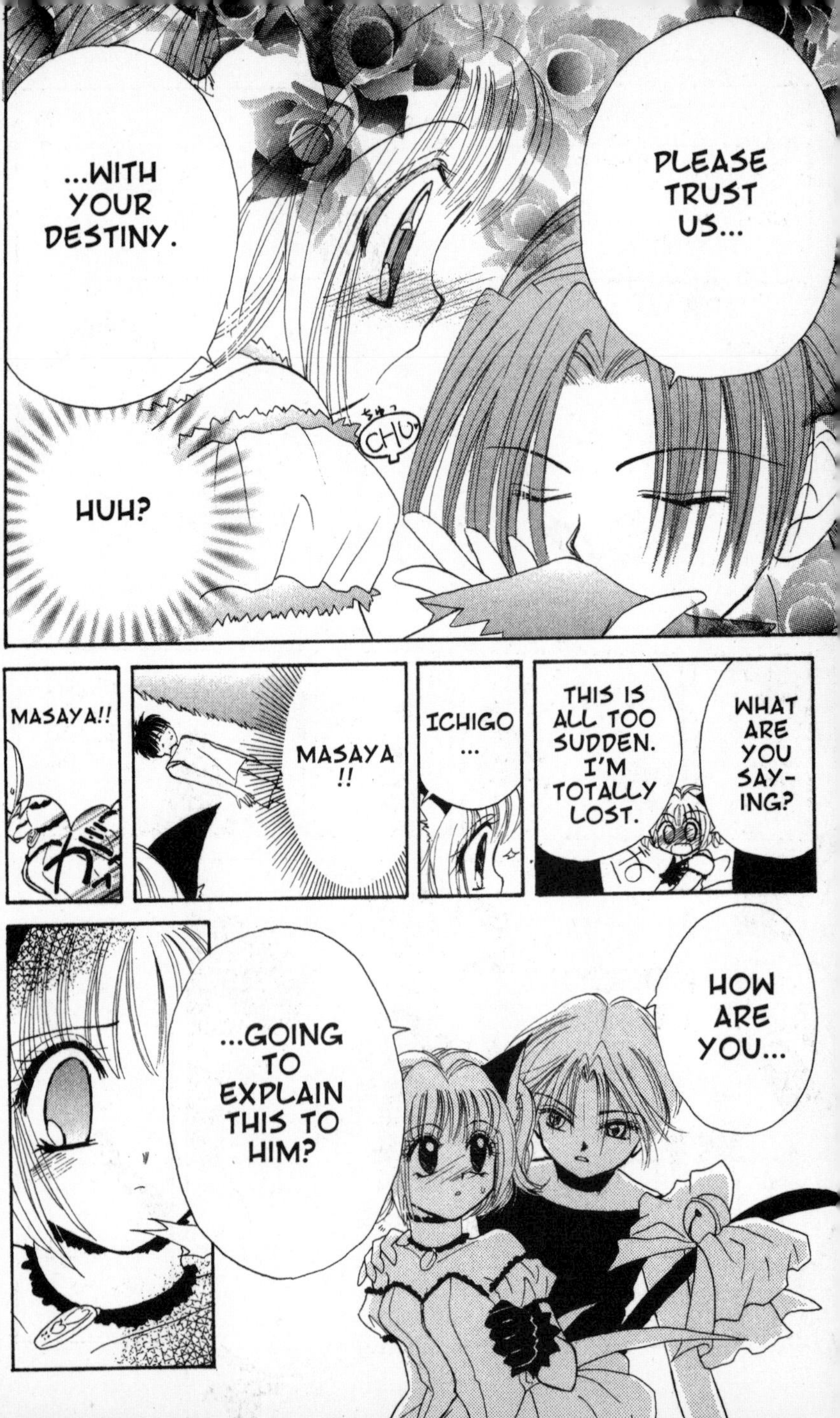
PLEASE TRUST US...
...WITH YOUR DESTINY.
CHU
HUH?
WHAT ARE YOU SAYING?
THIS IS ALL TOO SUDDEN. I'M TOTALLY LOST.
ICHIGO...
MASAYA!!
MASAYA!!
HOW ARE YOU...
...GOING TO EXPLAIN THIS TO HIM?

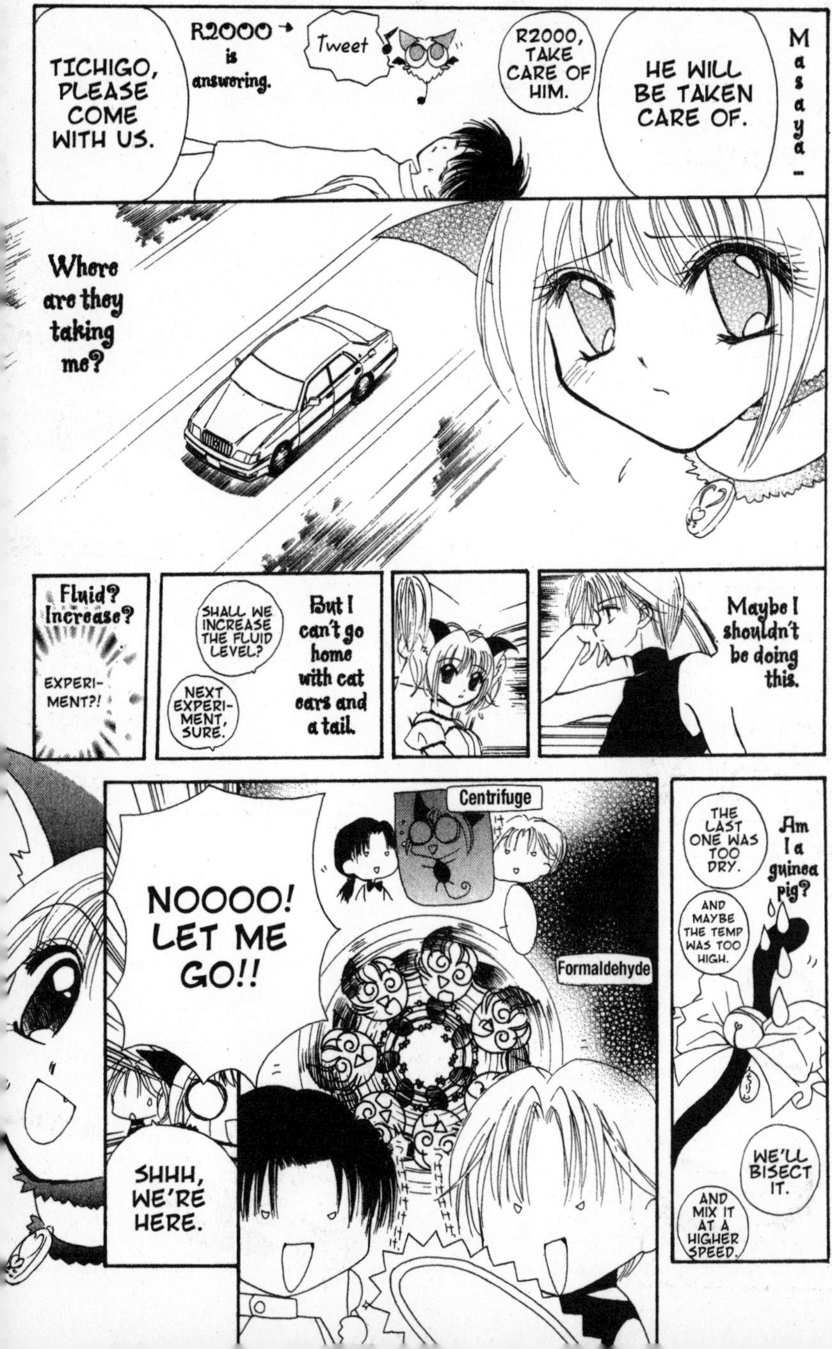
Masaya...
HE WILL BE TAKEN CARE OF.
R2000, TAKE CARE OF HIM.
Tweet
R2000 → is answering.
TICHIGO, PLEASE COME WITH US.
Where are they taking me?
Maybe I shouldn't be doing this.
But I can't go home with cat ears and a tail.
SHALL WE INCREASE THE FLUID LEVEL?
NEXT EXPERIMENT, SURE.
Fluid? Increase?
EXPERIMENT?!
Am I a guinea pig?
THE LAST ONE WAS TOO DRY.
AND MAYBE THE TEMP WAS TOO HIGH.
WE'LL BISECT IT.
AND MIX IT AT A HIGHER SPEED.
Centrifuge
Formaldehyde
NOOOO! LET ME GO!!
SHHH, WE'RE HERE.

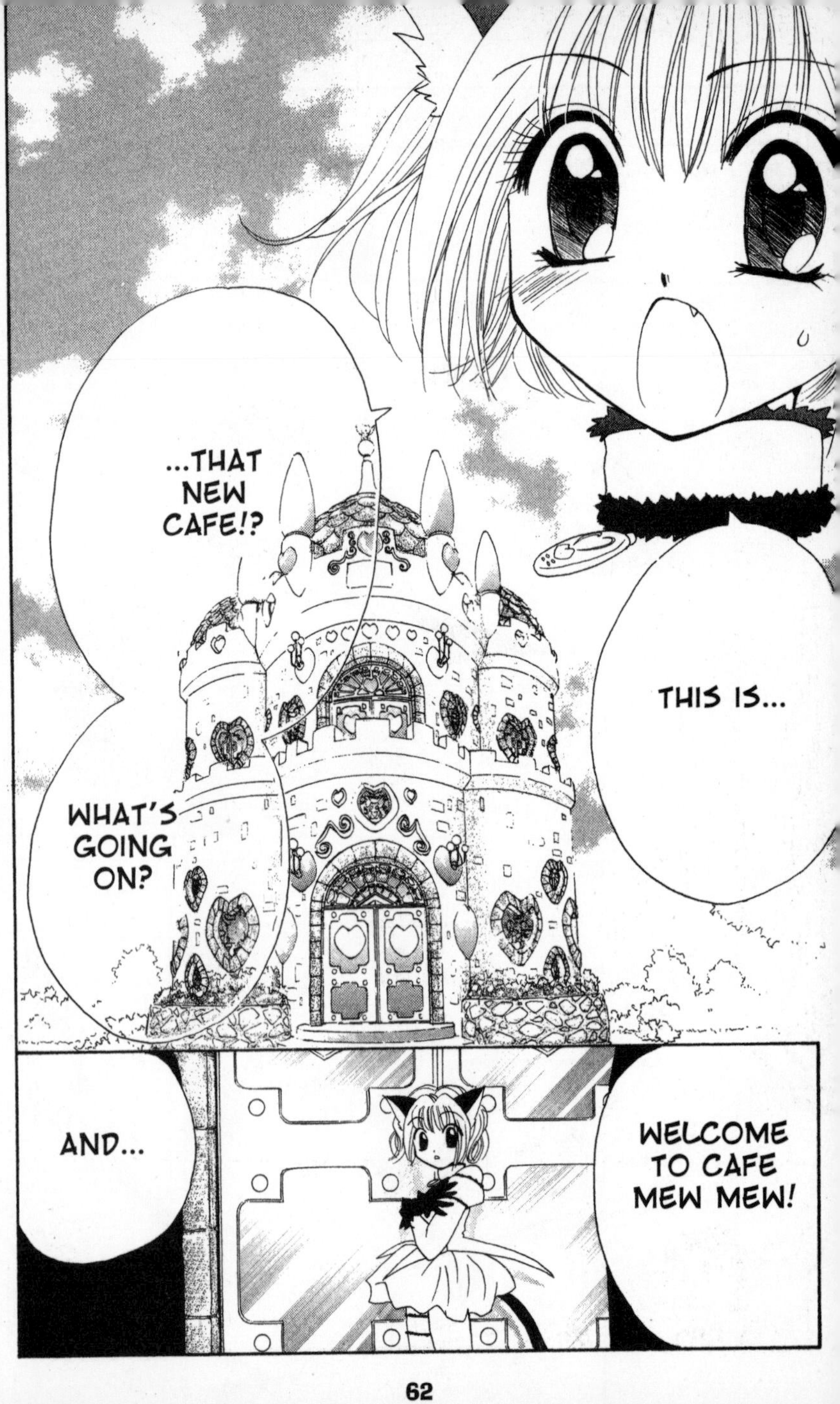
THIS IS...
...THAT NEW CAFE!?
WHAT'S GOING ON?
WELCOME TO CAFE MEW MEW!
AND...

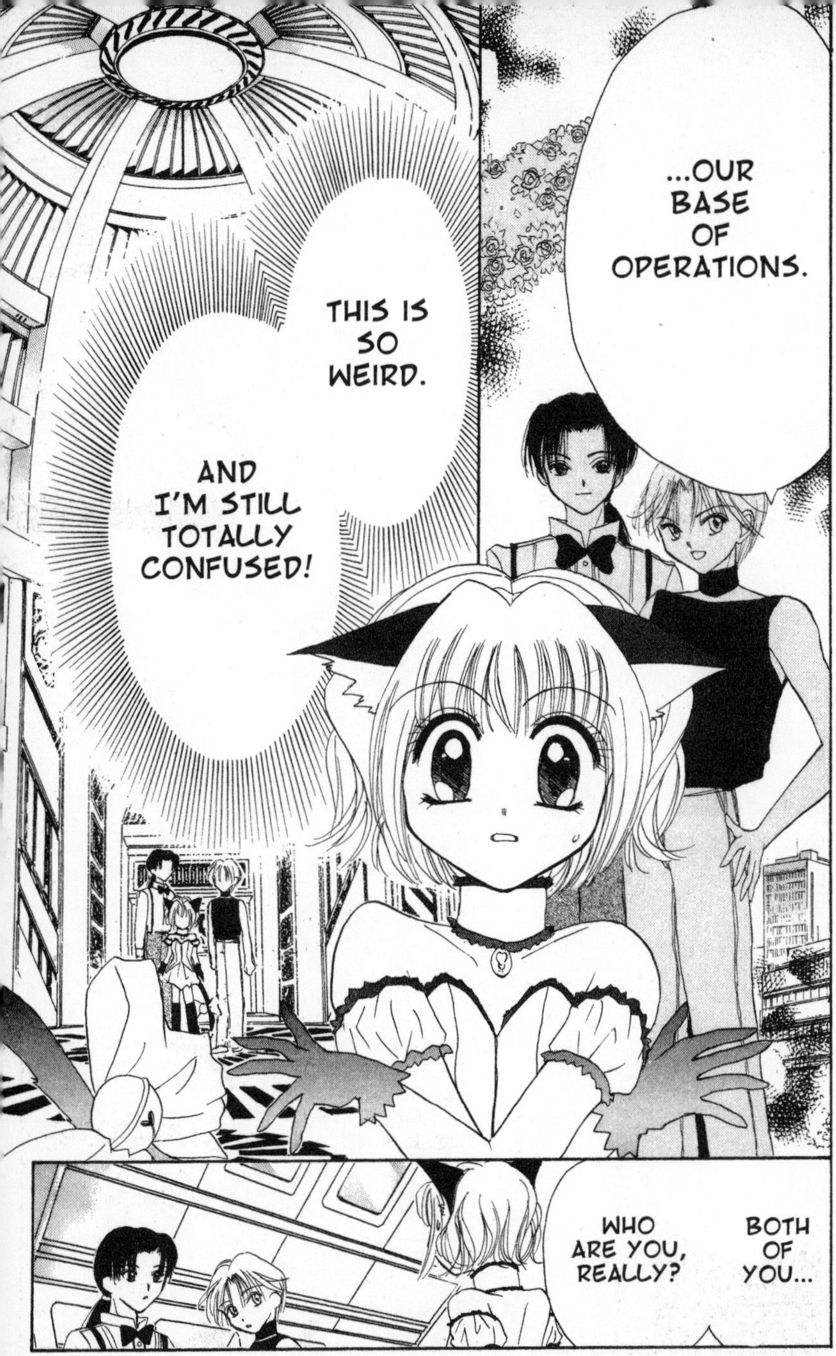
...OUR BASE OF OPERATIONS.
THIS IS SO WEIRD.
AND I'M STILL TOTALLY CONFUSED!
BOTH OF YOU...
WHO ARE YOU, REALLY?

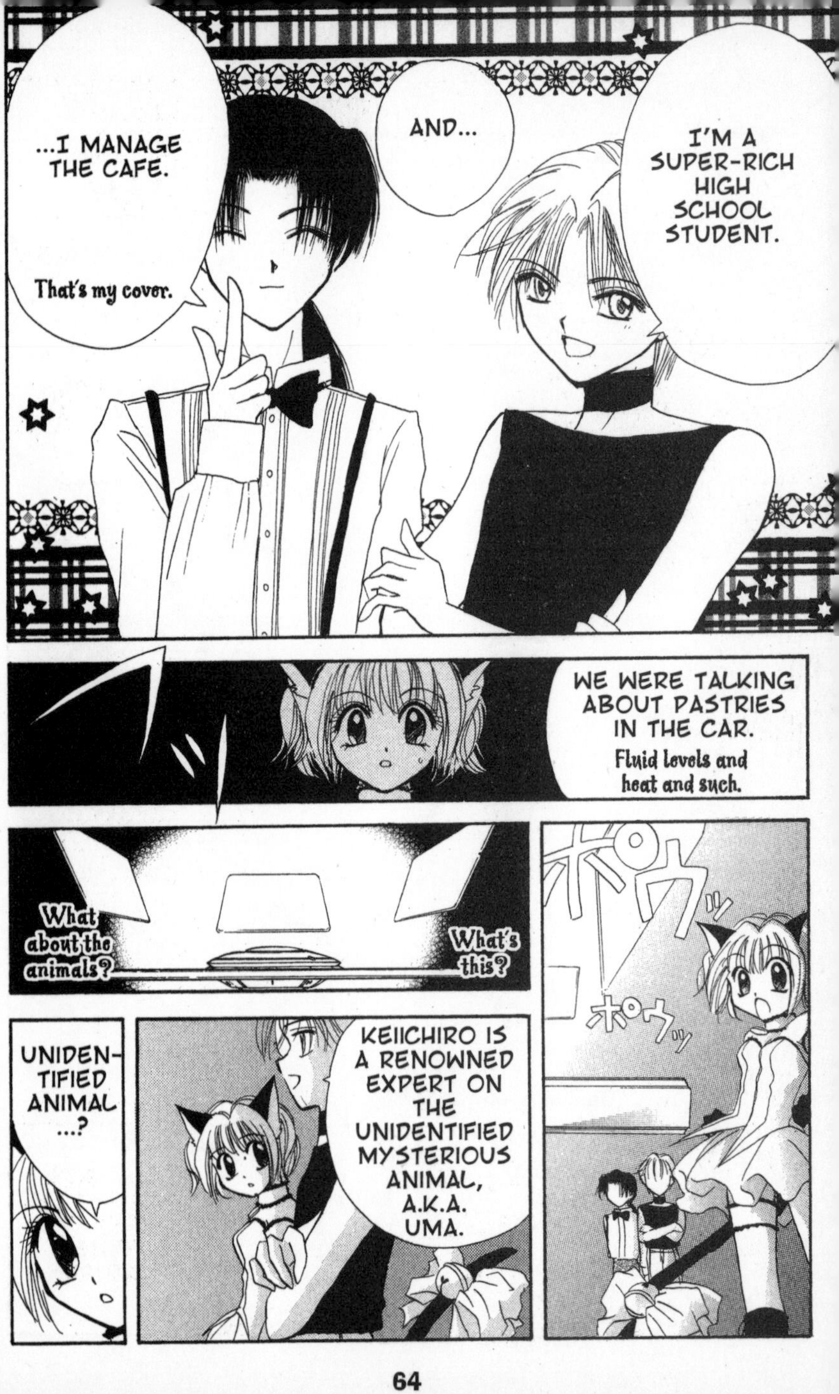
I'M A SUPER-RICH HIGH SCHOOL STUDENT.
AND...
...I MANAGE THE CAFE.
That's my cover.
WE WERE TALKING ABOUT PASTRIES IN THE CAR.
Fluid levels and heat and such.
ポウッ
ポウッ
What's this?
What about the animals?
KEIICHIRO IS A RENOWNED EXPERT ON THE UNIDENTIFIED MYSTERIOUS ANIMAL, A.K.A. UMA.
UNIDEN-TIFIED ANIMAL ...?

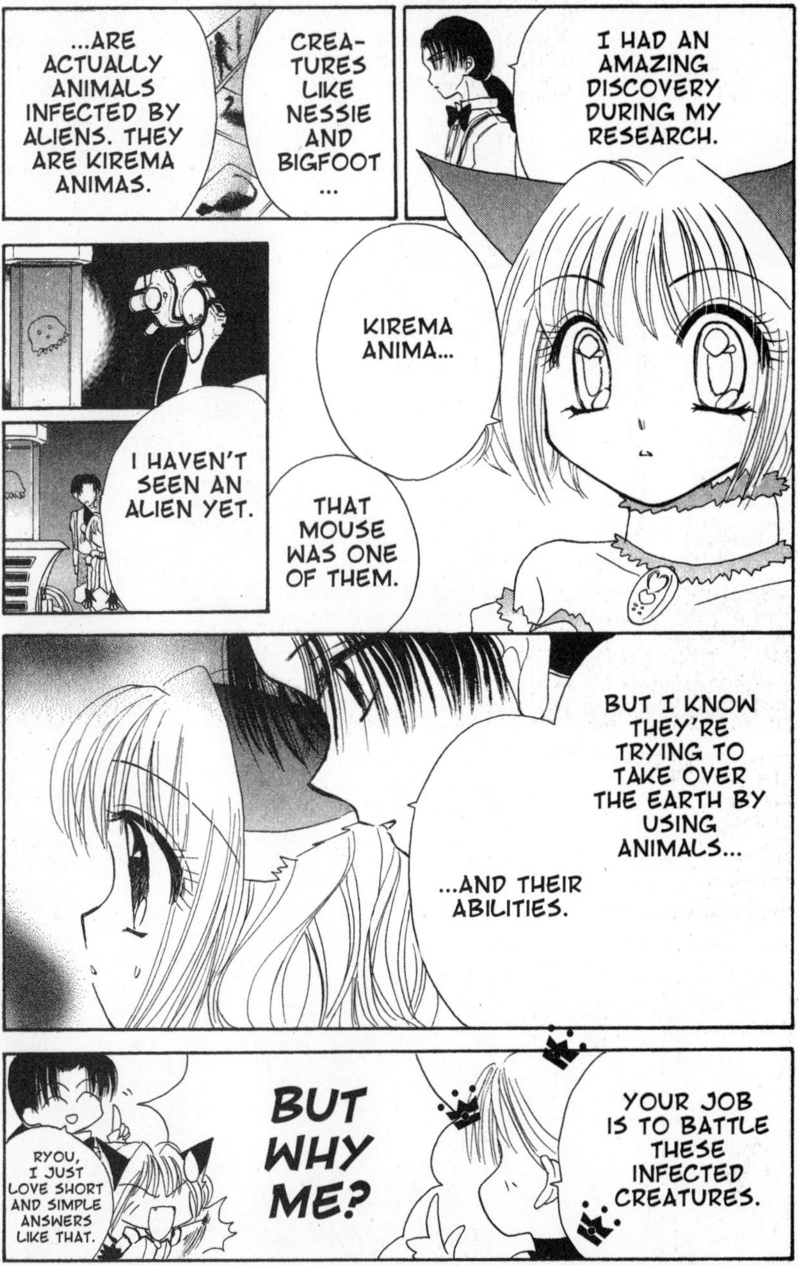
I HAD AN AMAZING DISCOVERY DURING MY RESEARCH.
CREATURES LIKE NESSIE AND BIGFOOT...
...ARE ACTUALLY ANIMALS INFECTED BY ALIENS. THEY ARE KIREMA ANIMAS.
KIREMA ANIMA...
THAT MOUSE WAS ONE OF THEM.
I HAVEN'T SEEN AN ALIEN YET.
BUT I KNOW THEY'RE TRYING TO TAKE OVER THE EARTH BY USING ANIMALS...
...AND THEIR ABILITIES.
YOUR JOB IS TO BATTLE THESE INFECTED CREATURES.
BUT WHY ME?
RYOU, I JUST LOVE SHORT AND SIMPLE ANSWERS LIKE THAT.

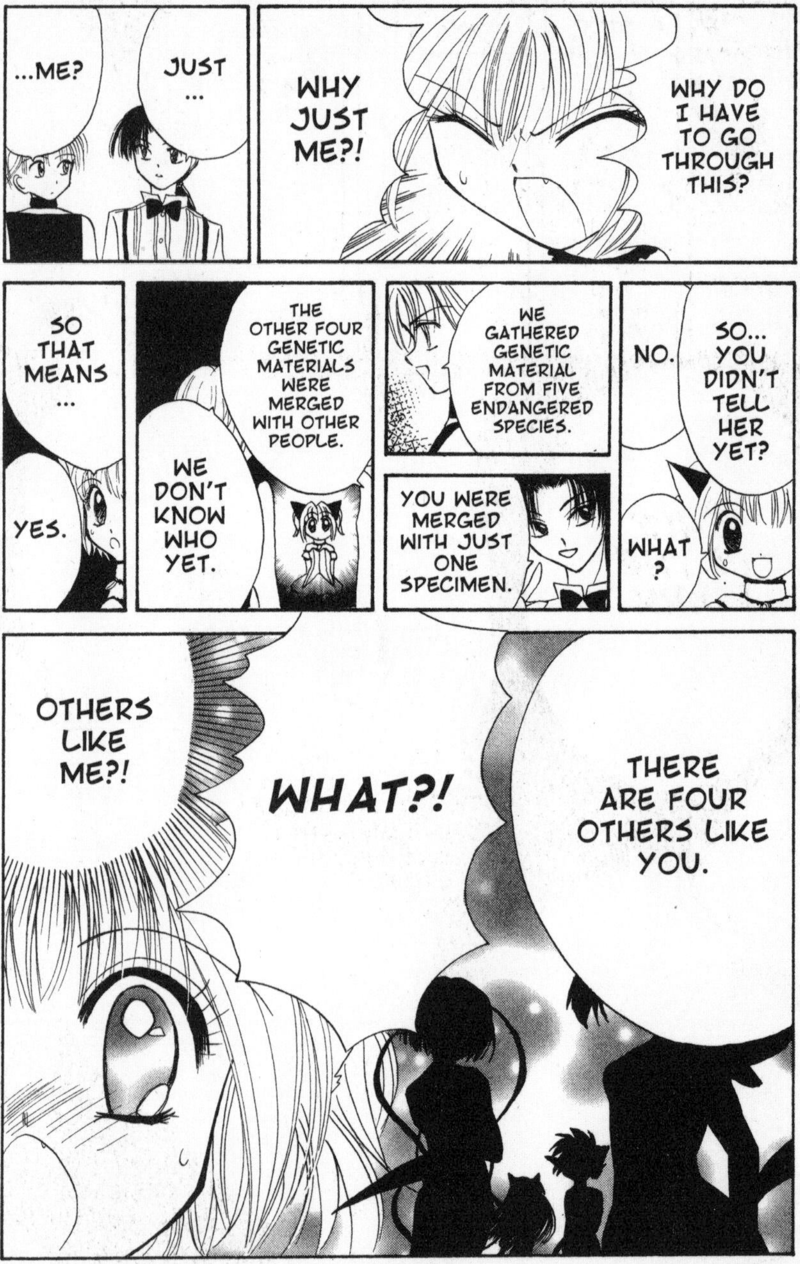
WHY DO I HAVE TO GO THROUGH THIS?
WHY JUST ME?!
JUST ...
...ME?
SO... YOU DIDN'T TELL HER YET?
NO.
WHAT ?
WE GATHERED GENETIC MATERIAL FROM FIVE ENDANGERED SPECIES.
YOU WERE MERGED WITH JUST ONE SPECIMEN.
THE OTHER FOUR GENETIC MATERIALS WERE MERGED WITH OTHER PEOPLE.
WE DON'T KNOW WHO YET.
SO THAT MEANS ...
YES.
THERE ARE FOUR OTHERS LIKE YOU.
WHAT?!
OTHERS LIKE ME?!

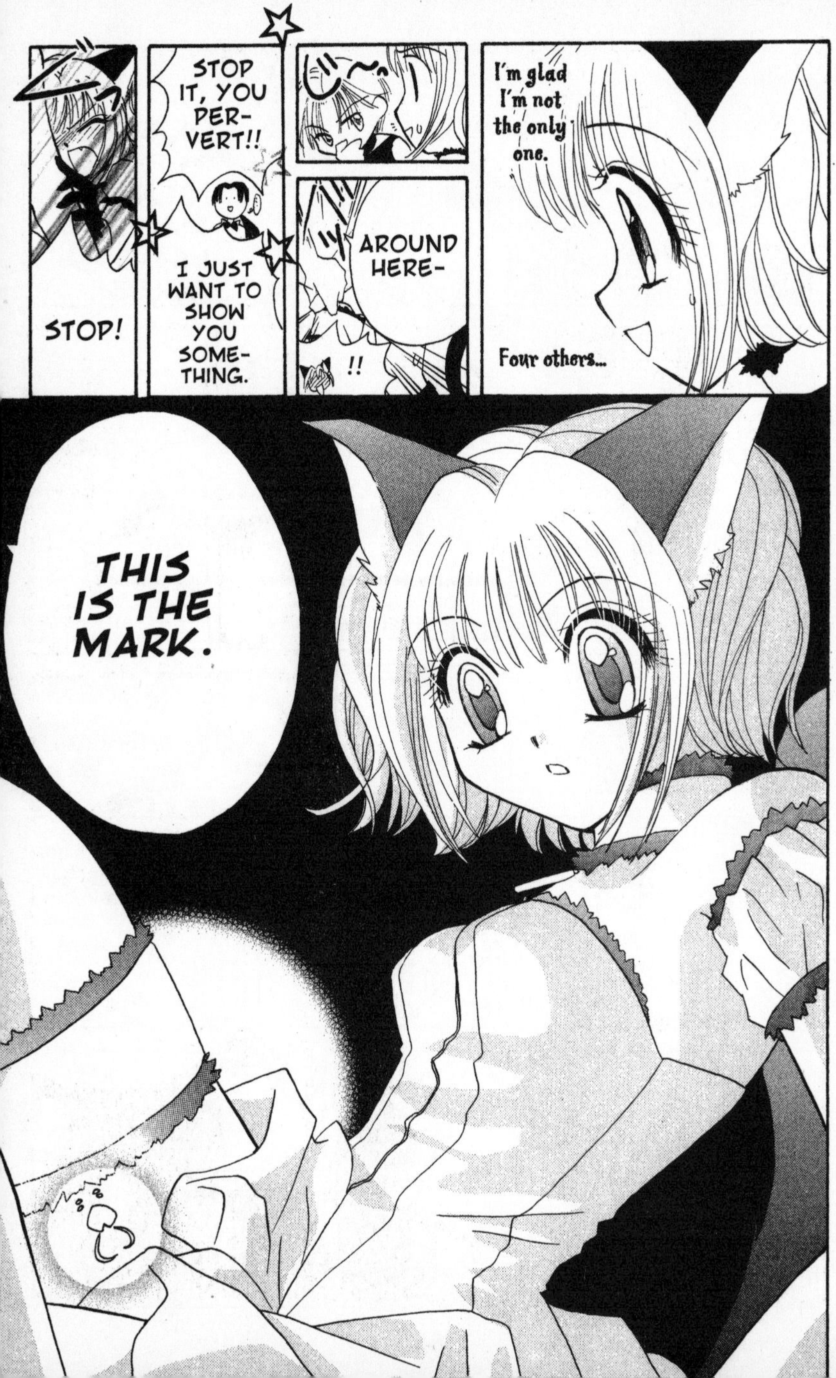
I'm glad I'm not the only one.
Four others...
AROUND HERE-
!!
STOP IT, YOU PER-VERT!!
I JUST WANT TO SHOW YOU SOME-THING.
STOP!
THIS IS THE MARK.

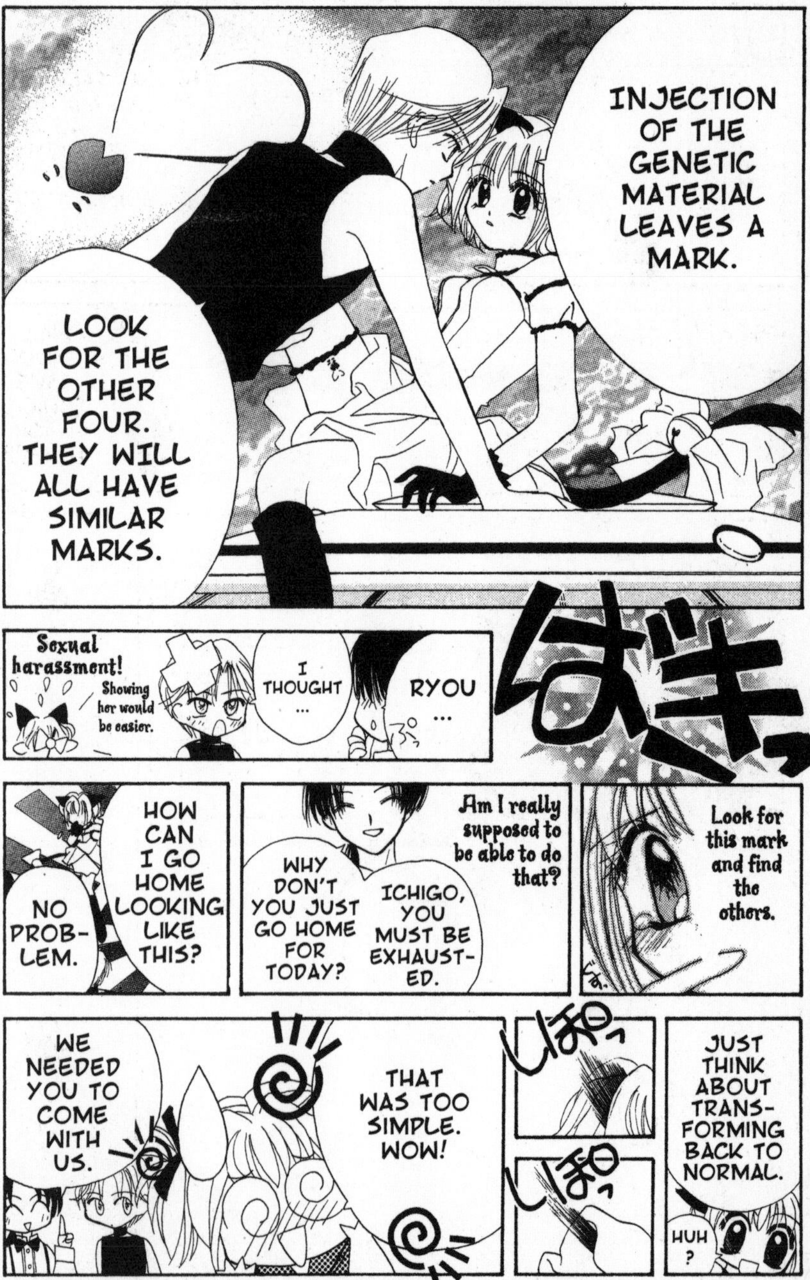
INJECTION OF THE GENETIC MATERIAL LEAVES A MARK.
LOOK FOR THE OTHER FOUR. THEY WILL ALL HAVE SIMILAR MARKS.
RYOU ...
I THOUGHT ...
Showing her would be easier.
Sexual harassment!
Look for this mark and find the others.
Am I really supposed to be able to do that?
ICHIGO, YOU MUST BE EXHAUST-ED.
WHY DON'T YOU JUST GO HOME FOR TODAY?
HOW CAN I GO HOME LOOKING LIKE THIS?
NO PROB-LEM.
JUST THINK ABOUT TRANS-FORMING BACK TO NORMAL.
HUH ?
THAT WAS TOO SIMPLE. WOW!
WE NEEDED YOU TO COME WITH US.

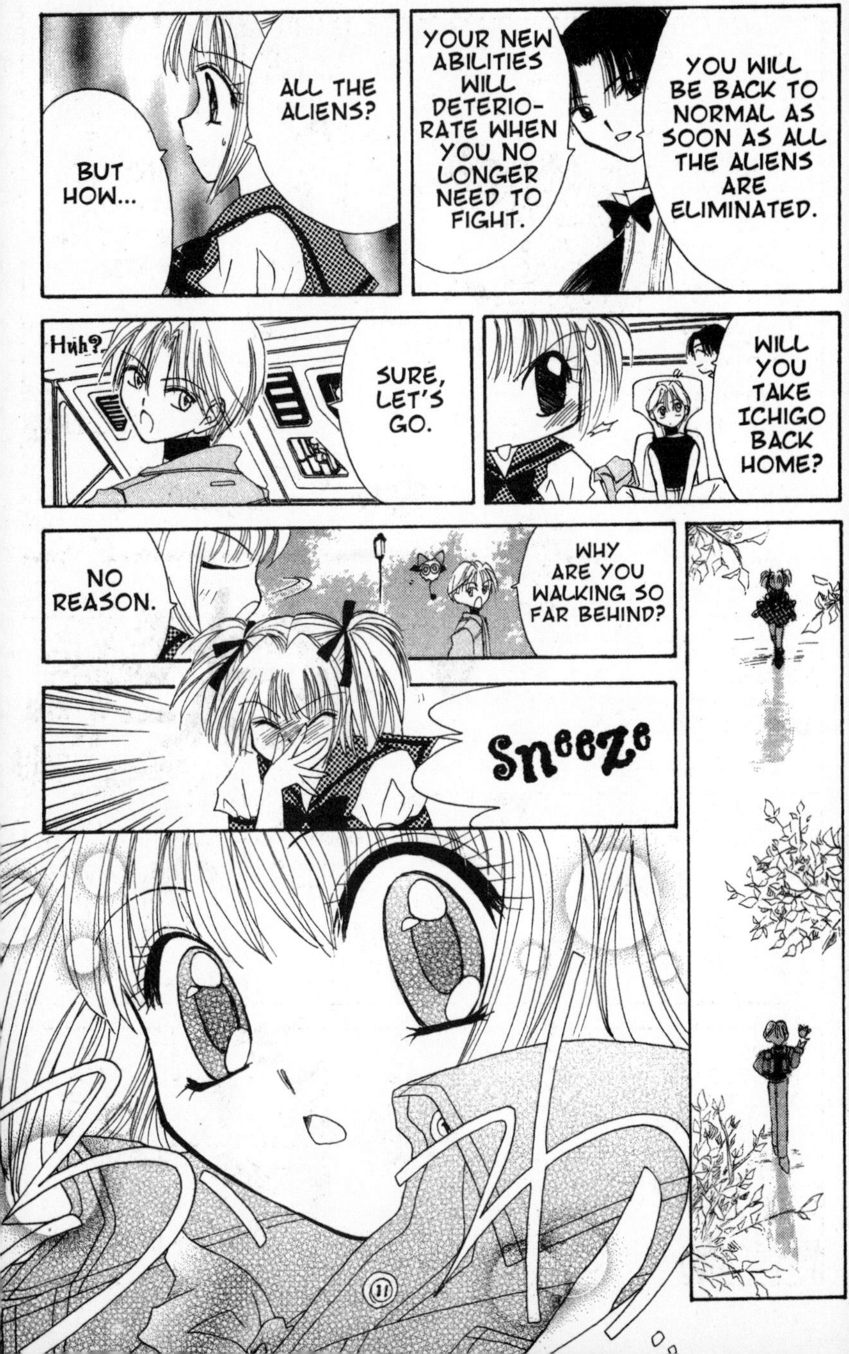
YOU WILL BE BACK TO NORMAL AS SOON AS ALL THE ALIENS ARE ELIMINATED.
YOUR NEW ABILITIES WILL DETERIO-RATE WHEN YOU NO LONGER NEED TO FIGHT.
ALL THE ALIENS?
BUT HOW...
WILL YOU TAKE ICHIGO BACK HOME?
SURE, LET'S GO.
Huh?
WHY ARE YOU WALKING SO FAR BEHIND?
NO REASON.
Sneeze

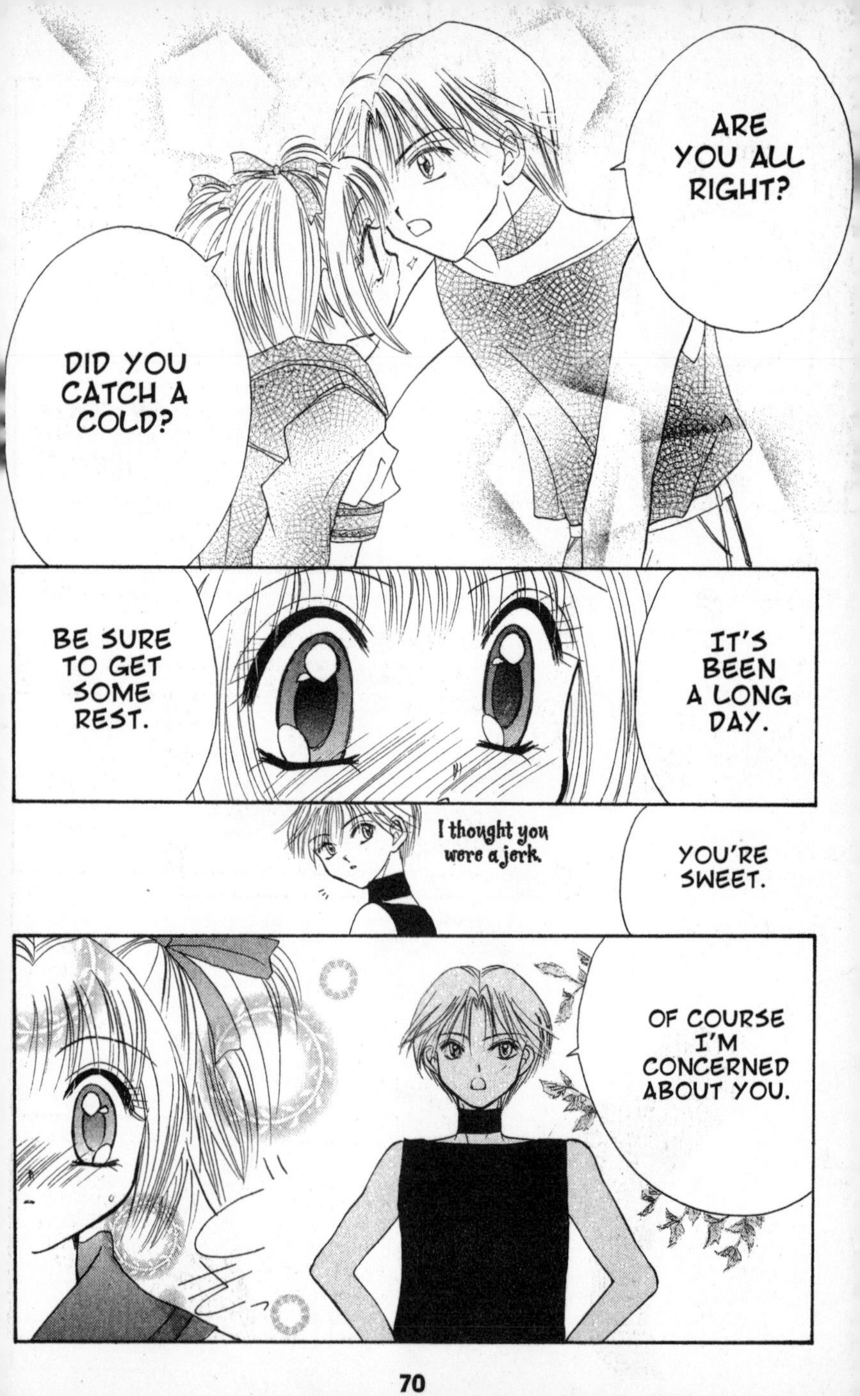
ARE YOU ALL RIGHT?
DID YOU CATCH A COLD?
IT'S BEEN A LONG DAY.
BE SURE TO GET SOME REST.
YOU'RE SWEET.
I thought you were a jerk.
OF COURSE I'M CONCERNED ABOUT YOU.

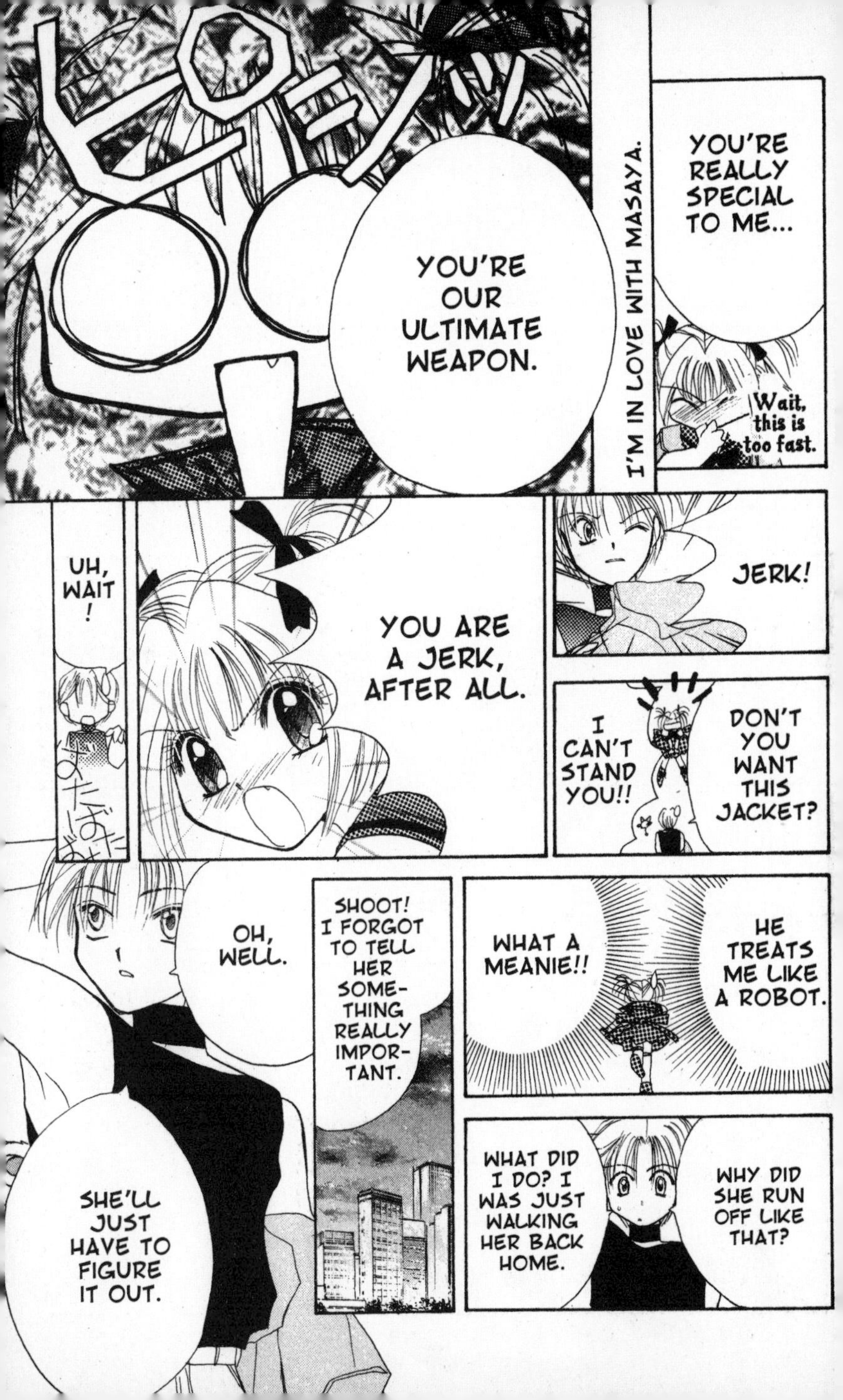
YOU'RE REALLY SPECIAL TO ME...
Wait, this is too fast.
I'M IN LOVE WITH MASAYA.
YOU'RE OUR ULTIMATE WEAPON.
JERK!
DON'T YOU WANT THIS JACKET?
I CAN'T STAND YOU!!
YOU ARE A JERK, AFTER ALL.
UH, WAIT!
HE TREATS ME LIKE A ROBOT.
WHAT A MEANIE!!
WHY DID SHE RUN OFF LIKE THAT?
WHAT DID I DO? I WAS JUST WALKING HER BACK HOME.
SHOOT! I FORGOT TO TELL HER SOME-THING REALLY IMPOR-TANT.
OH, WELL.
SHE'LL JUST HAVE TO FIGURE IT OUT.

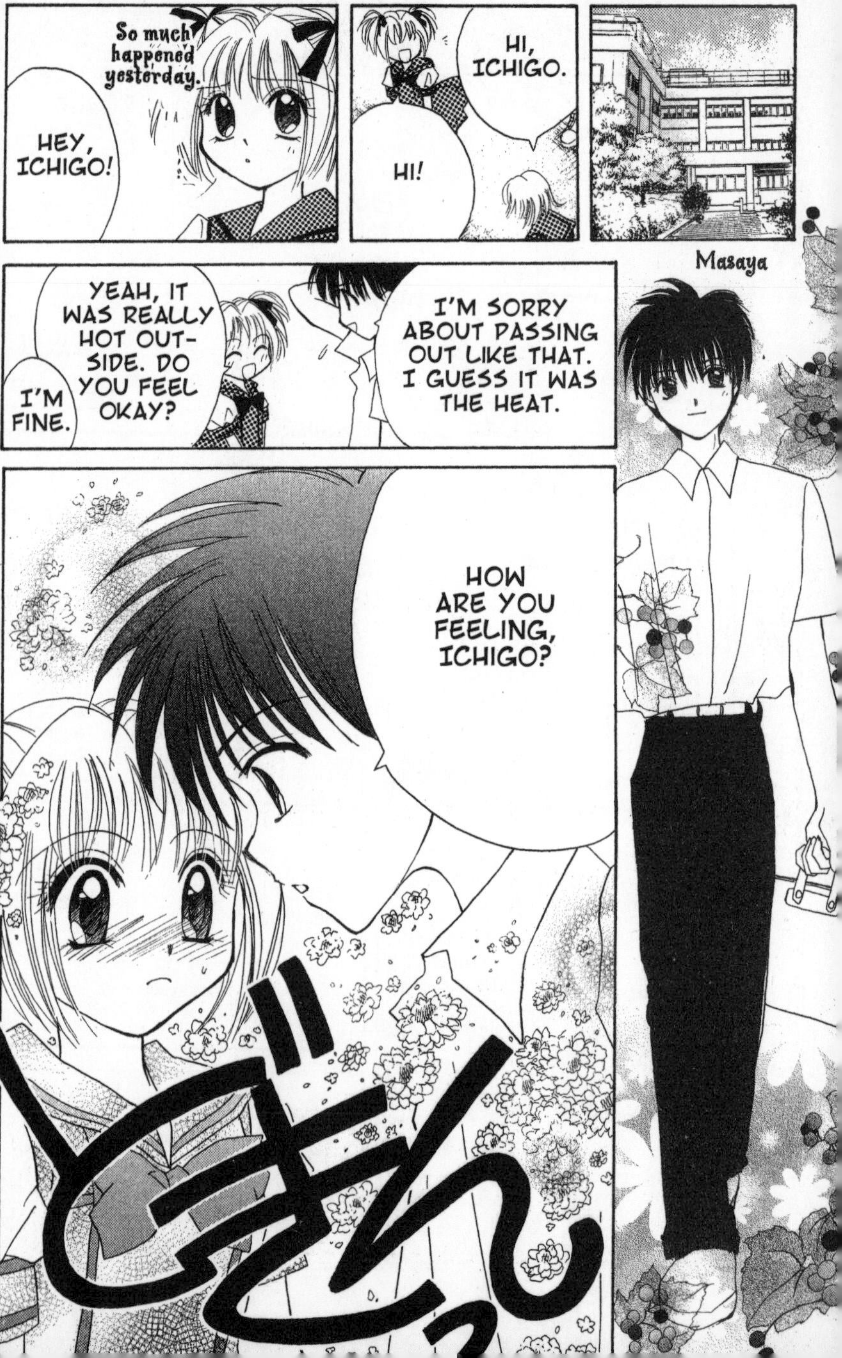
HI, ICHIGO.
HI!
So much happened yesterday.
HEY, ICHIGO!
Masaya
I'M SORRY ABOUT PASSING OUT LIKE THAT. I GUESS IT WAS THE HEAT.
YEAH, IT WAS REALLY HOT OUT-SIDE. DO YOU FEEL OKAY?
I'M FINE.
HOW ARE YOU FEELING, ICHIGO?
どきんっ

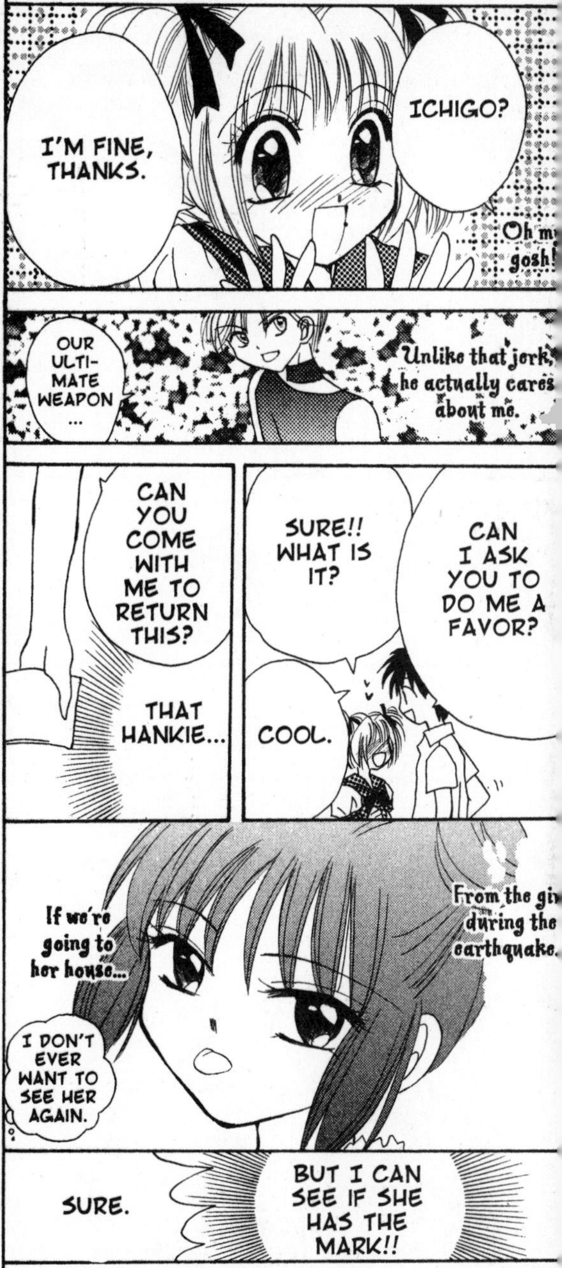
ICHIGO?
Oh m gosh!
I'M FINE, THANKS.
Unlike that jerk, he actually cares about me.
OUR ULTI-MATE WEAPON ...
CAN I ASK YOU TO DO ME A FAVOR?
SURE!! WHAT IS IT?
COOL.
CAN YOU COME WITH ME TO RETURN THIS?
THAT HANKIE...
From the gi during the earthquake.
If we're going to her house...
I DON'T EVER WANT TO SEE HER AGAIN.
BUT I CAN SEE IF SHE HAS THE MARK!!
SURE.

Project Meeting 1

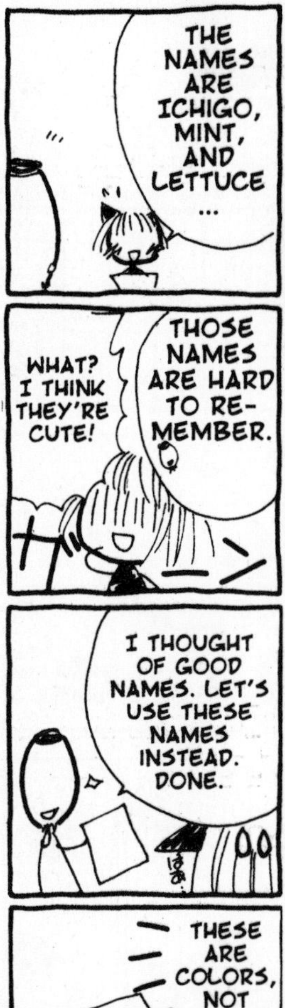
THE NAMES ARE ICHIGO, MINT, AND LETTUCE ...
THOSE NAMES ARE HARD TO RE-MEMBER.
WHAT? I THINK THEY'RE CUTE!
I THOUGHT OF GOOD NAMES. LET'S USE THESE NAMES INSTEAD. DONE.
THESE ARE COLORS, NOT NAMES!!
Character names:
Peach
Blue
Green

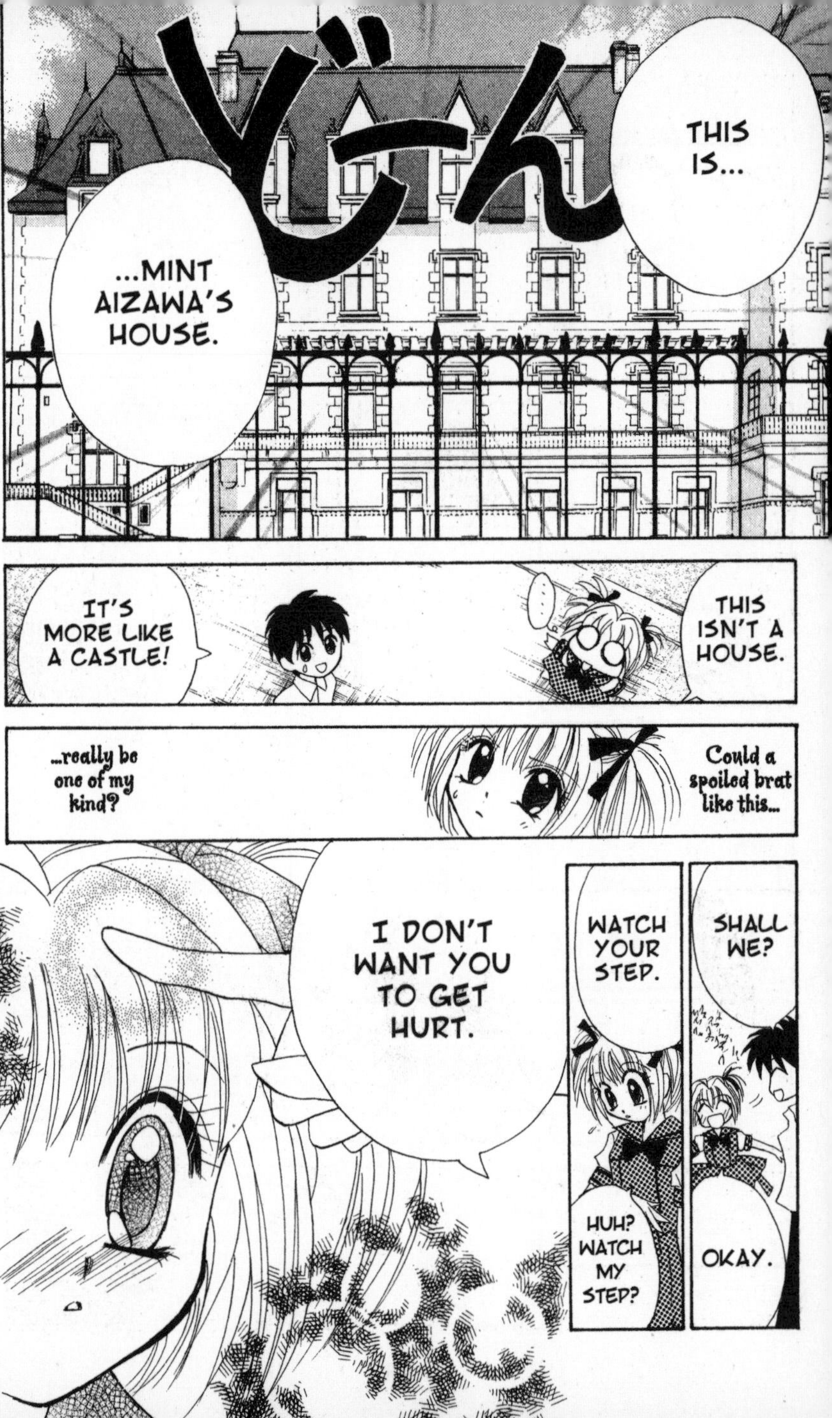
どん
THIS IS...
...MINT AIZAWA'S HOUSE.
THIS ISN'T A HOUSE.
...
IT'S MORE LIKE A CASTLE!
Could a spoiled brat like this...
...really be one of my kind?
SHALL WE?
OKAY.
WATCH YOUR STEP.
HUH? WATCH MY STEP?
I DON'T WANT YOU TO GET HURT.

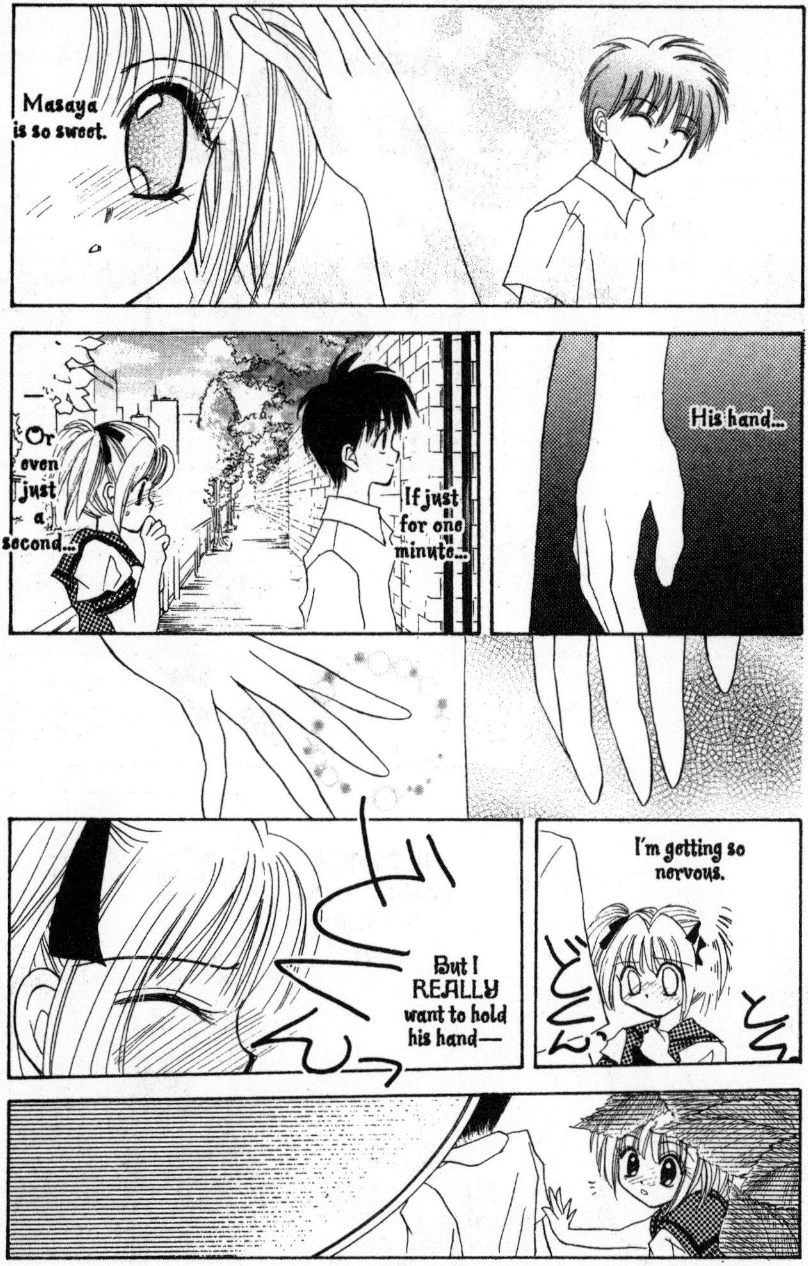
Masaya is so sweet.
His hand...
If just for one minute...
—Or even just a second...
I'm getting so nervous.
But I REALLY want to hold his hand—

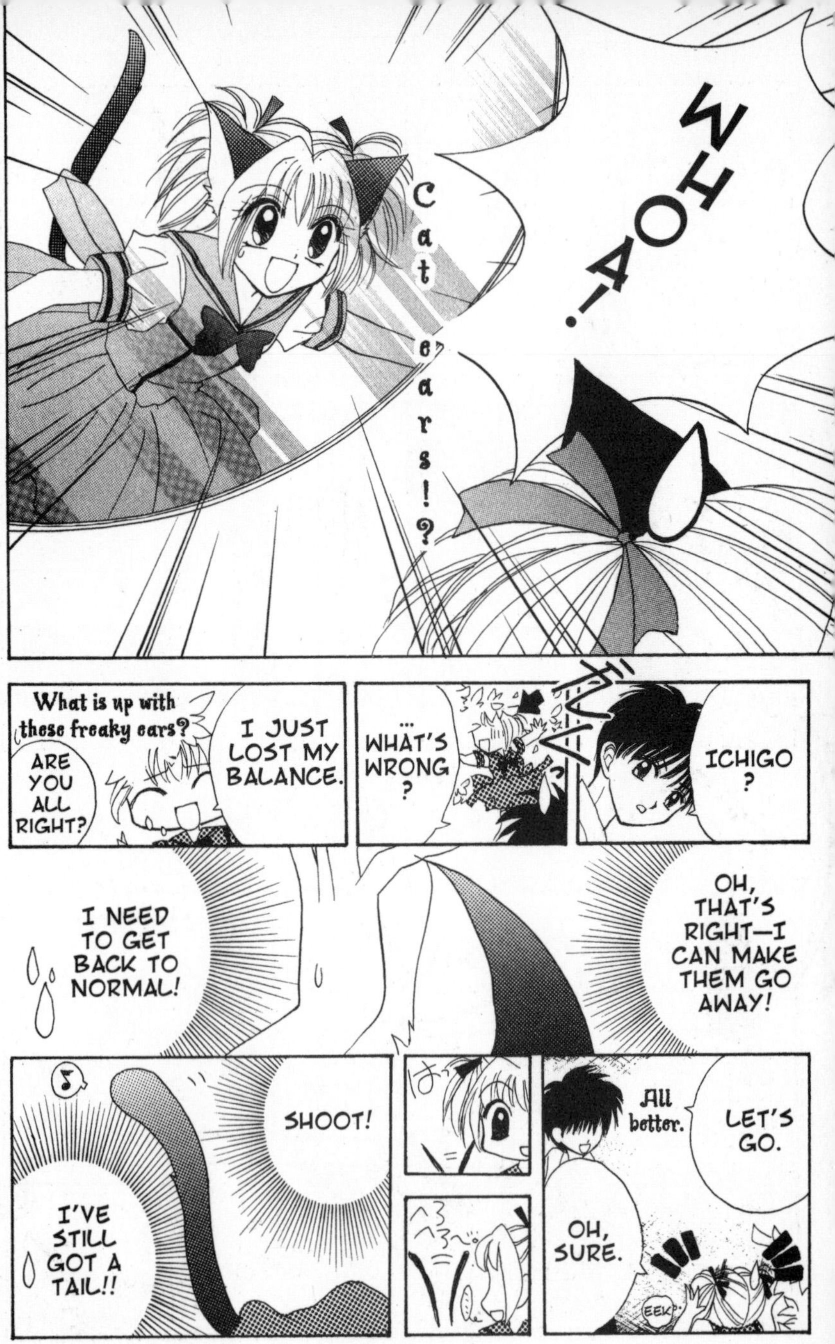
WHOA!
Cat ears!?
ICHIGO?
...WHAT'S WRONG?
I JUST LOST MY BALANCE.
What is up with these freaky ears?
ARE YOU ALL RIGHT?
OH, THAT'S RIGHT—I CAN MAKE THEM GO AWAY!
I NEED TO GET BACK TO NORMAL!
LET'S GO.
All better.
OH, SURE.
EEK
SHOOT!
I'VE STILL GOT A TAIL!!

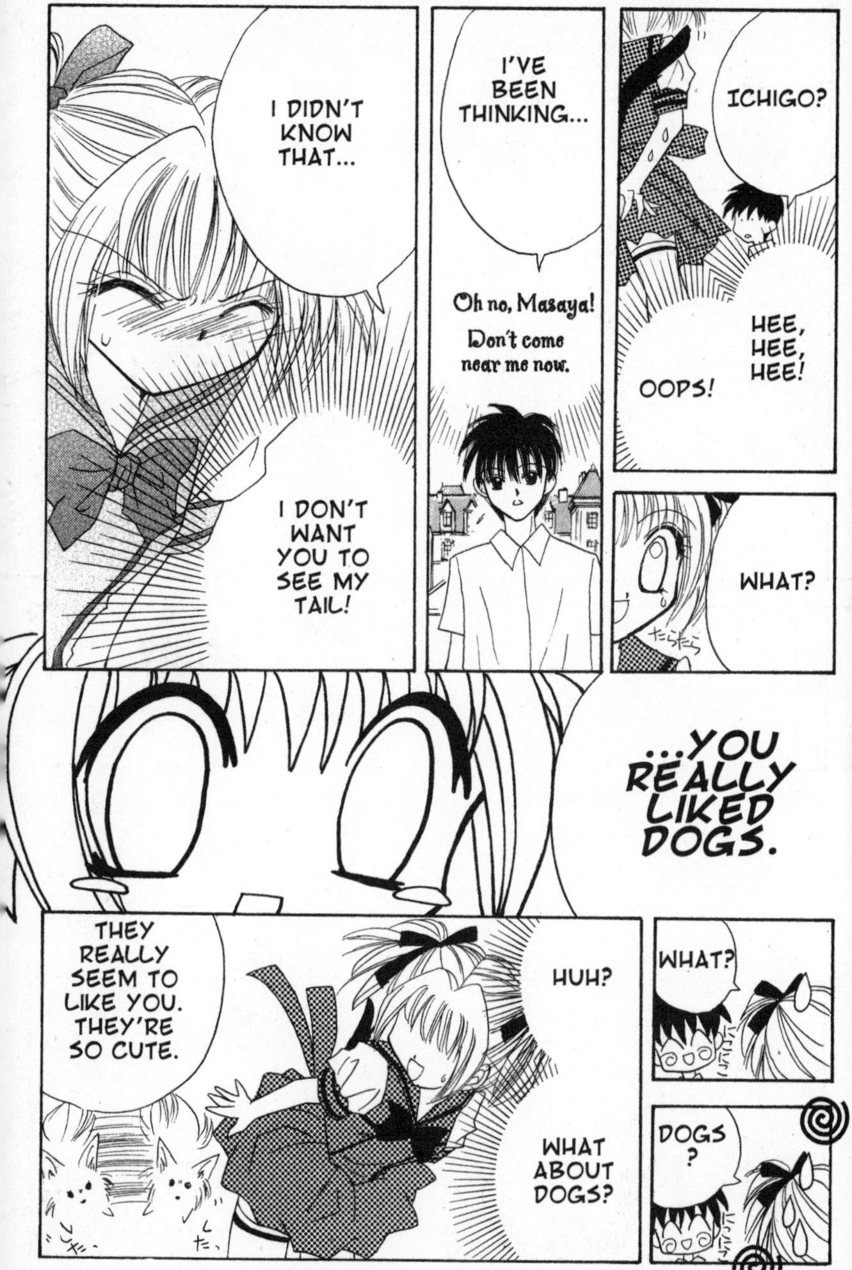
ICHIGO?
HEE, HEE, HEE!
OOPS!
WHAT?
I'VE BEEN THINKING...
Oh no, Masaya! Don't come near me now.
I DIDN'T KNOW THAT...
I DON'T WANT YOU TO SEE MY TAIL!
...YOU REALLY LIKED DOGS.
WHAT?
DOGS?
HUH?
THEY REALLY SEEM TO LIKE YOU. THEY'RE SO CUTE.
WHAT ABOUT DOGS?

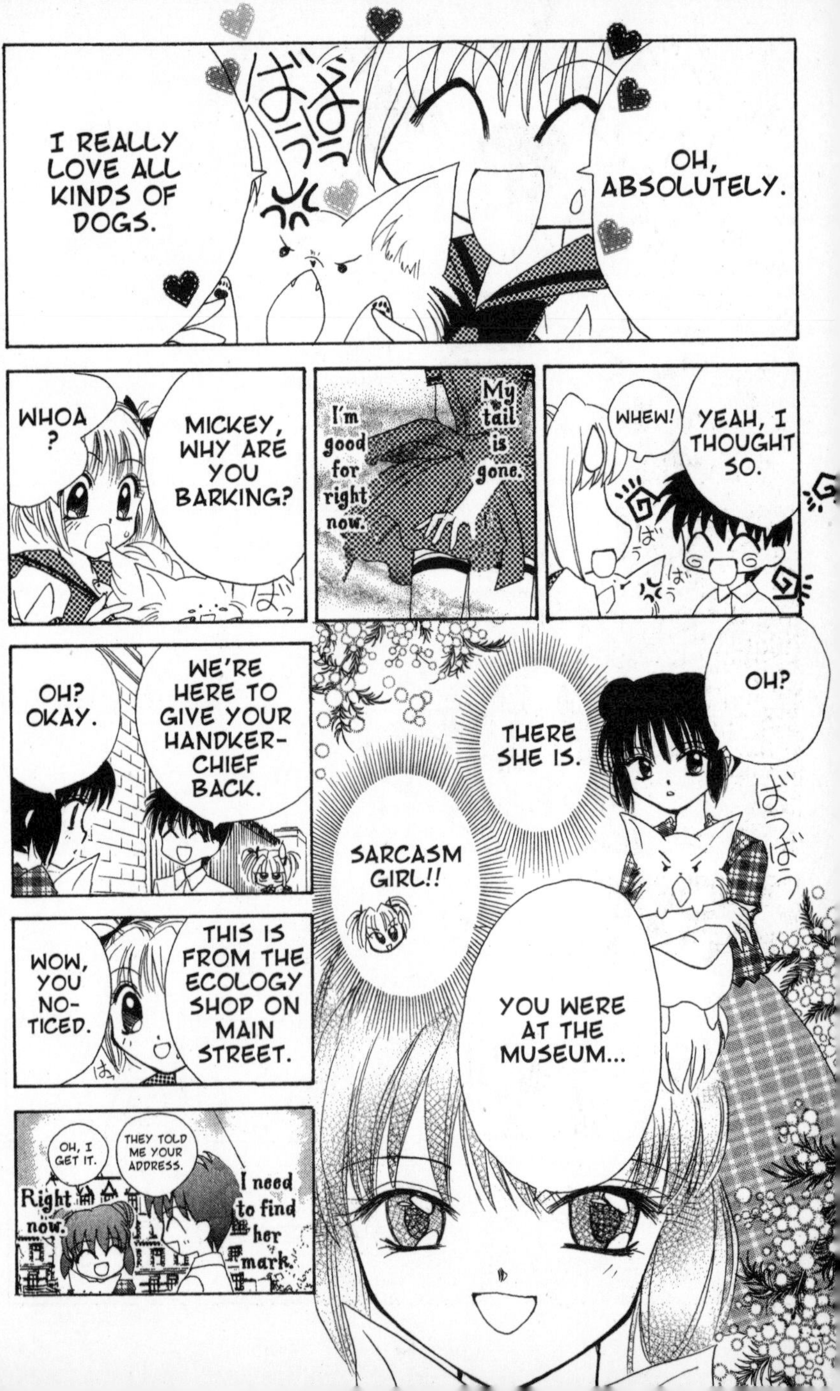
OH, ABSOLUTELY.
I REALLY LOVE ALL KINDS OF DOGS.
YEAH, I THOUGHT SO.
WHEW!
My tail is gone.
I'm good for right now.
MICKEY, WHY ARE YOU BARKING?
WHOA?
OH?
THERE SHE IS.
SARCASM GIRL!!
YOU WERE AT THE MUSEUM...
WE'RE HERE TO GIVE YOUR HANDKER-CHIEF BACK.
OH? OKAY.
THIS IS FROM THE ECOLOGY SHOP ON MAIN STREET.
WOW, YOU NO-TICED.
THEY TOLD ME YOUR ADDRESS.
OH, I GET IT.
I need to find her mark.
Right now.

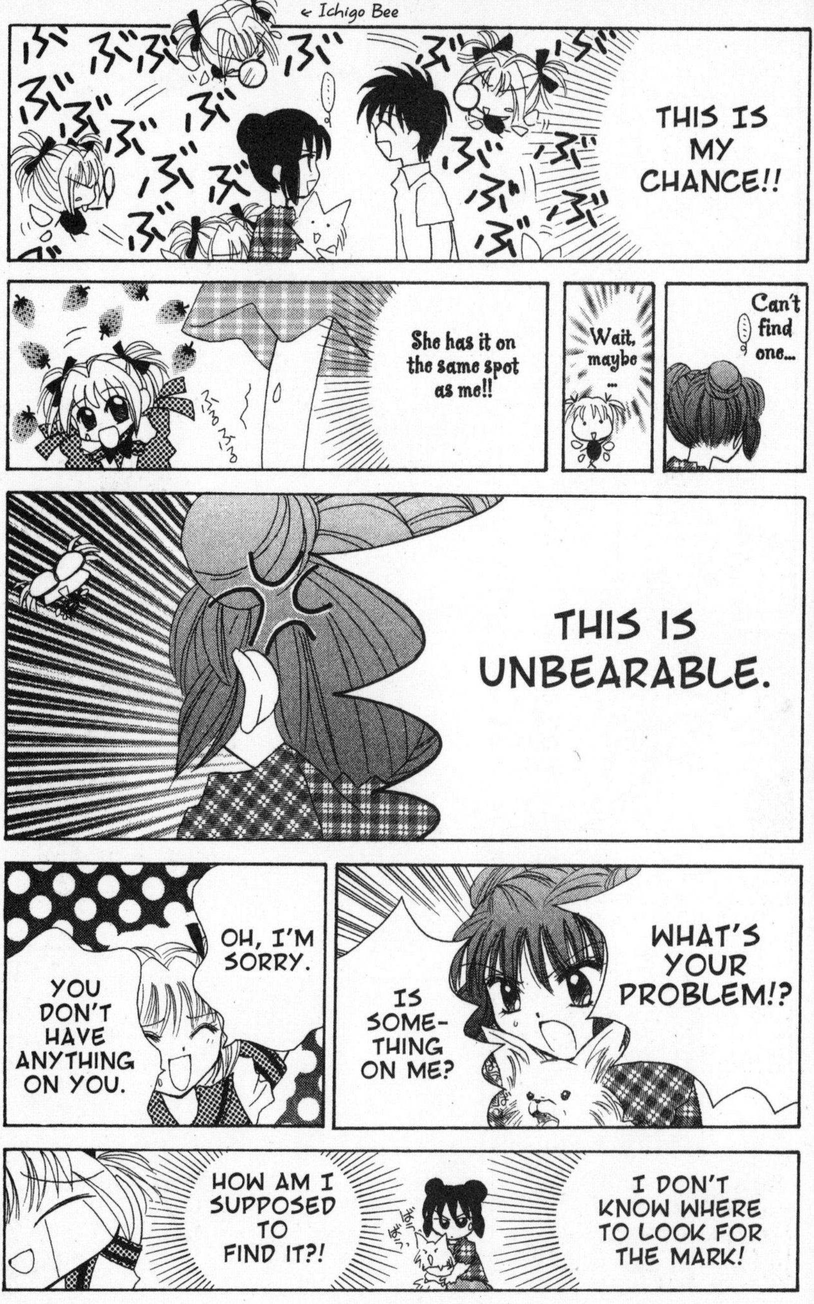
← Ichigo Bee
THIS IS MY CHANCE!!
Can't find one...
Wait, maybe ...
She has it on the same spot as me!!
THIS IS UNBEARABLE.
WHAT'S YOUR PROBLEM!?
IS SOME-THING ON ME?
OH, I'M SORRY.
YOU DON'T HAVE ANYTHING ON YOU.
I DON'T KNOW WHERE TO LOOK FOR THE MARK!
HOW AM I SUPPOSED TO FIND IT?!

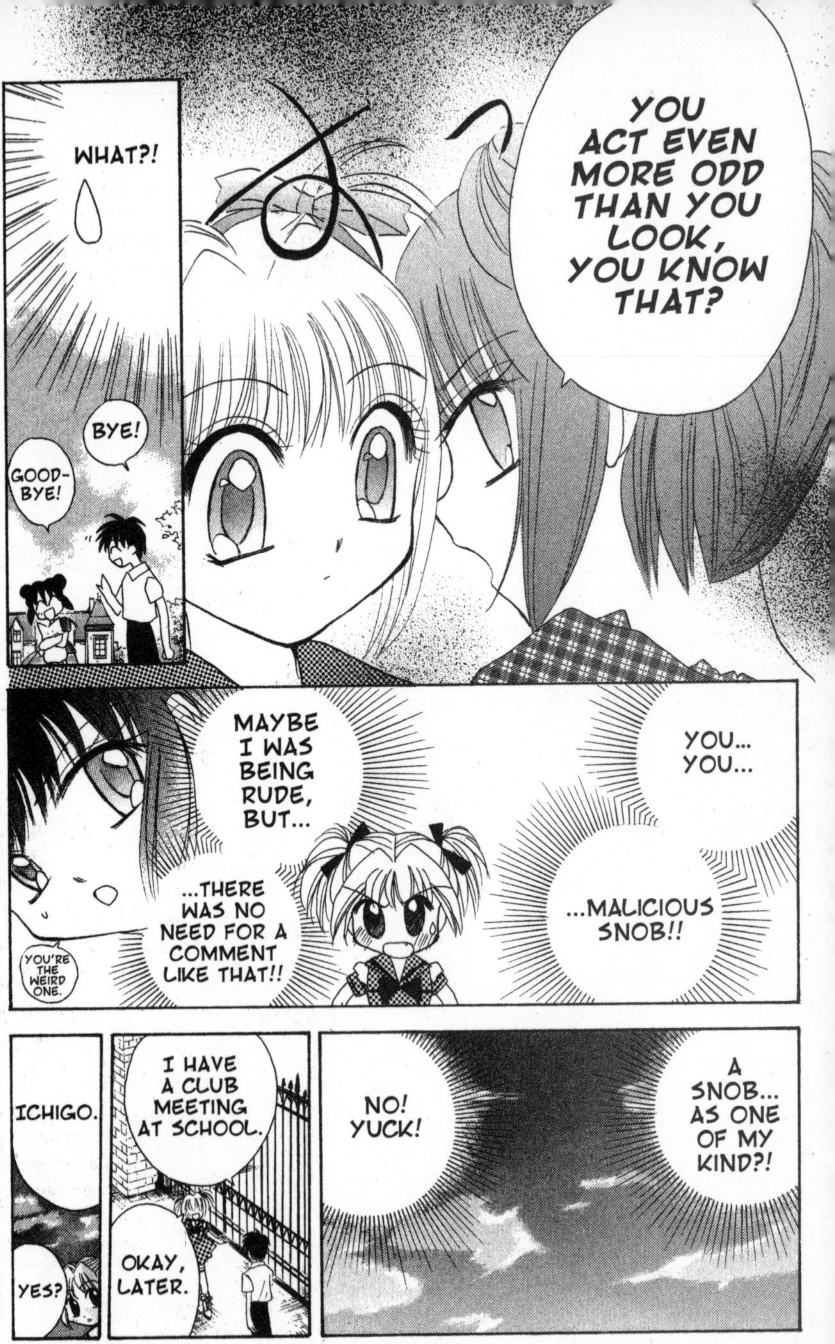
YOU ACT EVEN MORE ODD THAN YOU LOOK, YOU KNOW THAT?
WHAT?!
BYE!
GOOD-BYE!
YOU... YOU...
...MALICIOUS SNOB!!
MAYBE I WAS BEING RUDE, BUT...
...THERE WAS NO NEED FOR A COMMENT LIKE THAT!!
YOU'RE THE WEIRD ONE.
A SNOB... AS ONE OF MY KIND?!
NO! YUCK!
I HAVE A CLUB MEETING AT SCHOOL.
OKAY, LATER.
ICHIGO.
YES?

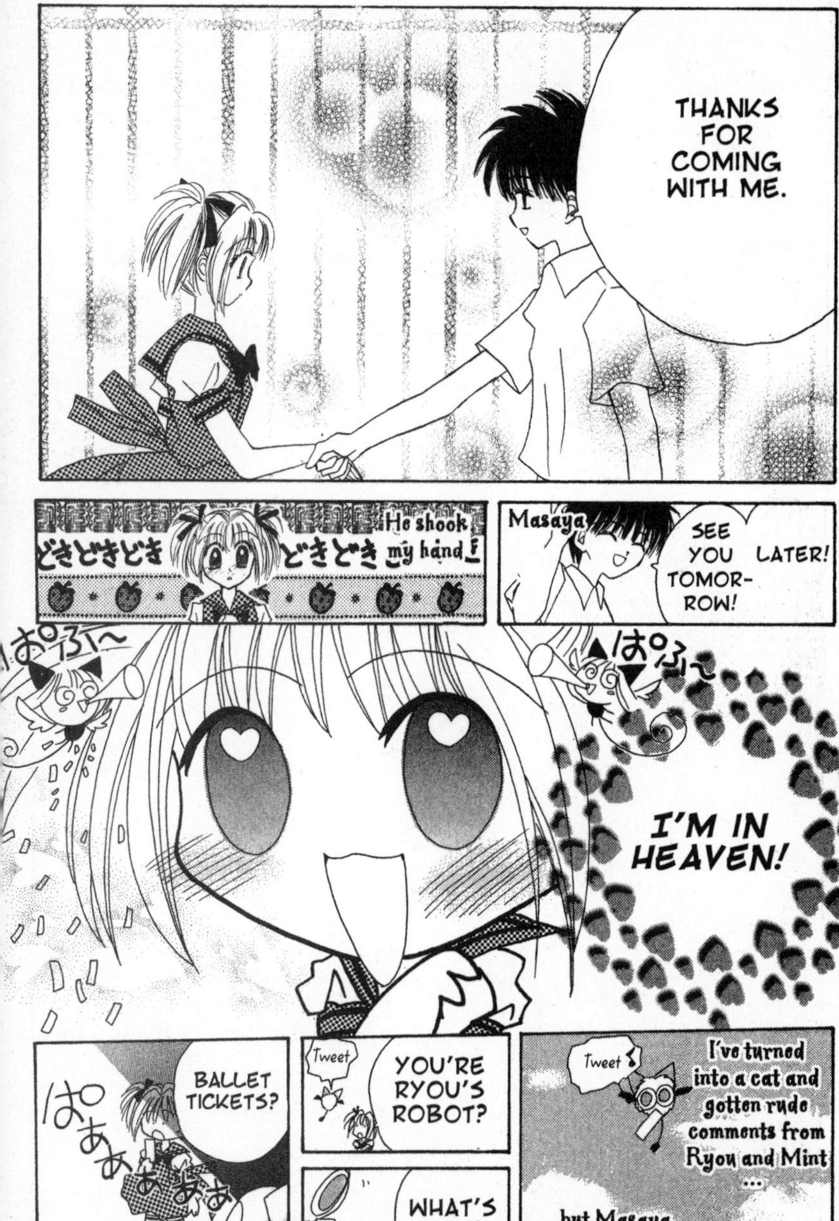
THANKS FOR COMING WITH ME.
Masaya
SEE YOU TOMORROW!
LATER!
どきどきどき
He shook my hand!
どきどき
ぱふ〜
I'M IN HEAVEN!
ぱふ〜
Tweet
I've turned into a cat and gotten rude comments from Ryou and Mint ...
... but Masaya just made my day!
Tweet
YOU'RE RYOU'S ROBOT?
WHAT'S THIS?
BALLET TICKETS?
ぱあああああ

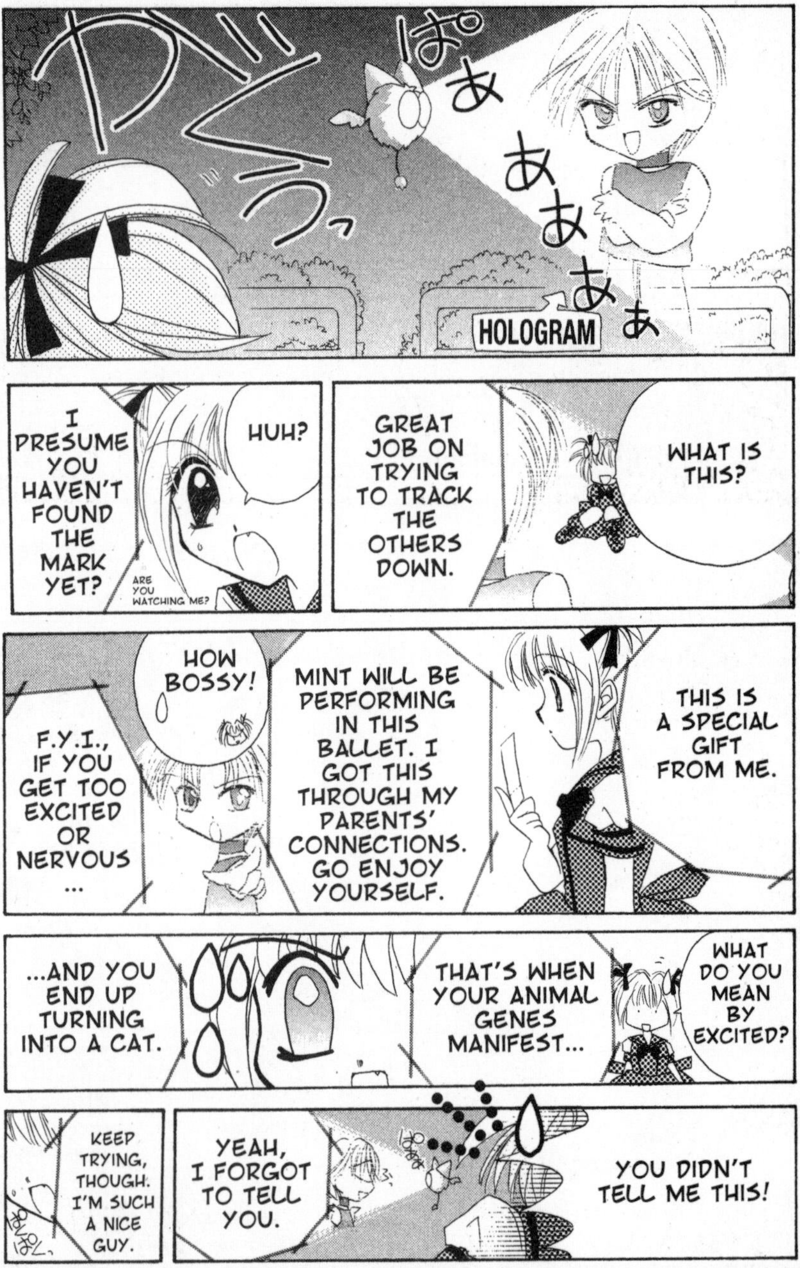
ぱぁあああぁ
やぐうっ
HOLOGRAM
WHAT IS THIS?
GREAT JOB ON TRYING TO TRACK THE OTHERS DOWN.
HUH?
I PRESUME YOU HAVEN'T FOUND THE MARK YET?
ARE YOU WATCHING ME?
THIS IS A SPECIAL GIFT FROM ME.
MINT WILL BE PERFORMING IN THIS BALLET. I GOT THIS THROUGH MY PARENTS' CONNECTIONS. GO ENJOY YOURSELF.
HOW BOSSY!
F.Y.I., IF YOU GET TOO EXCITED OR NERVOUS ...
WHAT DO YOU MEAN BY EXCITED?
THAT'S WHEN YOUR ANIMAL GENES MANIFEST...
...AND YOU END UP TURNING INTO A CAT.
YOU DIDN'T TELL ME THIS!
YEAH, I FORGOT TO TELL YOU.
KEEP TRYING, THOUGH. I'M SUCH A NICE GUY.

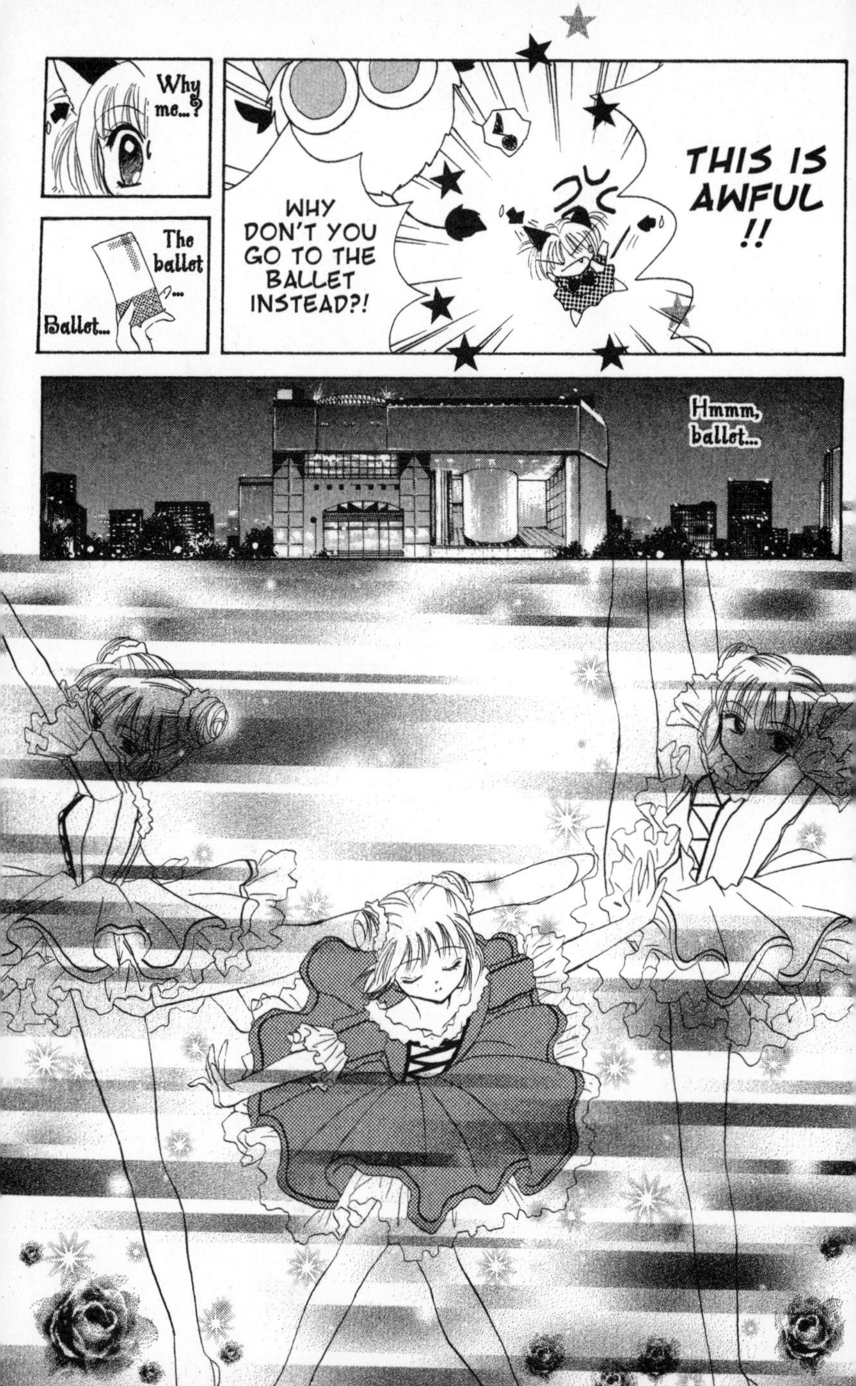
THIS IS AWFUL !!
WHY DON'T YOU GO TO THE BALLET INSTEAD?!
Why me...?
The ballet...
Ballet...
Hmmm, ballet...

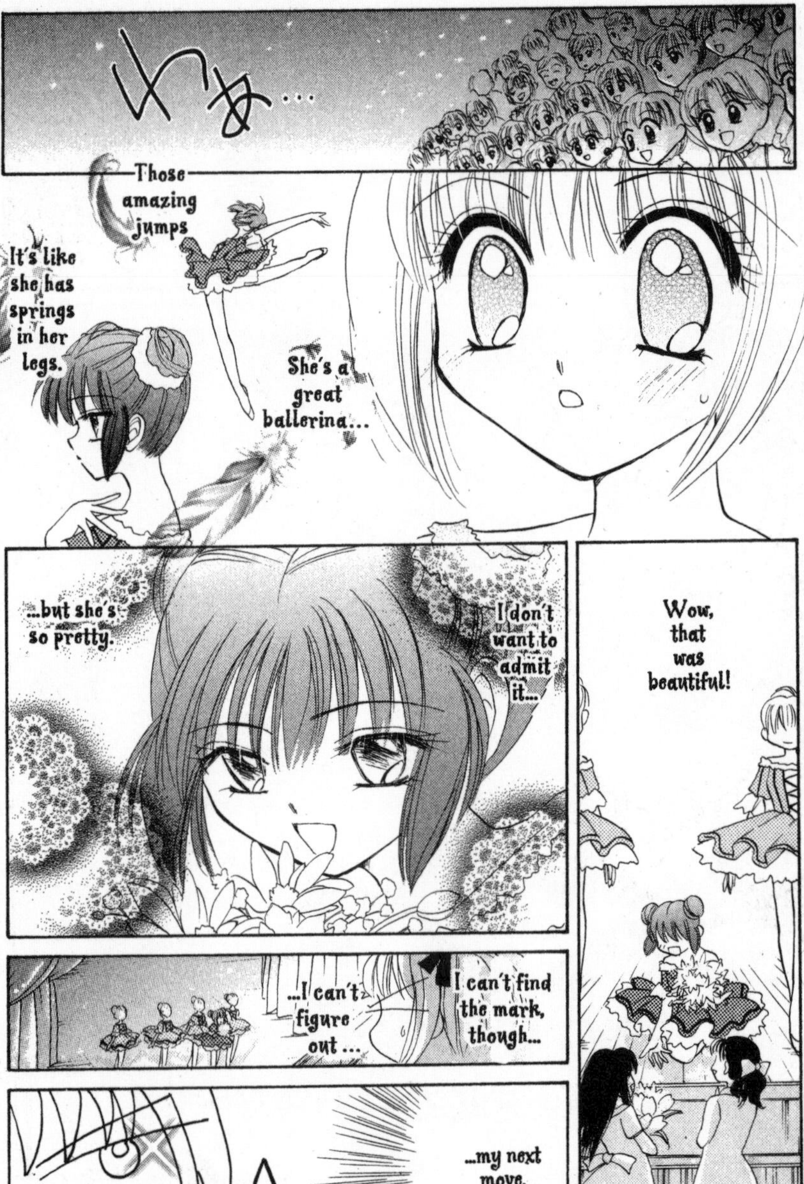
わぁ…
Those amazing jumps
It's like she has springs in her legs.
She's a great ballerina...
Wow, that was beautiful!
I don't want to admit it...
...but she's so pretty.
I can't find the mark, though...
...I can't figure out ...
...my next move.

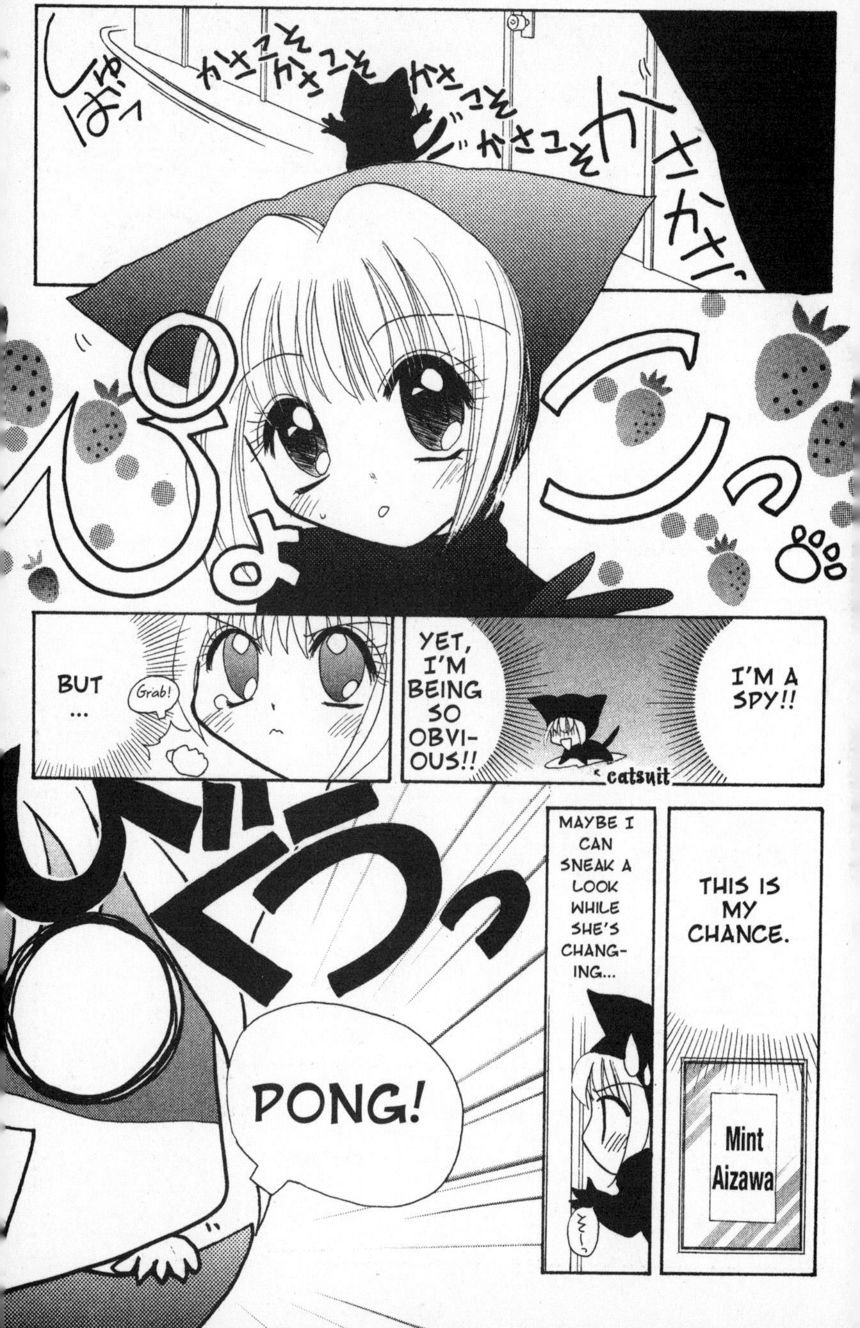
I'M A SPY!!
YET, I'M BEING SO OBVIOUS!!
catsuit
BUT ...
Grab!
THIS IS MY CHANCE.
Mint Aizawa
MAYBE I CAN SNEAK A LOOK WHILE SHE'S CHANGING...
PONG!

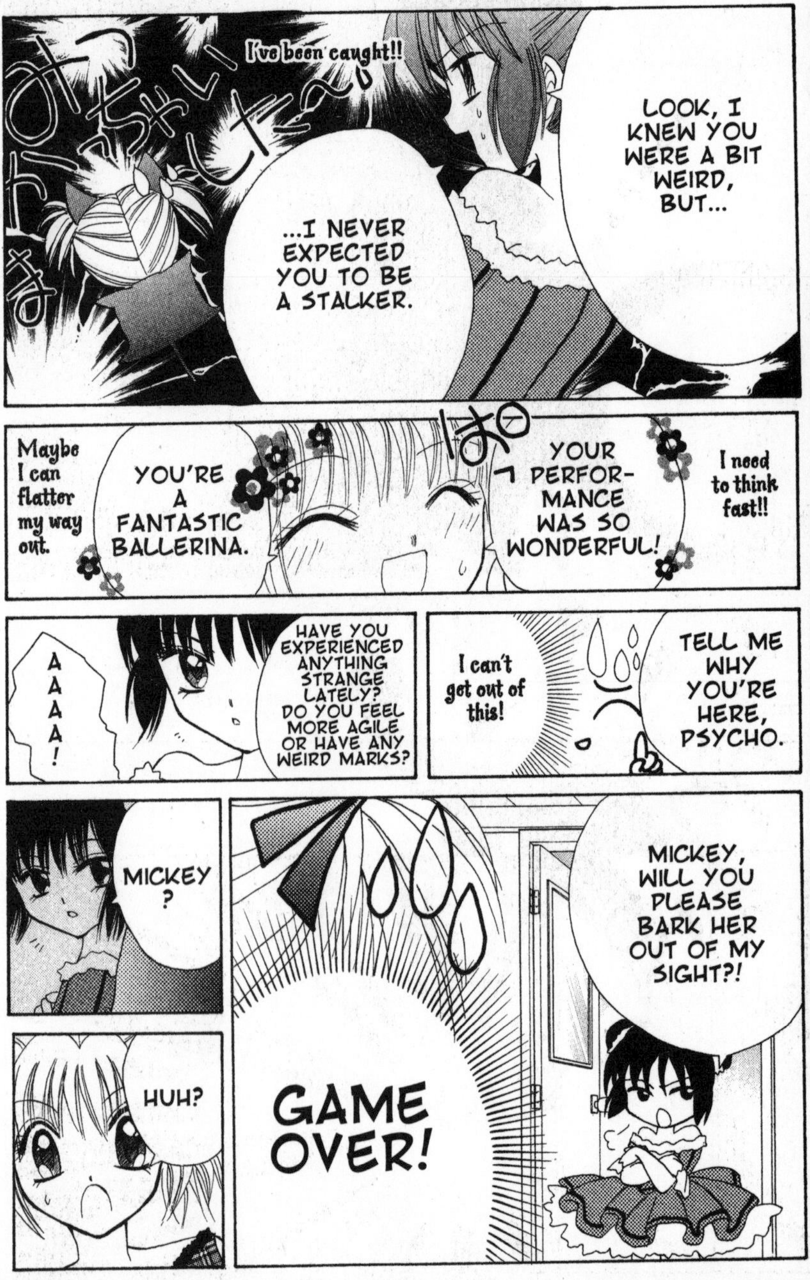
LOOK, I KNEW YOU WERE A BIT WEIRD, BUT...
I've been caught!!
...I NEVER EXPECTED YOU TO BE A STALKER.
I need to think fast!!
YOUR PERFORMANCE WAS SO WONDERFUL!
YOU'RE A FANTASTIC BALLERINA.
Maybe I can flatter my way out.
TELL ME WHY YOU'RE HERE, PSYCHO.
I can't get out of this!
HAVE YOU EXPERIENCED ANYTHING STRANGE LATELY? DO YOU FEEL MORE AGILE OR HAVE ANY WEIRD MARKS?
AAAA!
MICKEY, WILL YOU PLEASE BARK HER OUT OF MY SIGHT?!
GAME OVER!
MICKEY?
HUH?

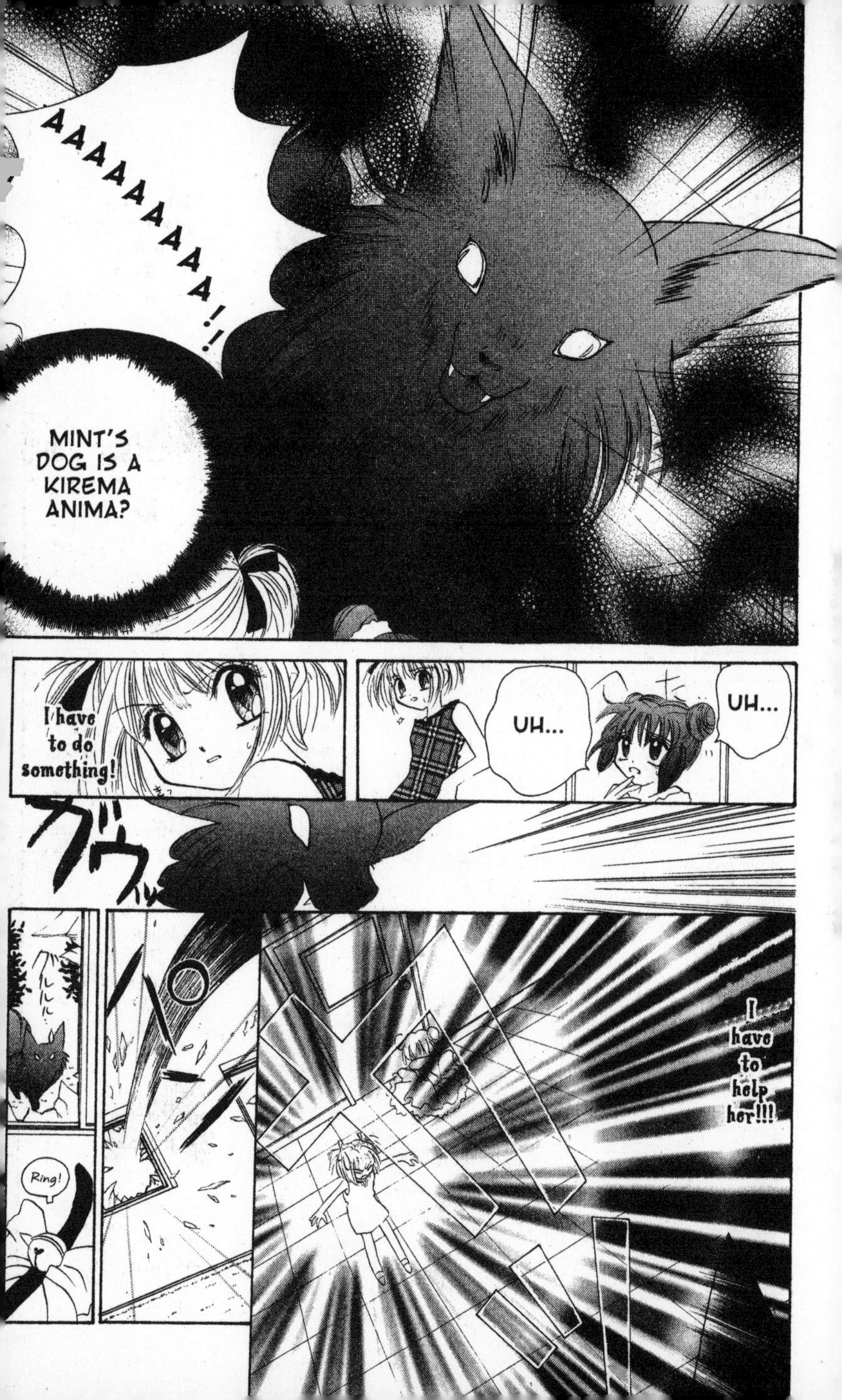
AAAAAAAAAAA!!
MINT'S DOG IS A KIREMA ANIMA?
UH...
UH...
I have to do something!
ガウッ
I have to help her!!!
Ring!

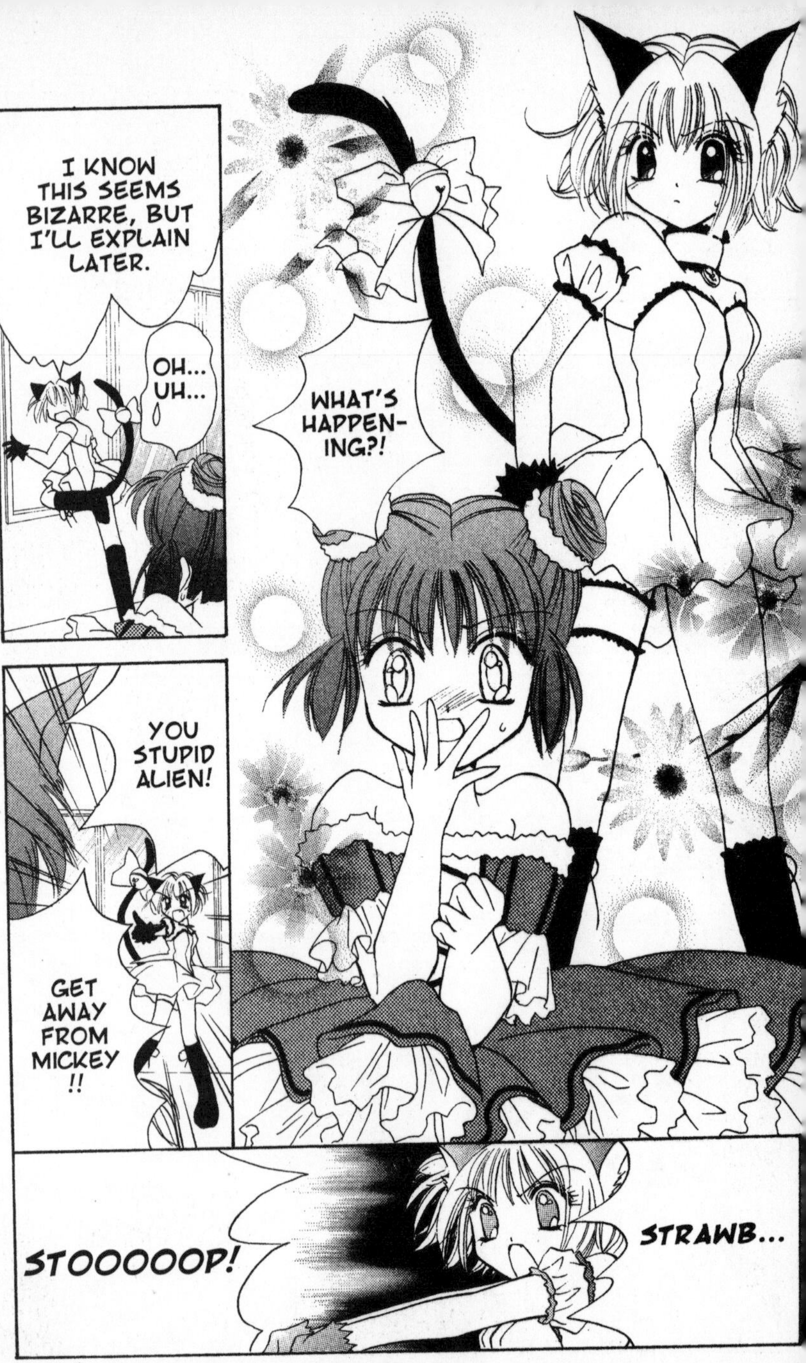
WHAT'S HAPPEN-ING?!
I KNOW THIS SEEMS BIZARRE, BUT I'LL EXPLAIN LATER.
OH... UH...
YOU STUPID ALIEN!
GET AWAY FROM MICKEY !!
STRAWB...
STOOOOOP!

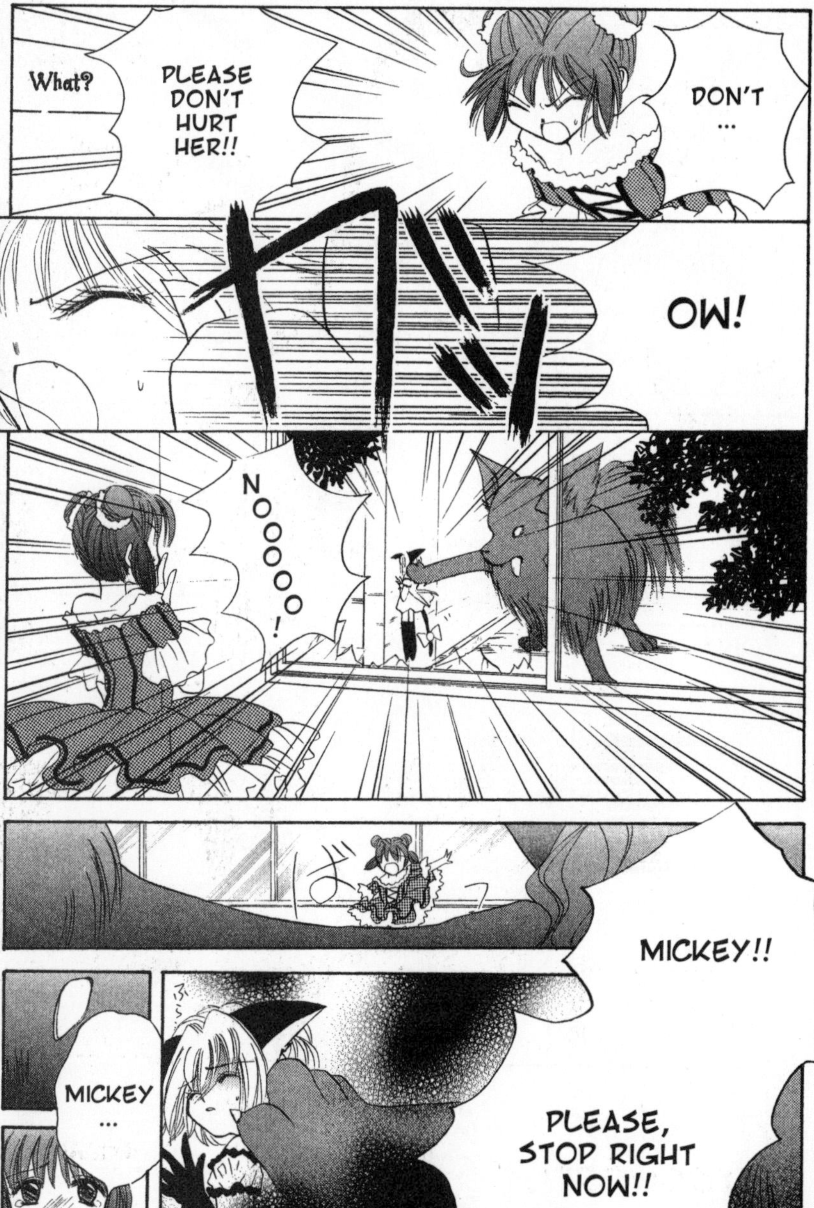
DON'T ...
PLEASE DON'T HURT HER!!
What?
OW!
NOOOOOO!
MICKEY!!
PLEASE, STOP RIGHT NOW!!
MICKEY ...

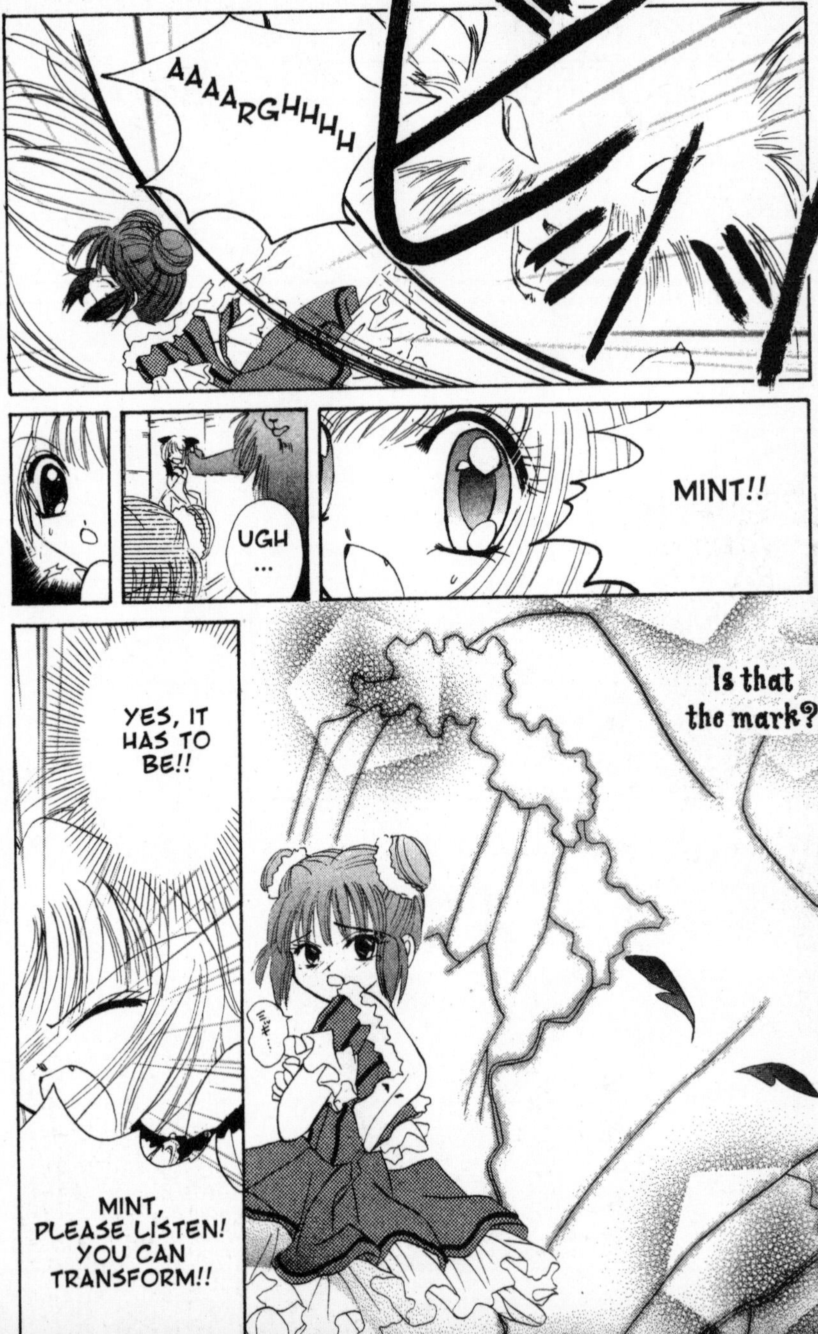
AAAARGHHHHH
MINT!!
UGH ...
Is that the mark?
YES, IT HAS TO BE!!
MINT, PLEASE LISTEN! YOU CAN TRANSFORM!!

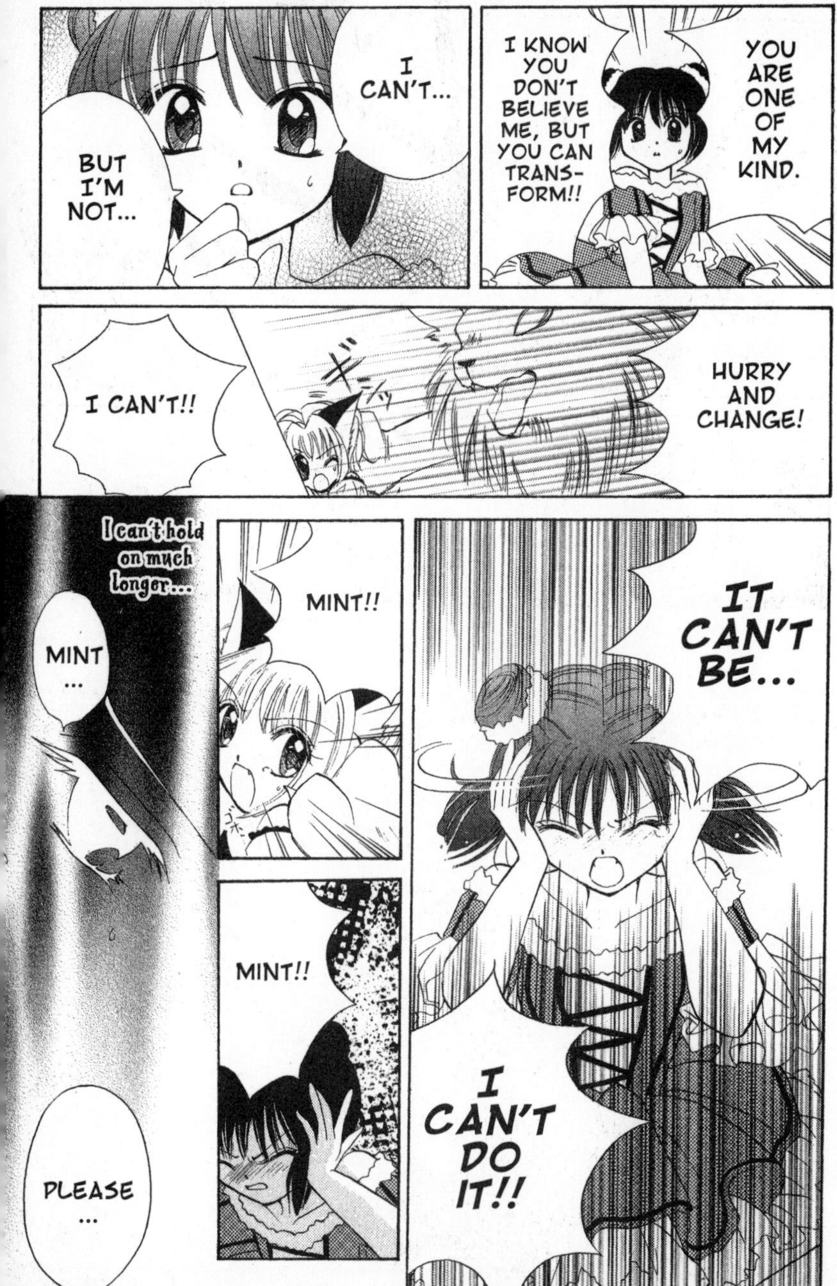
YOU ARE ONE OF MY KIND.
I KNOW YOU DON'T BELIEVE ME, BUT YOU CAN TRANS-FORM!!
I CAN'T...
BUT I'M NOT...
HURRY AND CHANGE!
I CAN'T!!
IT CAN'T BE...
I CAN'T DO IT!!
MINT!!
MINT!!
I can't hold on much longer...
MINT ...
PLEASE ...

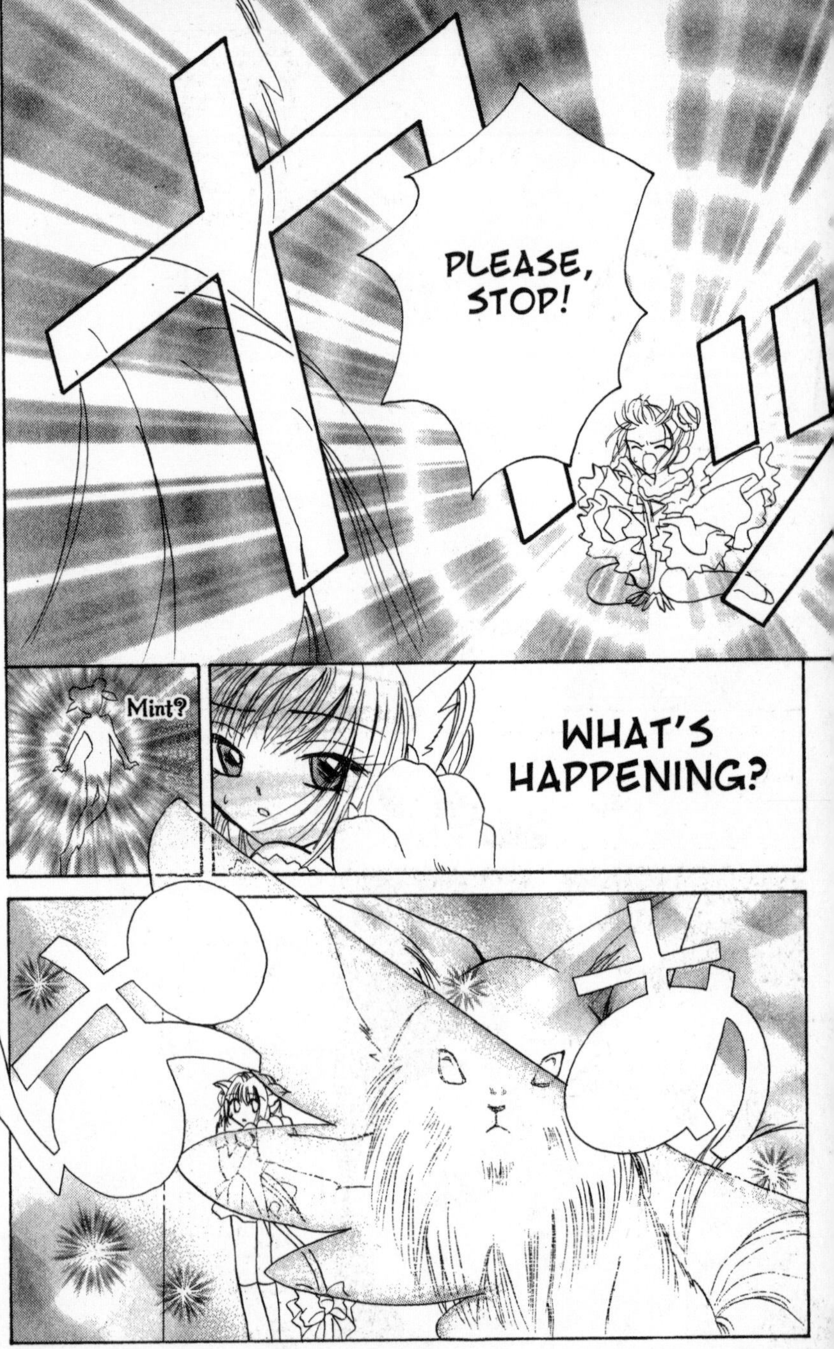
PLEASE, STOP!
WHAT'S HAPPENING?
Mint?

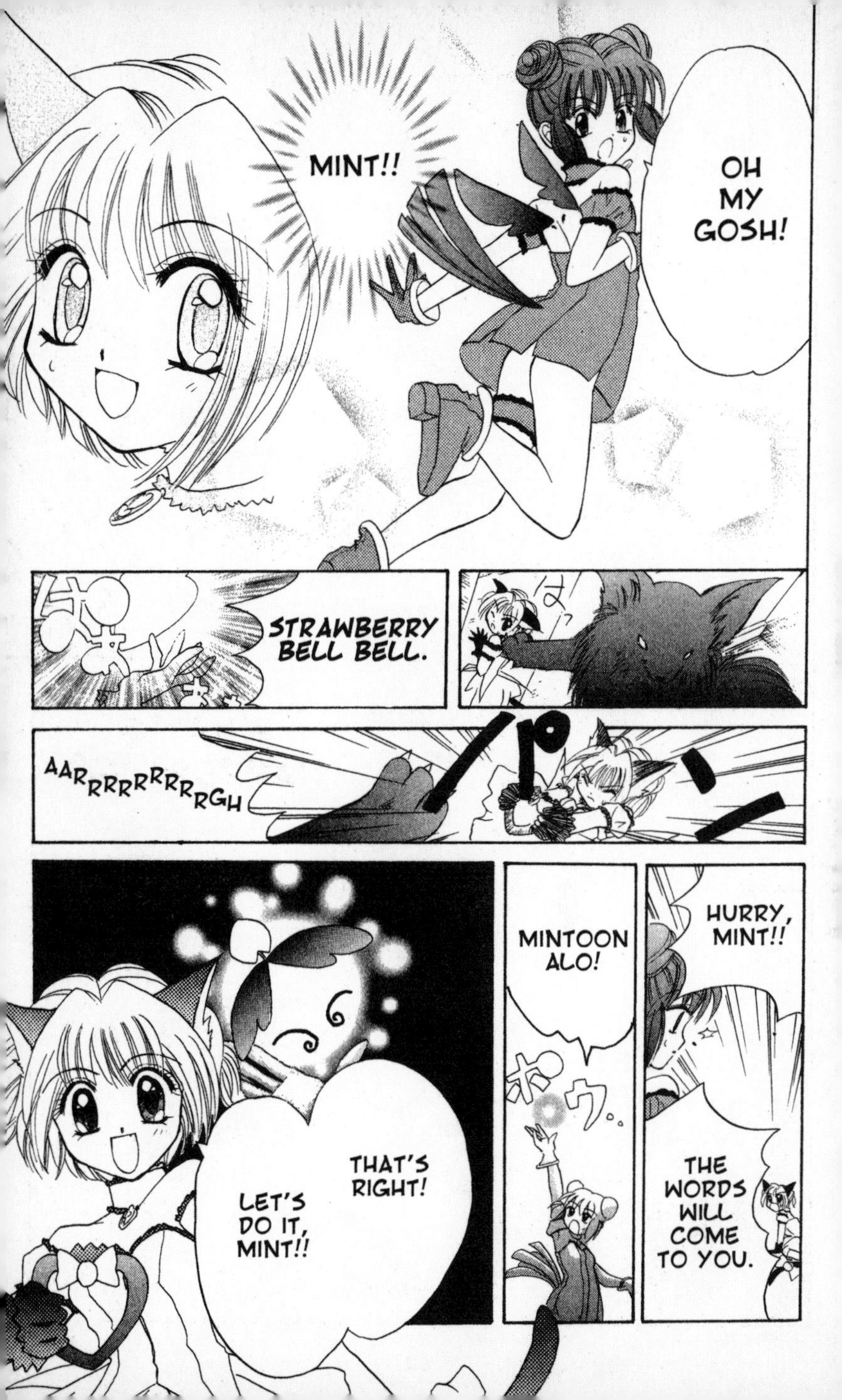
OH MY GOSH!
MINT!!
はっ
STRAWBERRY BELL BELL.
パ
AARRRRRRRRRGH
HURRY, MINT!!
THE WORDS WILL COME TO YOU.
MINTOON ALO!
ホウ
THAT'S RIGHT!
LET'S DO IT, MINT!!

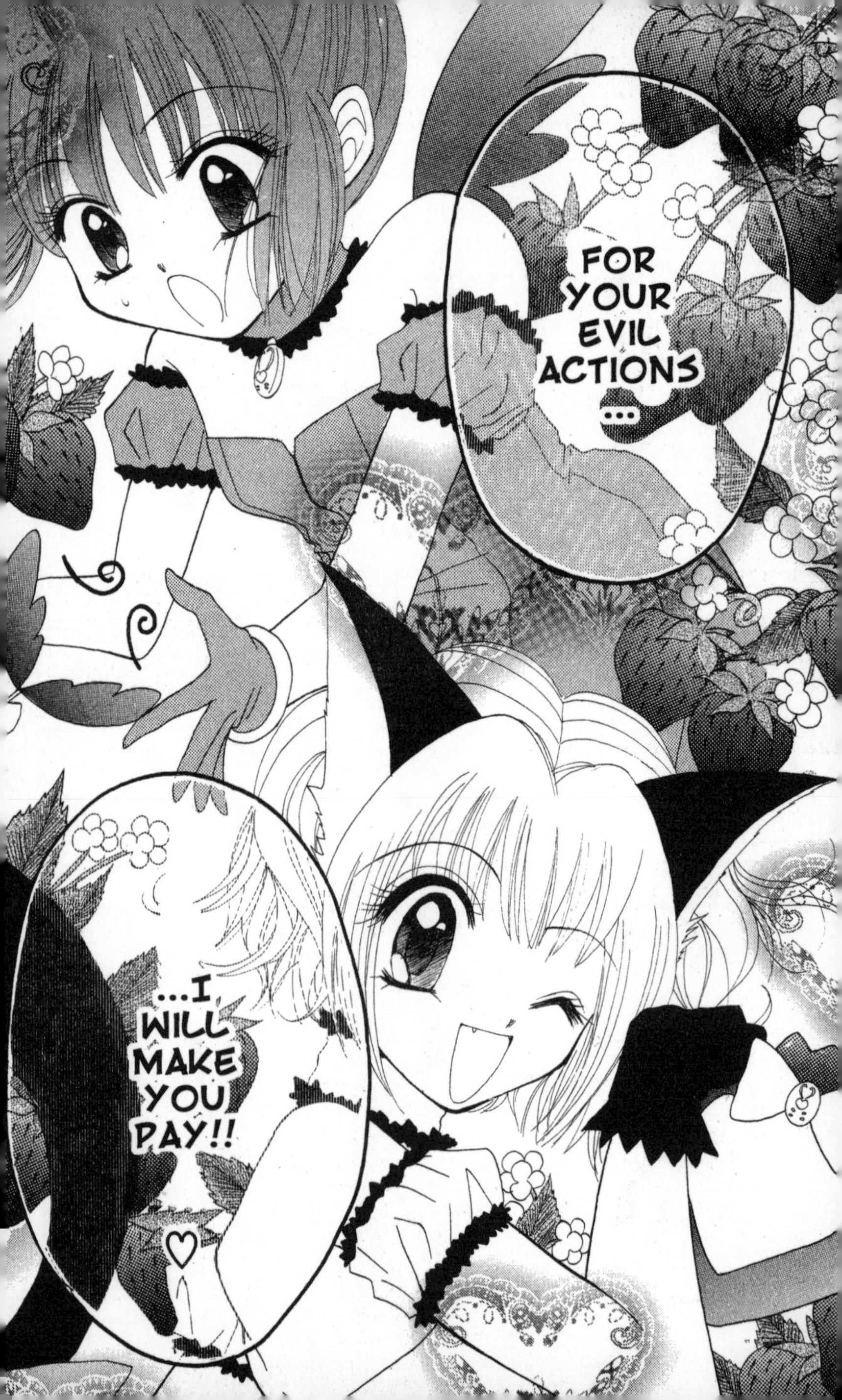
FOR YOUR EVIL ACTIONS ...
...I WILL MAKE YOU PAY!! ♡

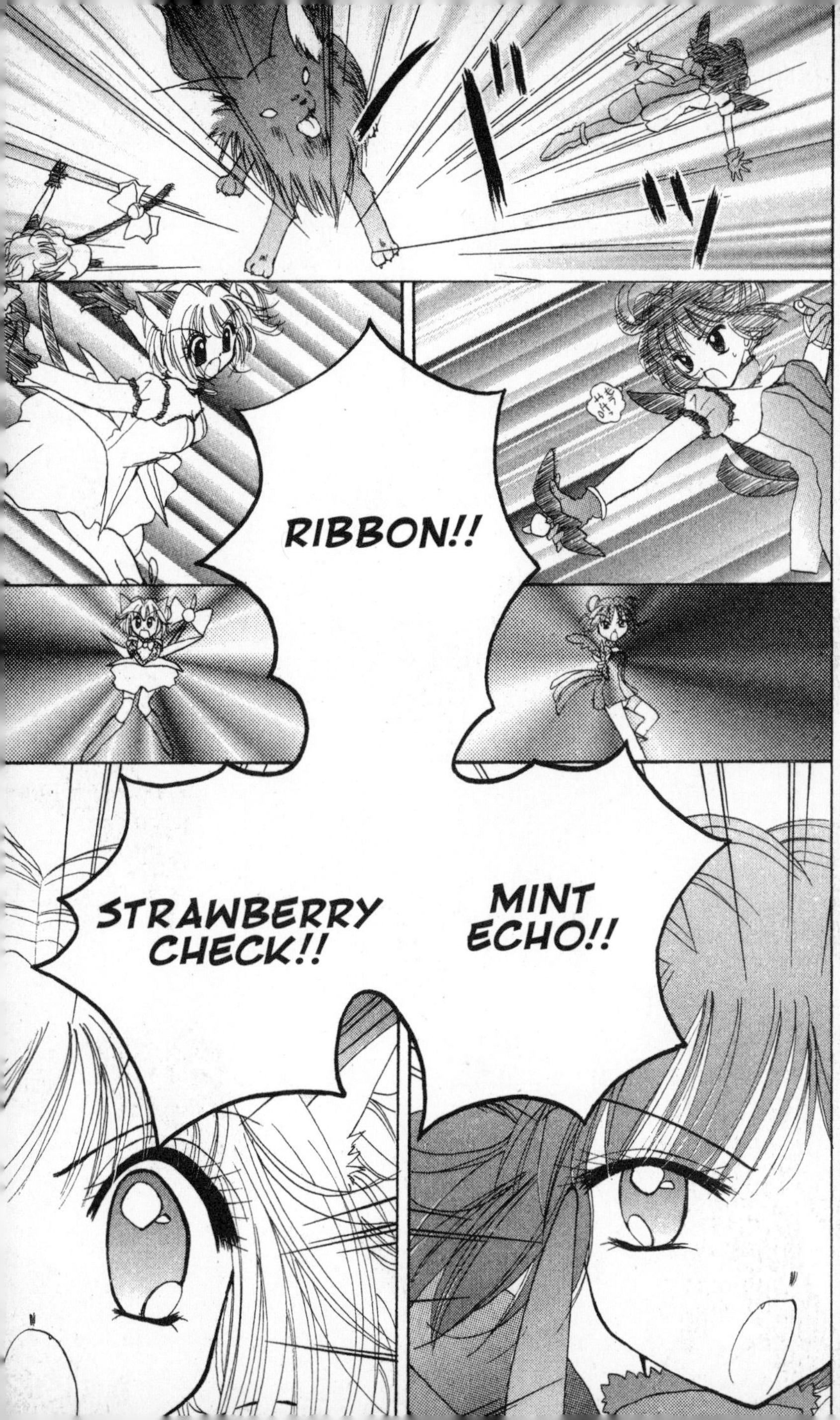
RIBBON!!
MINT ECHO!!
STRAWBERRY CHECK!!

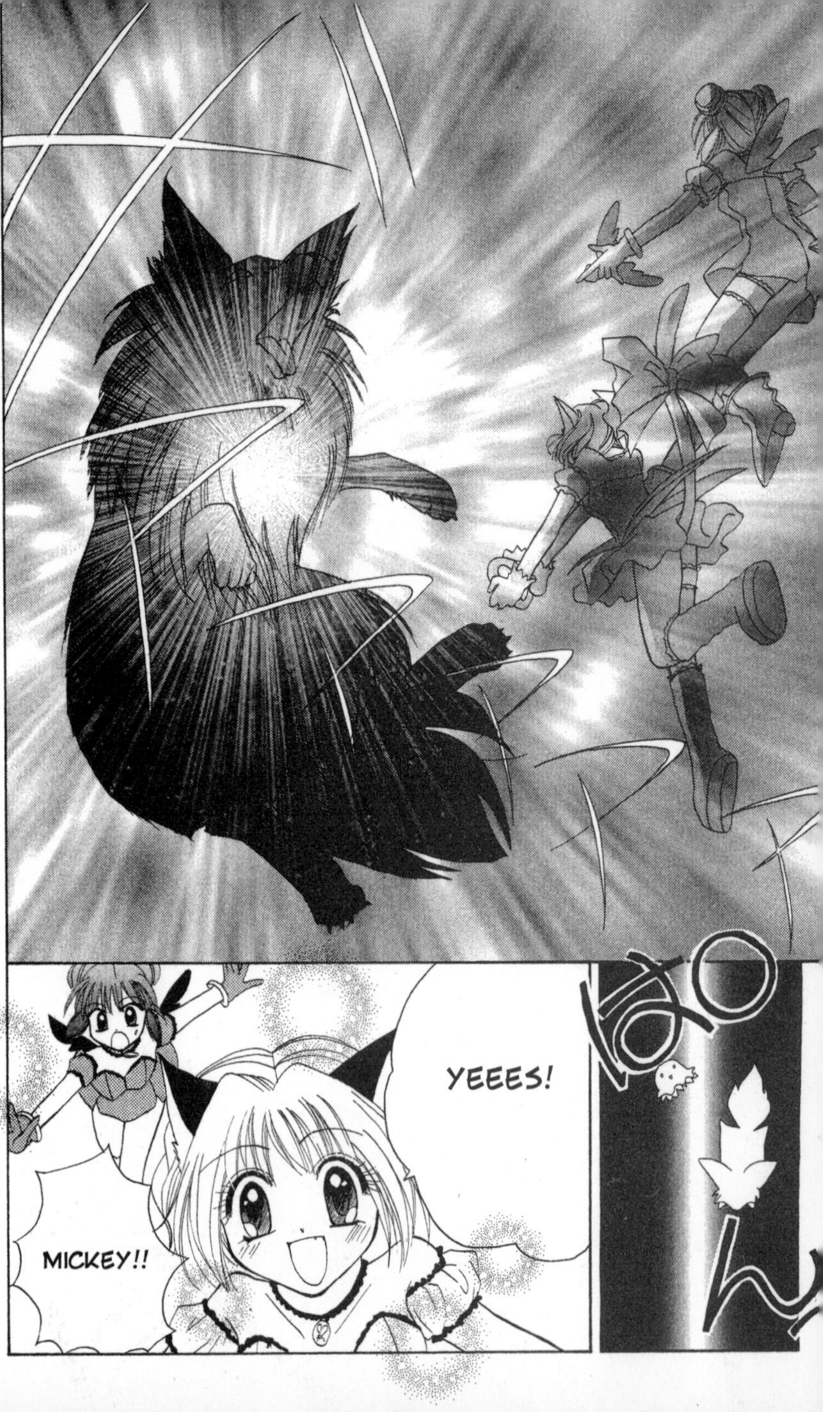
YEEES!
MICKEY!!

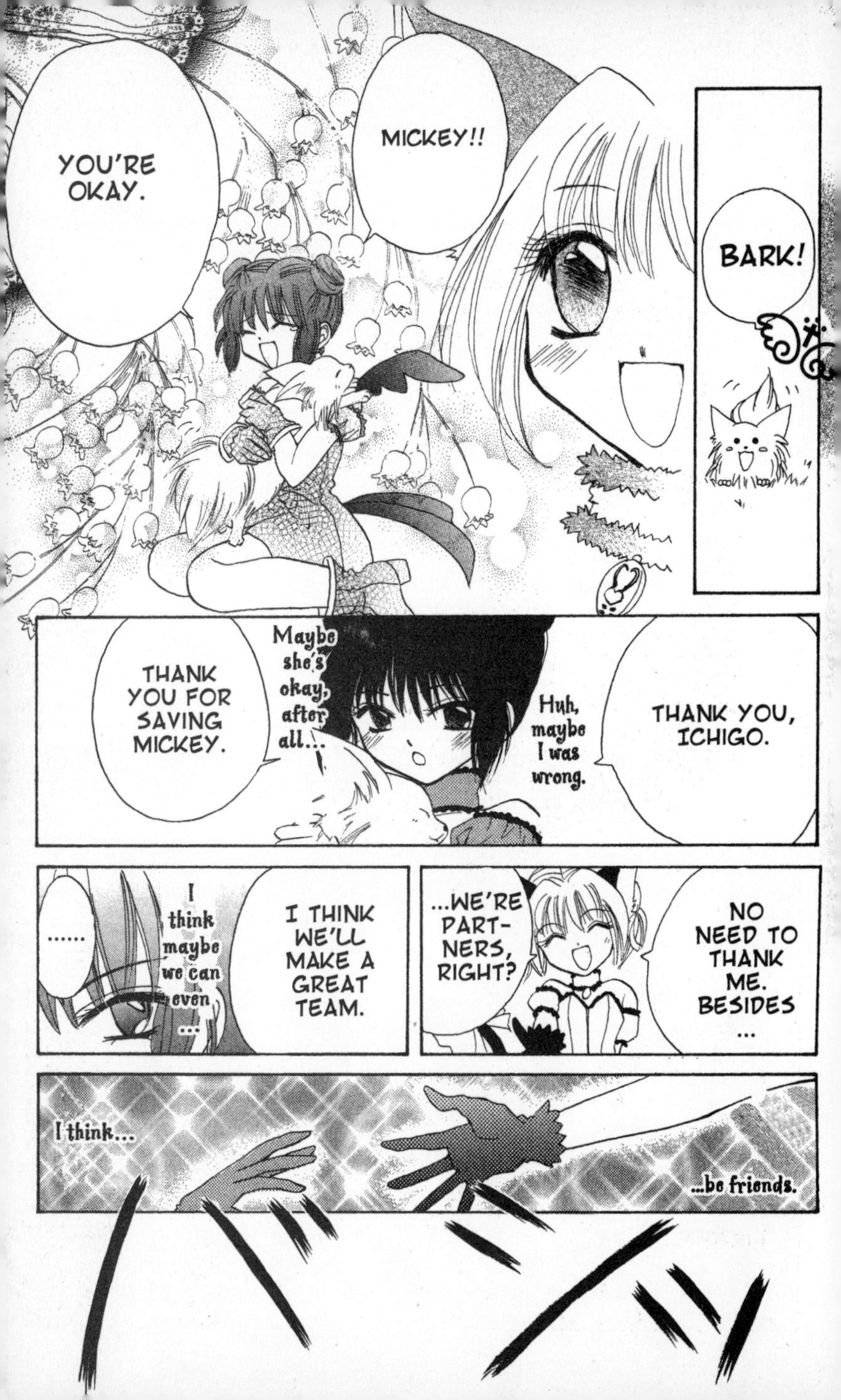

BARK!
MICKEY!!
YOU'RE OKAY.
THANK YOU, ICHIGO.
Huh, maybe I was wrong.
Maybe she's okay, after all...
THANK YOU FOR SAVING MICKEY.
NO NEED TO THANK ME. BESIDES ...
...WE'RE PART-NERS, RIGHT?
I THINK WE'LL MAKE A GREAT TEAM.
I think maybe we can even ...
......
I think...
...be friends.

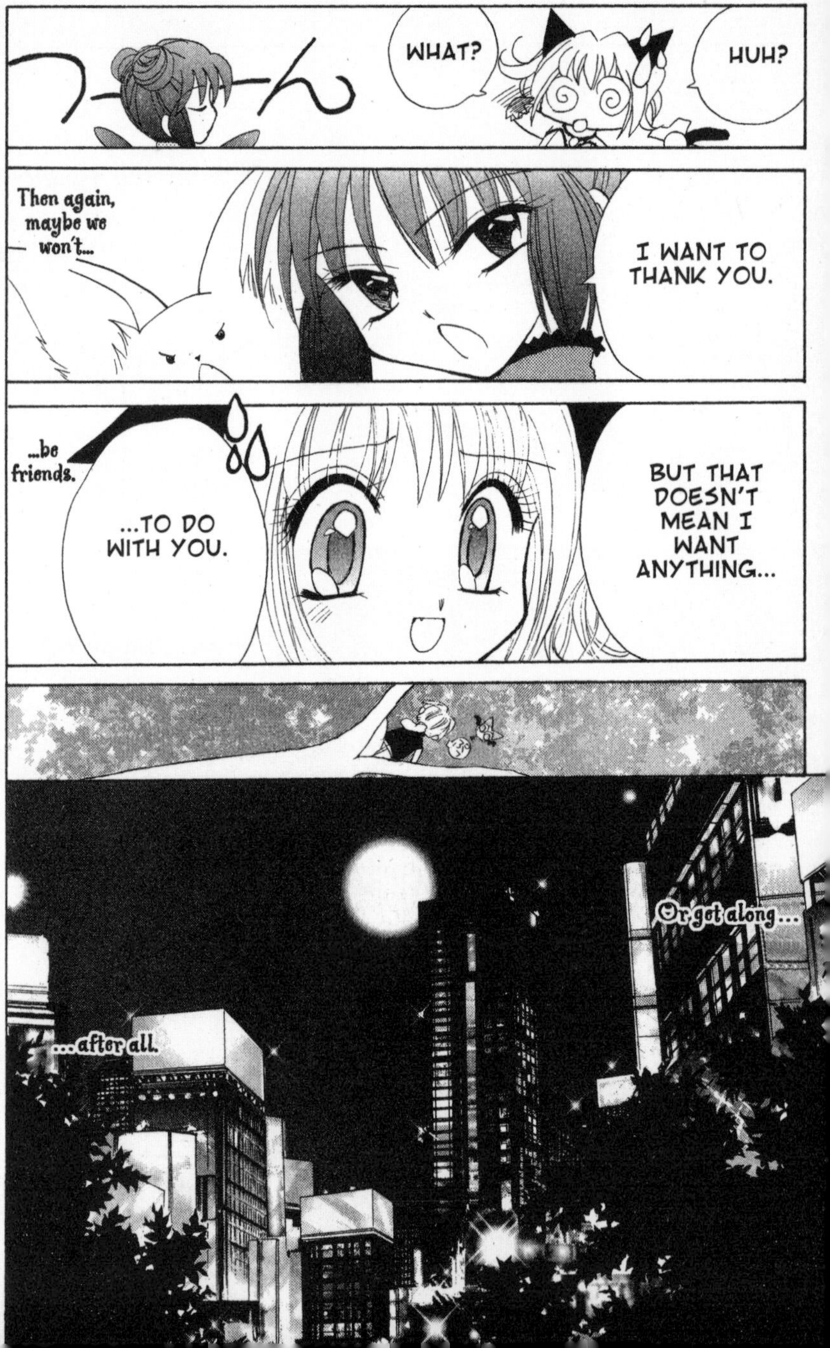
HUH?
WHAT?
つーん
I WANT TO THANK YOU.
Then again, maybe we won't...
BUT THAT DOESN'T MEAN I WANT ANYTHING...
...TO DO WITH YOU.
...be friends.
Or got along...
...after all.

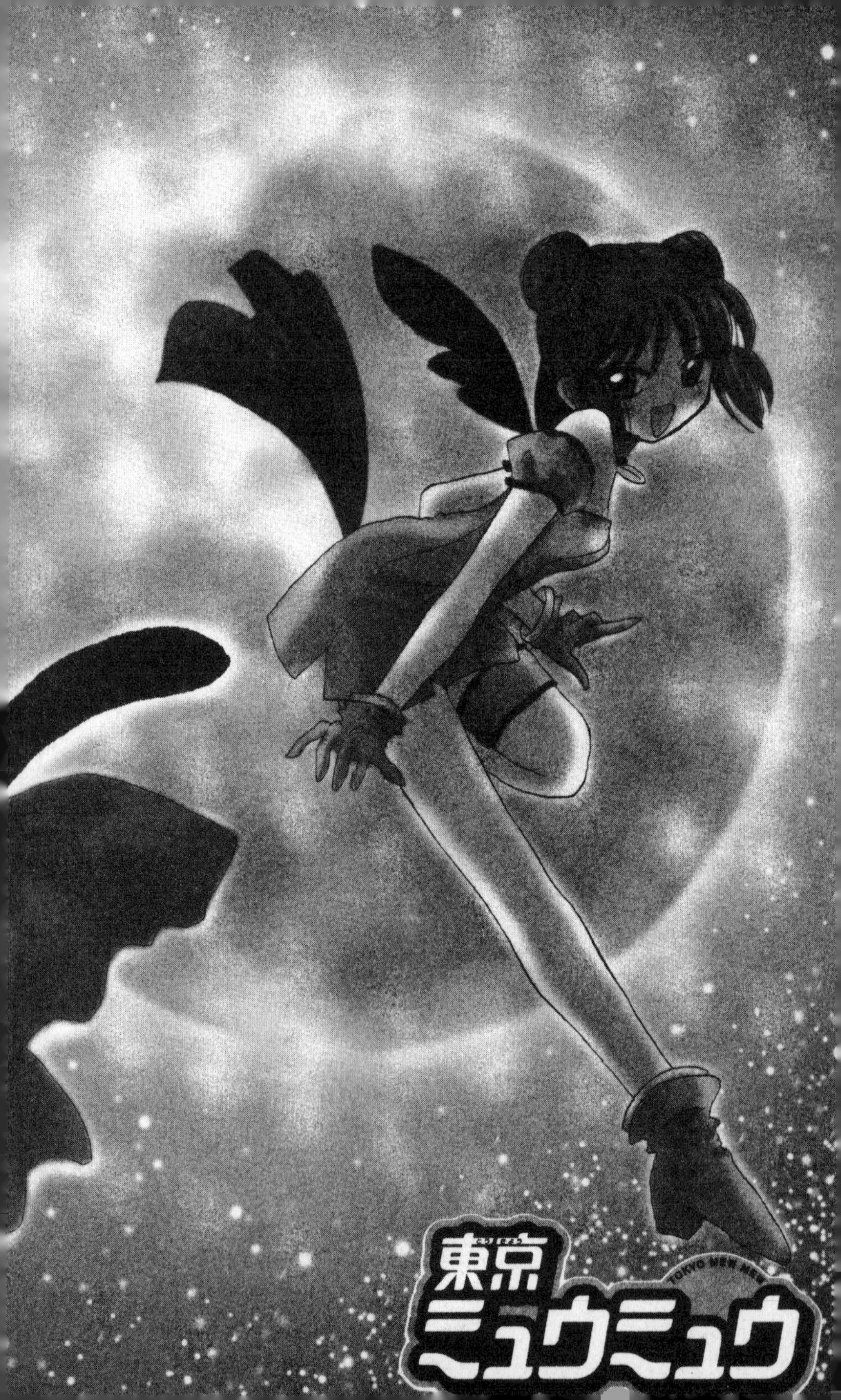
東京ミュウミュウ
TOKYO MEW MEW

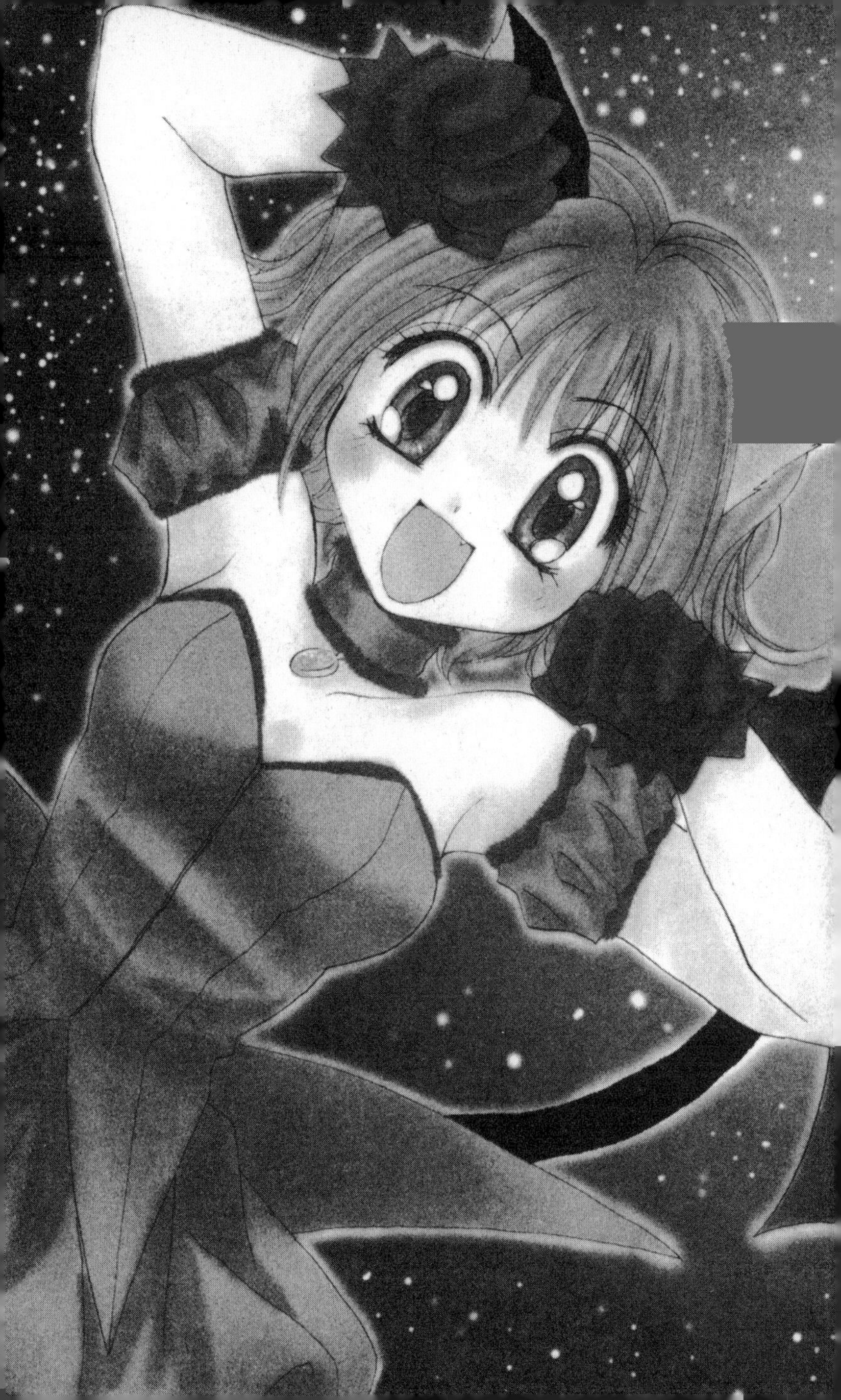

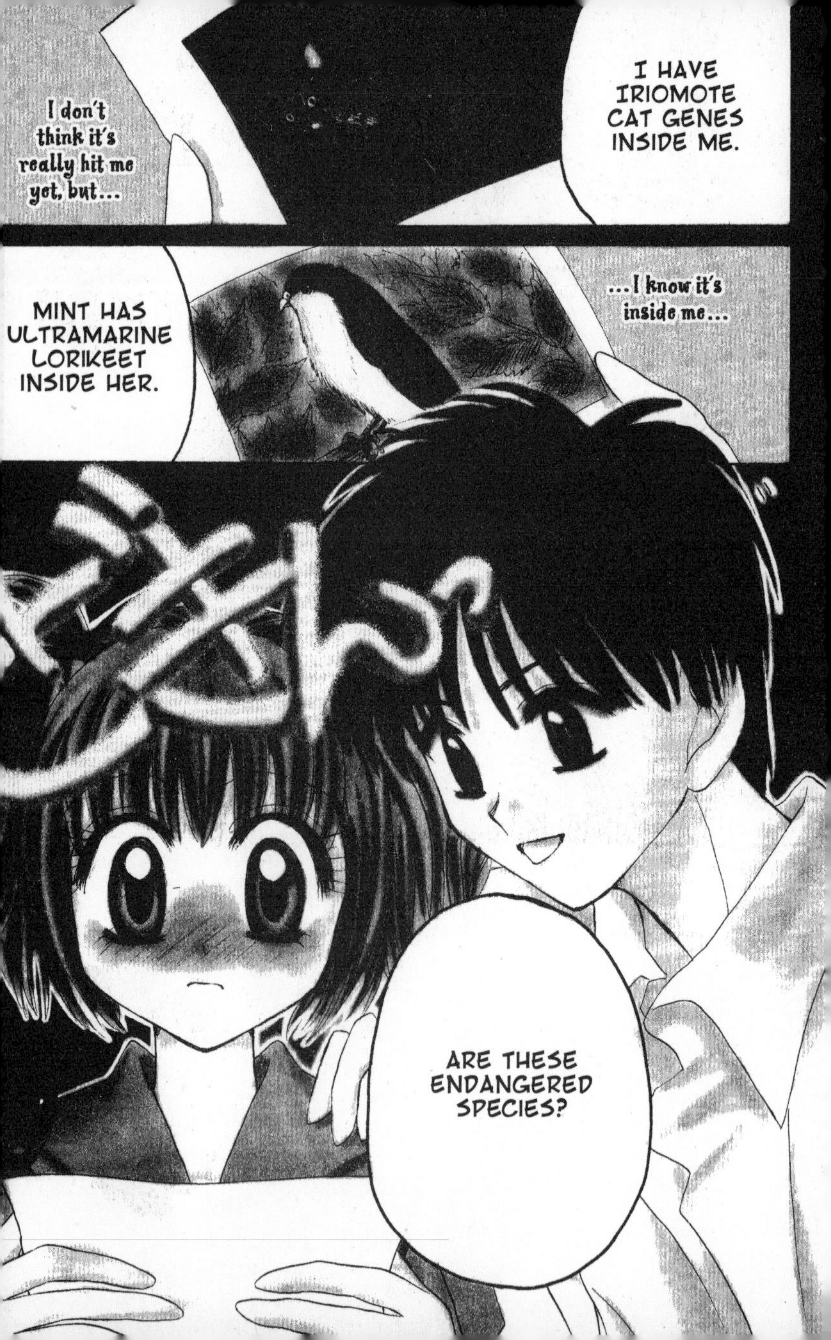
I HAVE IRIOMOTE CAT GENES INSIDE ME.
I don't think it's really hit me yet, but...
...I know it's inside me...
MINT HAS ULTRAMARINE LORIKEET INSIDE HER.
ARE THESE ENDANGERED SPECIES?

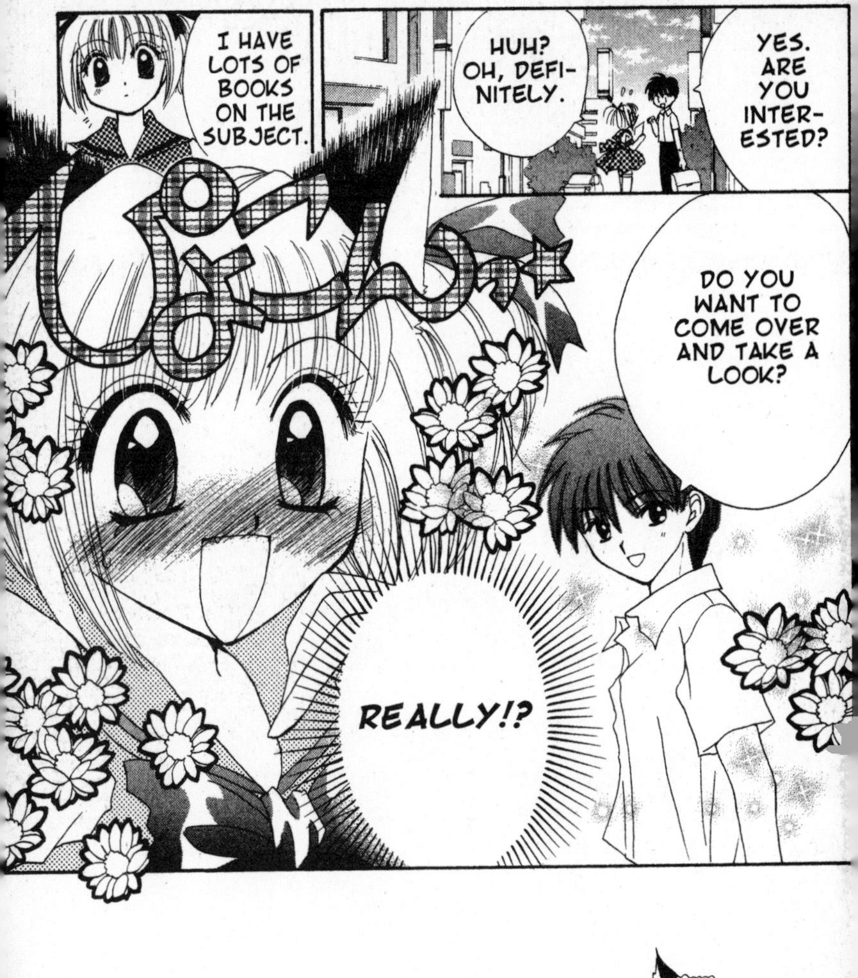
YES. ARE YOU INTERESTED?
HUH? OH, DEFINITELY.
I HAVE LOTS OF BOOKS ON THE SUBJECT.
DO YOU WANT TO COME OVER AND TAKE A LOOK?
REALLY!?

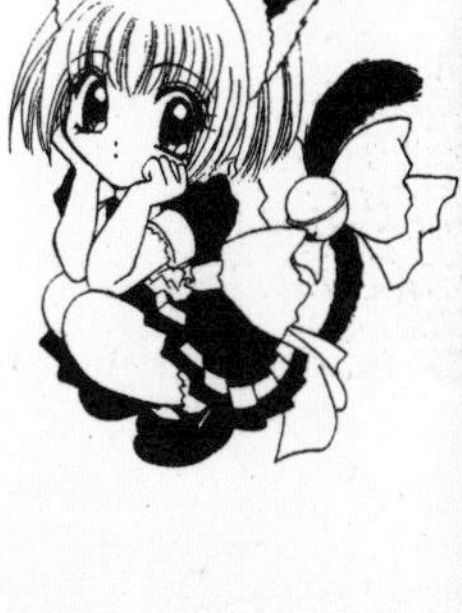

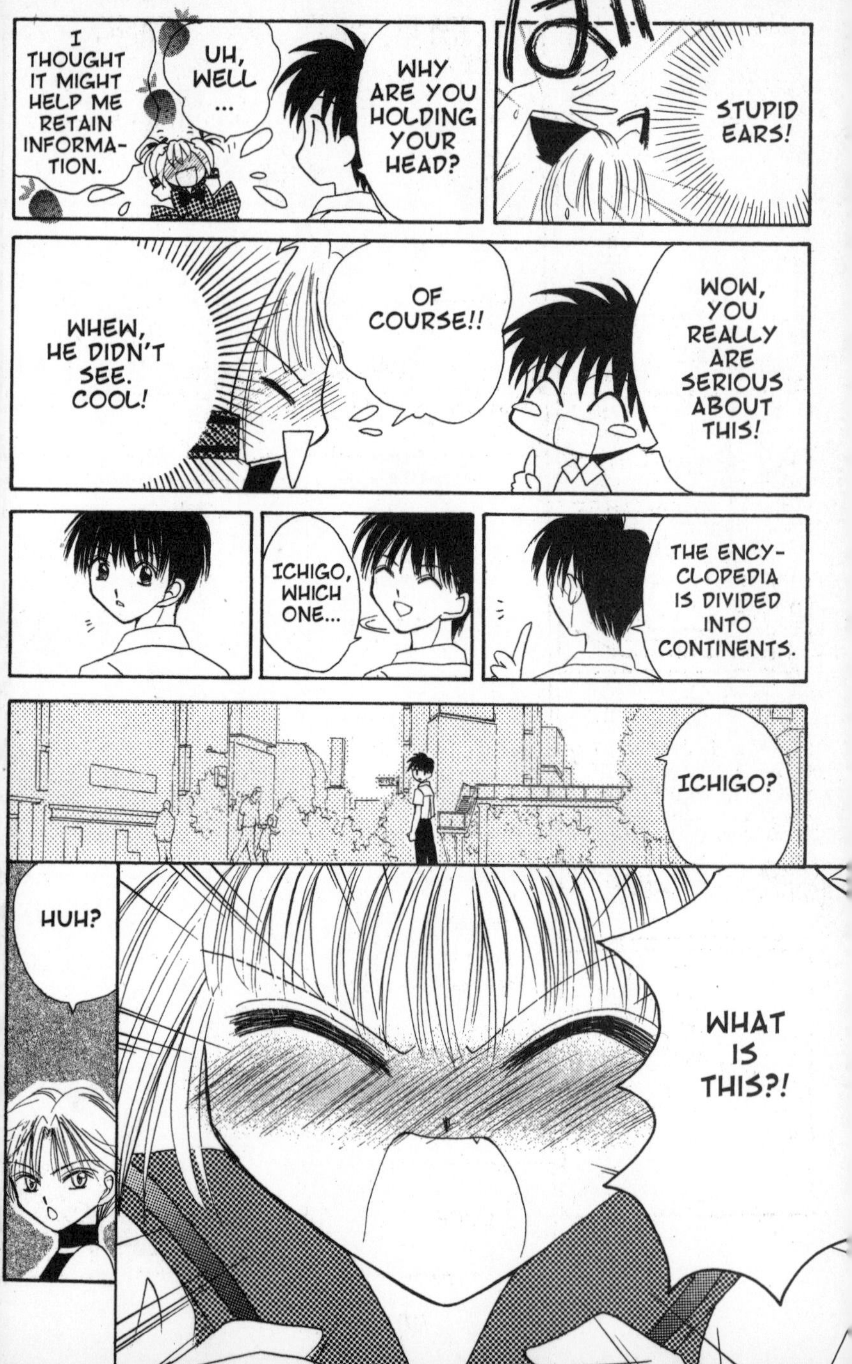
STUPID EARS!
WHY ARE YOU HOLDING YOUR HEAD?
UH, WELL ...
I THOUGHT IT MIGHT HELP ME RETAIN INFORMA-TION.
WOW, YOU REALLY ARE SERIOUS ABOUT THIS!
OF COURSE!!
WHEW, HE DIDN'T SEE. COOL!
THE ENCY-CLOPEDIA IS DIVIDED INTO CONTINENTS.
ICHIGO, WHICH ONE...
ICHIGO?
WHAT IS THIS?!
HUH?

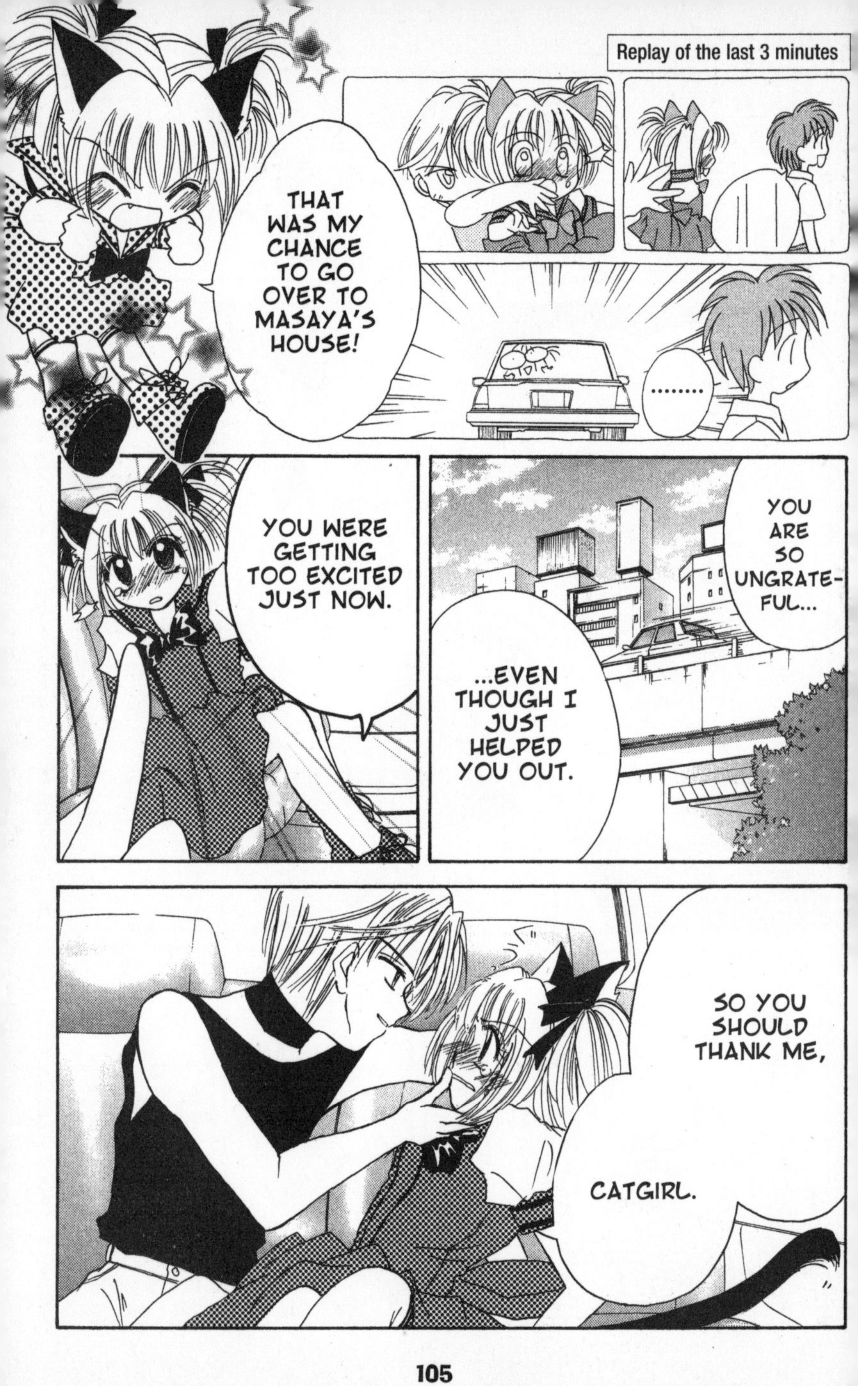
Replay of the last 3 minutes
....
THAT WAS MY CHANCE TO GO OVER TO MASAYA'S HOUSE!
YOU ARE SO UNGRATE-FUL...
...EVEN THOUGH I JUST HELPED YOU OUT.
YOU WERE GETTING TOO EXCITED JUST NOW.
SO YOU SHOULD THANK ME,
CATGIRL.

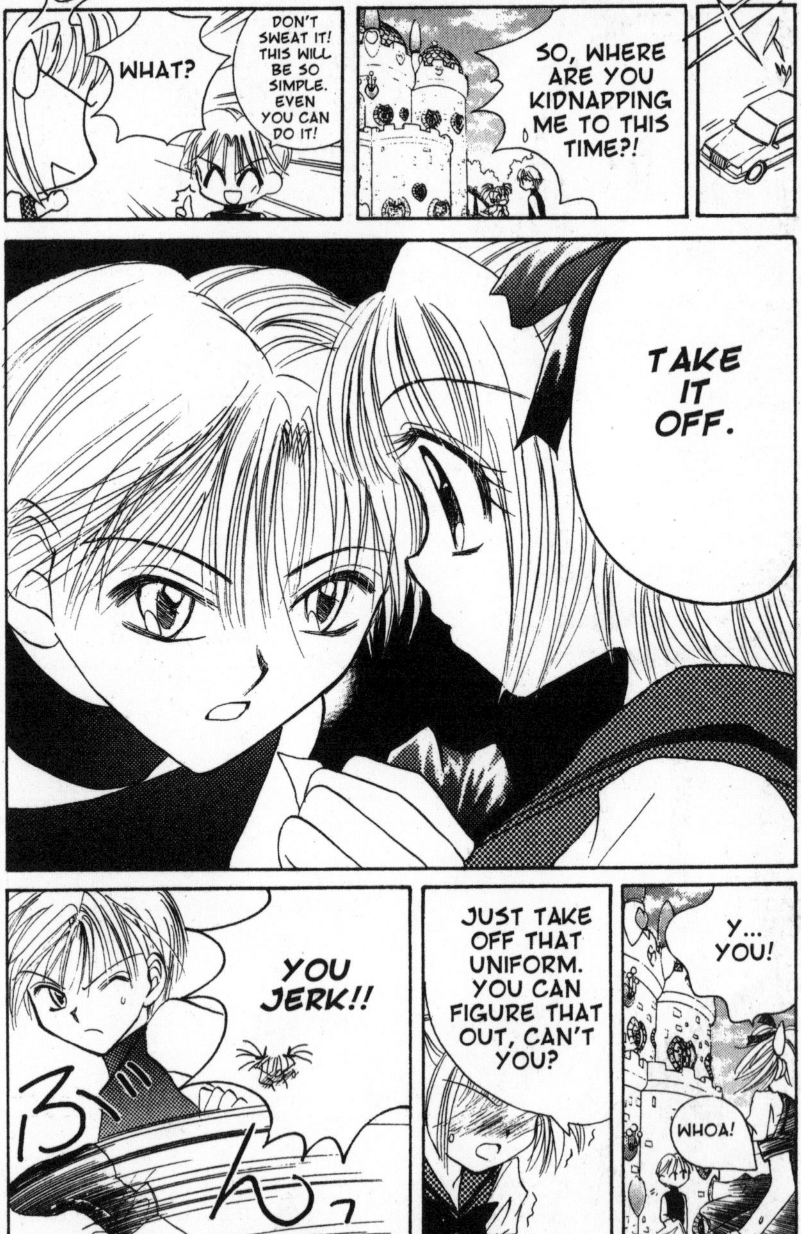
SO, WHERE ARE YOU KIDNAPPING ME TO THIS TIME?!
DON'T SWEAT IT! THIS WILL BE SO SIMPLE. EVEN YOU CAN DO IT!
WHAT?
TAKE IT OFF.
Y... YOU!
WHOA!
JUST TAKE OFF THAT UNIFORM. YOU CAN FIGURE THAT OUT, CAN'T YOU?
YOU JERK!!

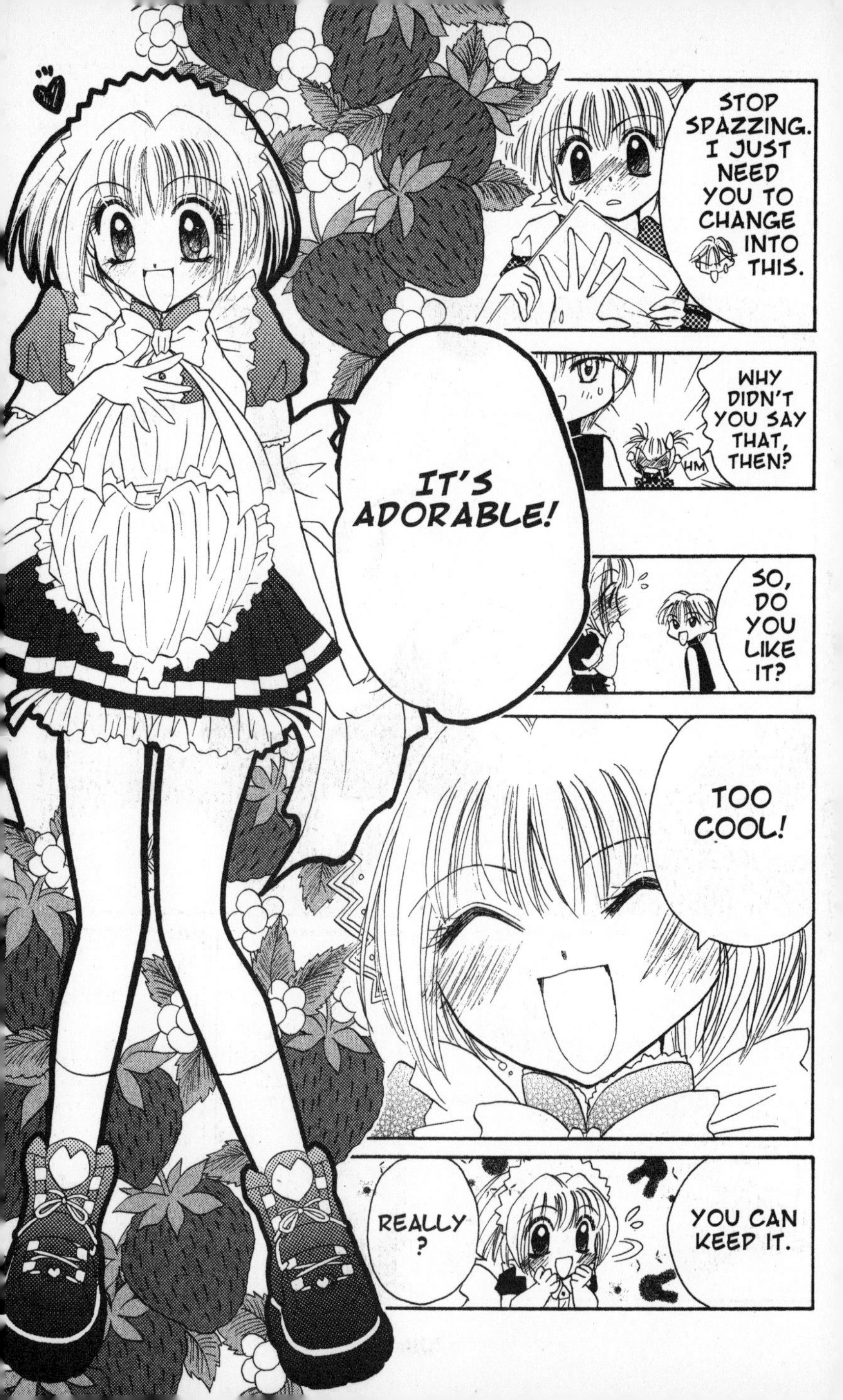
STOP SPAZZING. I JUST NEED YOU TO CHANGE INTO THIS.
WHY DIDN'T YOU SAY THAT, THEN?
HM
SO, DO YOU LIKE IT?
TOO COOL!
YOU CAN KEEP IT.
REALLY?
IT'S ADORABLE!

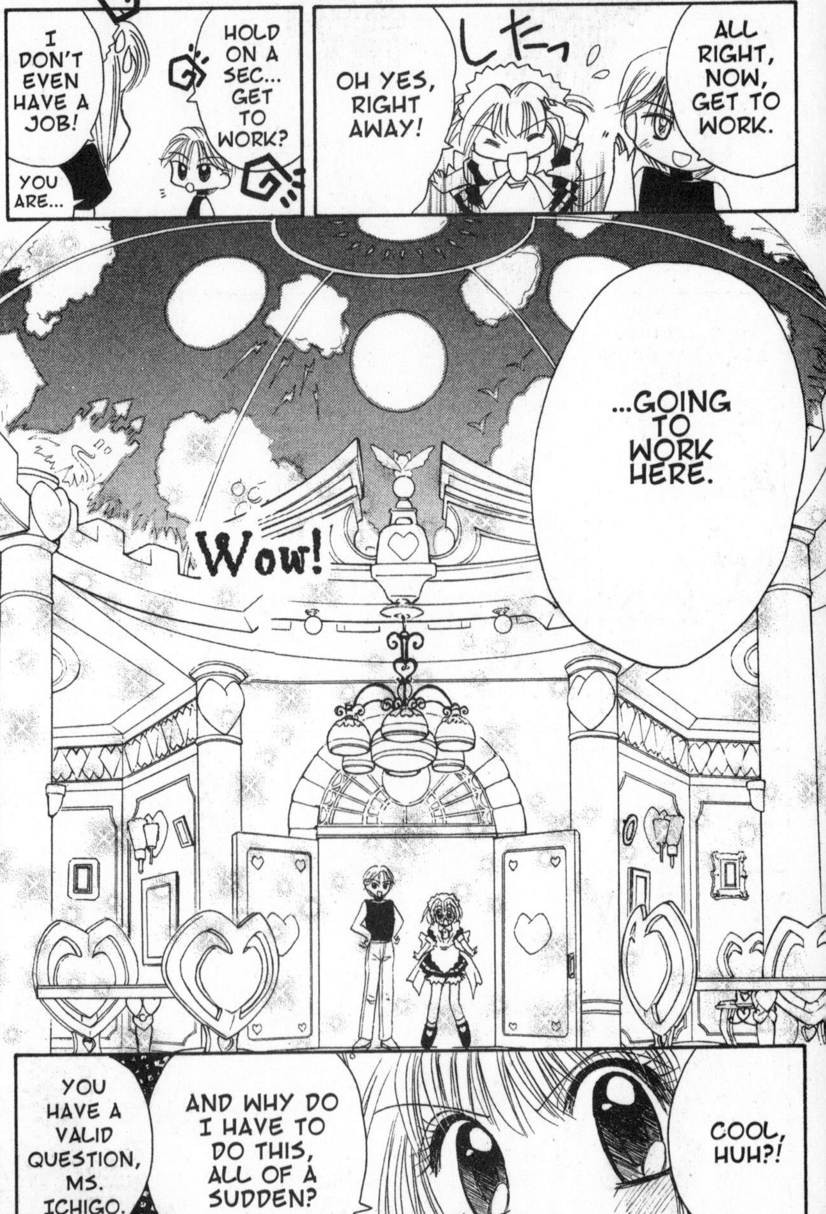
ALL RIGHT, NOW, GET TO WORK.
したーっ
OH YES, RIGHT AWAY!
HOLD ON A SEC... GET TO WORK?
I DON'T EVEN HAVE A JOB!
YOU ARE...
...GOING TO WORK HERE.
Wow!
COOL, HUH?!
AND WHY DO I HAVE TO DO THIS, ALL OF A SUDDEN?
YOU HAVE A VALID QUESTION, MS. ICHIGO.

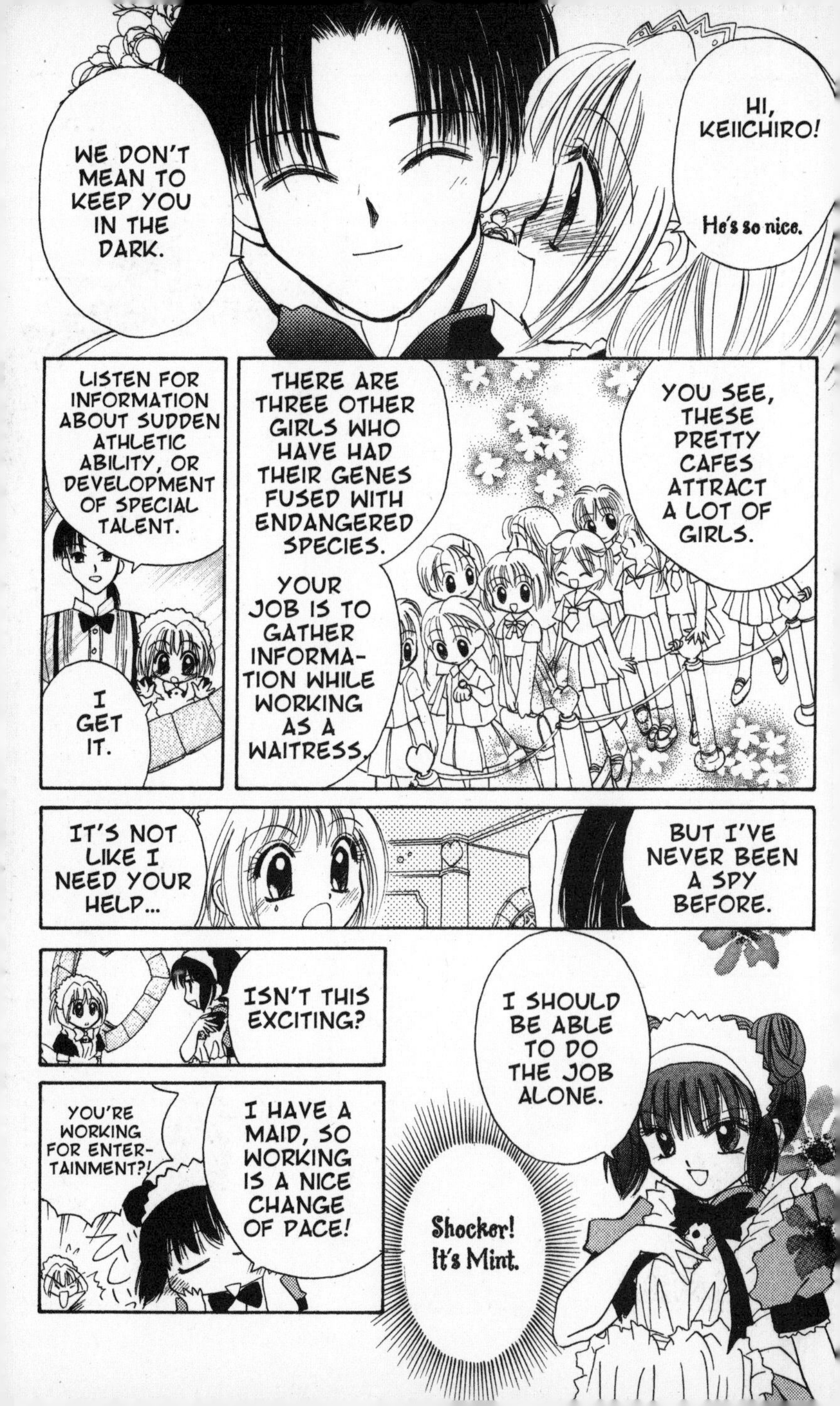

HI, KEIICHIRO!
He's so nice.
WE DON'T MEAN TO KEEP YOU IN THE DARK.
YOU SEE, THESE PRETTY CAFES ATTRACT A LOT OF GIRLS.
THERE ARE THREE OTHER GIRLS WHO HAVE HAD THEIR GENES FUSED WITH ENDANGERED SPECIES.
YOUR JOB IS TO GATHER INFORMATION WHILE WORKING AS A WAITRESS.
LISTEN FOR INFORMATION ABOUT SUDDEN ATHLETIC ABILITY, OR DEVELOPMENT OF SPECIAL TALENT.
I GET IT.
BUT I'VE NEVER BEEN A SPY BEFORE.
IT'S NOT LIKE I NEED YOUR HELP...
I SHOULD BE ABLE TO DO THE JOB ALONE.
Shocker! It's Mint.
ISN'T THIS EXCITING?
I HAVE A MAID, SO WORKING IS A NICE CHANGE OF PACE!
YOU'RE WORKING FOR ENTERTAINMENT?!

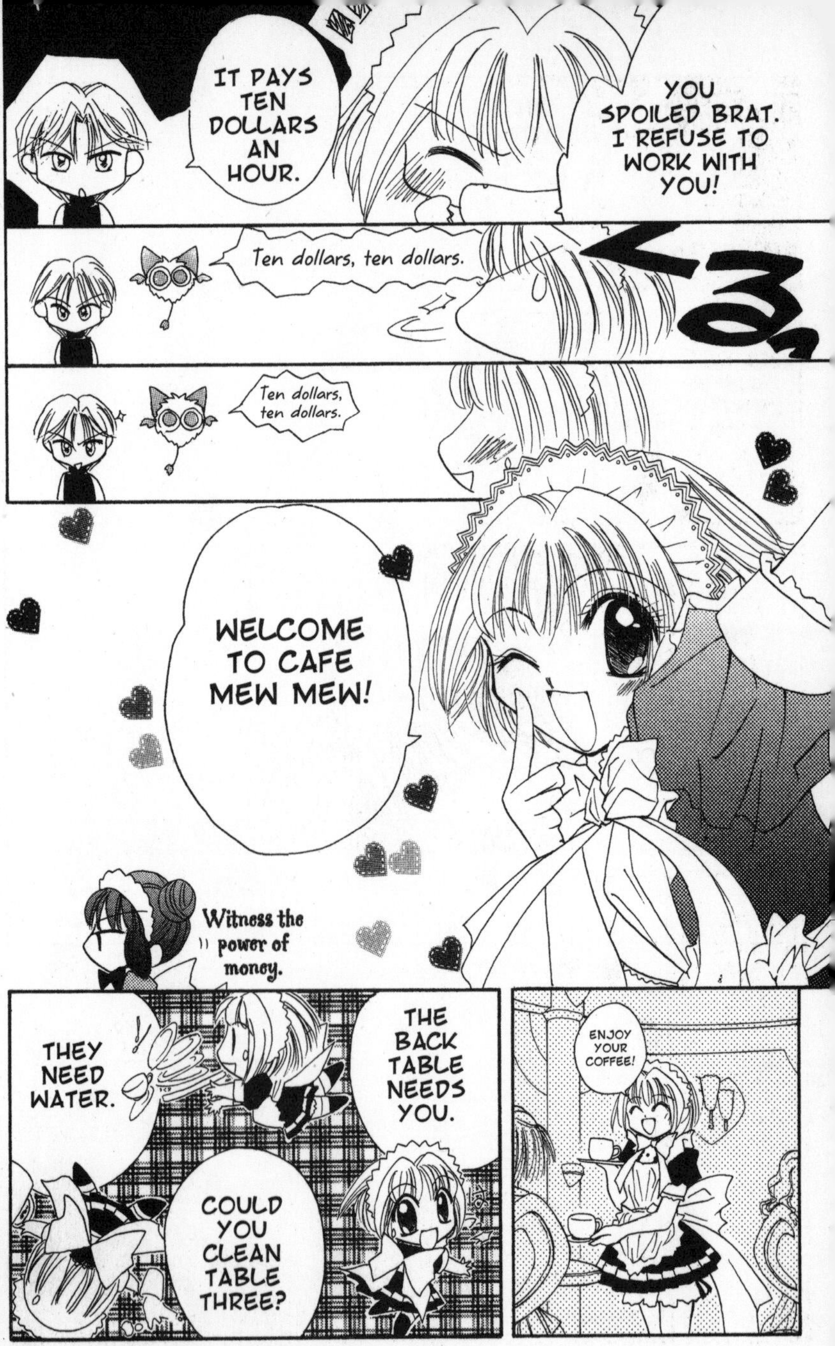
YOU SPOILED BRAT. I REFUSE TO WORK WITH YOU!
IT PAYS TEN DOLLARS AN HOUR.
くる
Ten dollars, ten dollars.
Ten dollars, ten dollars.
WELCOME TO CAFE MEW MEW!
Witness the power of money.
ENJOY YOUR COFFEE!
THE BACK TABLE NEEDS YOU.
THEY NEED WATER.
COULD YOU CLEAN TABLE THREE?

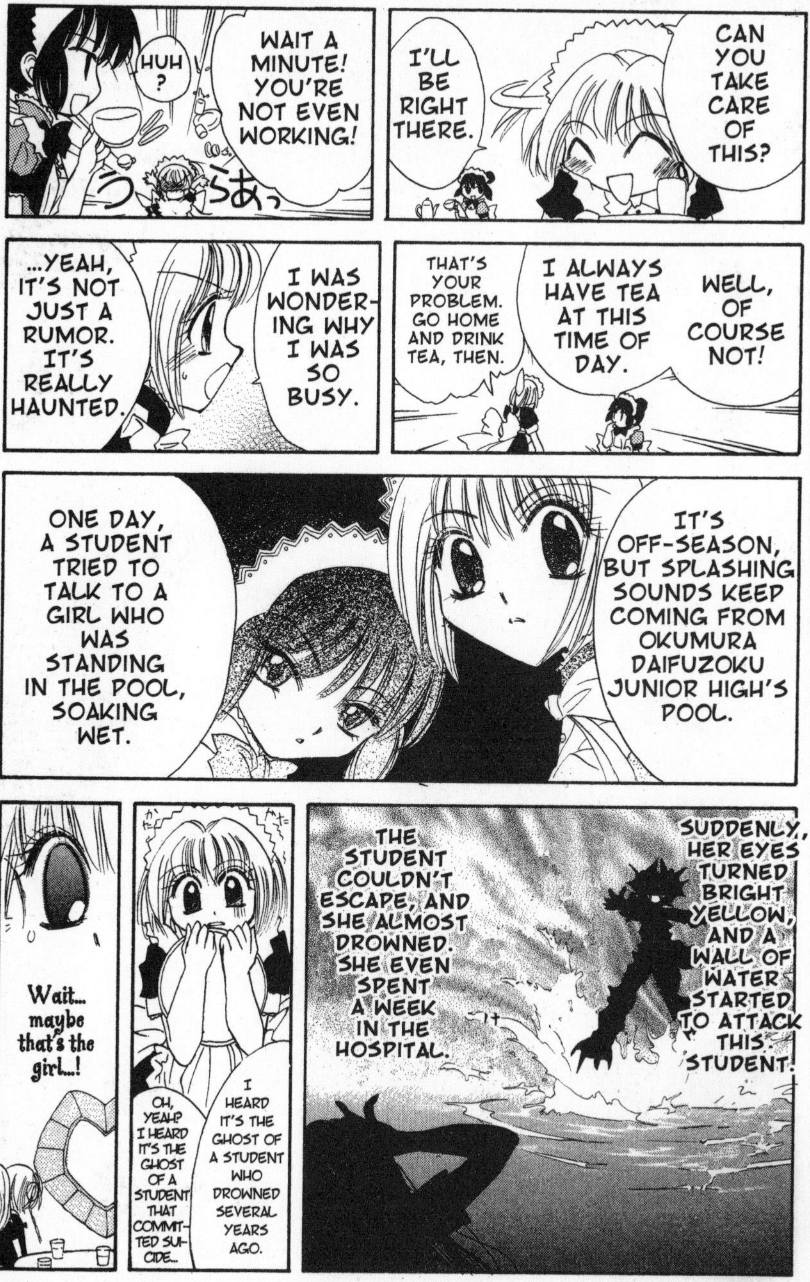
CAN YOU TAKE CARE OF THIS?
I'LL BE RIGHT THERE.
WAIT A MINUTE! YOU'RE NOT EVEN WORKING!
HUH ?
うらあっ
WELL, OF COURSE NOT!
I ALWAYS HAVE TEA AT THIS TIME OF DAY.
THAT'S YOUR PROBLEM. GO HOME AND DRINK TEA, THEN.
I WAS WONDER-ING WHY I WAS SO BUSY.
...YEAH, IT'S NOT JUST A RUMOR. IT'S REALLY HAUNTED.
IT'S OFF-SEASON, BUT SPLASHING SOUNDS KEEP COMING FROM OKUMURA DAIFUZOKU JUNIOR HIGH'S POOL.
ONE DAY, A STUDENT TRIED TO TALK TO A GIRL WHO WAS STANDING IN THE POOL, SOAKING WET.
SUDDENLY, HER EYES TURNED BRIGHT YELLOW, AND A WALL OF WATER STARTED TO ATTACK THIS STUDENT!
THE STUDENT COULDN'T ESCAPE, AND SHE ALMOST DROWNED. SHE EVEN SPENT A WEEK IN THE HOSPITAL.
I HEARD IT'S THE GHOST OF A STUDENT WHO DROWNED SEVERAL YEARS AGO.
OH, YEAH? I HEARD IT'S THE GHOST OF A STUDENT THAT COMMIT-TED SUI-CIDE...
Wait... maybe that's the girl...!

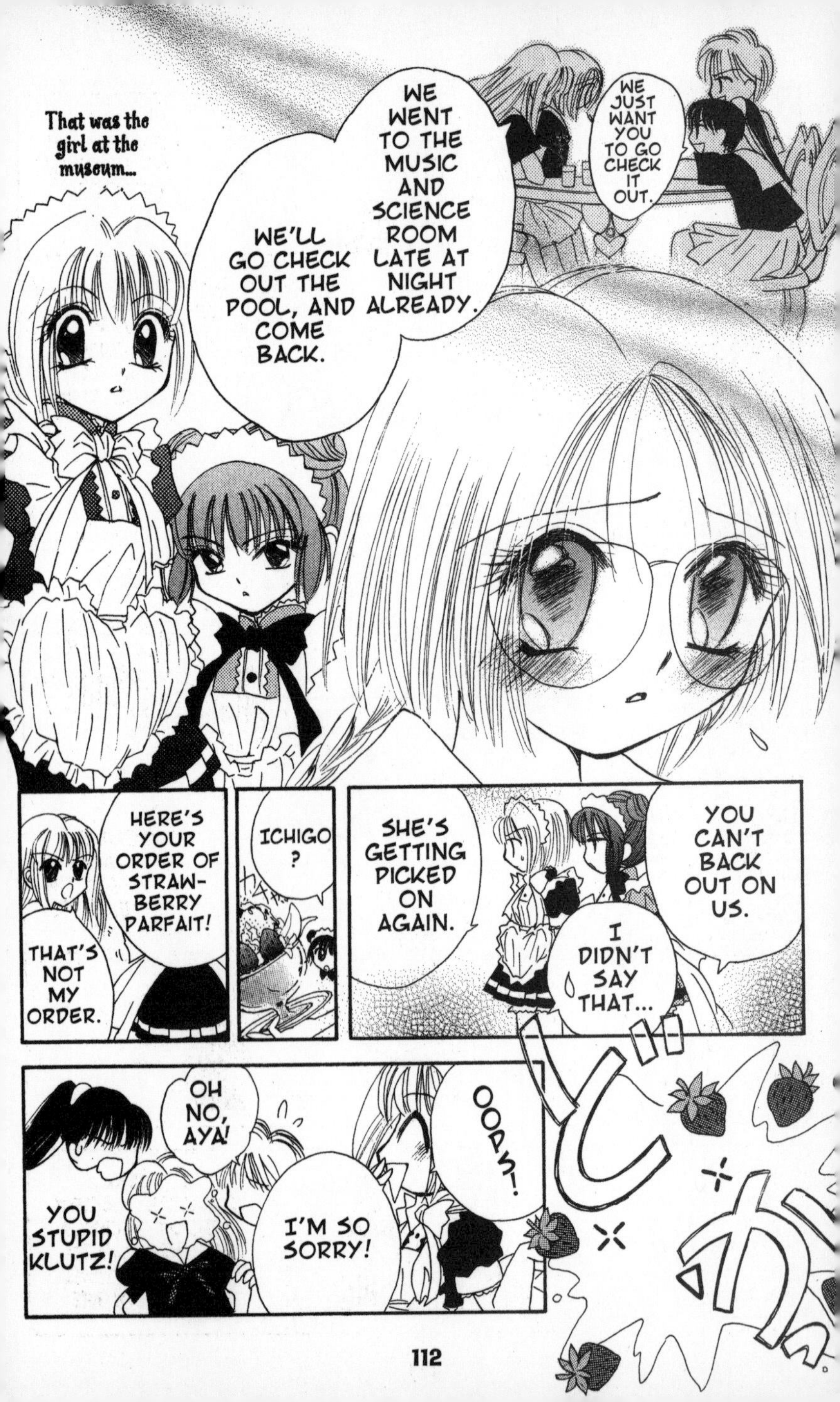

WE JUST WANT YOU TO GO CHECK IT OUT.
WE WENT TO THE MUSIC AND SCIENCE ROOM LATE AT NIGHT ALREADY.
WE'LL GO CHECK OUT THE POOL, AND COME BACK.
That was the girl at the museum...
YOU CAN'T BACK OUT ON US.
I DIDN'T SAY THAT...
SHE'S GETTING PICKED ON AGAIN.
ICHIGO?
HERE'S YOUR ORDER OF STRAW-BERRY PARFAIT!
THAT'S NOT MY ORDER.
OOPS!
I'M SO SORRY!
OH NO, AYA!
YOU STUPID KLUTZ!

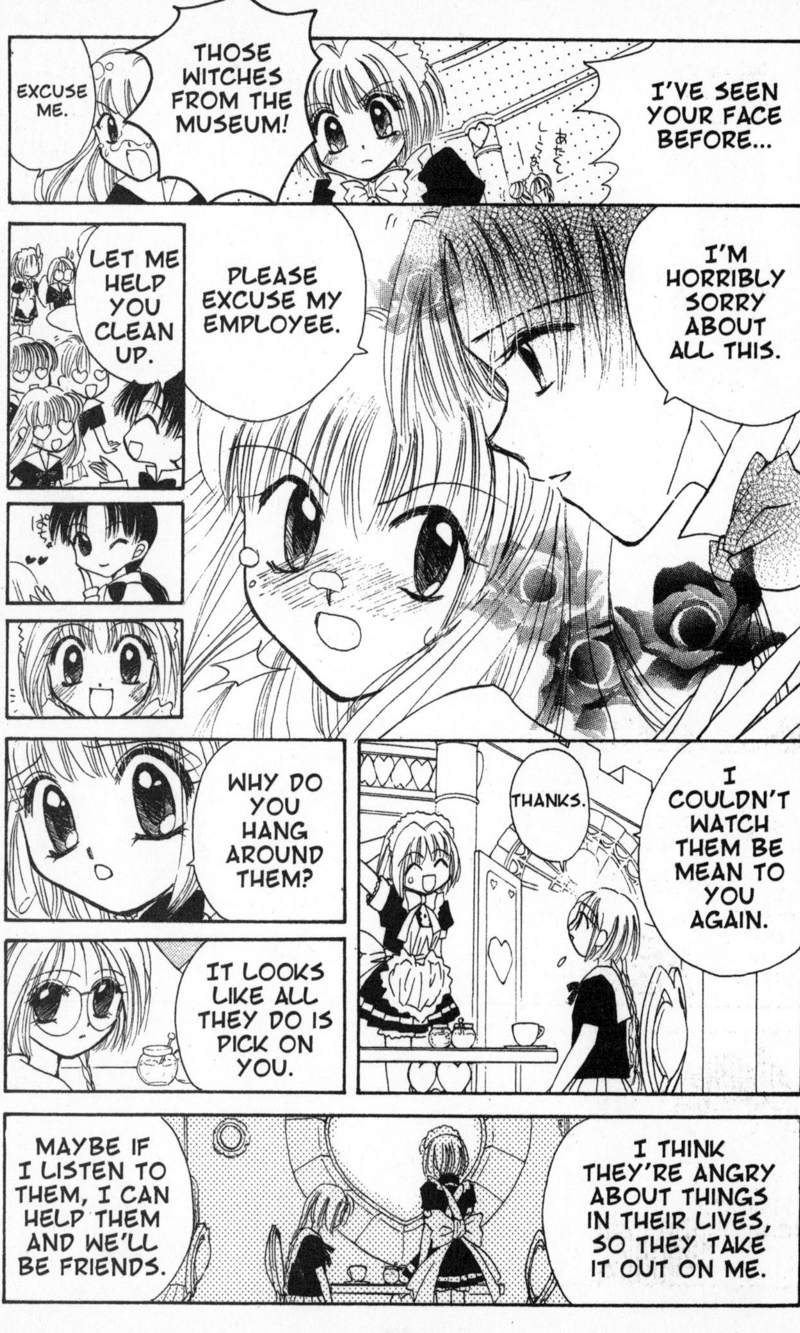
I'VE SEEN YOUR FACE BEFORE...
THOSE WITCHES FROM THE MUSEUM!
EXCUSE ME.
I'M HORRIBLY SORRY ABOUT ALL THIS.
PLEASE EXCUSE MY EMPLOYEE.
LET ME HELP YOU CLEAN UP.
I COULDN'T WATCH THEM BE MEAN TO YOU AGAIN.
THANKS.
WHY DO YOU HANG AROUND THEM?
IT LOOKS LIKE ALL THEY DO IS PICK ON YOU.
I THINK THEY'RE ANGRY ABOUT THINGS IN THEIR LIVES, SO THEY TAKE IT OUT ON ME.
MAYBE IF I LISTEN TO THEM, I CAN HELP THEM AND WE'LL BE FRIENDS.

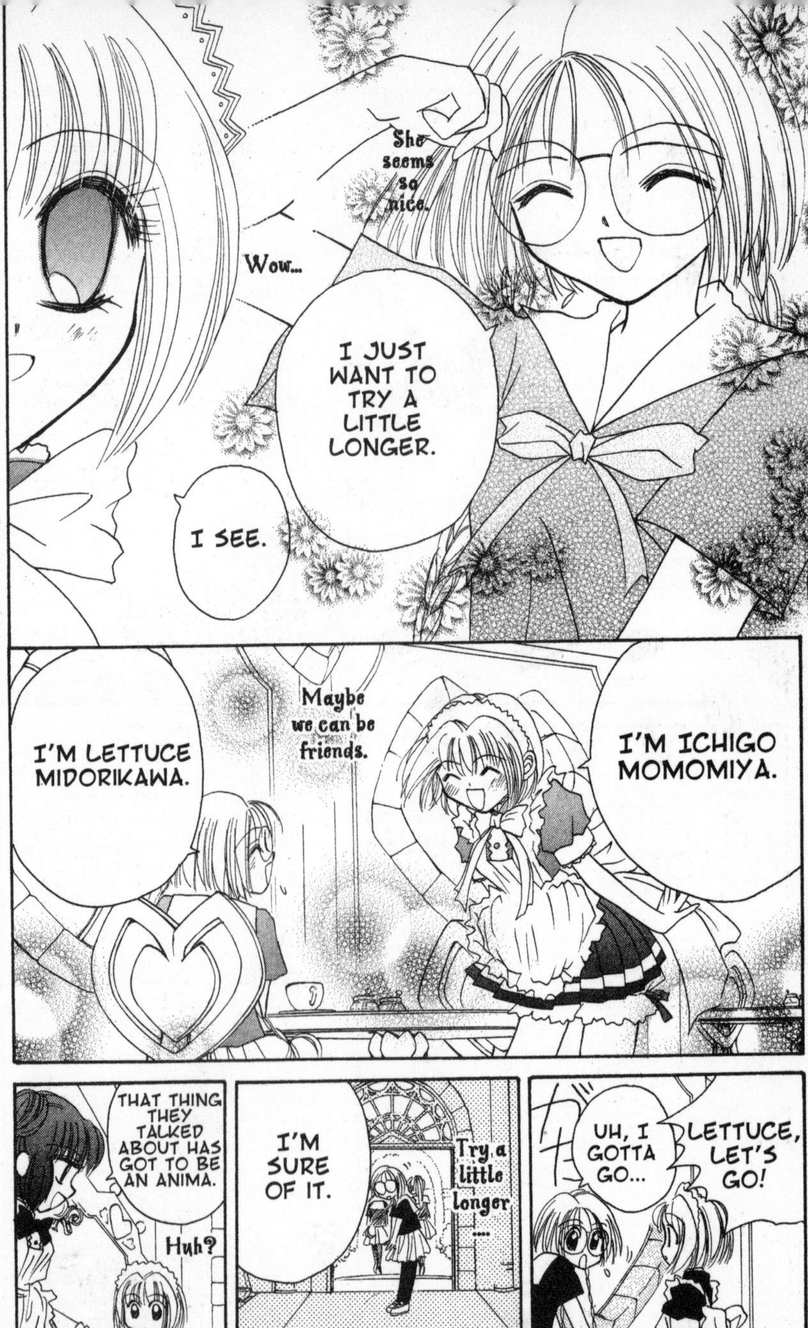
She seems so nice.
Wow...
I JUST WANT TO TRY A LITTLE LONGER.
I SEE.
I'M ICHIGO MOMOMIYA.
Maybe we can be friends.
I'M LETTUCE MIDORIKAWA.
LETTUCE, LET'S GO!
UH, I GOTTA GO...
Try a little longer....
I'M SURE OF IT.
THAT THING THEY TALKED ABOUT HAS GOT TO BE AN ANIMA.
Huh?

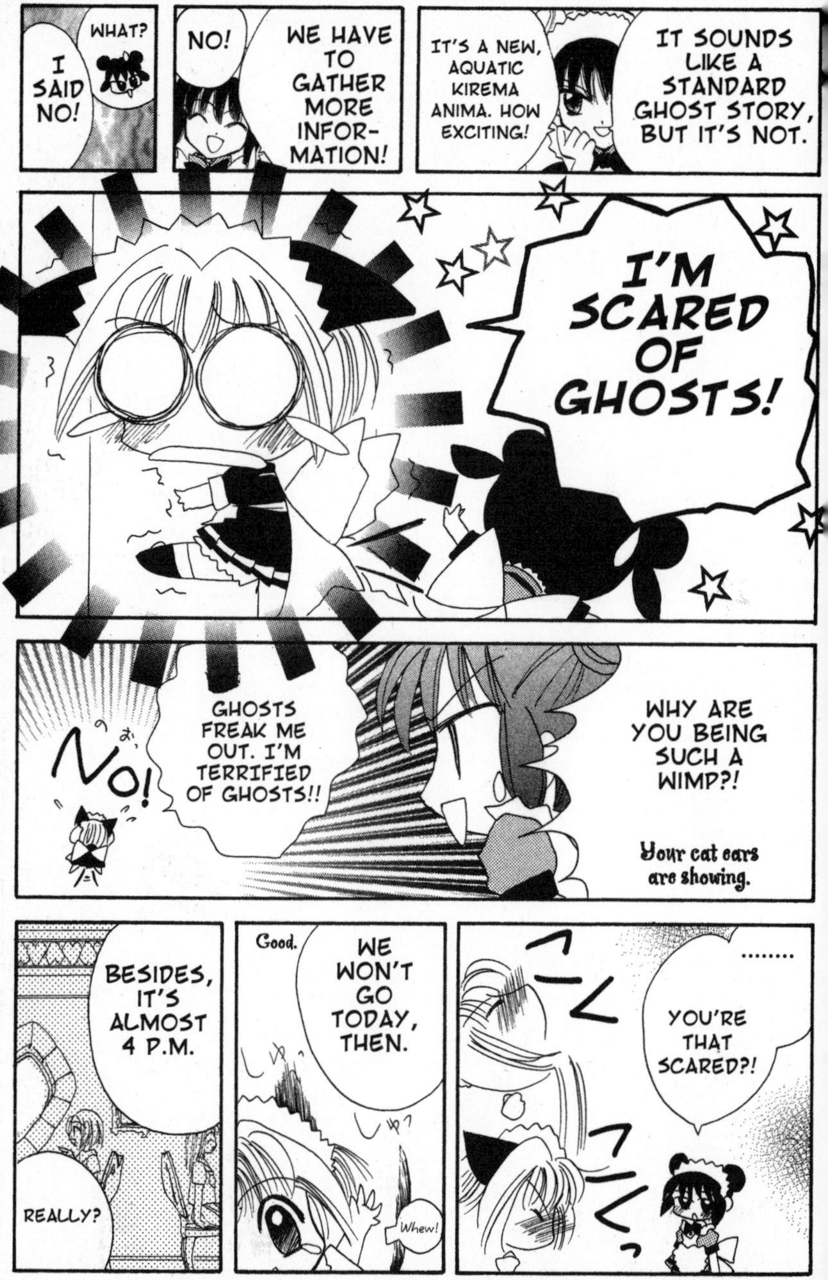
IT SOUNDS LIKE A STANDARD GHOST STORY, BUT IT'S NOT.
IT'S A NEW, AQUATIC KIREMA ANIMA. HOW EXCITING!
WE HAVE TO GATHER MORE INFORMATION!
NO!
WHAT?
I SAID NO!
I'M SCARED OF GHOSTS!
WHY ARE YOU BEING SUCH A WIMP?!
Your cat ears are showing.
GHOSTS FREAK ME OUT. I'M TERRIFIED OF GHOSTS!!
NO!
....
YOU'RE THAT SCARED?!
WE WON'T GO TODAY, THEN.
Good.
Whew!
BESIDES, IT'S ALMOST 4 P.M.
REALLY?

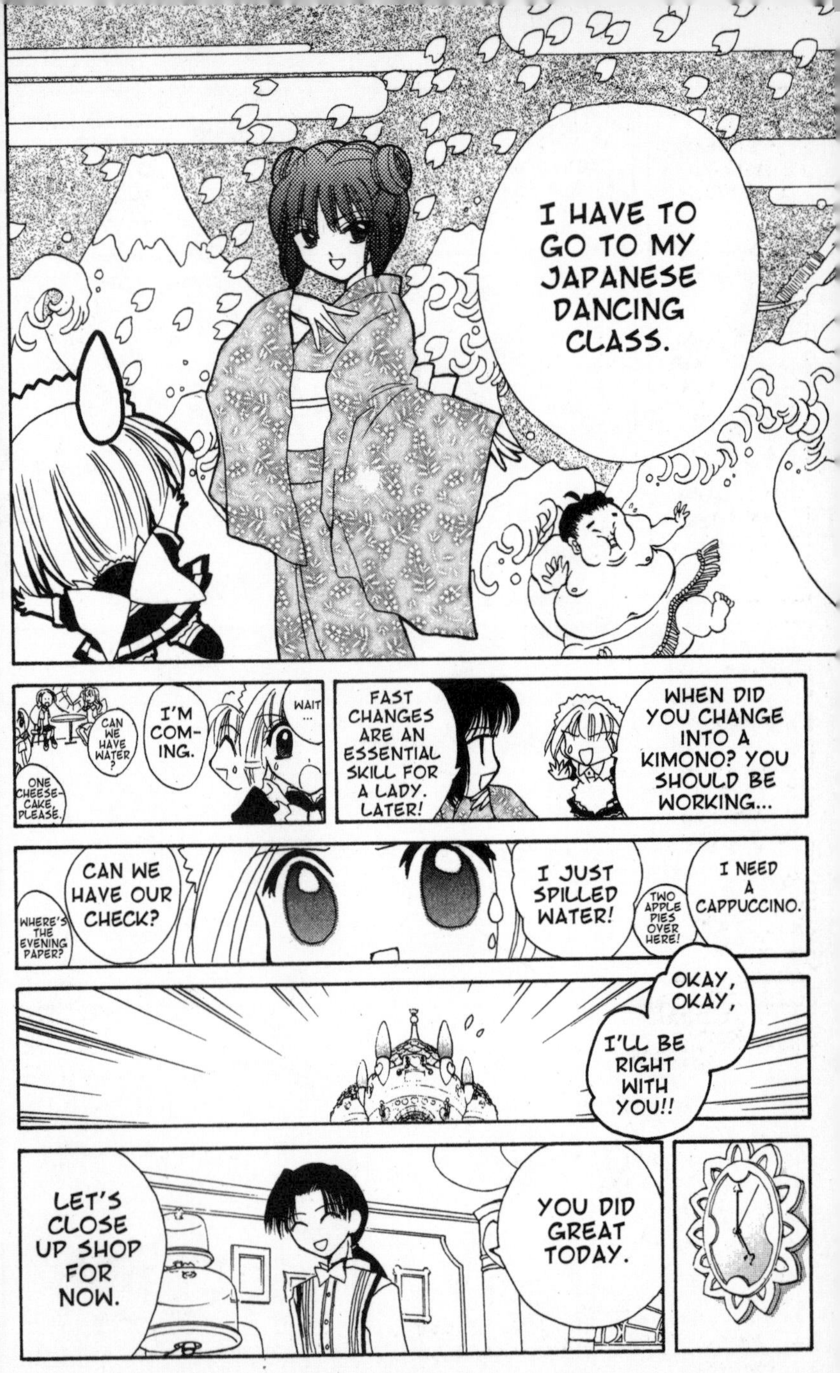
I HAVE TO GO TO MY JAPANESE DANCING CLASS.
WHEN DID YOU CHANGE INTO A KIMONO? YOU SHOULD BE WORKING...
FAST CHANGES ARE AN ESSENTIAL SKILL FOR A LADY. LATER!
WAIT...
I'M COM-ING.
CAN WE HAVE WATER?
ONE CHEESE-CAKE, PLEASE.
I NEED A CAPPUCCINO.
TWO APPLE PIES OVER HERE!
I JUST SPILLED WATER!
CAN WE HAVE OUR CHECK?
WHERE'S THE EVENING PAPER?
OKAY, OKAY, I'LL BE RIGHT WITH YOU!!
YOU DID GREAT TODAY.
LET'S CLOSE UP SHOP FOR NOW.

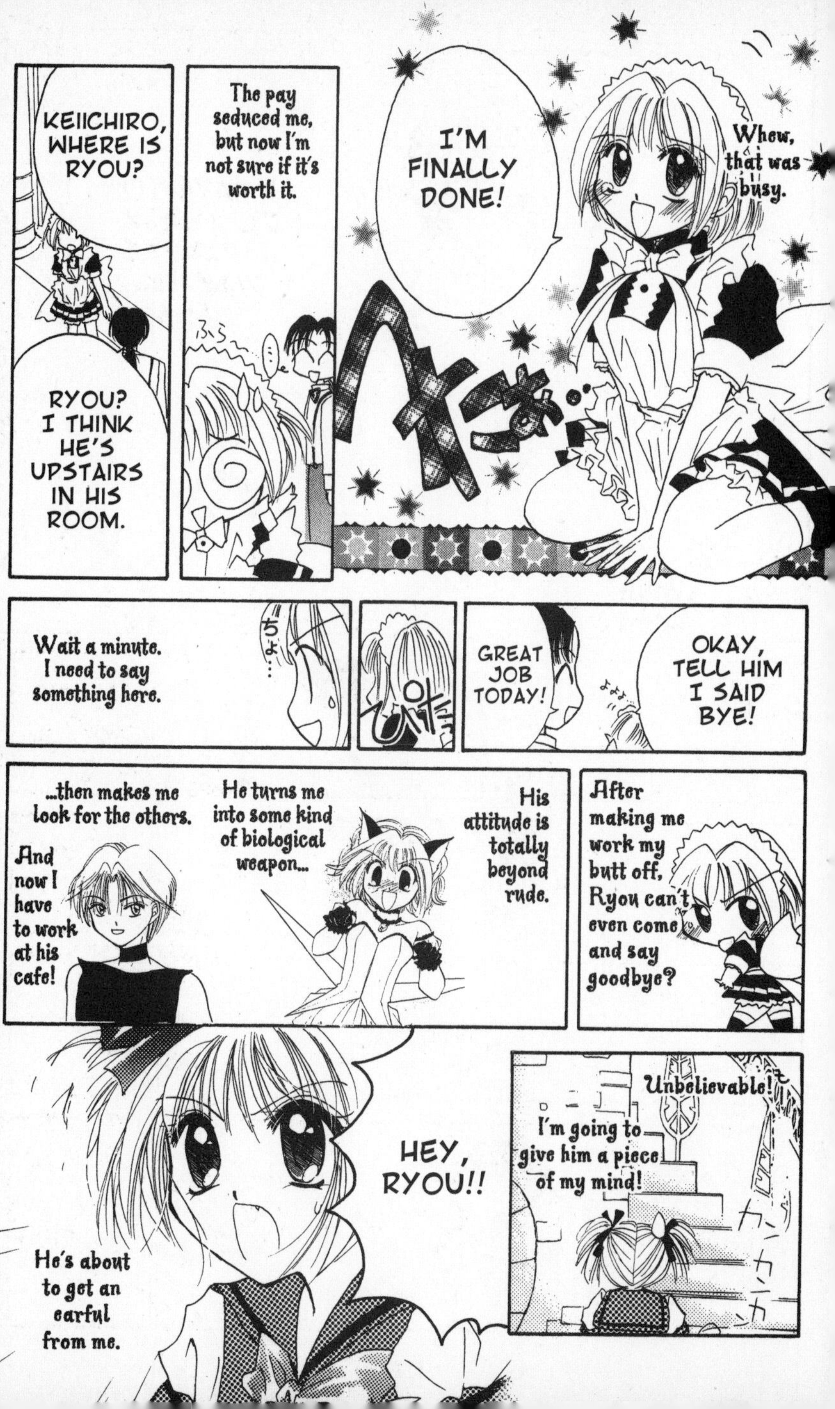

Whew, that was busy.
I'M FINALLY DONE!
The pay seduced me, but now I'm not sure if it's worth it.
…
ふら
KEIICHIRO, WHERE IS RYOU?
RYOU? I THINK HE'S UPSTAIRS IN HIS ROOM.
OKAY, TELL HIM I SAID BYE!
GREAT JOB TODAY!
ちょ…
Wait a minute. I need to say something here.
After making me work my butt off, Ryou can't even come and say goodbye?
His attitude is totally beyond rude.
He turns me into some kind of biological weapon...
...then makes me look for the others.
And now I have to work at his cafe!
Unbelievable!
I'm going to give him a piece of my mind!
HEY, RYOU!!
He's about to get an earful from me.

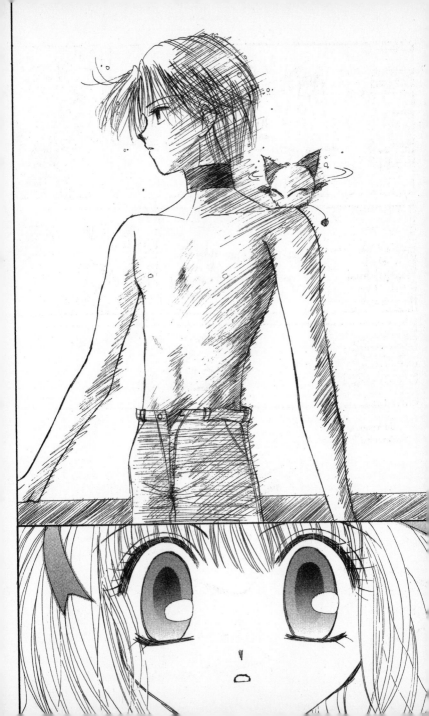

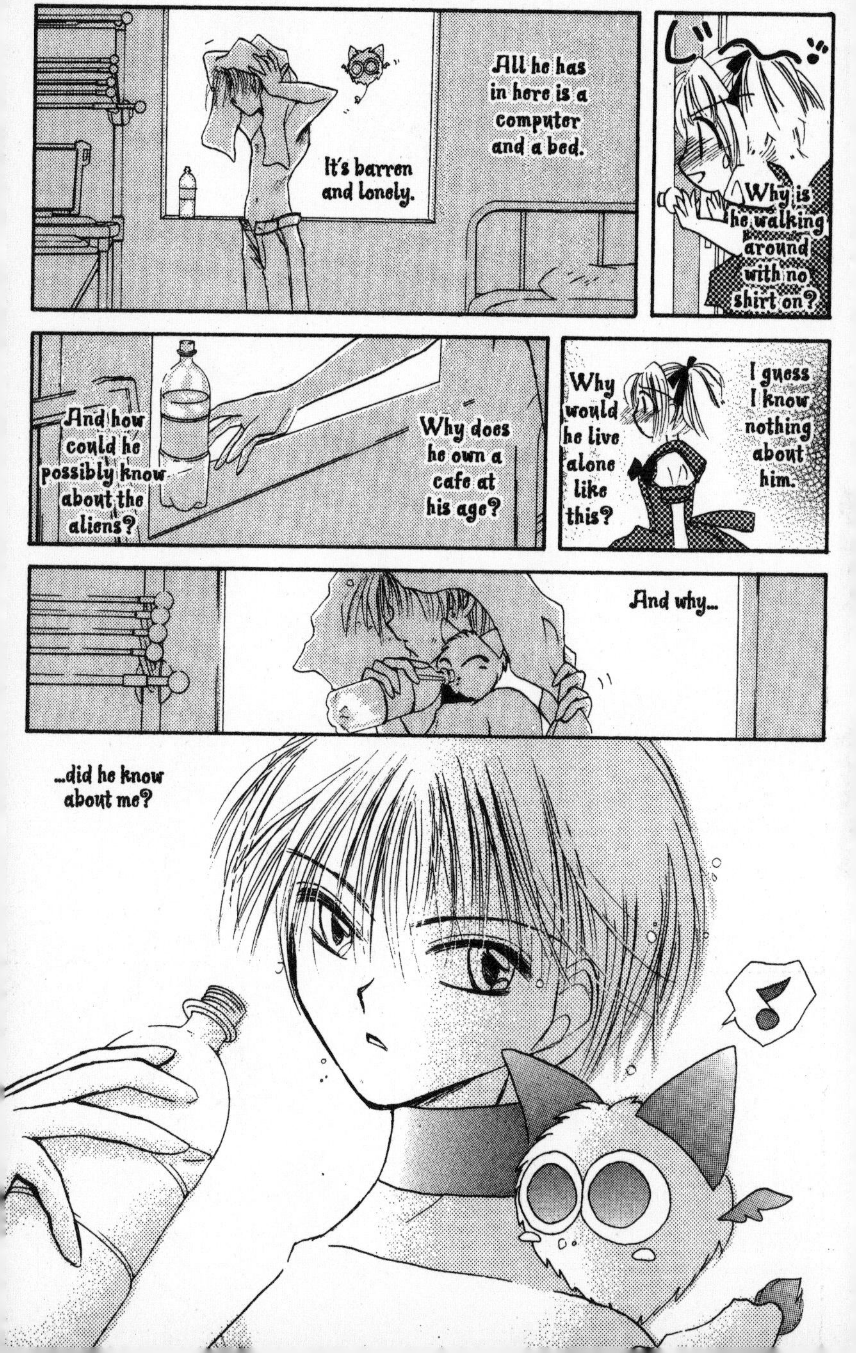

じ〜
Why is he walking around with no shirt on?
All he has in here is a computer and a bed.
It's barren and lonely.
I guess I know nothing about him.
Why would he live alone like this?
Why does he own a cafe at his age?
And how could he possibly know about the aliens?
And why...
...did he know about me?

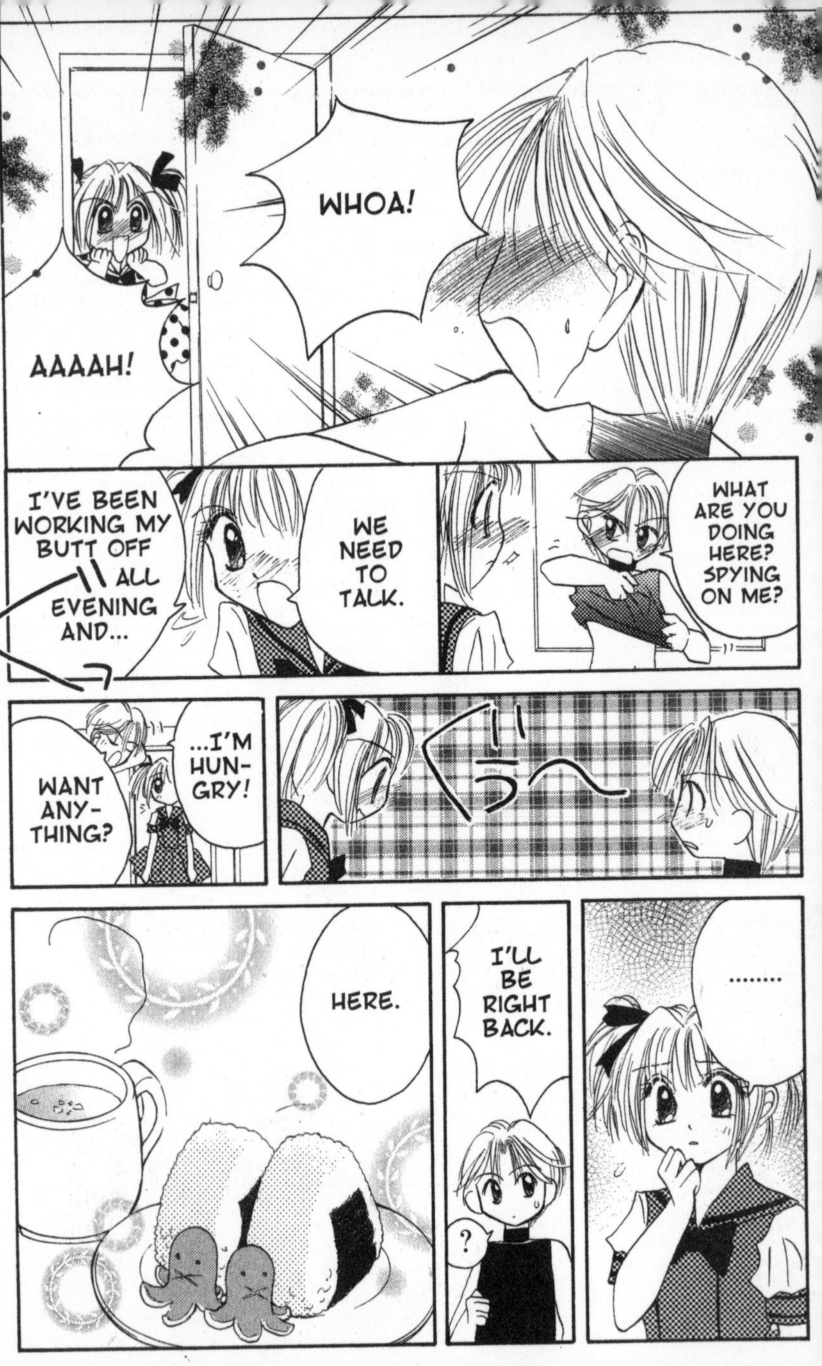
WHOA!
AAAAH!
WHAT ARE YOU DOING HERE? SPYING ON ME?
WE NEED TO TALK.
I'VE BEEN WORKING MY BUTT OFF ALL EVENING AND...
ぐう〜
...I'M HUN-GRY!
WANT ANY-THING?
....
I'LL BE RIGHT BACK.
?
HERE.

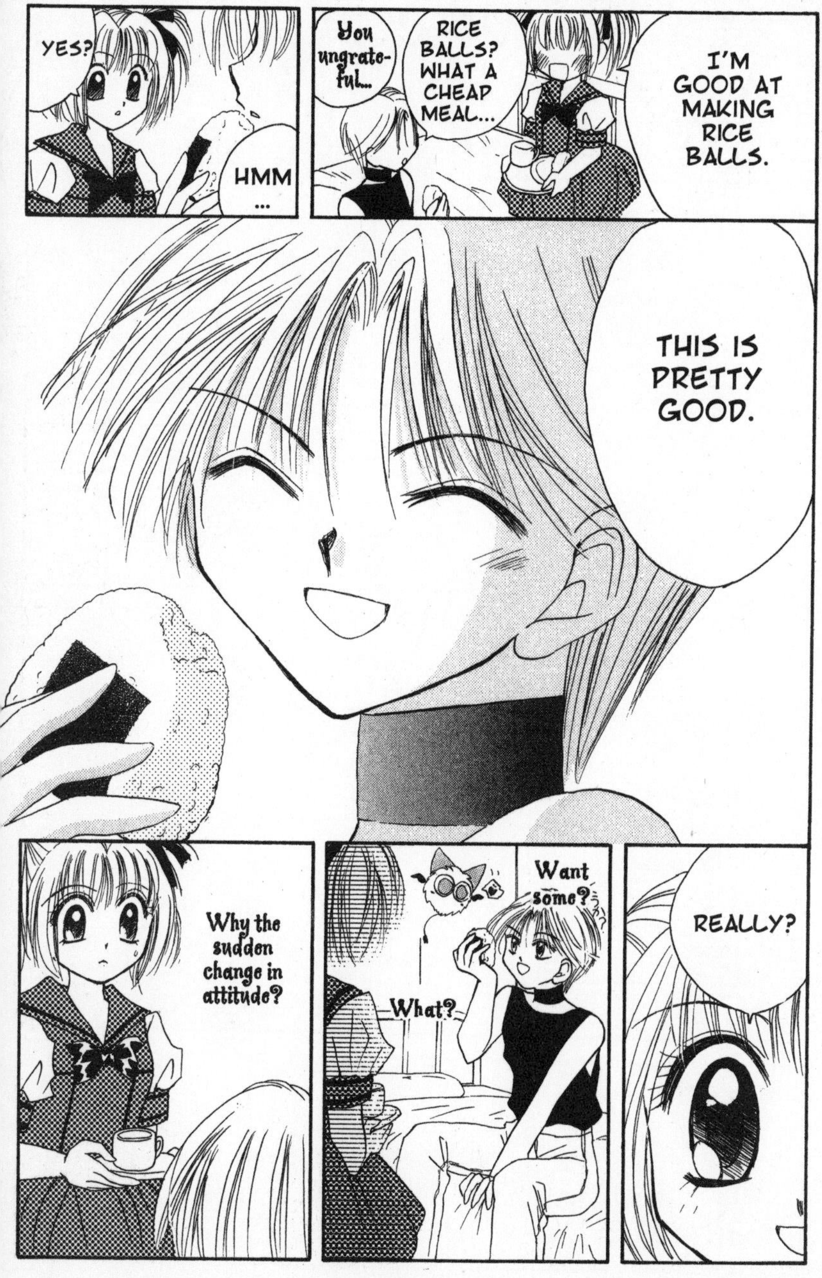
I'M GOOD AT MAKING RICE BALLS.
RICE BALLS? WHAT A CHEAP MEAL...
You ungrateful...
YES?
HMM ...
THIS IS PRETTY GOOD.
REALLY?
Want some?
What?
Why the sudden change in attitude?

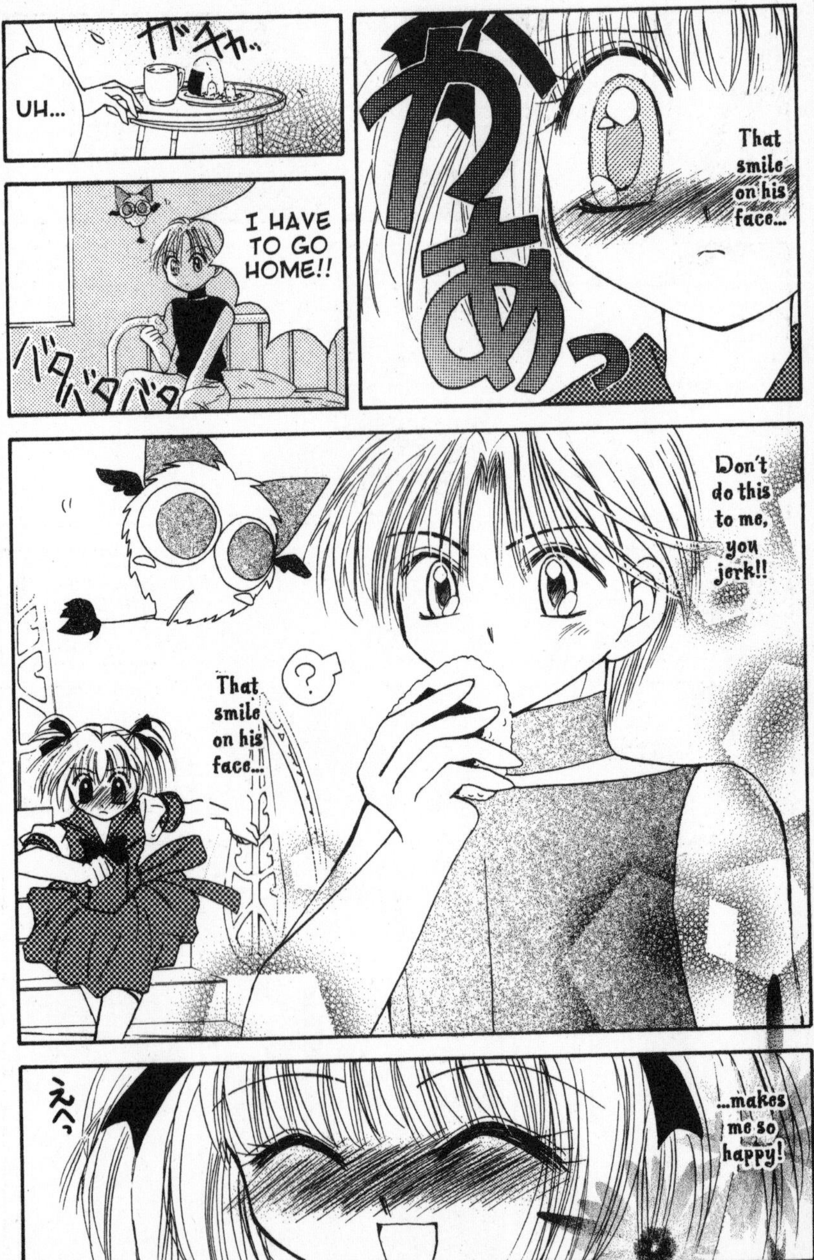

がぁっ
That smile on his face...
ガチャ
UH...
I HAVE TO GO HOME!!
バタバタバタ
Don't do this to me, you jerk!!
?
That smile on his face...
...makes me so happy!
えへっ

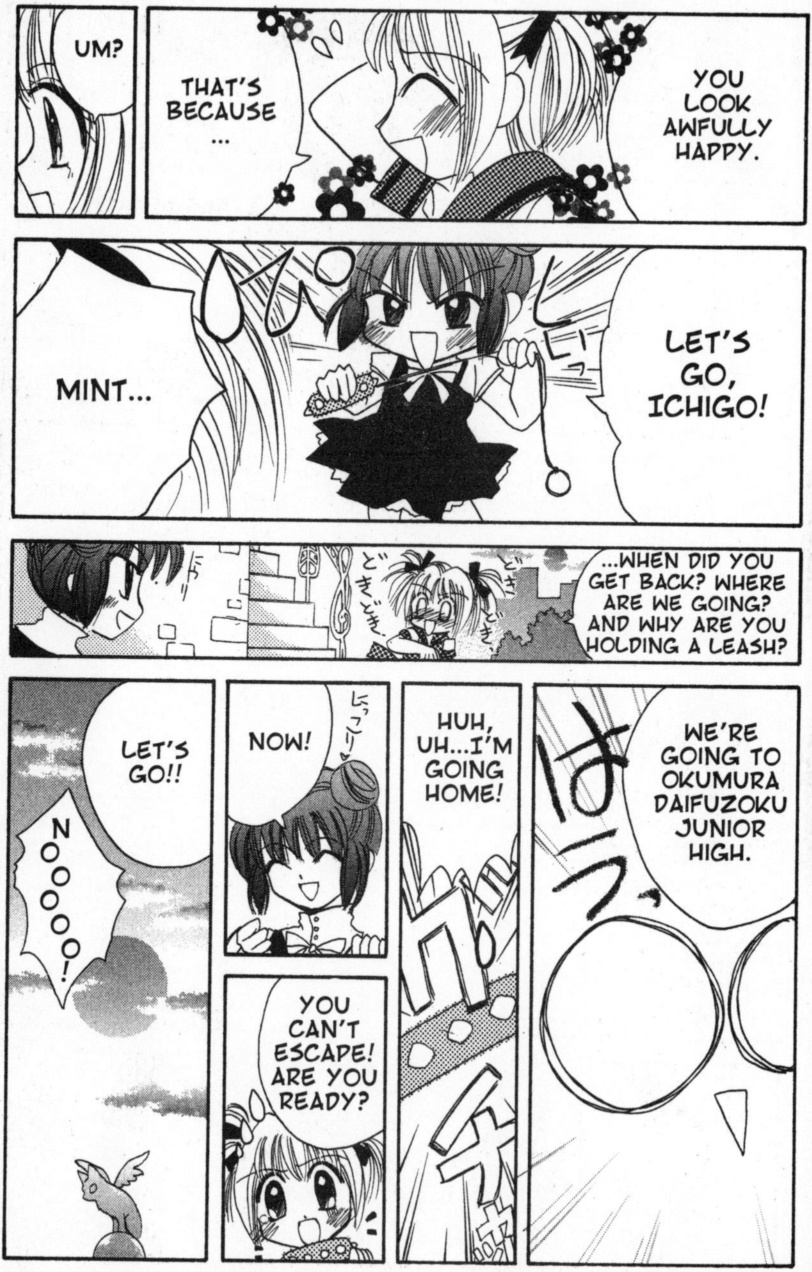
YOU LOOK AWFULLY HAPPY.
THAT'S BECAUSE ...
UM?
LET'S GO, ICHIGO!
MINT...
...WHEN DID YOU GET BACK? WHERE ARE WE GOING? AND WHY ARE YOU HOLDING A LEASH?
WE'RE GOING TO OKUMURA DAIFUZOKU JUNIOR HIGH.
HUH, UH...I'M GOING HOME!
NOW!
YOU CAN'T ESCAPE! ARE YOU READY?
LET'S GO!!
NOOOOOO!

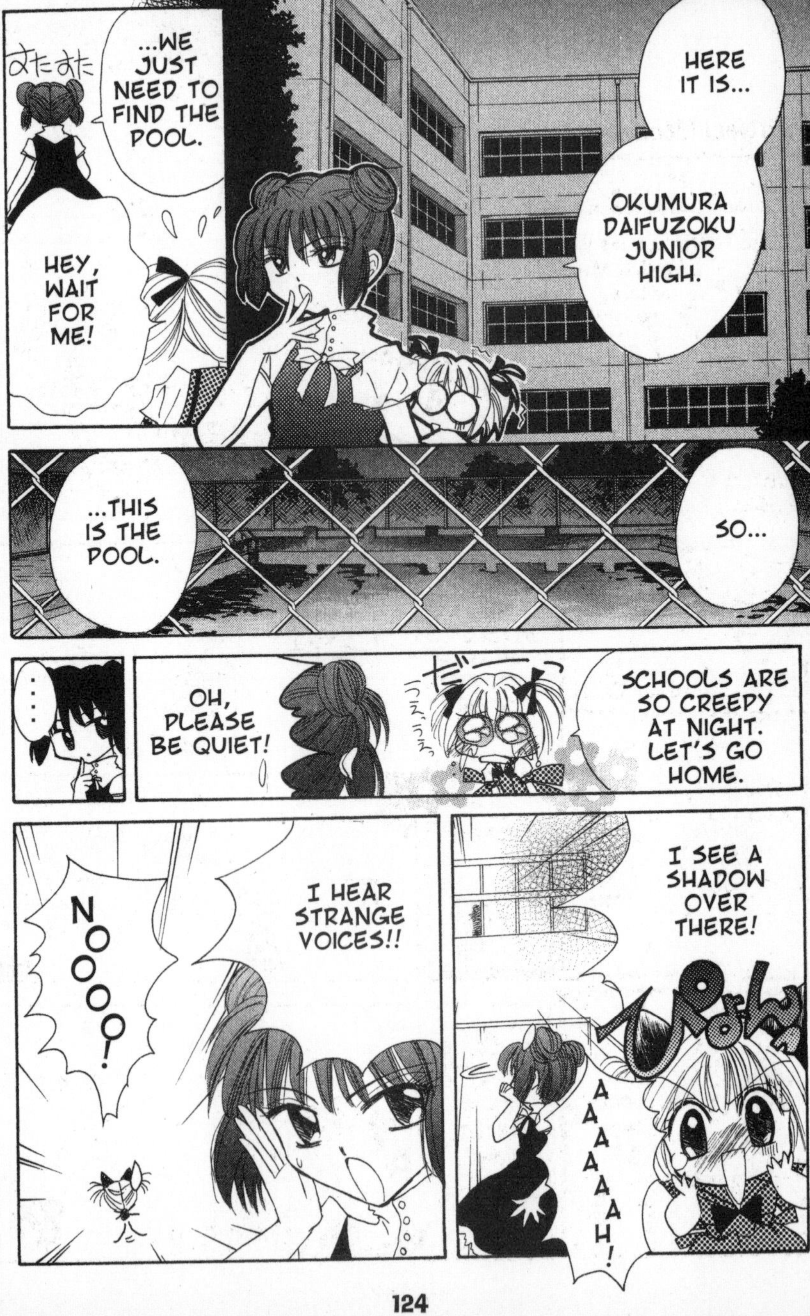
HERE IT IS...
OKUMURA DAIFUZOKU JUNIOR HIGH.
...WE JUST NEED TO FIND THE POOL.
HEY, WAIT FOR ME!
SO...
...THIS IS THE POOL.
SCHOOLS ARE SO CREEPY AT NIGHT. LET'S GO HOME.
OH, PLEASE BE QUIET!
....
I SEE A SHADOW OVER THERE!
AAAAAAH!
I HEAR STRANGE VOICES!!
NOOOO!

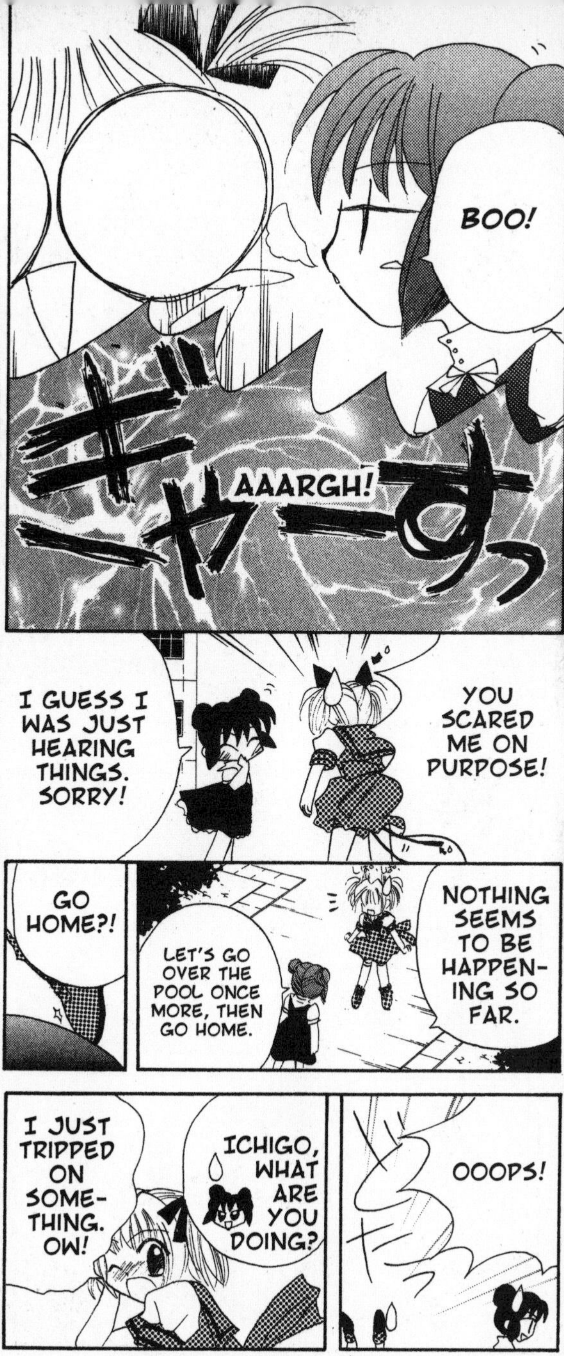
BOO!
AAARGH!
ギャーっ
YOU SCARED ME ON PURPOSE!
I GUESS I WAS JUST HEARING THINGS. SORRY!
NOTHING SEEMS TO BE HAPPENING SO FAR.
LET'S GO OVER THE POOL ONCE MORE, THEN GO HOME.
GO HOME?!
OOOPS!
ICHIGO, WHAT ARE YOU DOING?
I JUST TRIPPED ON SOMETHING. OW!

Project Meeting 3

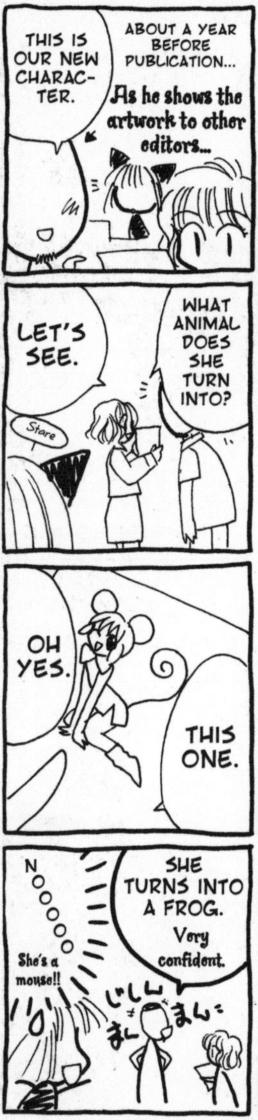
ABOUT A YEAR BEFORE PUBLICATION...
THIS IS OUR NEW CHARACTER.
As he shows the artwork to other editors...
WHAT ANIMAL DOES SHE TURN INTO?
LET'S SEE.
Stare
OH YES.
THIS ONE.
SHE TURNS INTO A FROG.
Very confident.
NOOOOOO
She's a mouse!!
じしんまんまん

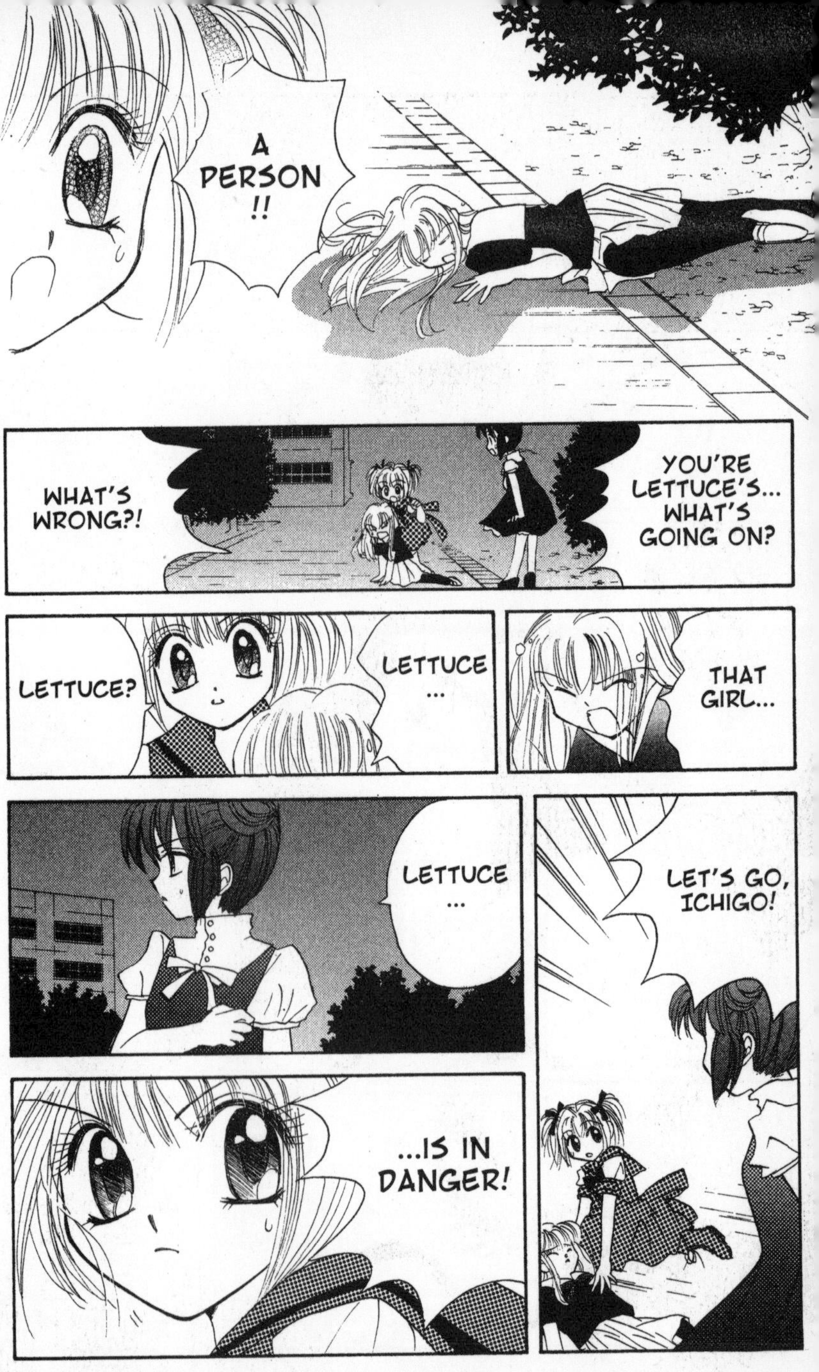
A PERSON !!
YOU'RE LETTUCE'S... WHAT'S GOING ON?
WHAT'S WRONG?!
THAT GIRL...
LETTUCE ...
LETTUCE?
LET'S GO, ICHIGO!
LETTUCE ...
...IS IN DANGER!

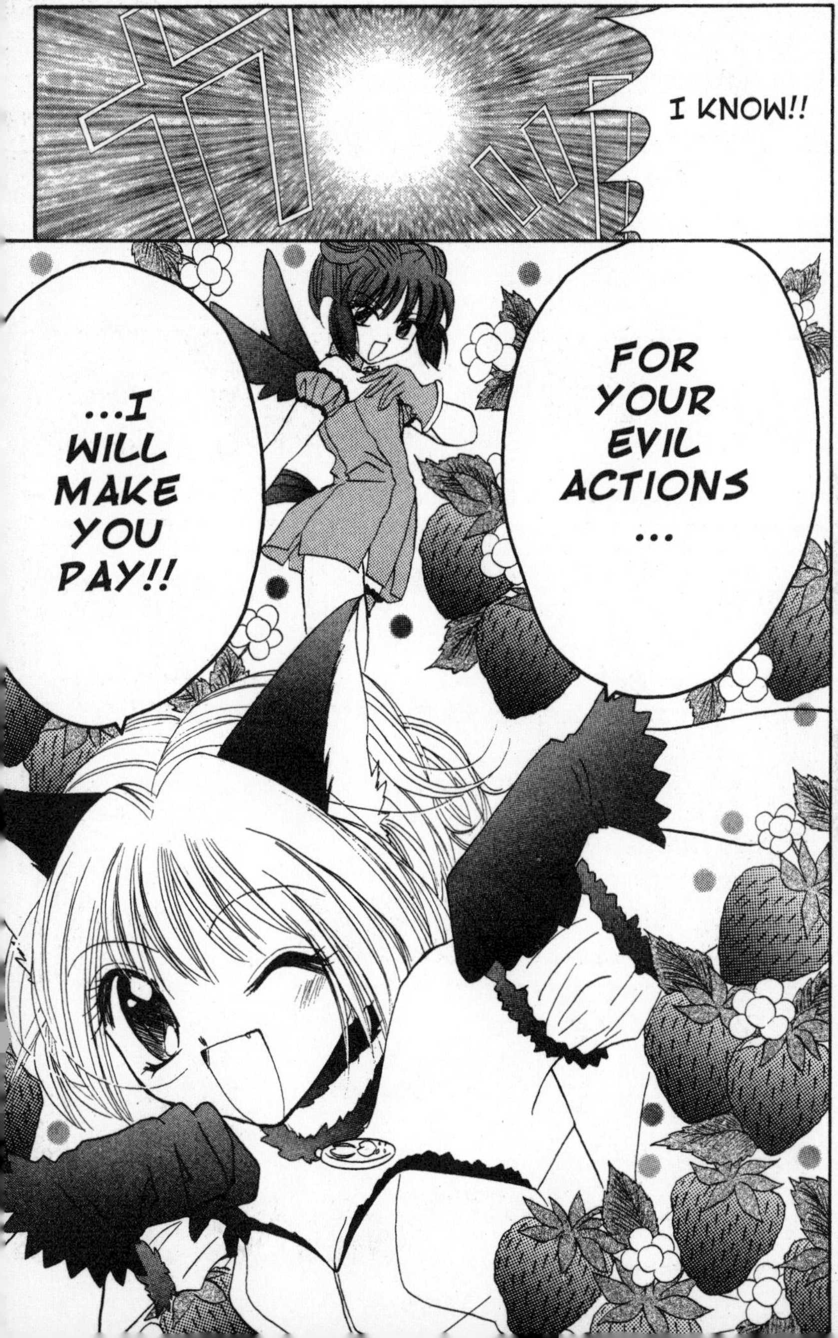
I KNOW!!
FOR YOUR EVIL ACTIONS ...
...I WILL MAKE YOU PAY!!

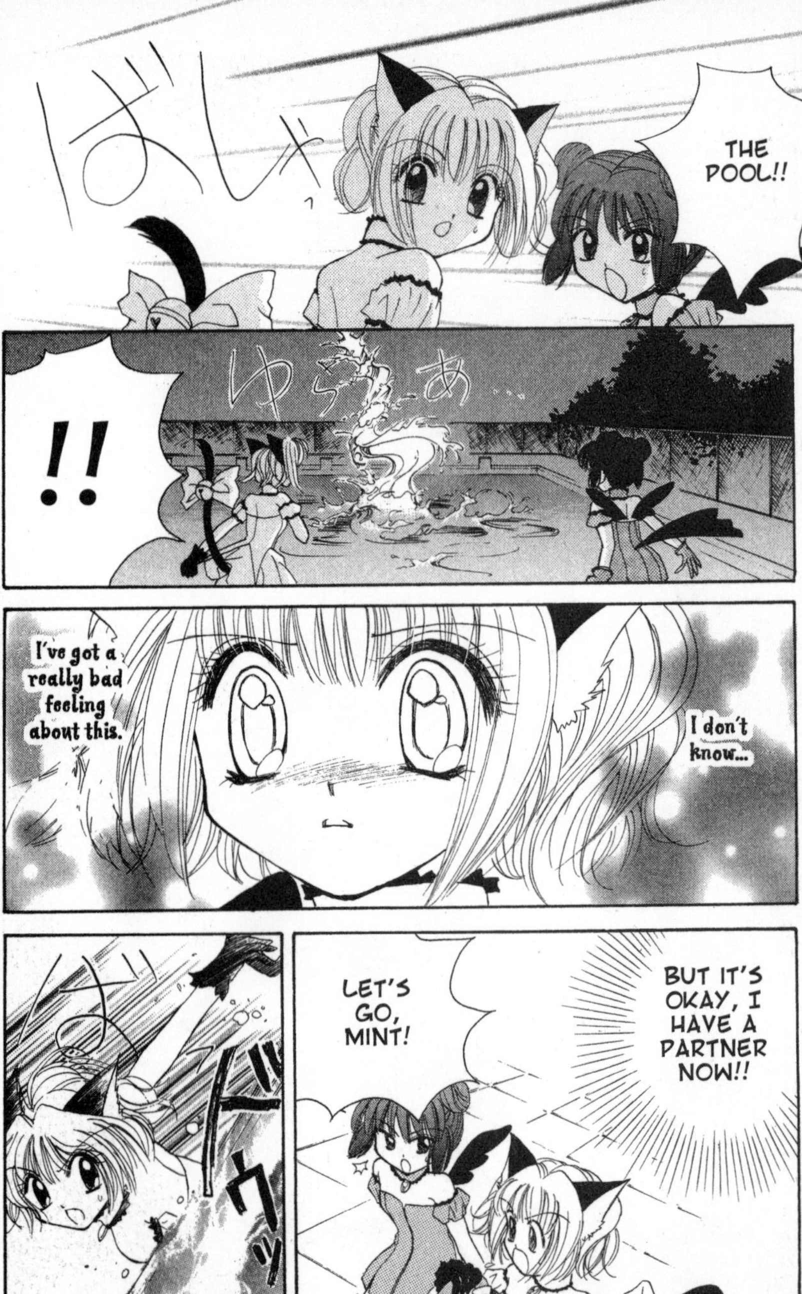
THE POOL!!
!!
I don't know...
I've got a really bad feeling about this.
BUT IT'S OKAY, I HAVE A PARTNER NOW!!
LET'S GO, MINT!

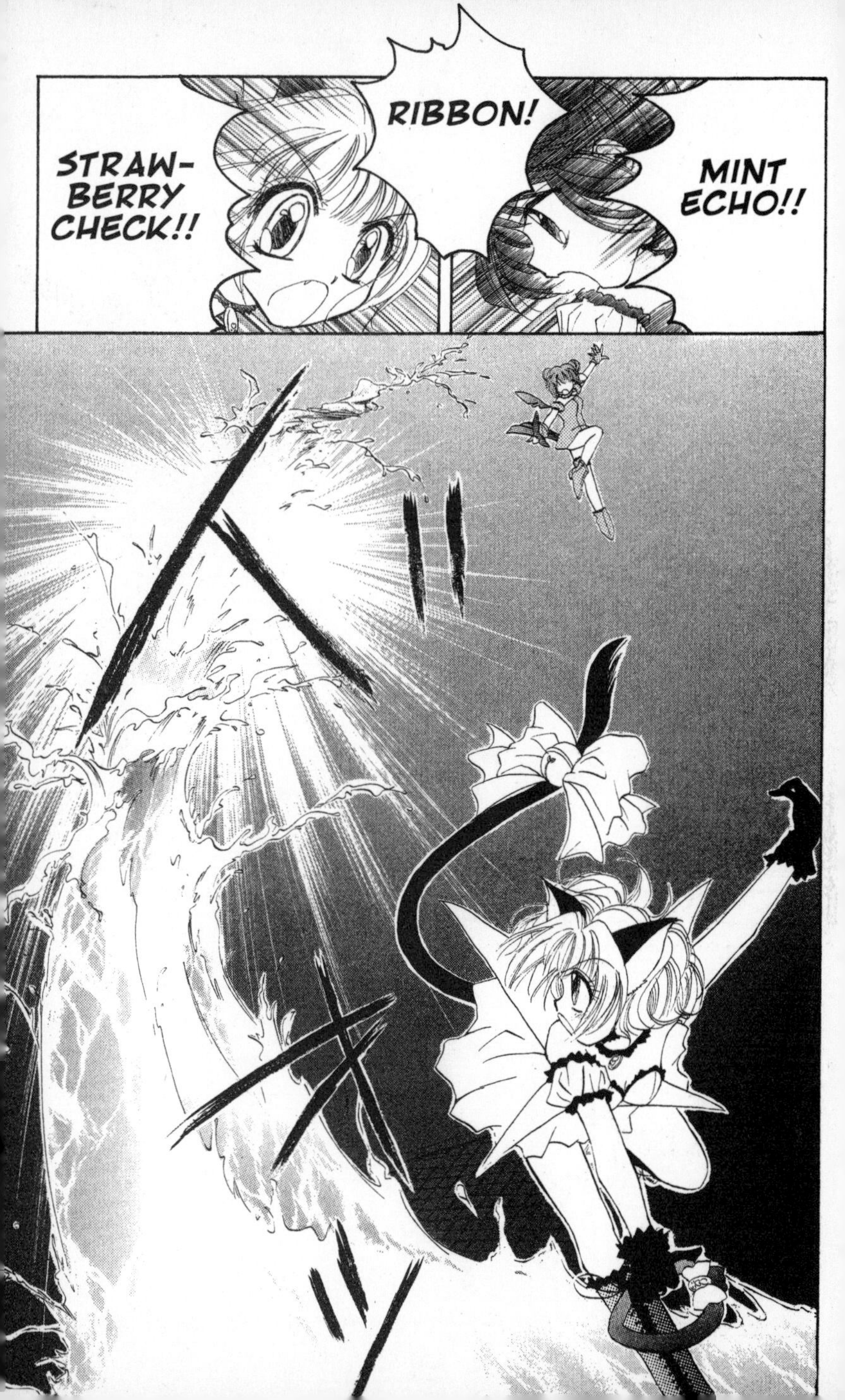
RIBBON!
MINT ECHO!!
STRAW-BERRY CHECK!!

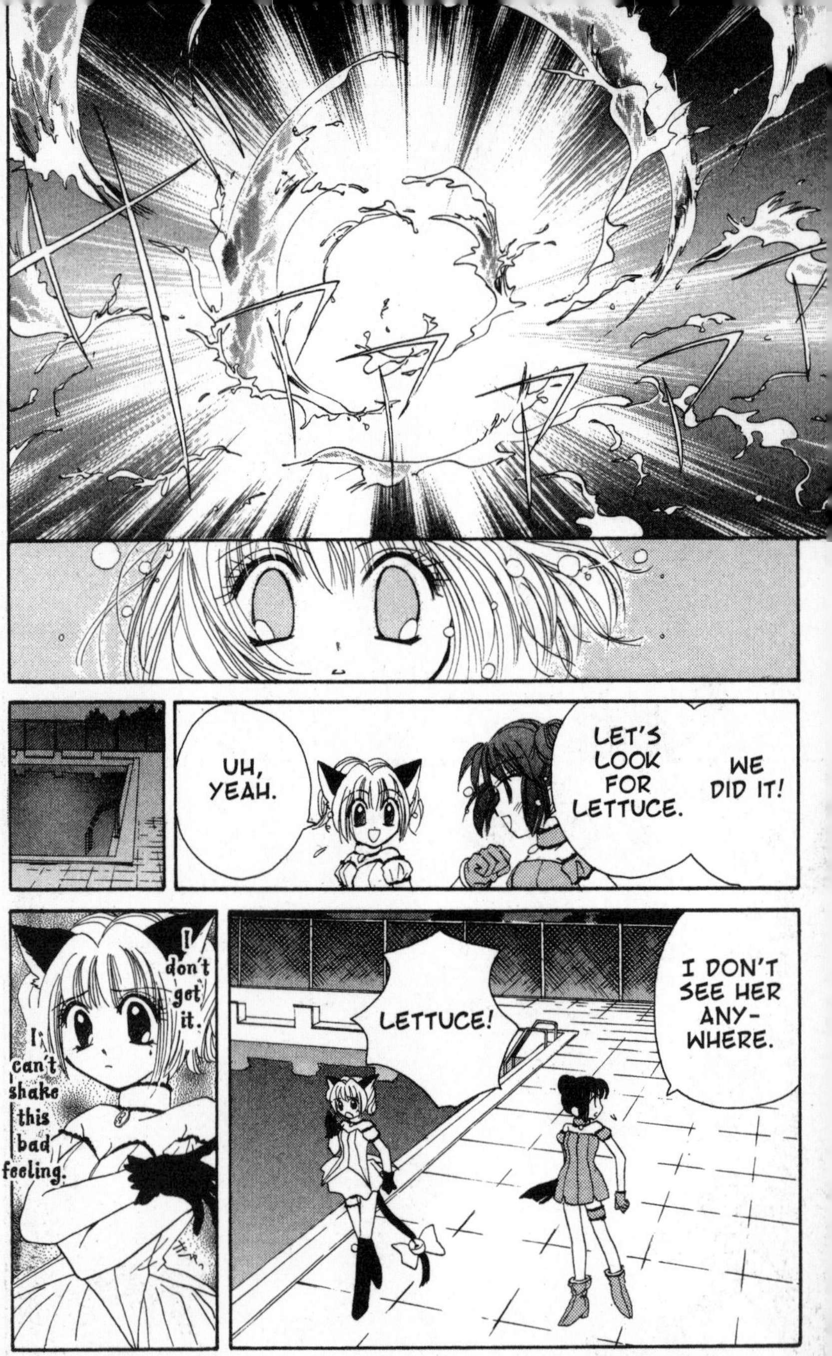
WE DID IT!
LET'S LOOK FOR LETTUCE.
UH, YEAH.
I DON'T SEE HER ANY-WHERE.
LETTUCE!
I don't get it.
I can't shake this bad feeling.

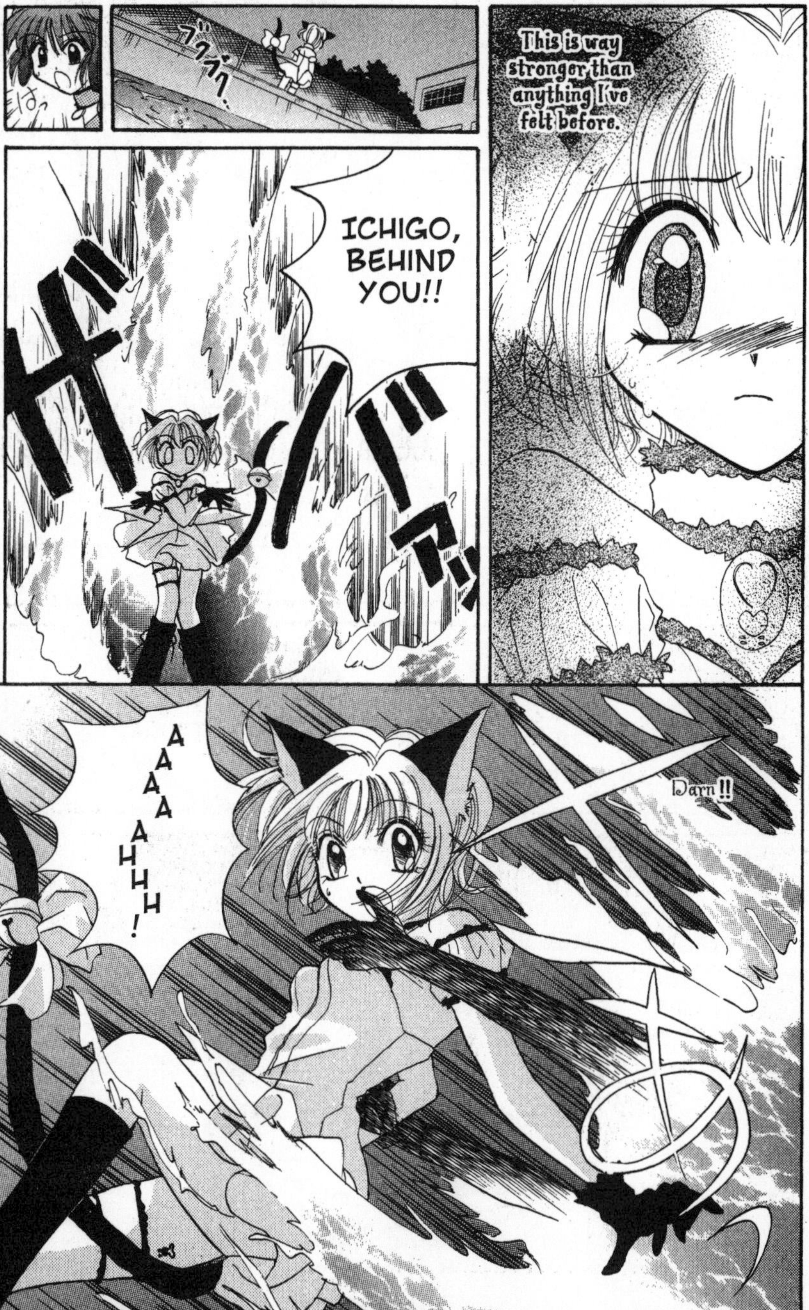
This is way stronger than anything I've felt before.
ブクブク
はっ
ICHIGO, BEHIND YOU!!
ザバーッ
Darn!!
AAAAAHHHH!

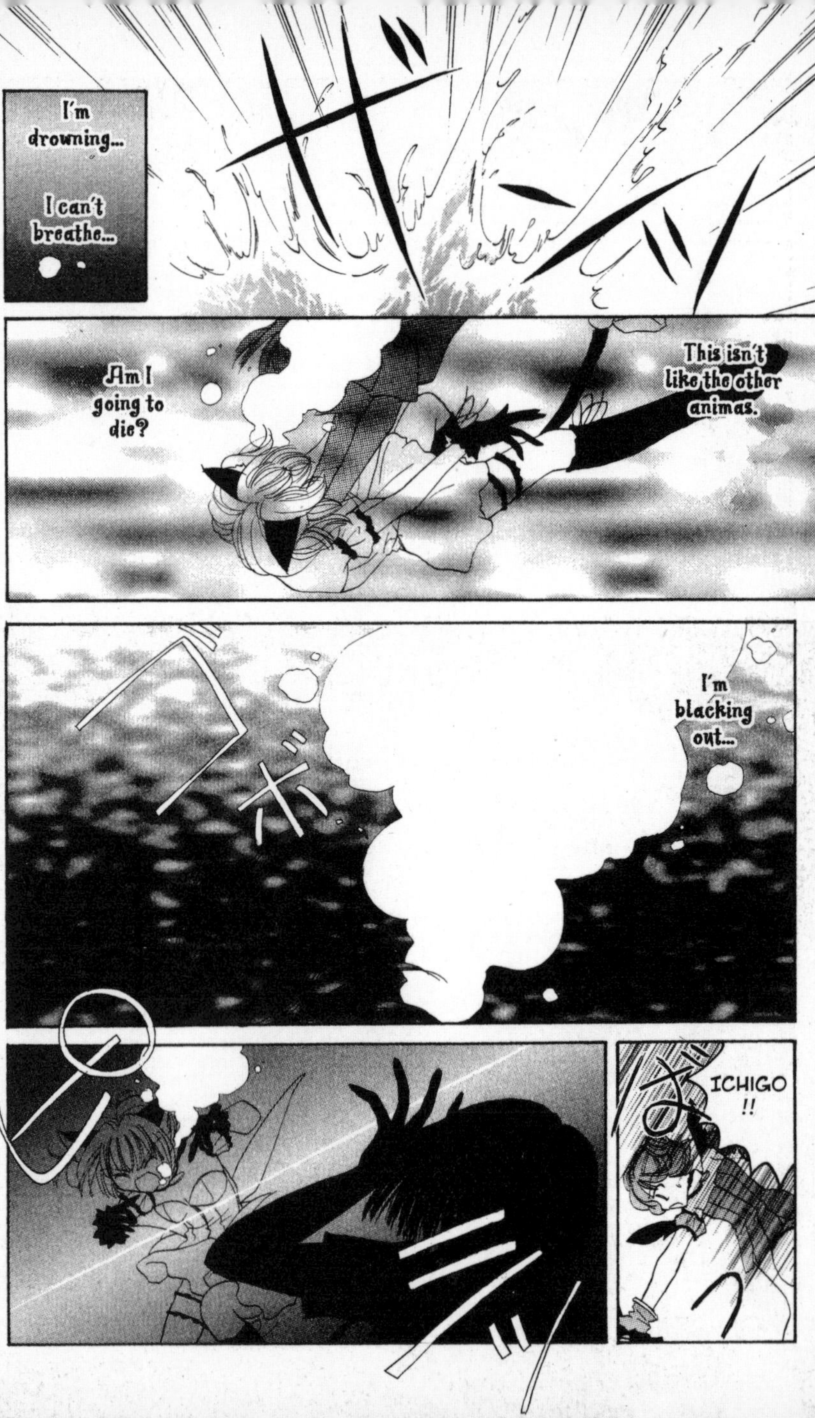
I'm drowning...
I can't breathe...
This isn't like the other animas.
Am I going to die?
I'm blacking out...
ICHIGO !!

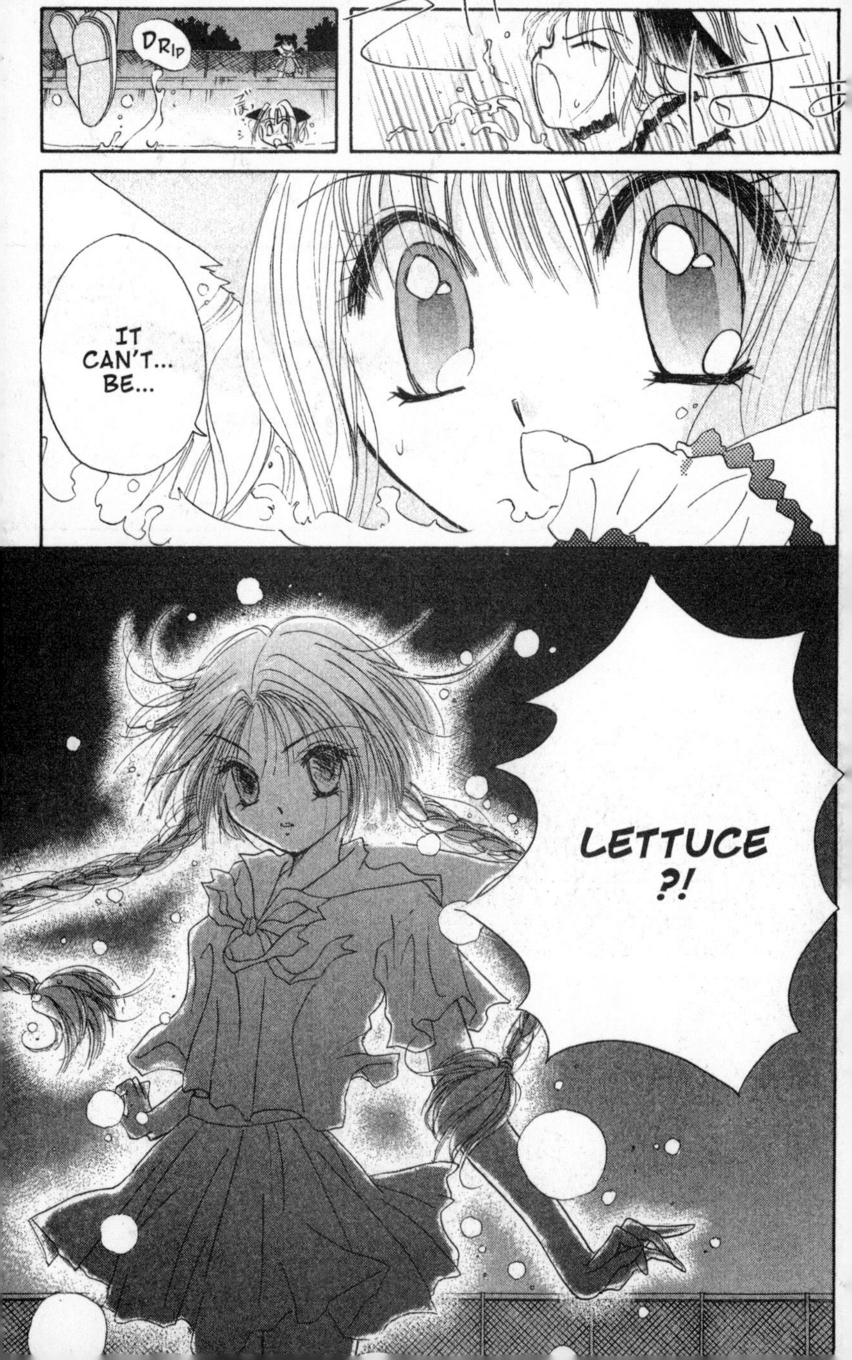
DRIP
IT CAN'T... BE...
LETTUCE ?!

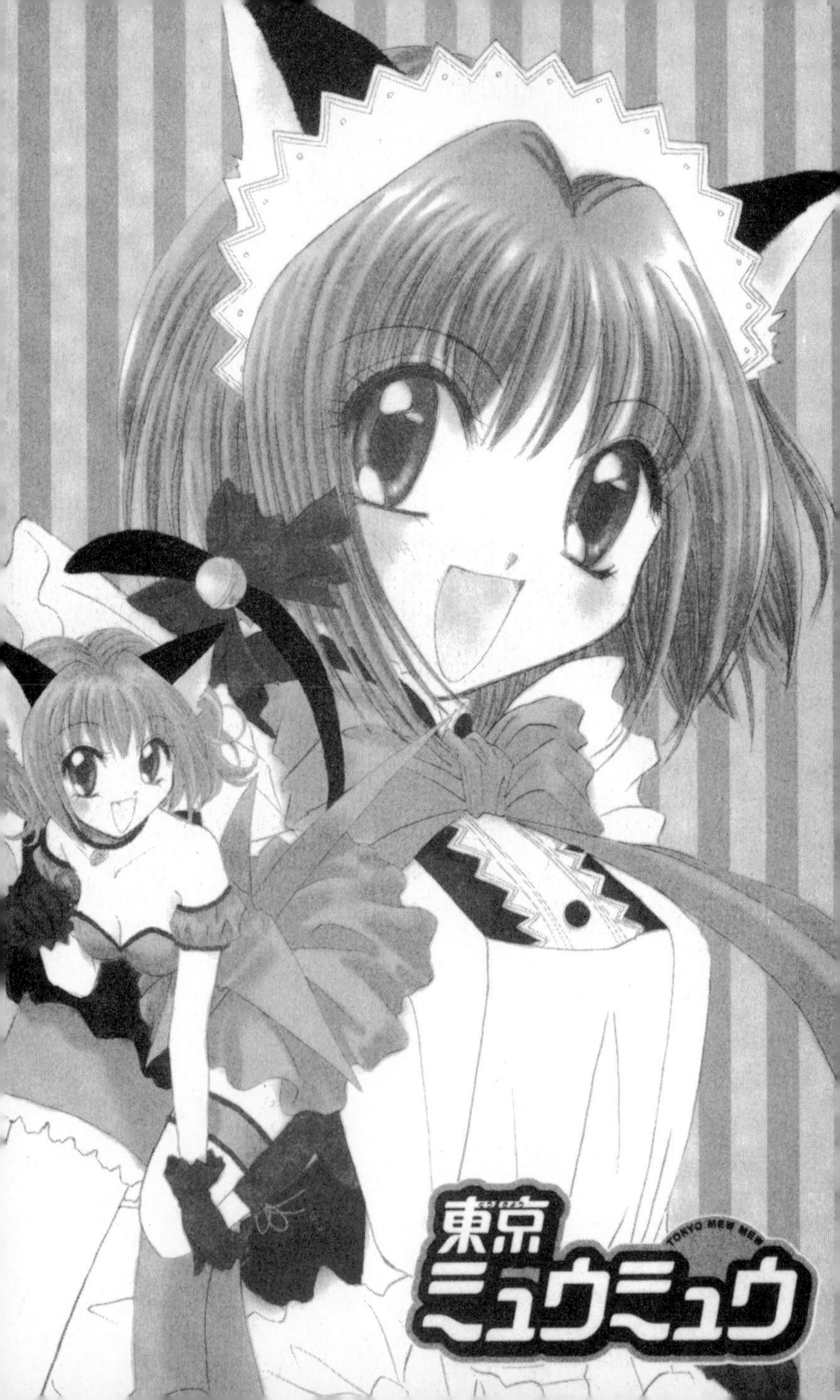
東京ミュウミュウ
TOKYO MEW MEW

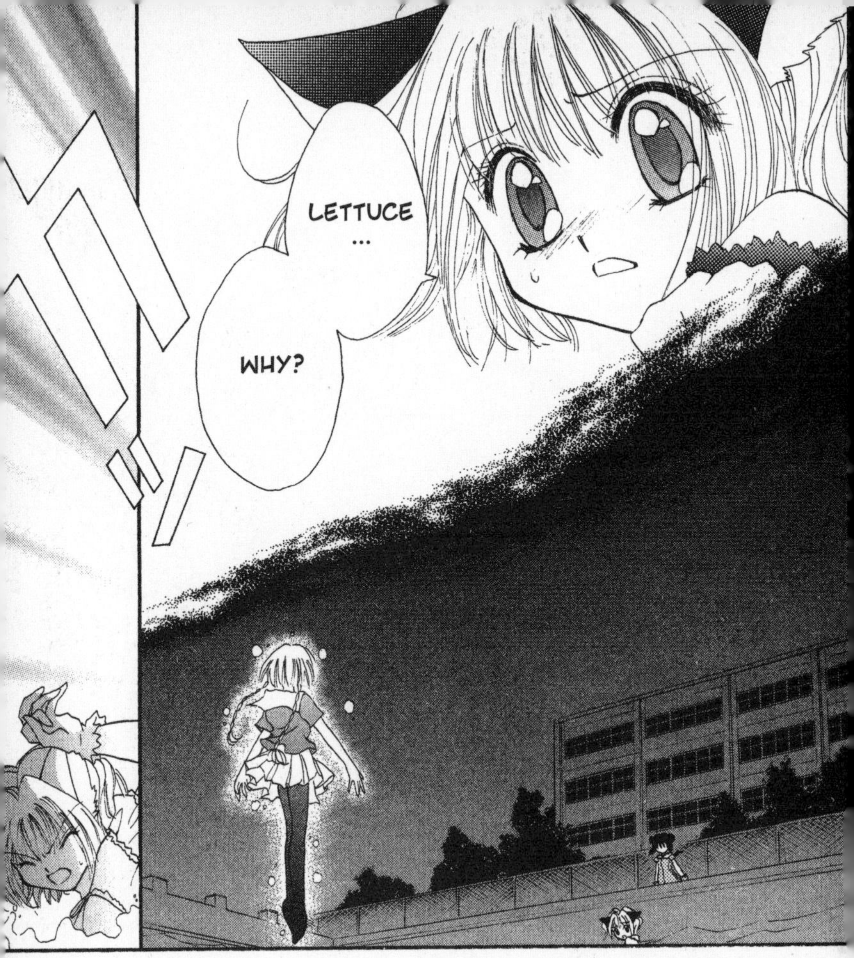
LETTUCE
...
WHY?

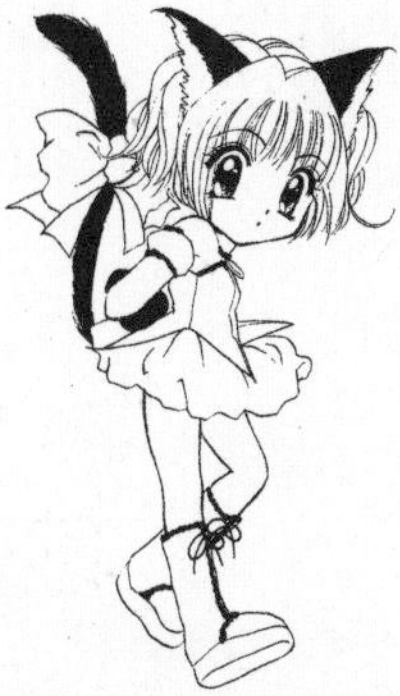

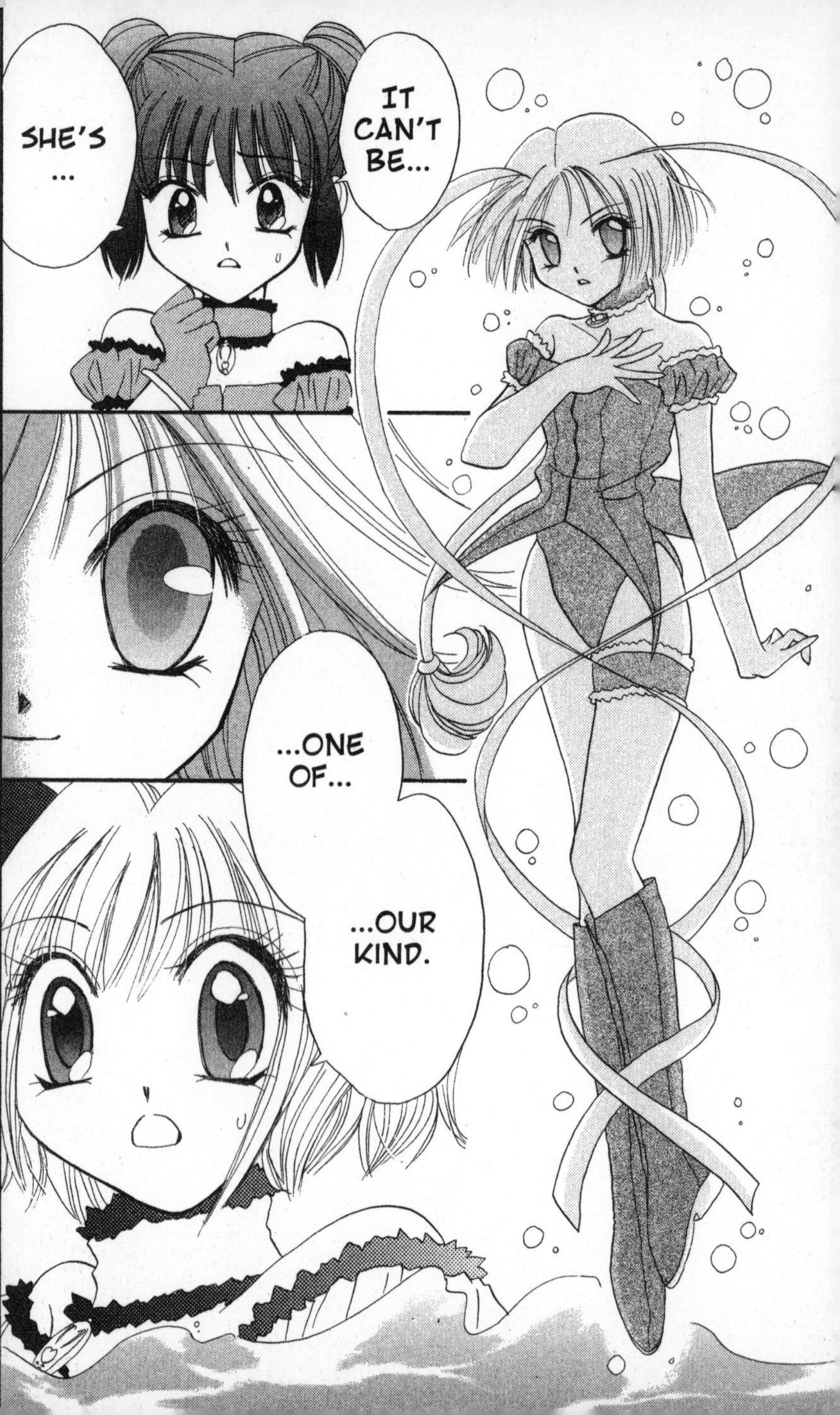
IT CAN'T BE...
SHE'S ...
...ONE OF...
...OUR KIND.

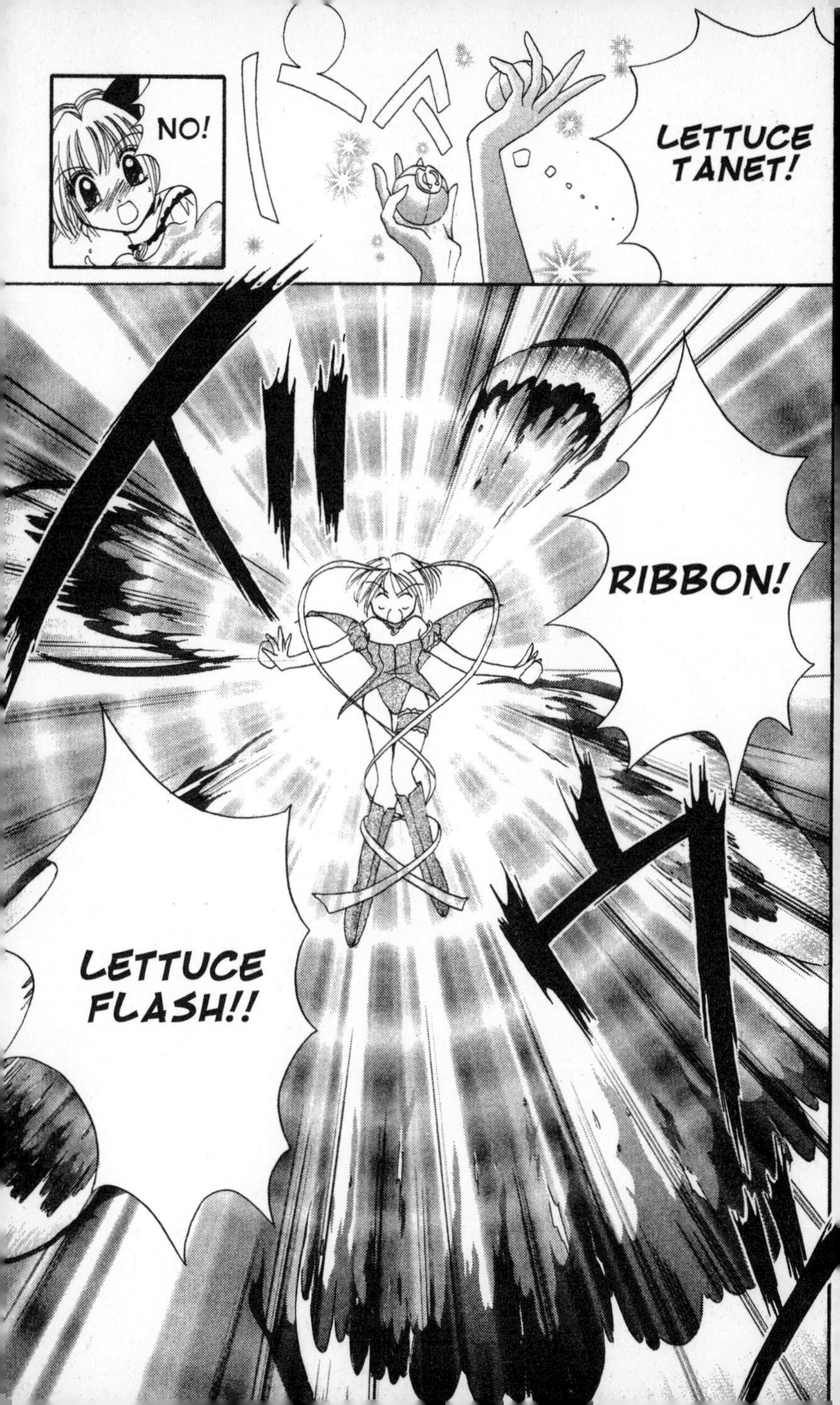
LETTUCE TANET!
NO!
RIBBON!
LETTUCE FLASH!!

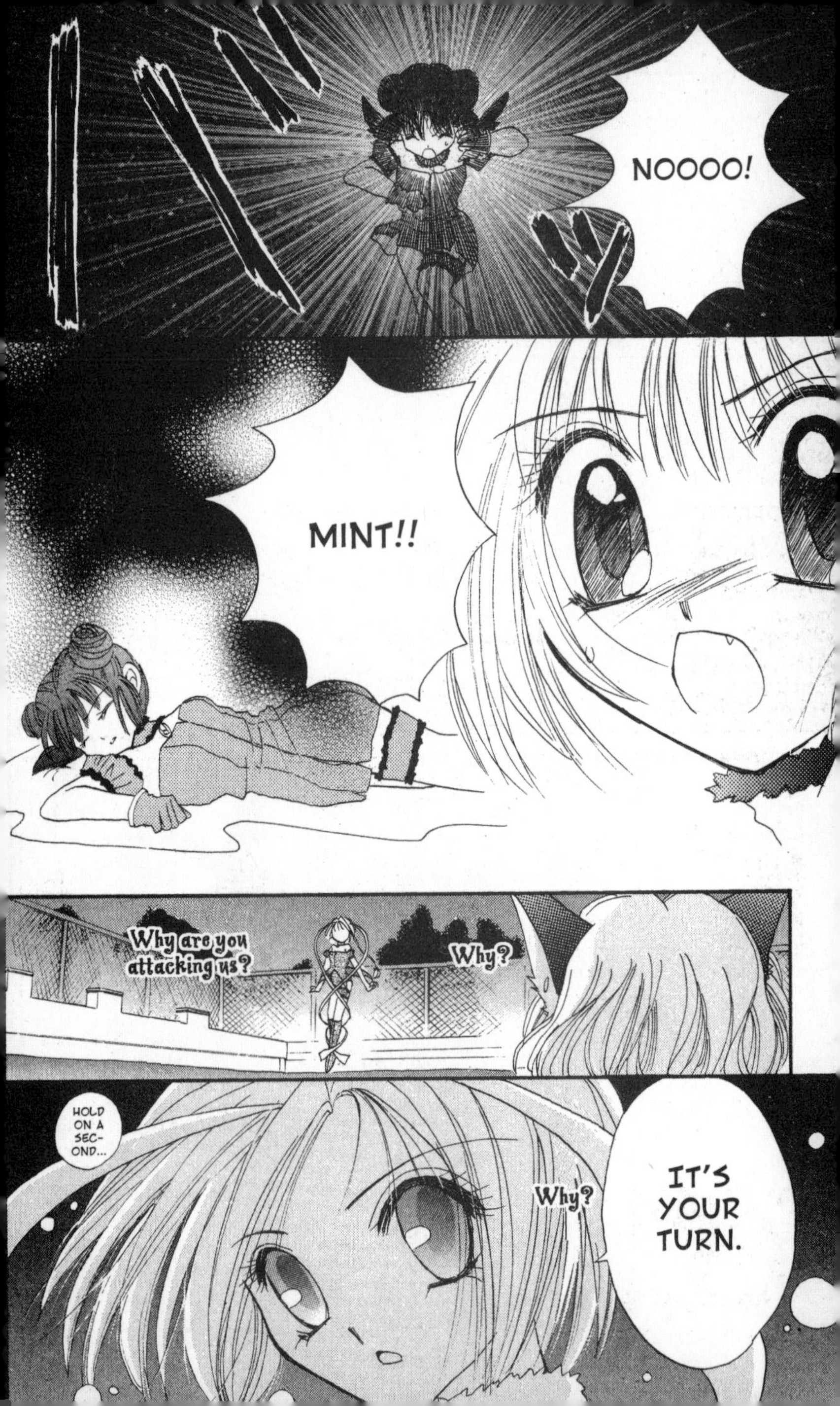
NOOOO!
MINT!!
Why?
Why are you attacking us?
IT'S YOUR TURN.
Why?
HOLD ON A SEC-OND...

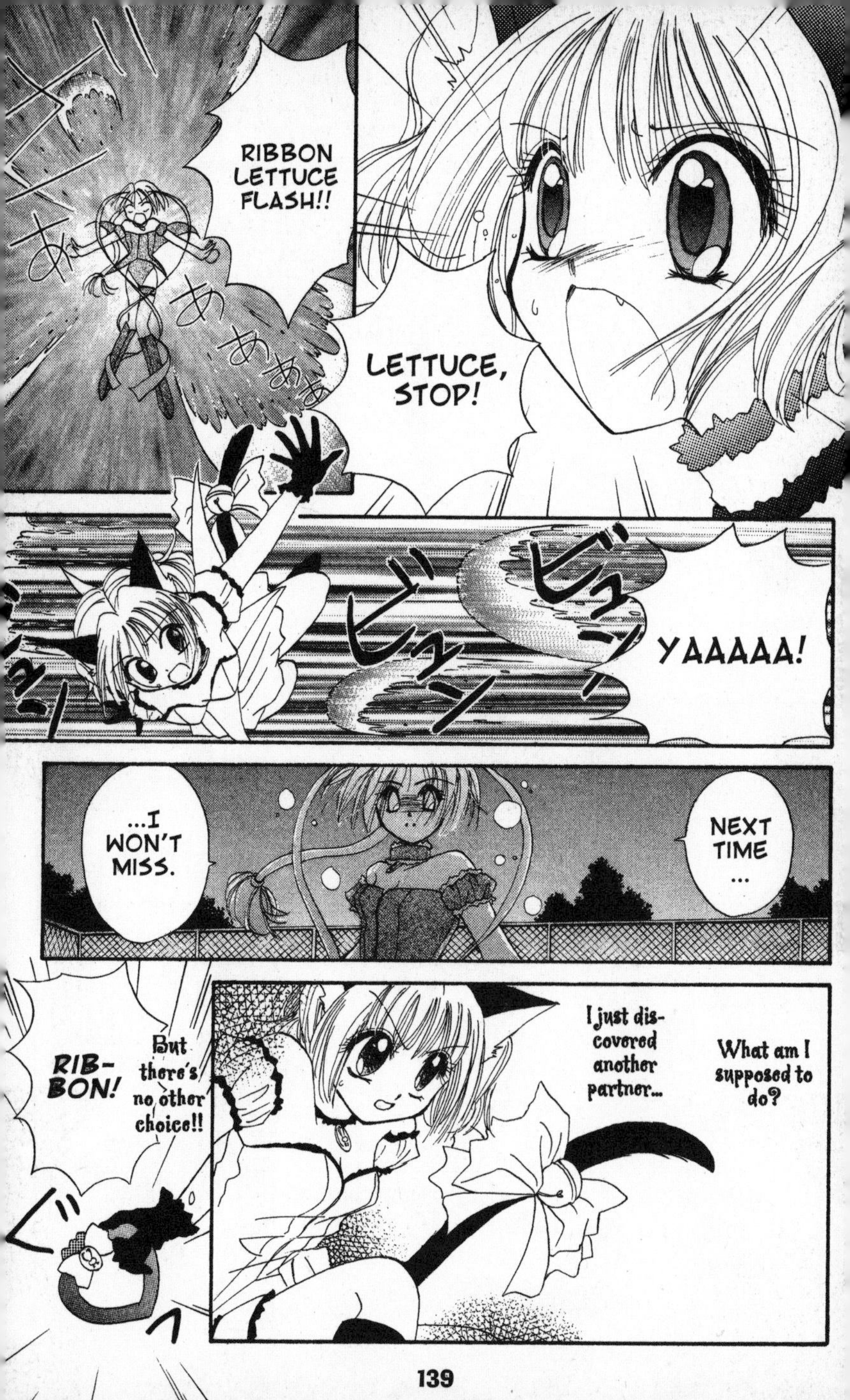
LETTUCE, STOP!
RIBBON LETTUCE FLASH!!
YAAAAA!
NEXT TIME ...
...I WON'T MISS.
What am I supposed to do?
I just discovered another partner...
But there's no other choice!!
RIB-BON!

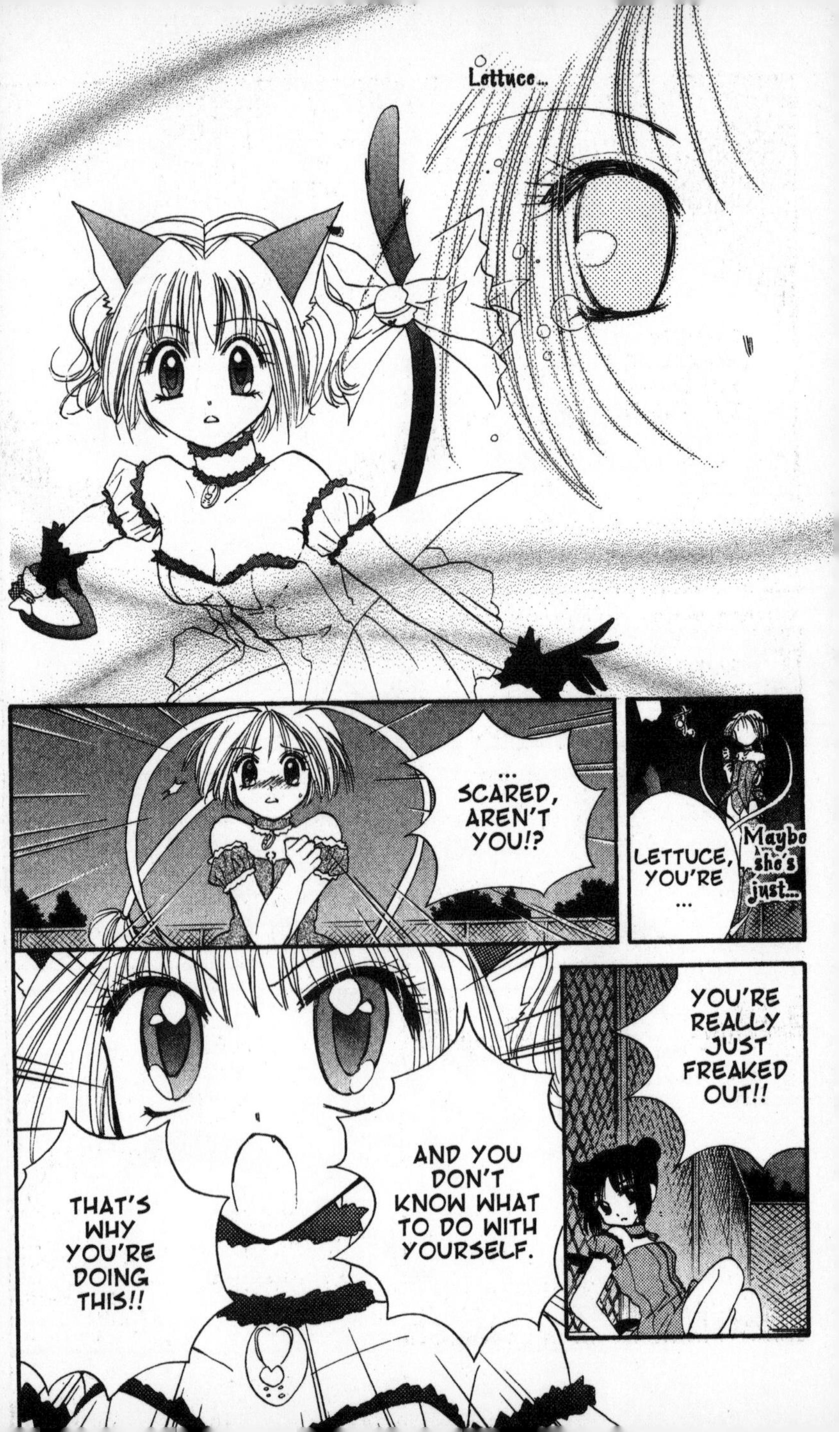
Lettuce...
Maybe she's just...
LETTUCE, YOU'RE ...
... SCARED, AREN'T YOU!?
YOU'RE REALLY JUST FREAKED OUT!!
AND YOU DON'T KNOW WHAT TO DO WITH YOURSELF.
THAT'S WHY YOU'RE DOING THIS!!

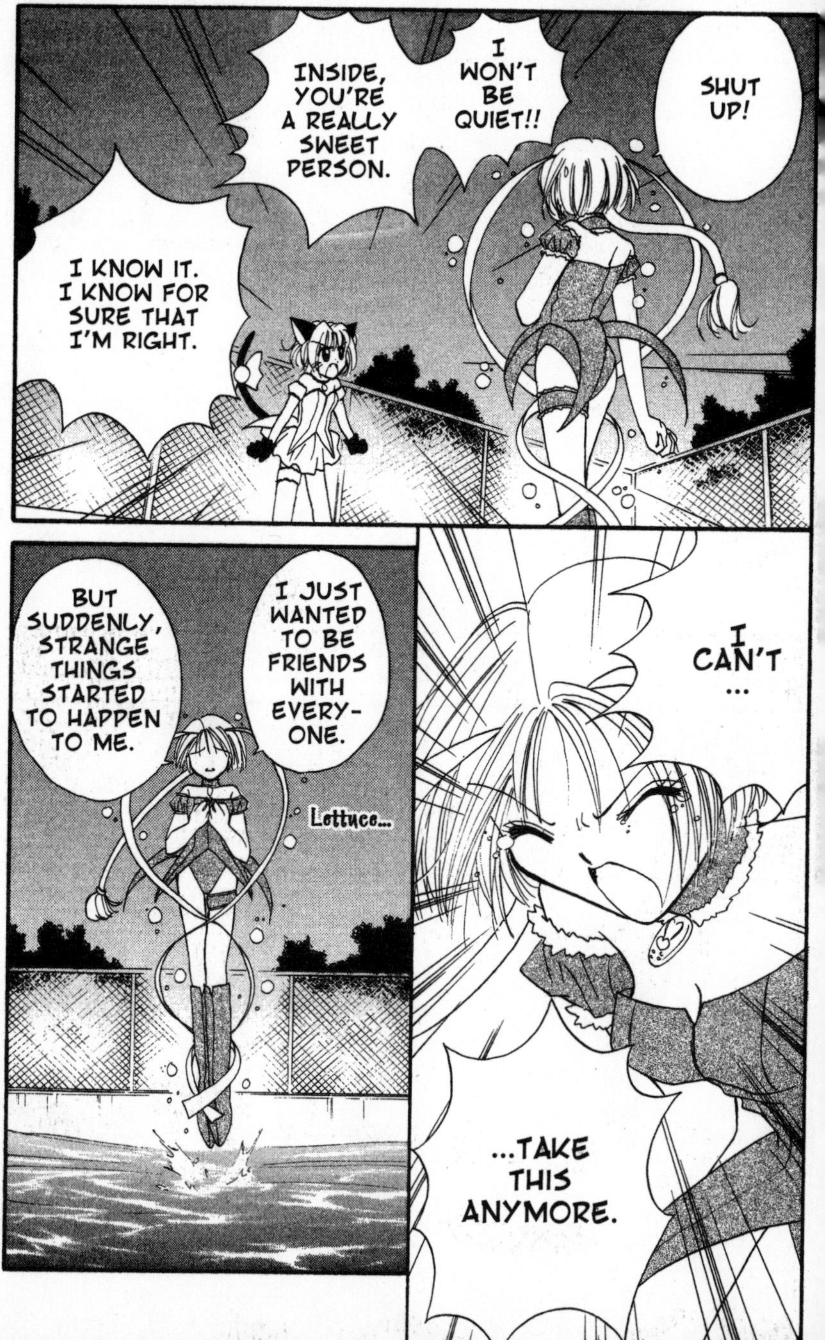
SHUT UP!
I WON'T BE QUIET!!
INSIDE, YOU'RE A REALLY SWEET PERSON.
I KNOW IT. I KNOW FOR SURE THAT I'M RIGHT.
I CAN'T ...
...TAKE THIS ANYMORE.
I JUST WANTED TO BE FRIENDS WITH EVERY-ONE.
BUT SUDDENLY, STRANGE THINGS STARTED TO HAPPEN TO ME.
Lettuce...

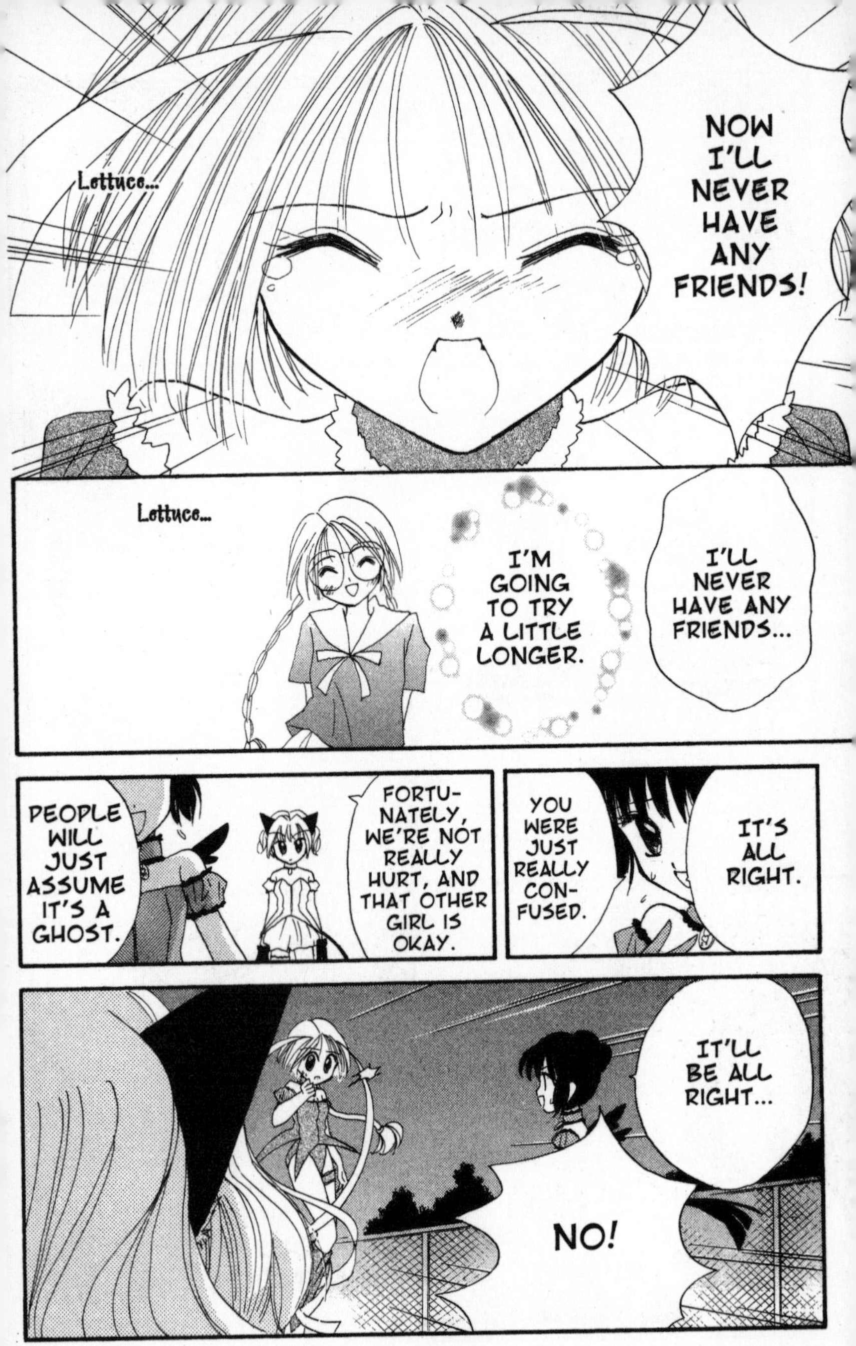

NOW I'LL NEVER HAVE ANY FRIENDS!
Lettuce...
I'LL NEVER HAVE ANY FRIENDS...
I'M GOING TO TRY A LITTLE LONGER.
Lettuce...
IT'S ALL RIGHT.
YOU WERE JUST REALLY CON-FUSED.
FORTU-NATELY, WE'RE NOT REALLY HURT, AND THAT OTHER GIRL IS OKAY.
PEOPLE WILL JUST ASSUME IT'S A GHOST.
IT'LL BE ALL RIGHT...
NO!

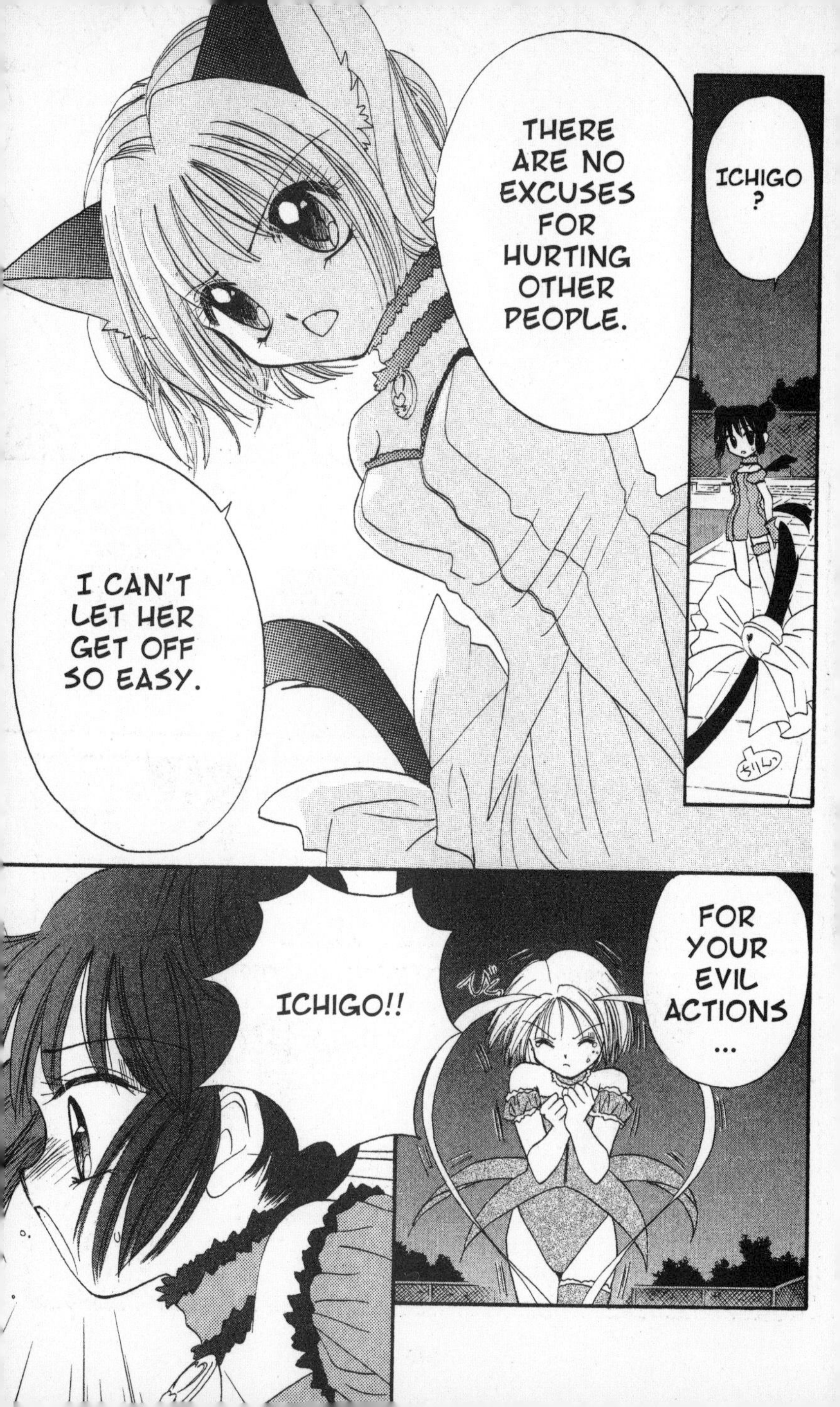
ICHIGO?
THERE ARE NO EXCUSES FOR HURTING OTHER PEOPLE.
I CAN'T LET HER GET OFF SO EASY.
FOR YOUR EVIL ACTIONS...
ICHIGO!!

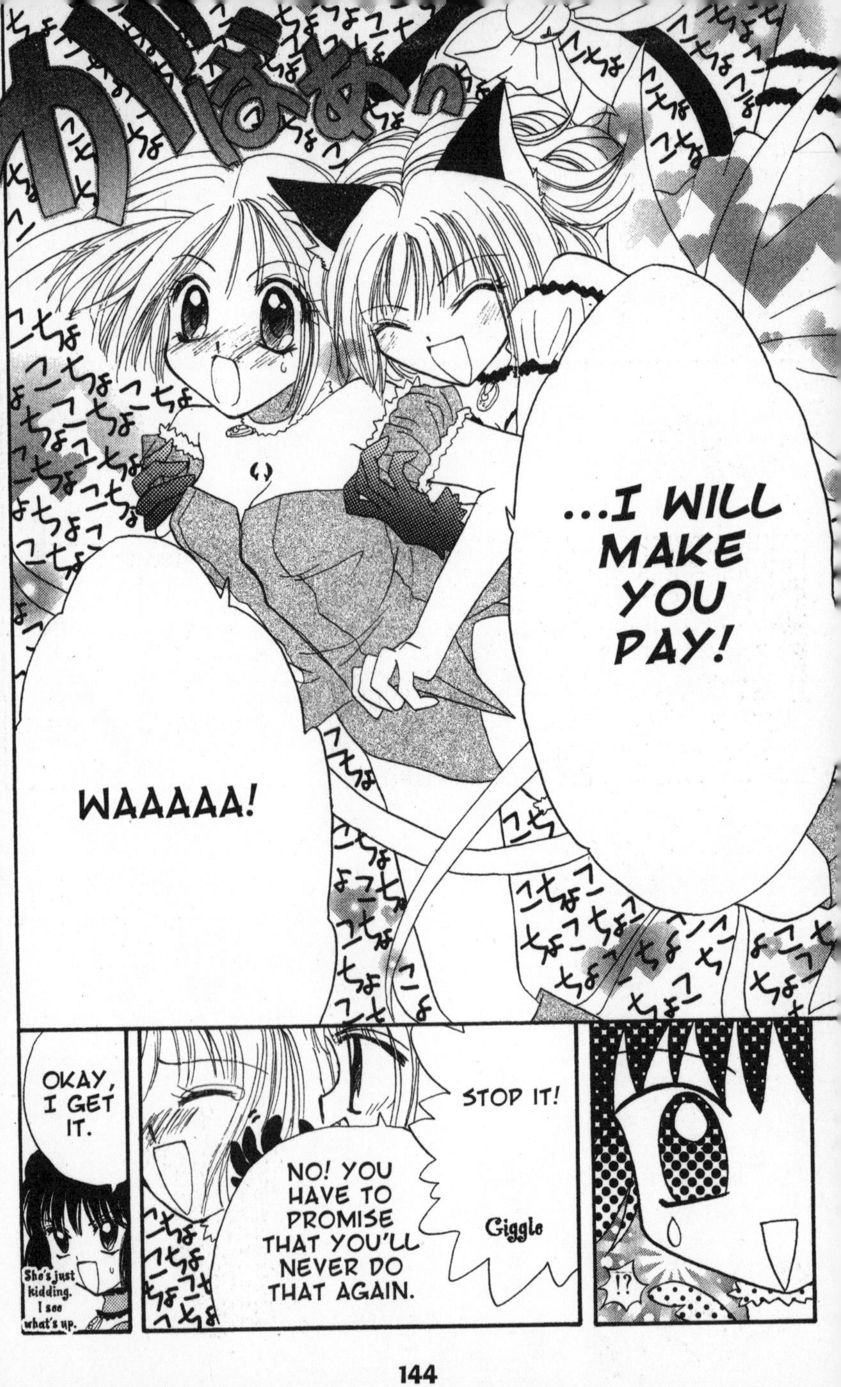
...I WILL MAKE YOU PAY!
WAAAAA!
!?
STOP IT!
NO! YOU HAVE TO PROMISE THAT YOU'LL NEVER DO THAT AGAIN.
Giggle
OKAY, I GET IT.
She's just kidding. I see what's up.

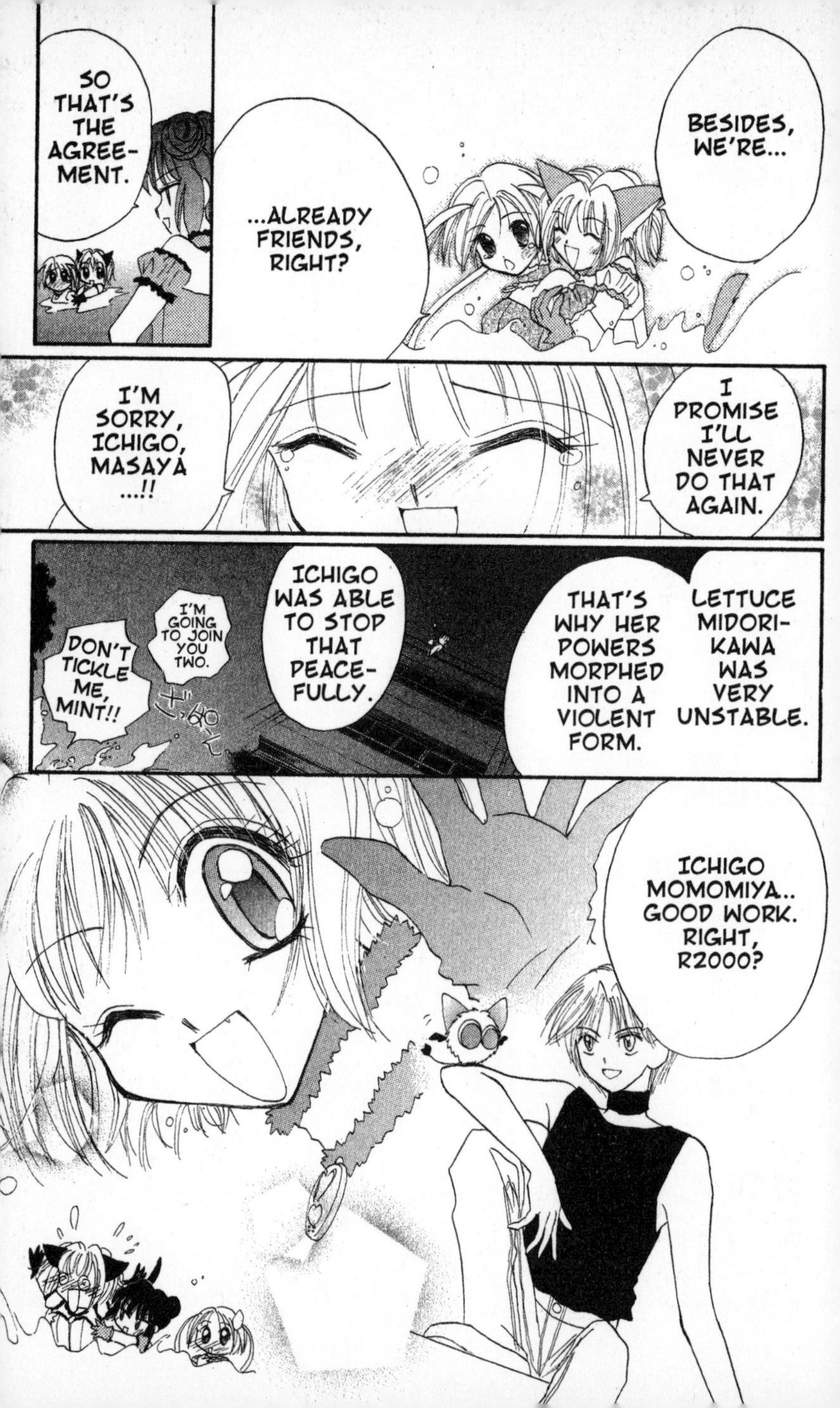

BESIDES, WE'RE...
...ALREADY FRIENDS, RIGHT?
SO THAT'S THE AGREE-MENT.
I PROMISE I'LL NEVER DO THAT AGAIN.
I'M SORRY, ICHIGO, MASAYA ...!!
LETTUCE MIDORI-KAWA WAS VERY UNSTABLE.
THAT'S WHY HER POWERS MORPHED INTO A VIOLENT FORM.
ICHIGO WAS ABLE TO STOP THAT PEACE-FULLY.
I'M GOING TO JOIN YOU TWO.
DON'T TICKLE ME, MINT!!
ICHIGO MOMOMIYA.. GOOD WORK. RIGHT, R2000?

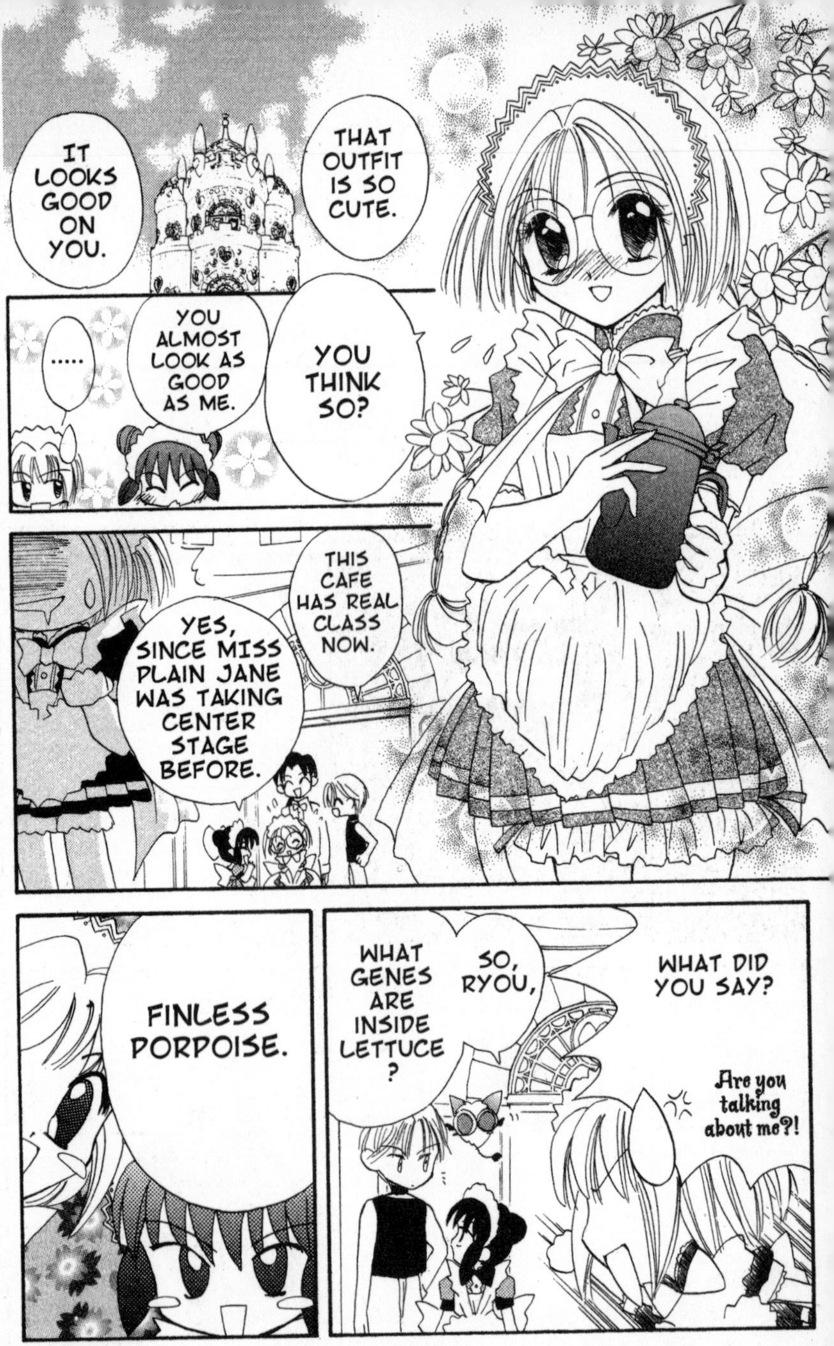
THAT OUTFIT IS SO CUTE.
IT LOOKS GOOD ON YOU.
YOU THINK SO?
YOU ALMOST LOOK AS GOOD AS ME.
......
THIS CAFE HAS REAL CLASS NOW.
YES, SINCE MISS PLAIN JANE WAS TAKING CENTER STAGE BEFORE.
WHAT DID YOU SAY?
Are you talking about me?!
SO, RYOU,
WHAT GENES ARE INSIDE LETTUCE ?
FINLESS PORPOISE.

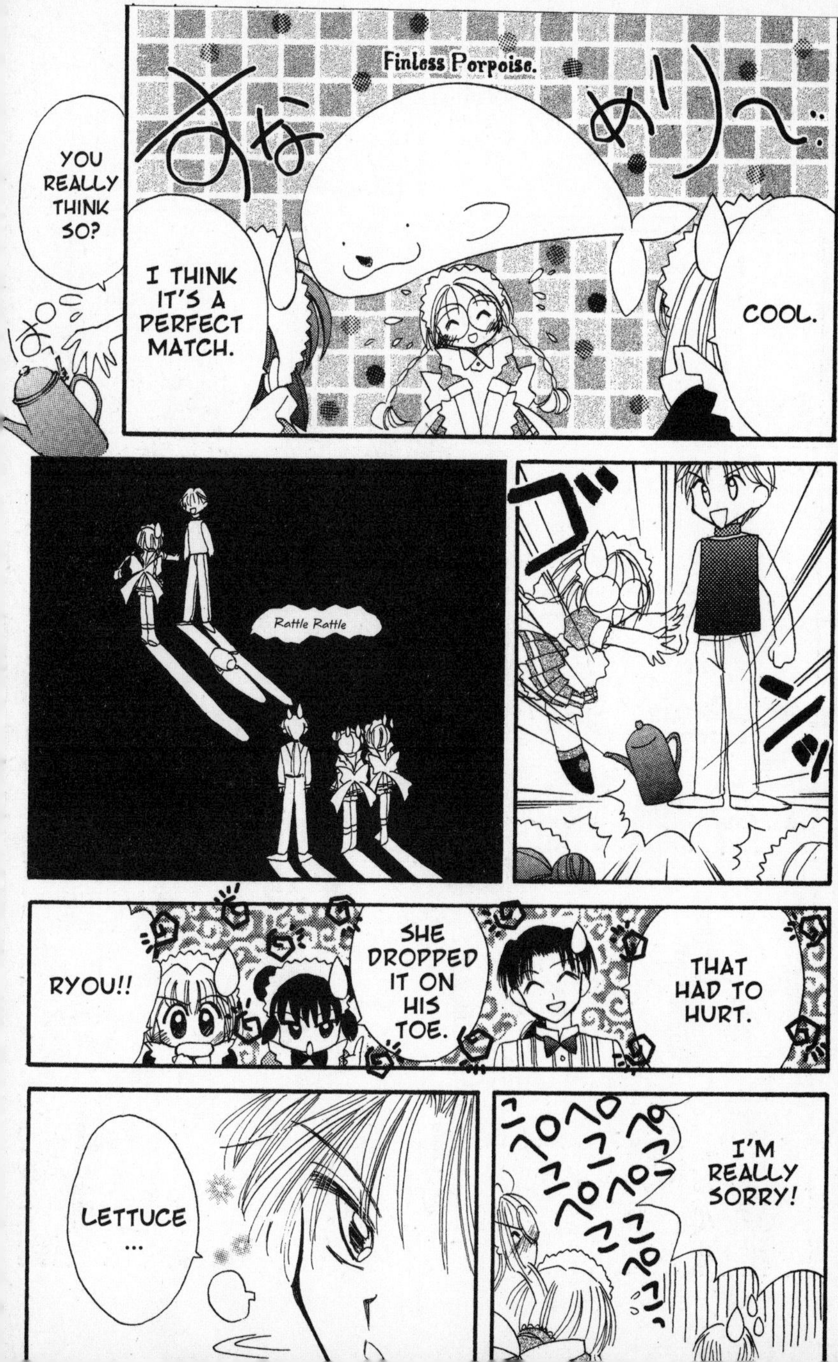
Finless Porpoise.
COOL.
I THINK IT'S A PERFECT MATCH.
YOU REALLY THINK SO?
Rattle Rattle
THAT HAD TO HURT.
SHE DROPPED IT ON HIS TOE.
RYOU!!
I'M REALLY SORRY!
LETTUCE ...

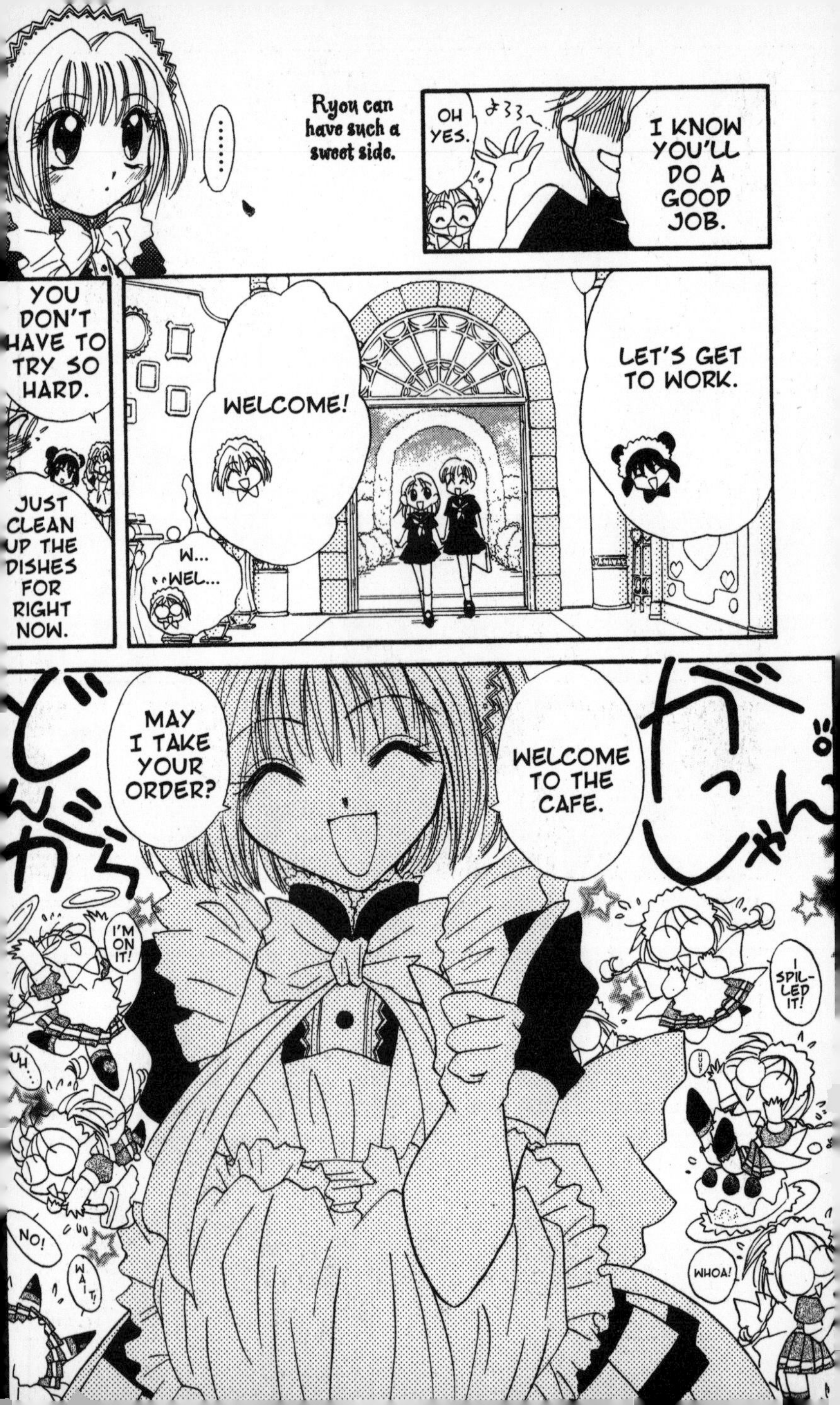
I KNOW YOU'LL DO A GOOD JOB.
よろろ～
OH YES.
Ryou can have such a sweet side.
......
LET'S GET TO WORK.
WELCOME!
W... WEL...
YOU DON'T HAVE TO TRY SO HARD.
JUST CLEAN UP THE DISHES FOR RIGHT NOW.
がっしゃん
WELCOME TO THE CAFE.
MAY I TAKE YOUR ORDER?
どんがら
I SPILLED IT!
HUH?
WHOA!
I'M ON IT!
UH...
NO!
WAIT!

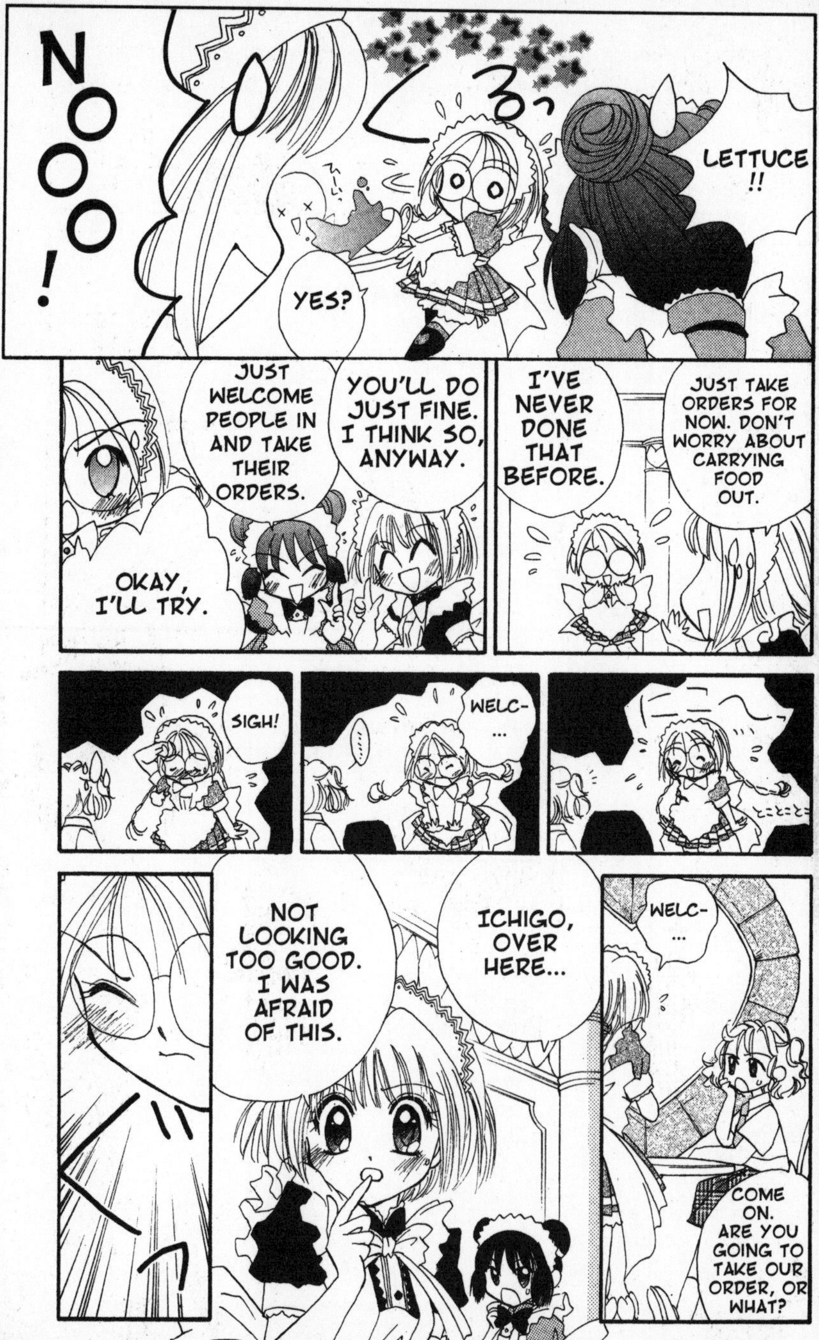
LETTUCE !!
YES?
NOOOO!
JUST TAKE ORDERS FOR NOW. DON'T WORRY ABOUT CARRYING FOOD OUT.
I'VE NEVER DONE THAT BEFORE.
YOU'LL DO JUST FINE. I THINK SO, ANYWAY.
JUST WELCOME PEOPLE IN AND TAKE THEIR ORDERS.
OKAY, I'LL TRY.
WELC- ...
...
SIGH!
WELC- ...
COME ON. ARE YOU GOING TO TAKE OUR ORDER, OR WHAT?
ICHIGO, OVER HERE...
NOT LOOKING TOO GOOD. I WAS AFRAID OF THIS.

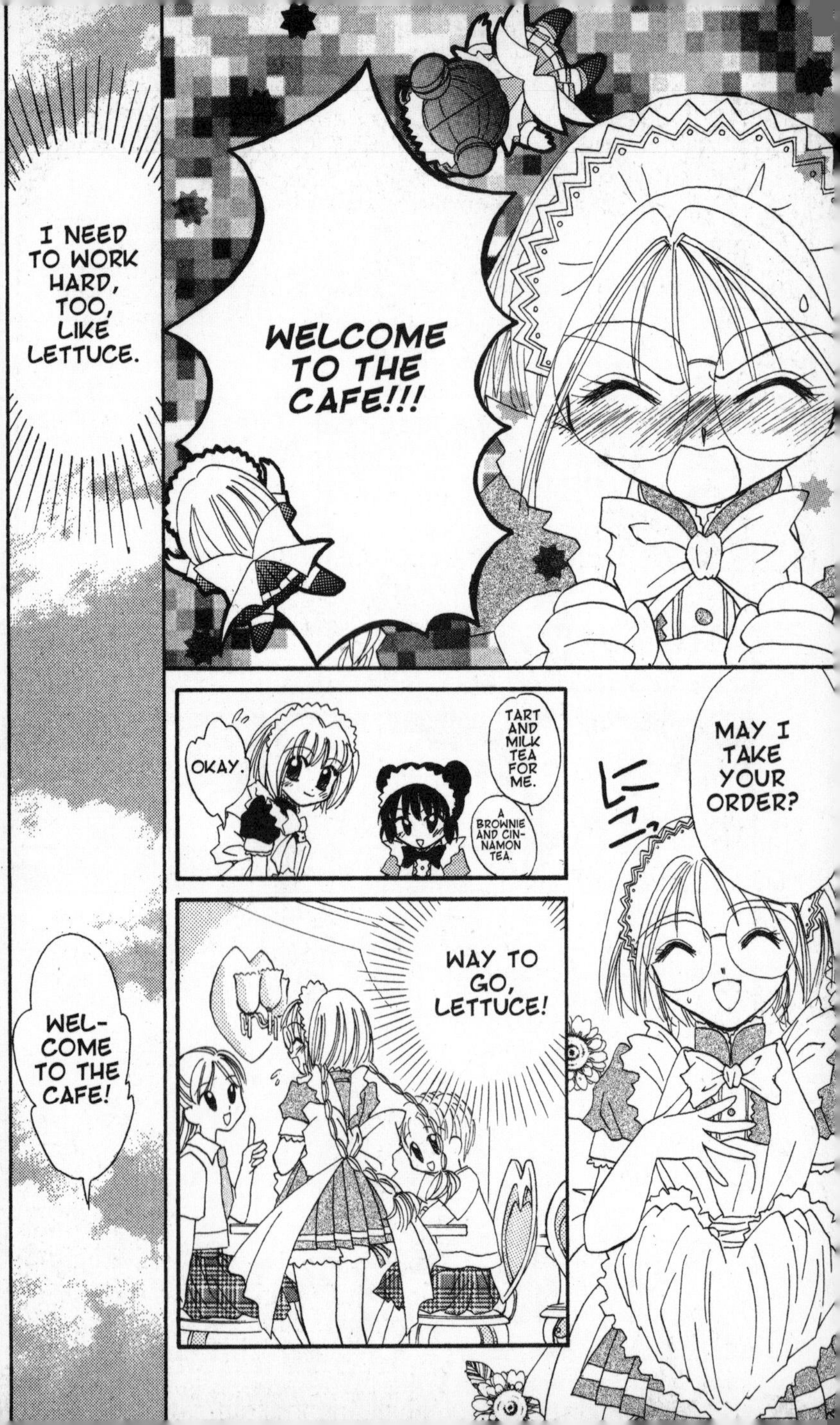
WELCOME TO THE CAFE!!!
MAY I TAKE YOUR ORDER?
TART AND MILK TEA FOR ME.
A BROWNIE AND CINNAMON TEA.
OKAY.
WAY TO GO, LETTUCE!
I NEED TO WORK HARD, TOO, LIKE LETTUCE.
WELCOME TO THE CAFE!

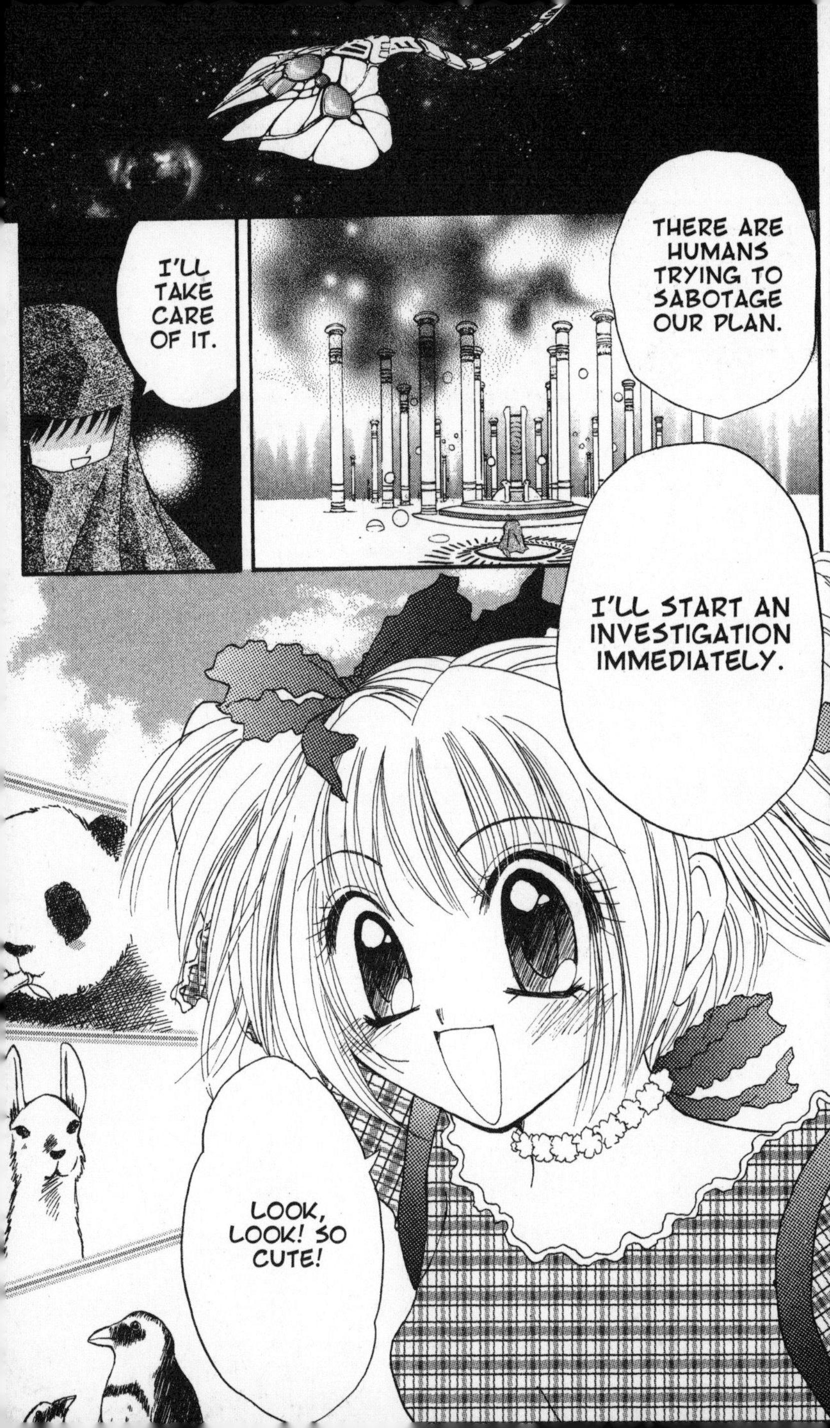
THERE ARE HUMANS TRYING TO SABOTAGE OUR PLAN.
I'LL TAKE CARE OF IT.
I'LL START AN INVESTIGATION IMMEDIATELY.
LOOK, LOOK! SO CUTE!

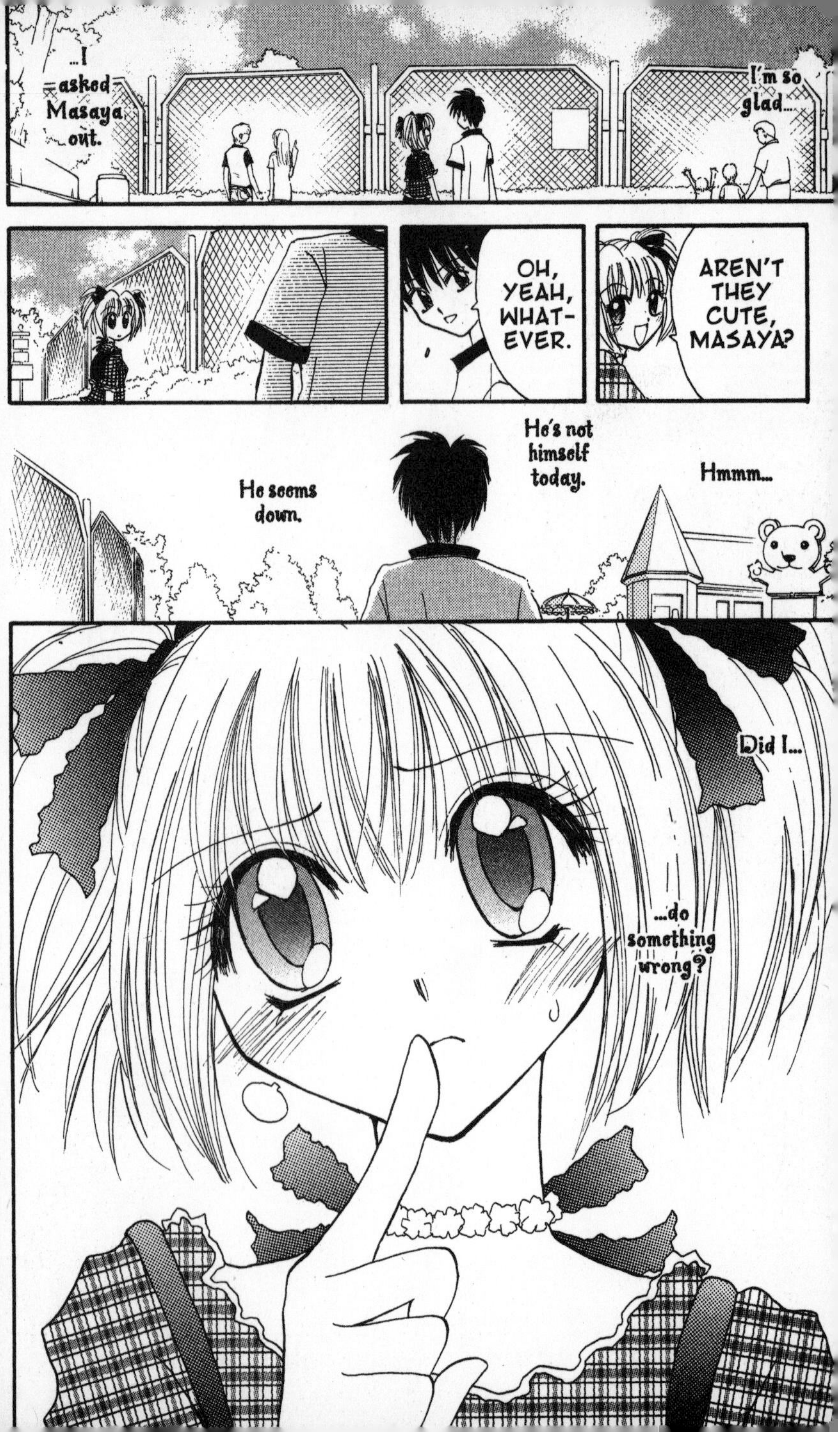
I'm so glad...
...I asked Masaya out.
AREN'T THEY CUTE, MASAYA?
OH, YEAH, WHATEVER.
Hmmm...
He's not himself today.
He seems down.
Did I...
...do something wrong?

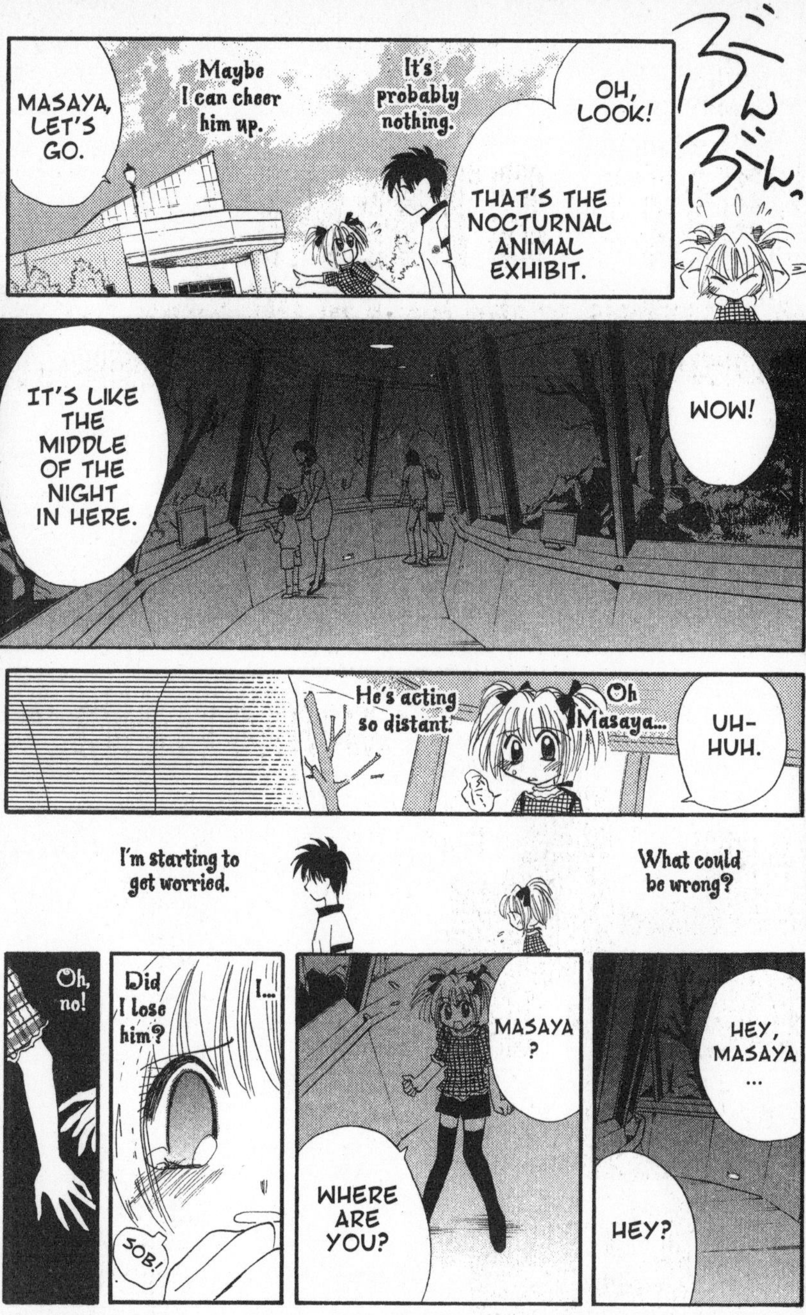
ぶんぶん
OH, LOOK!
THAT'S THE NOCTURNAL ANIMAL EXHIBIT.
It's probably nothing.
Maybe I can cheer him up.
MASAYA, LET'S GO.
WOW!
IT'S LIKE THE MIDDLE OF THE NIGHT IN HERE.
UH-HUH.
Oh Masaya...
He's acting so distant.
What could be wrong?
I'm starting to get worried.
HEY, MASAYA ...
HEY?
MASAYA ?
WHERE ARE YOU?
I...
Did I lose him?
SOB!
Oh, no!

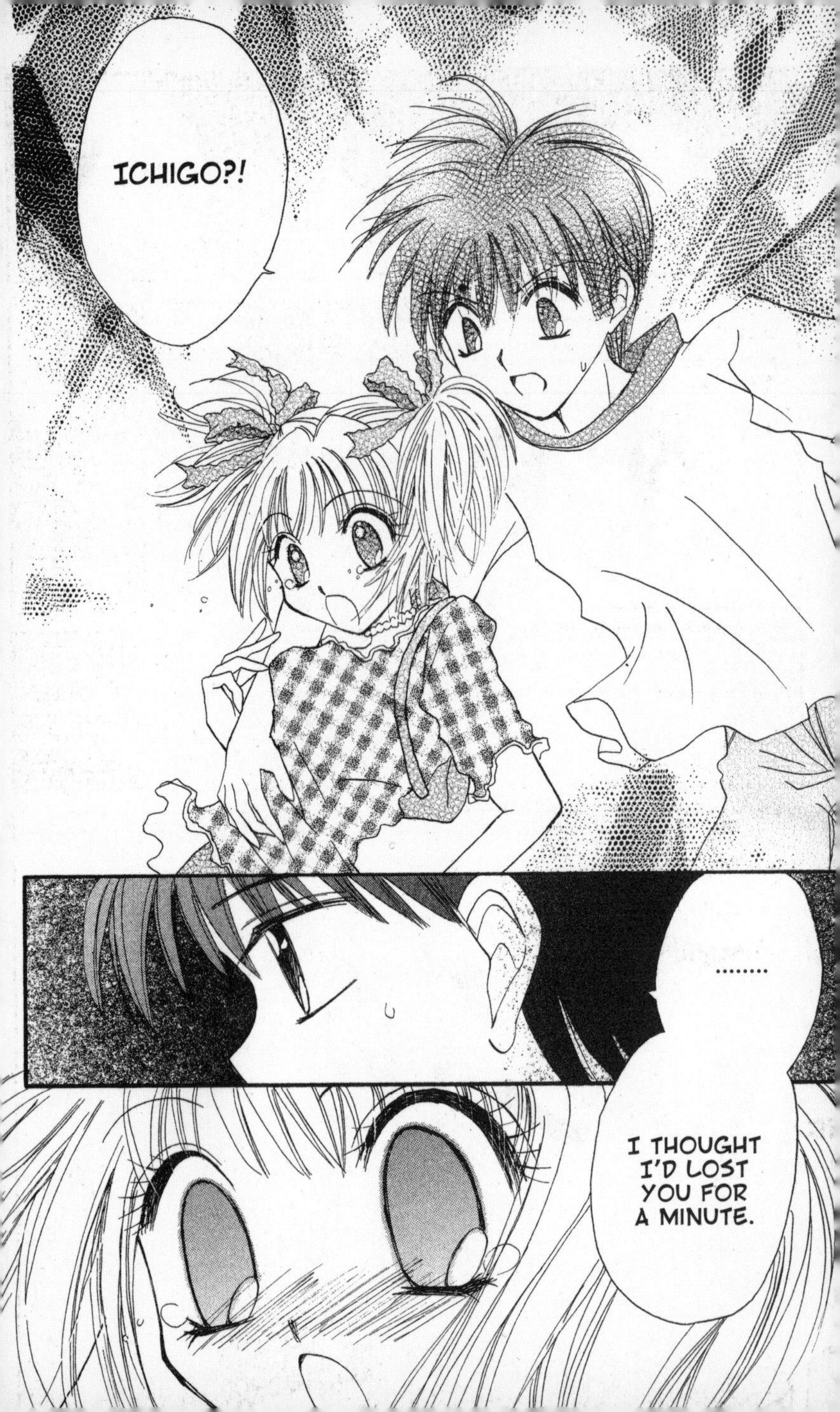
ICHIGO?!
....
I THOUGHT I'D LOST YOU FOR A MINUTE.

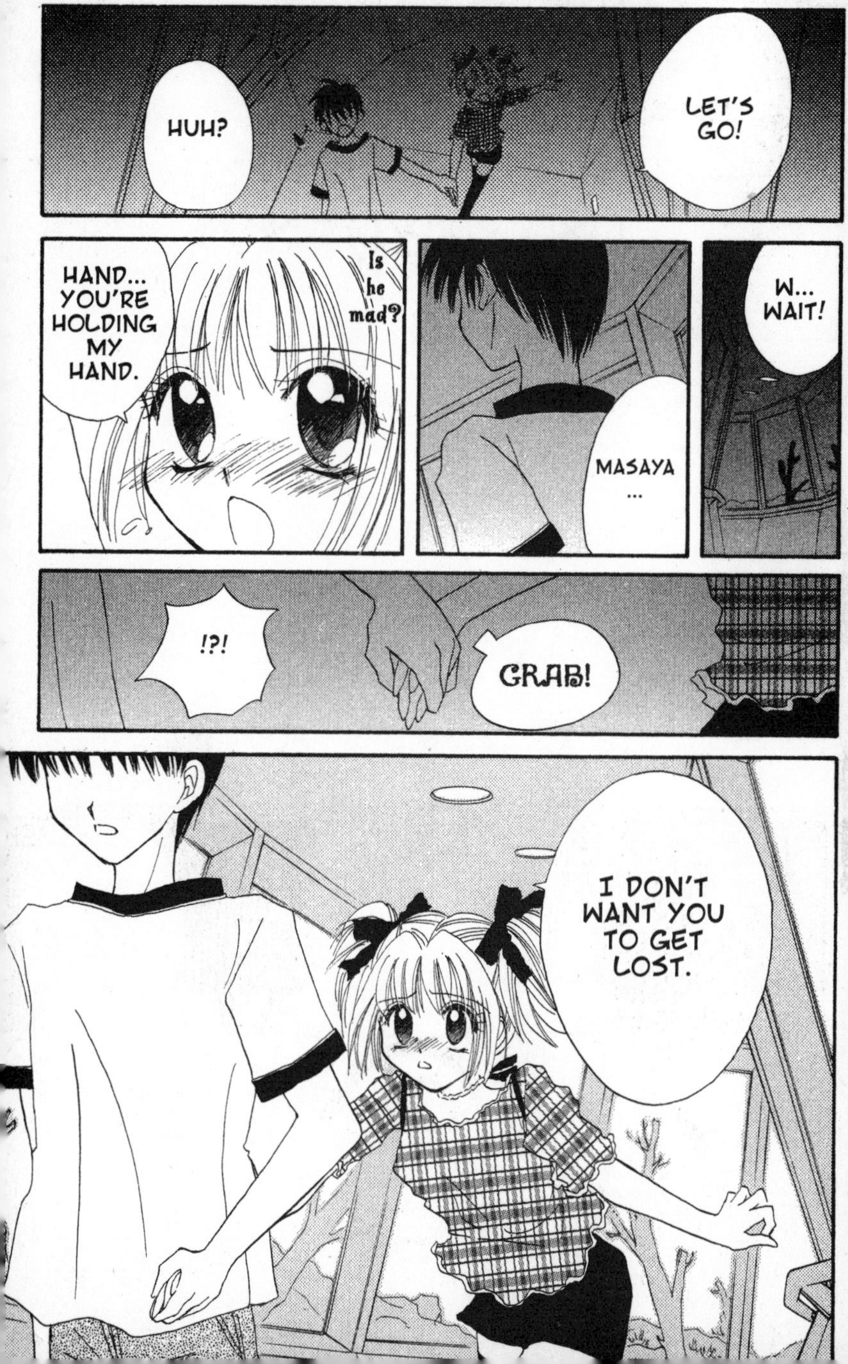
LET'S GO!
HUH?
W... WAIT!
MASAYA ...
Is he mad?
HAND... YOU'RE HOLDING MY HAND.
GRAB!
!?!
I DON'T WANT YOU TO GET LOST.

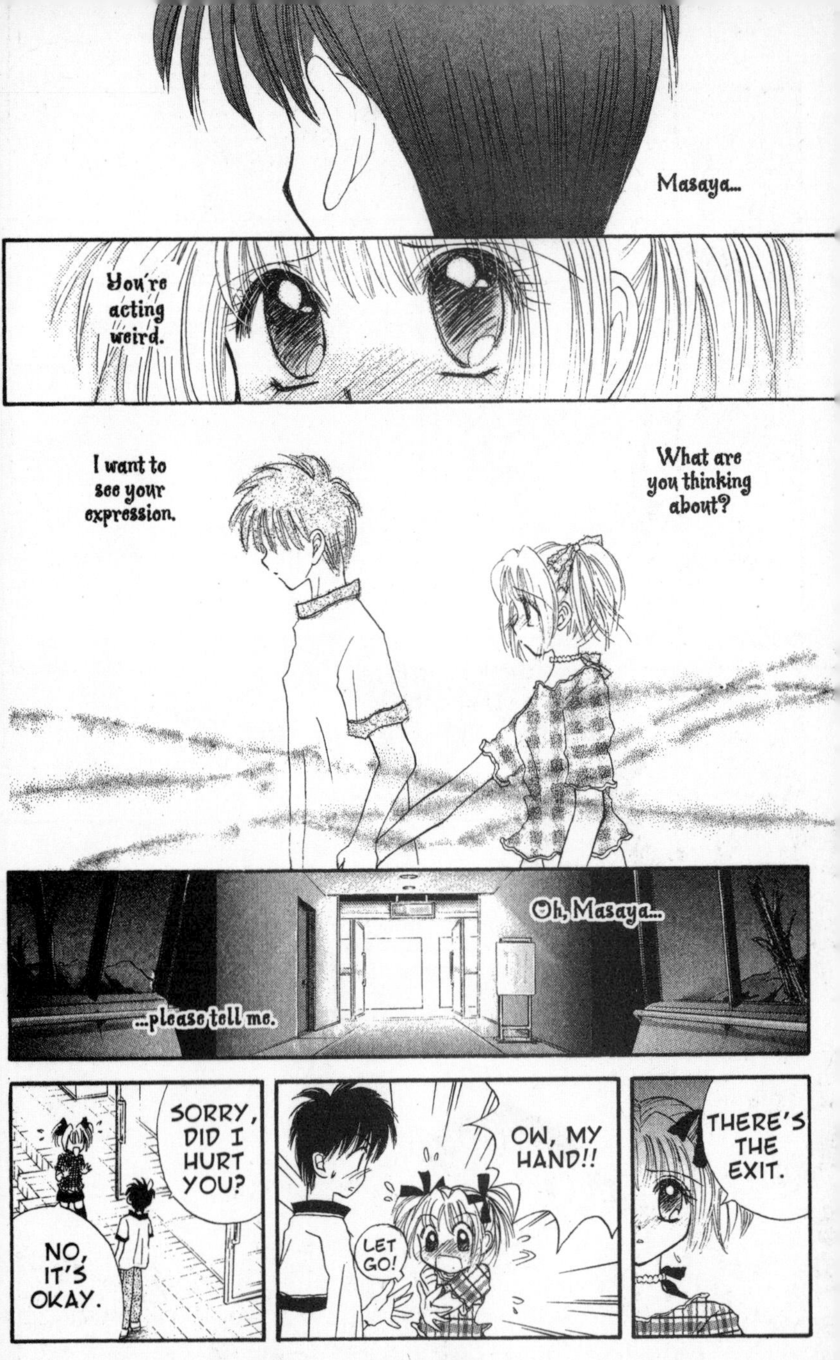
Masaya...
You're acting weird.
What are you thinking about?
I want to see your expression.
Oh, Masaya...
...please tell me.
THERE'S THE EXIT.
OW, MY HAND!!
LET GO!
SORRY, DID I HURT YOU?
NO, IT'S OKAY.

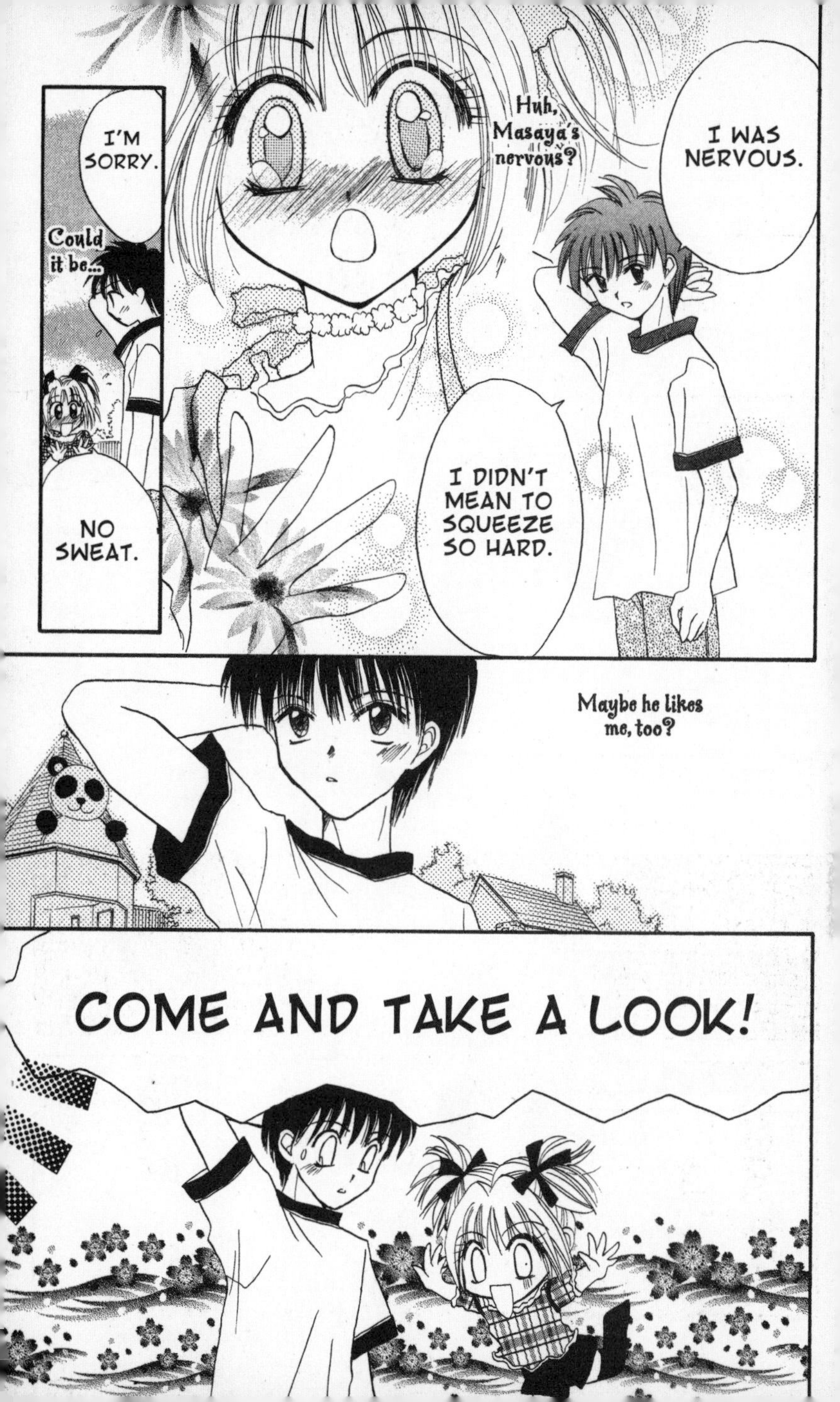

I WAS NERVOUS.
Huh, Masaya's nervous?
I DIDN'T MEAN TO SQUEEZE SO HARD.
I'M SORRY.
Could it be...
NO SWEAT.
Maybe he likes me, too?
COME AND TAKE A LOOK!

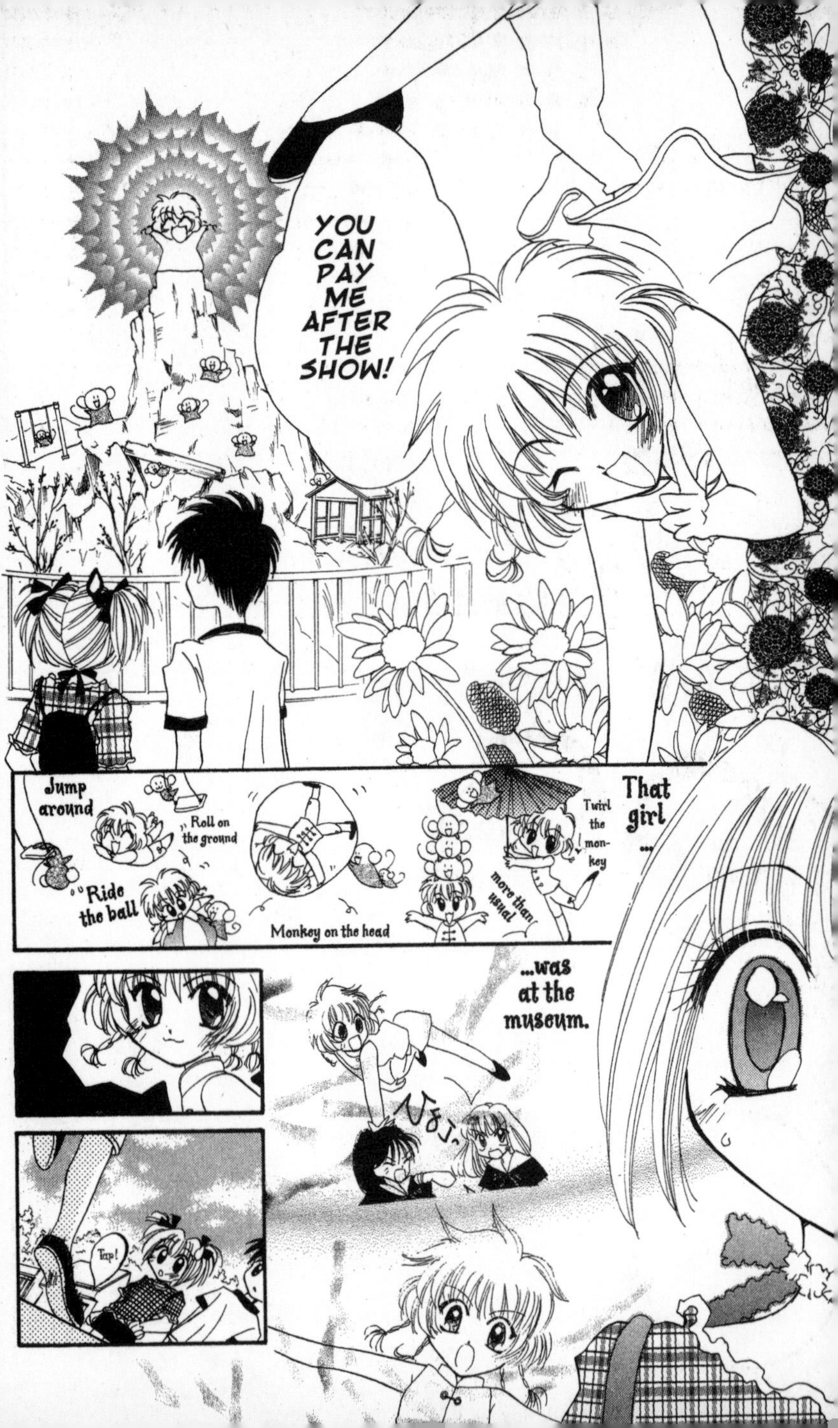
YOU CAN PAY ME AFTER THE SHOW!
That girl...
Twirl the monkey
more than usual
Monkey on the head
Roll on the ground
Ride the ball
Jump around
...was at the museum.
Tap!

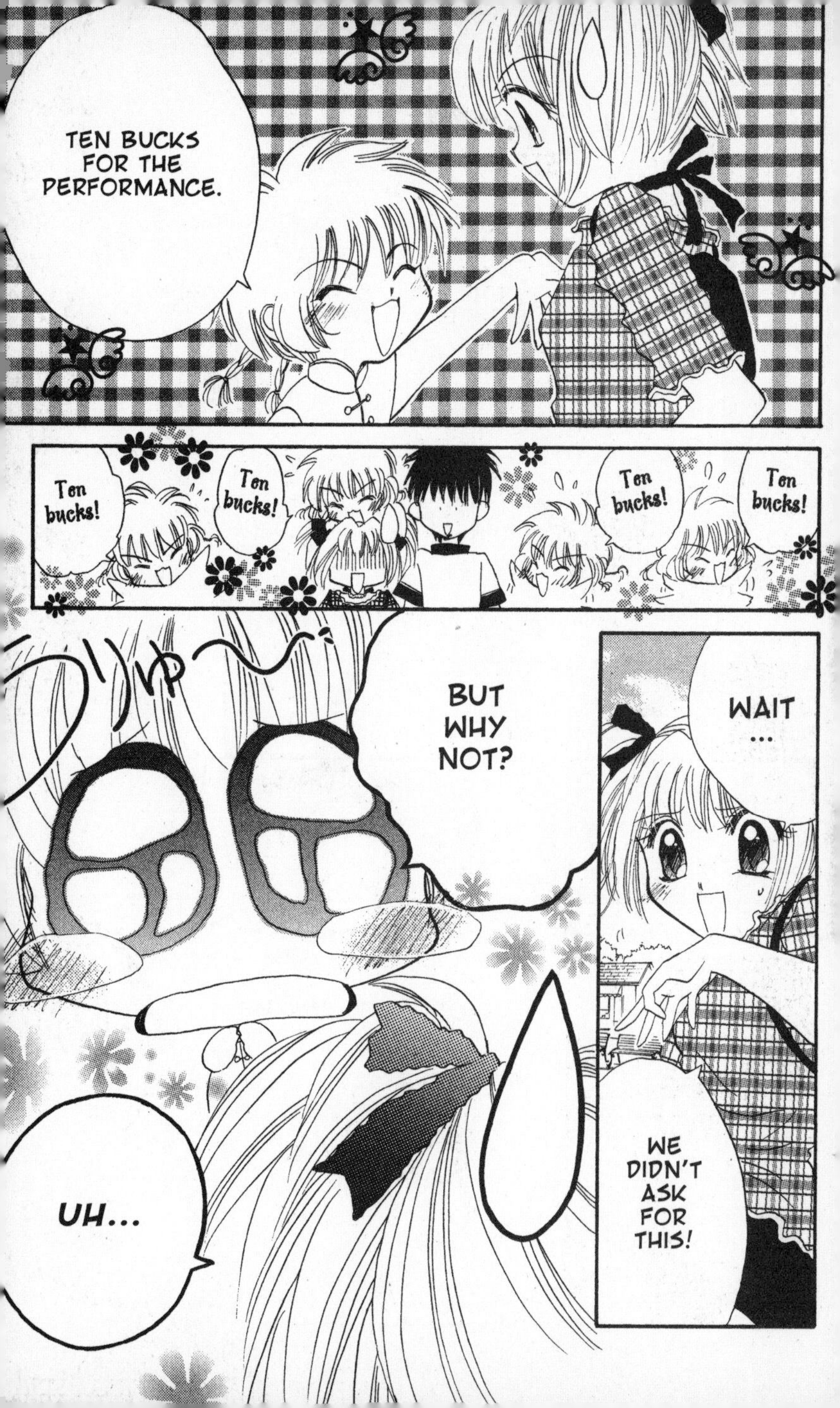
TEN BUCKS FOR THE PERFORMANCE.
Ten bucks!
Ten bucks!
Ten bucks!
Ten bucks!
WAIT ...
WE DIDN'T ASK FOR THIS!
うりゅ〜〜
BUT WHY NOT?
UH...

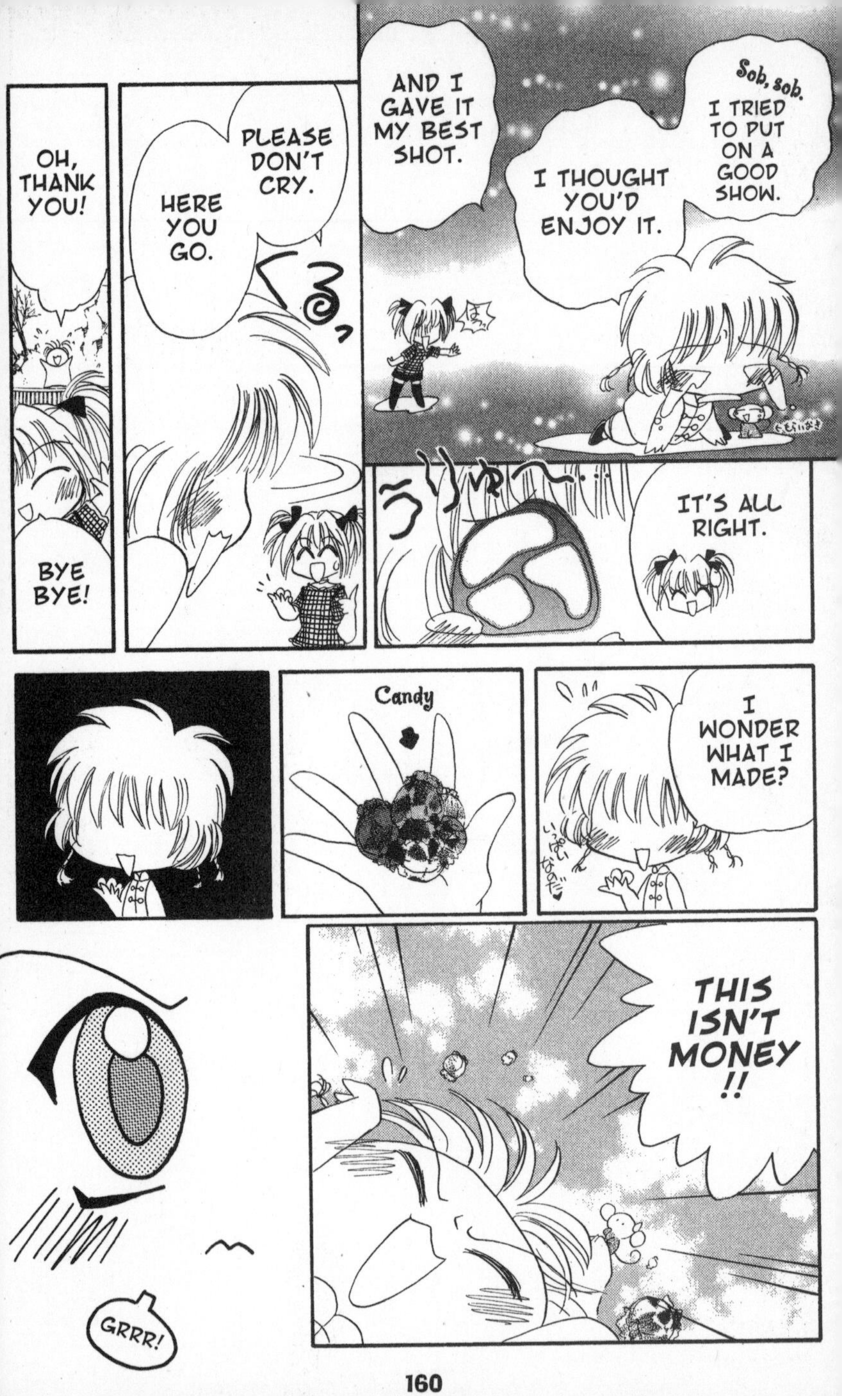
Sob, sob.
I TRIED TO PUT ON A GOOD SHOW.
I THOUGHT YOU'D ENJOY IT.
AND I GAVE IT MY BEST SHOT.
IT'S ALL RIGHT.
PLEASE DON'T CRY.
HERE YOU GO.
OH, THANK YOU!
BYE BYE!
I WONDER WHAT I MADE?
Candy
THIS ISN'T MONEY!!
GRRR!

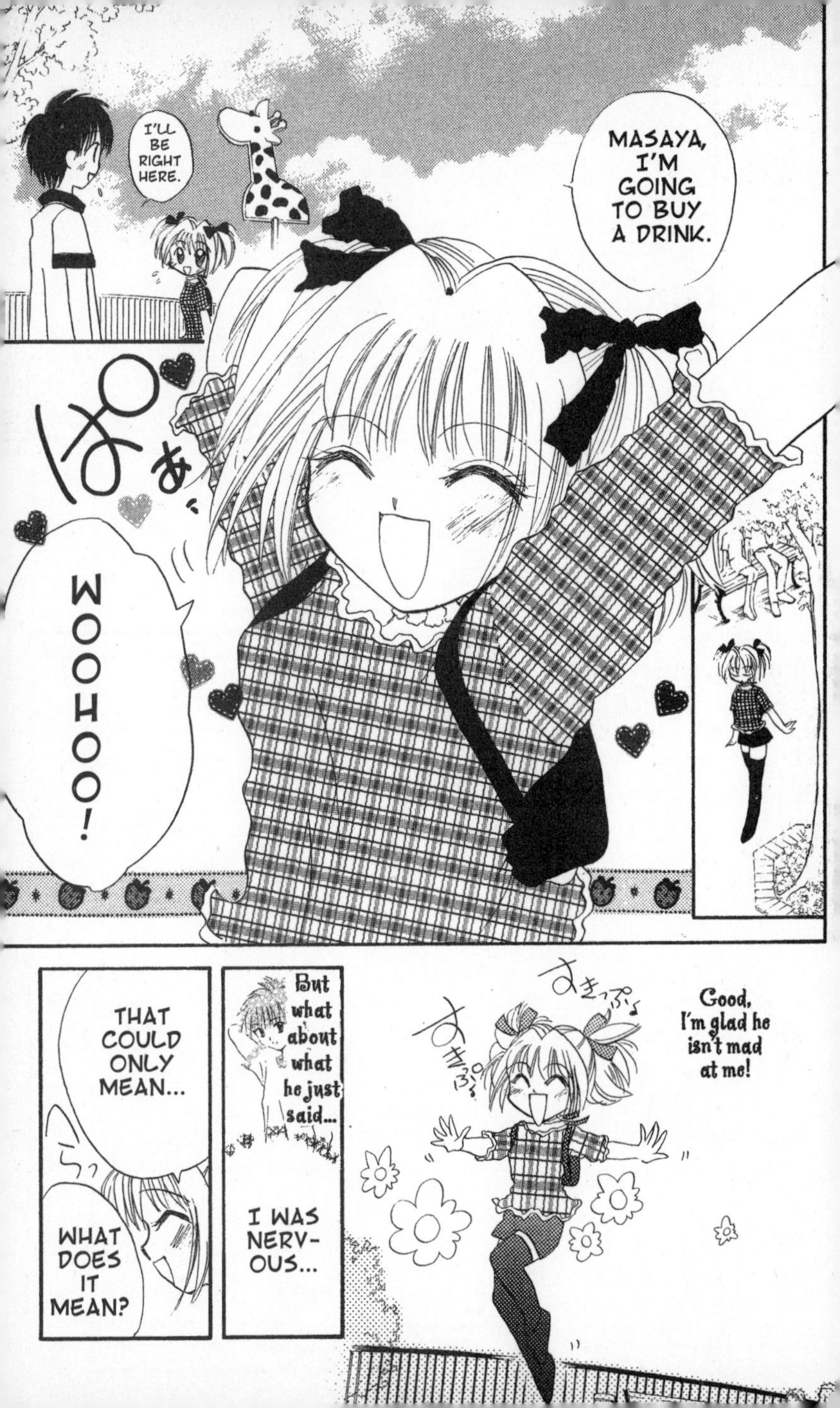

MASAYA, I'M GOING TO BUY A DRINK.
I'LL BE RIGHT HERE.
WOOHOO!
Good, I'm glad he isn't mad at me!
すきっぷ
すきっぷ
But what about what he just said...
I WAS NERV-OUS...
THAT COULD ONLY MEAN...
WHAT DOES IT MEAN?

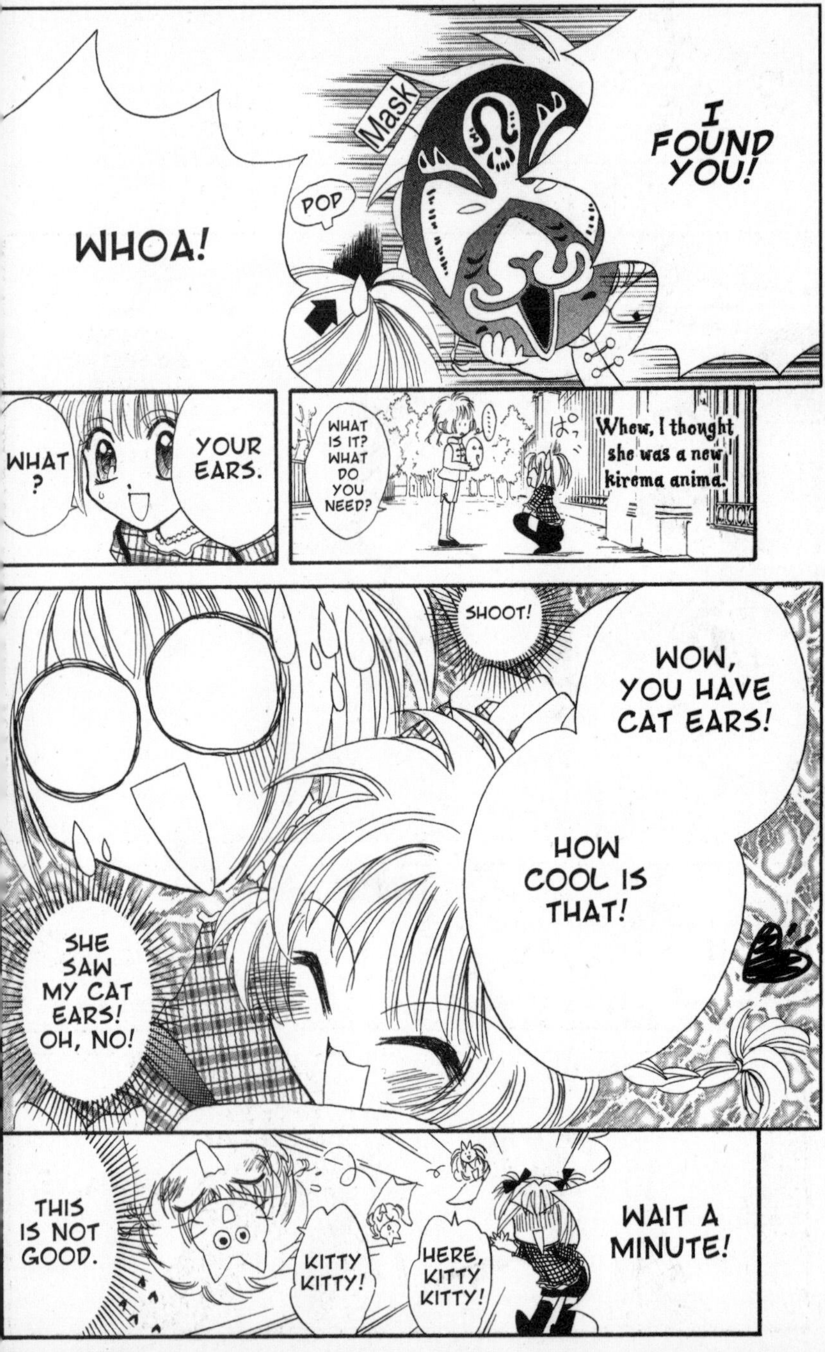
I FOUND YOU!
Mask
POP
WHOA!
Whew, I thought she was a new kirema anima.
ぱっ
...
WHAT IS IT? WHAT DO YOU NEED?
YOUR EARS.
WHAT?
SHOOT!
WOW, YOU HAVE CAT EARS!
HOW COOL IS THAT!
SHE SAW MY CAT EARS! OH, NO!
WAIT A MINUTE!
HERE, KITTY KITTY!
KITTY KITTY!
THIS IS NOT GOOD.

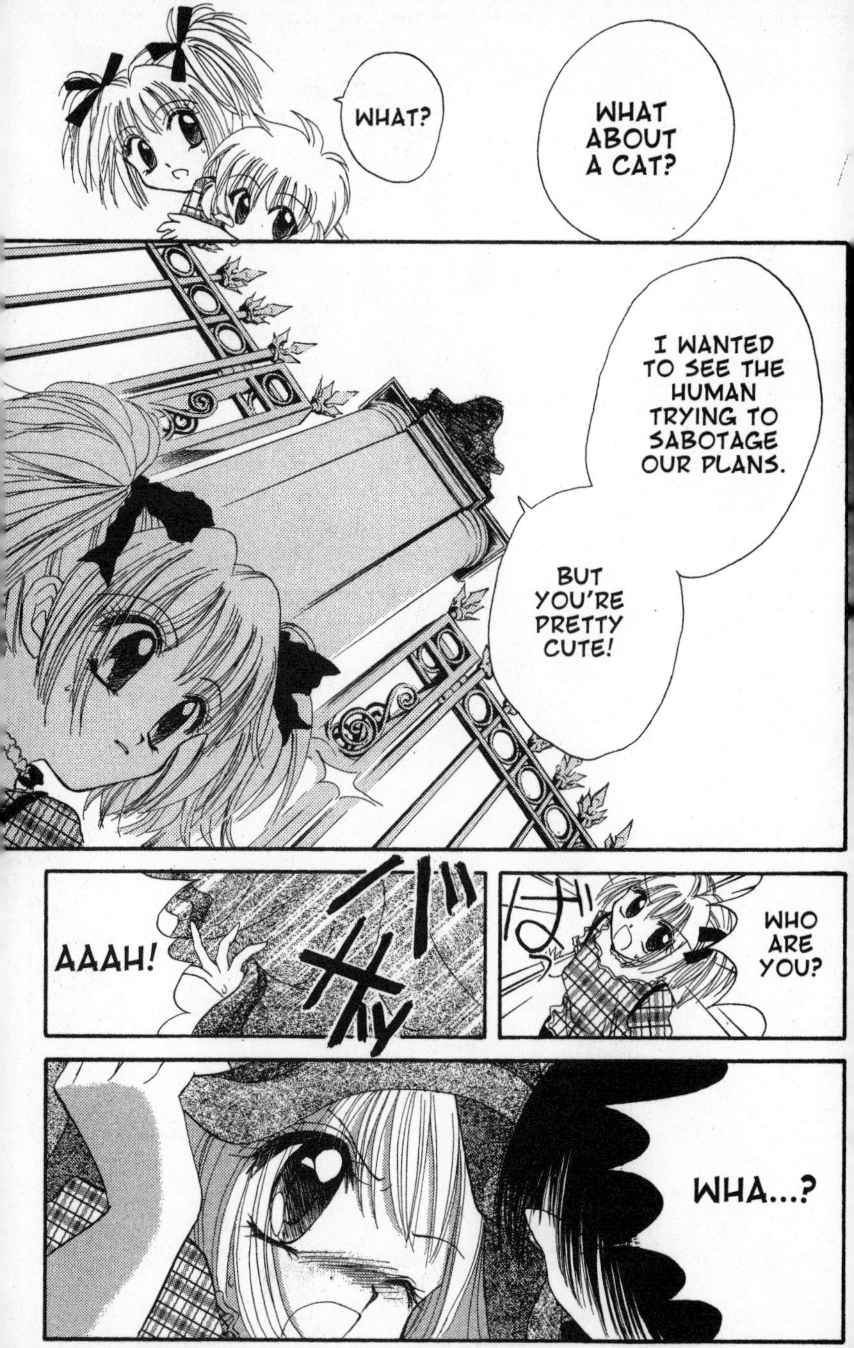
WHAT ABOUT A CAT?
WHAT?
I WANTED TO SEE THE HUMAN TRYING TO SABOTAGE OUR PLANS.
BUT YOU'RE PRETTY CUTE!
WHO ARE YOU?
AAAH!
WHA...?

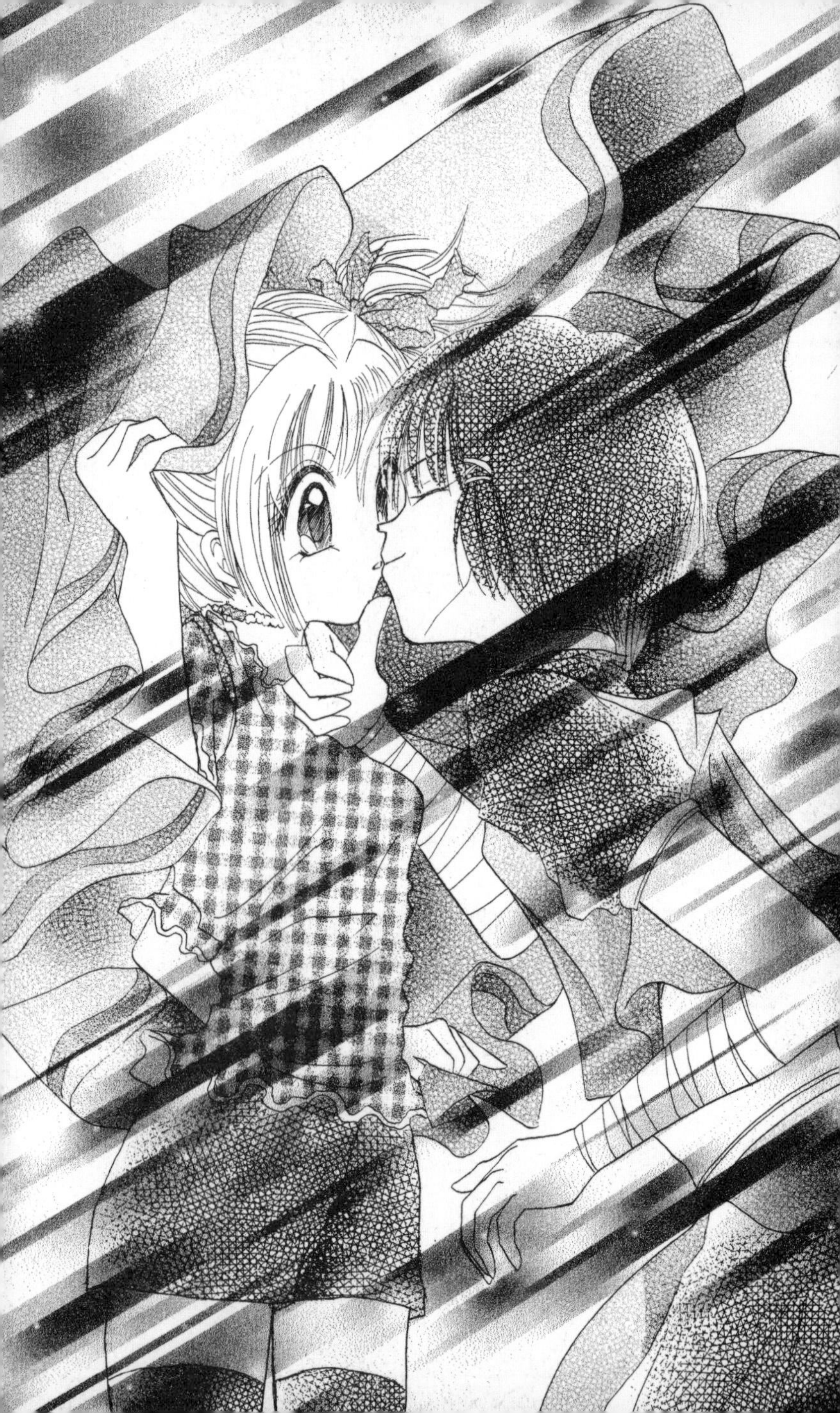

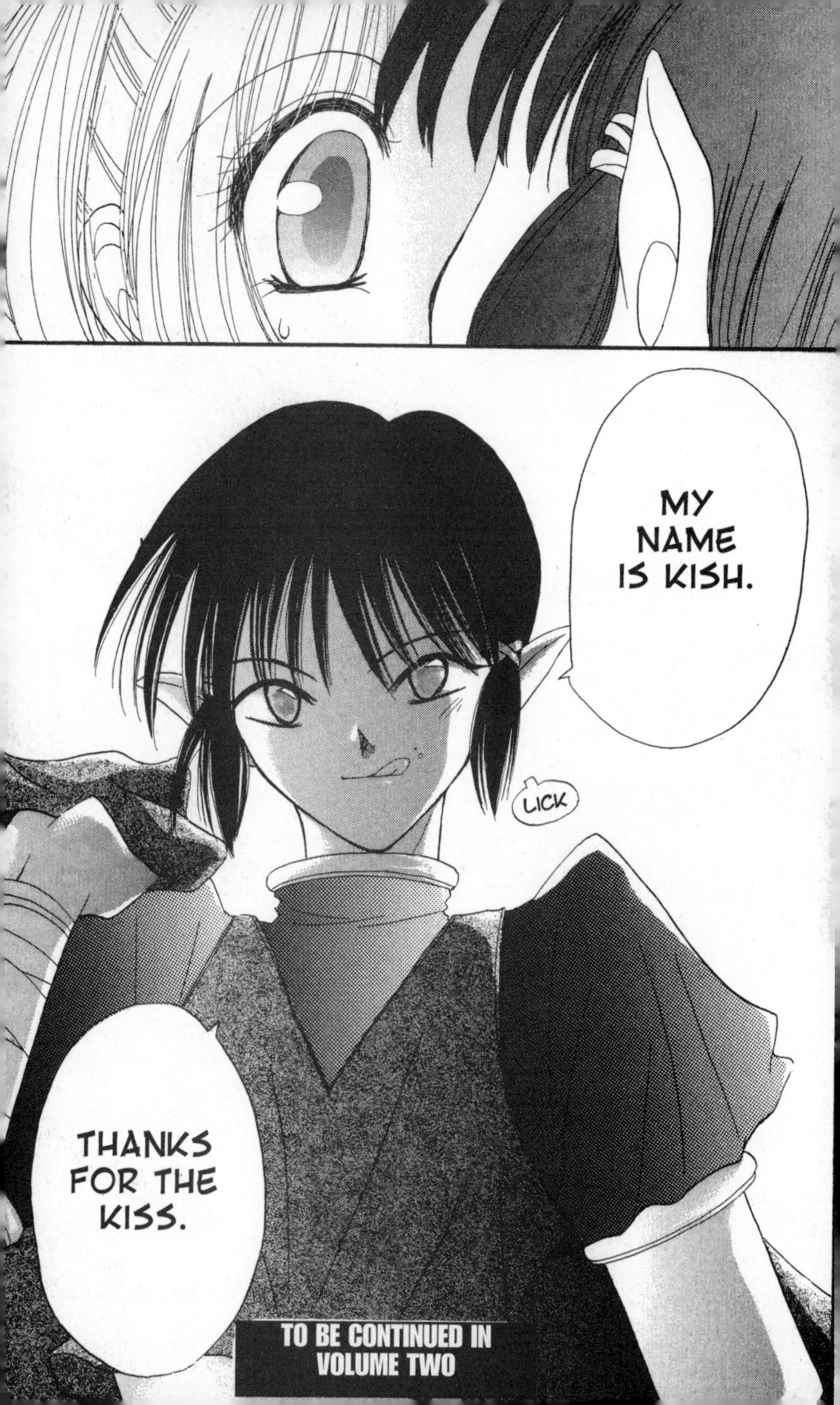
MY NAME IS KISH.
LICK
THANKS FOR THE KISS.
TO BE CONTINUED IN VOLUME TWO

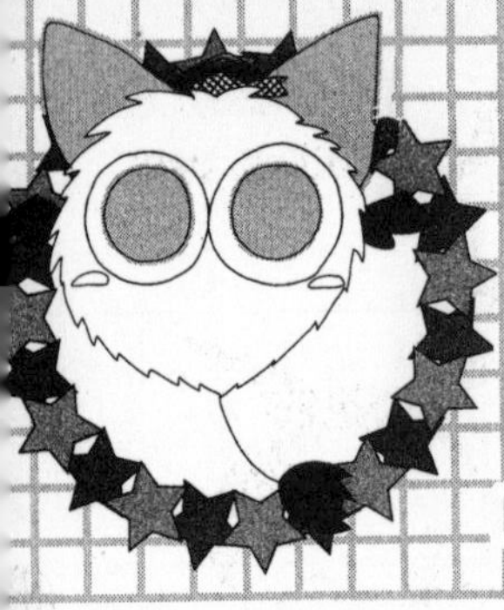

MASHA'S TOKYO MEW MEW

ENDANGERED SPECIES FILE

WHAT ARE ENDANGERED SPECIES?
ENDANGERED SPECIES ARE ANIMALS THAT ARE ON THE BRINK OF EXTINCTION. THERE ARE CURRENTLY 2,580 ENDANGERED SPECIES. THEIR NUMBERS ARE DECLINING FROM POACHING AND LOSS OF HABITAT. EVERYONE, LET'S ALL WORK TOGETHER TO SAVE ANIMALS FROM EXTINCTION!

FILE 3

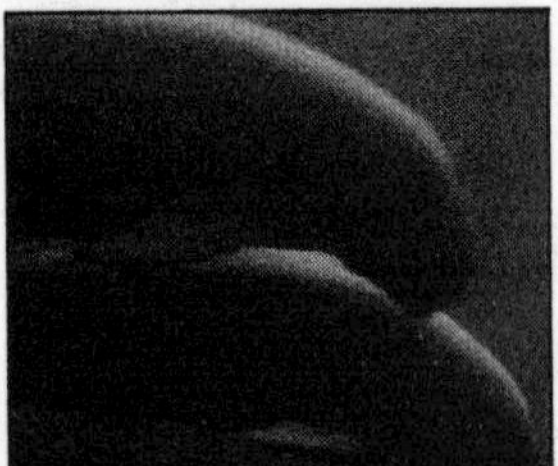

FINLESS PORPOISE NEOPHOCAENA PHOCAENOIDES

SIZE: AVERAGES 5 FEET, WEIGHS ABOUT 88 LBS.

HABITAT: ITS HABITAT SPANS FROM THE OCEANS OF JAPAN TO IRAN. KNOWN FOR ITS ADORABLE SMOOTH FACE, IT WAS NAMED A JAPANESE NATURAL MONUMENT IN 1930. UNLIKE OTHER PORPOISES, IT TRAVELS IN GROUPS INSTEAD OF LARGE PODS. IT IS HUNTED FOR ITS BLUBBER AND MEAT. FISHERMEN ALSO CATCH IT TO PREVENT IT FROM HARMING THEIR FISHING NETS. ITS NUMBERS IN THE WILD ARE STEADILY DECLINING.

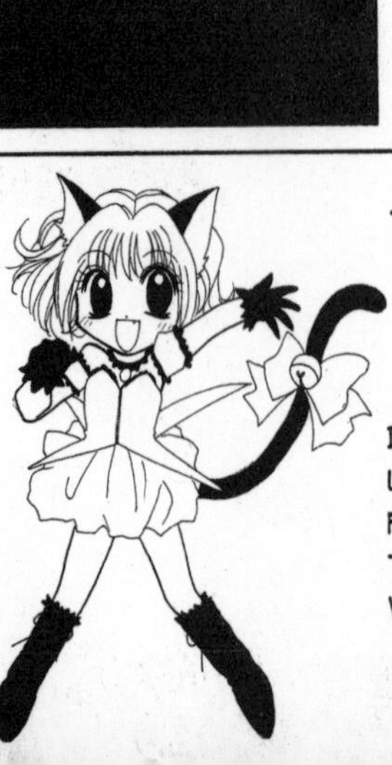

TO PREVENT THIS ATROCITY, ICHIGO AND HER FRIENDS HAVE ALL BEEN FUSED WITH THE GENETIC MATERIAL OF VARIOUS ENDANGERED SPECIES.

IRIOMOTE CAT	ICHIGO
ULTRAMARINE LORIKEET	MINT
FINLESS PORPOISE	LETTUCE

THE OTHER TWO CHARACTERS WILL BE INTRODUCED IN LATER VOLUMES.

ENJOY THE ADVENTURES OF THESE 5 SUPERHEROES!

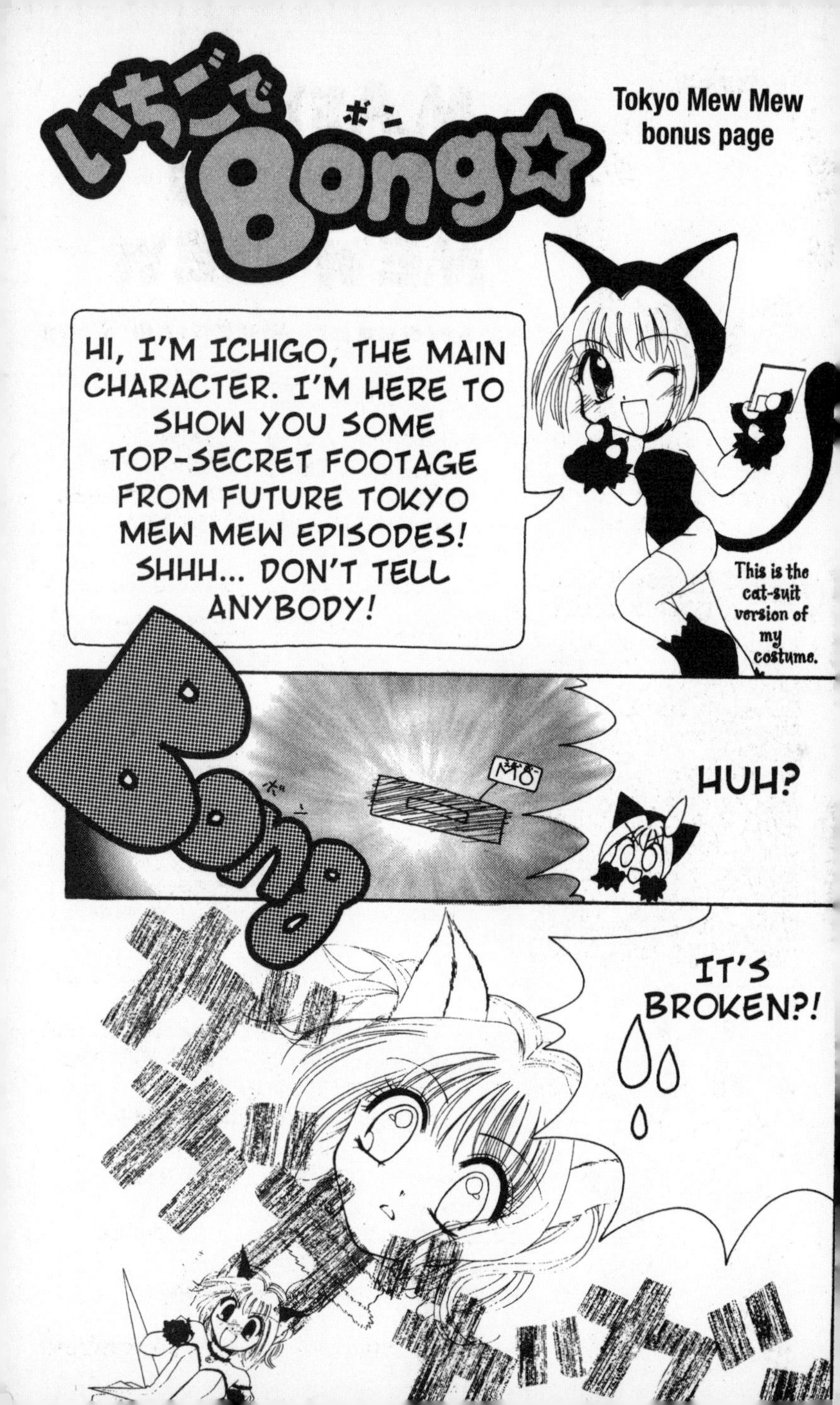

いちごでBong☆
ボン
Tokyo Mew Mew bonus page
HI, I'M ICHIGO, THE MAIN CHARACTER. I'M HERE TO SHOW YOU SOME TOP-SECRET FOOTAGE FROM FUTURE TOKYO MEW MEW EPISODES! SHHH... DON'T TELL ANYBODY!
This is the cat-suit version of my costume.
Bong
MO
HUH?
IT'S BROKEN?!

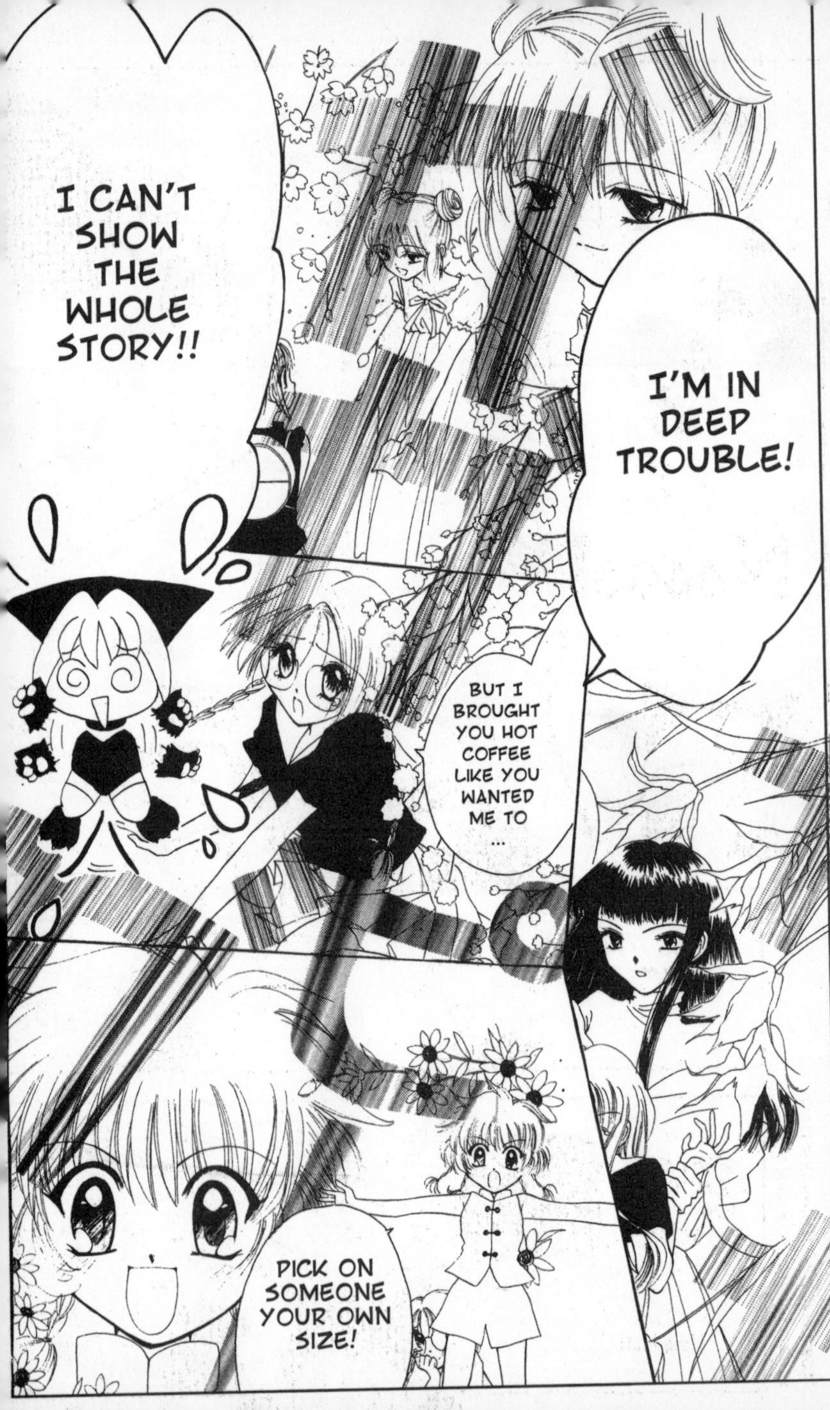
I'M IN DEEP TROUBLE!
I CAN'T SHOW THE WHOLE STORY!!
BUT I BROUGHT YOU HOT COFFEE LIKE YOU WANTED ME TO ...
PICK ON SOMEONE YOUR OWN SIZE!

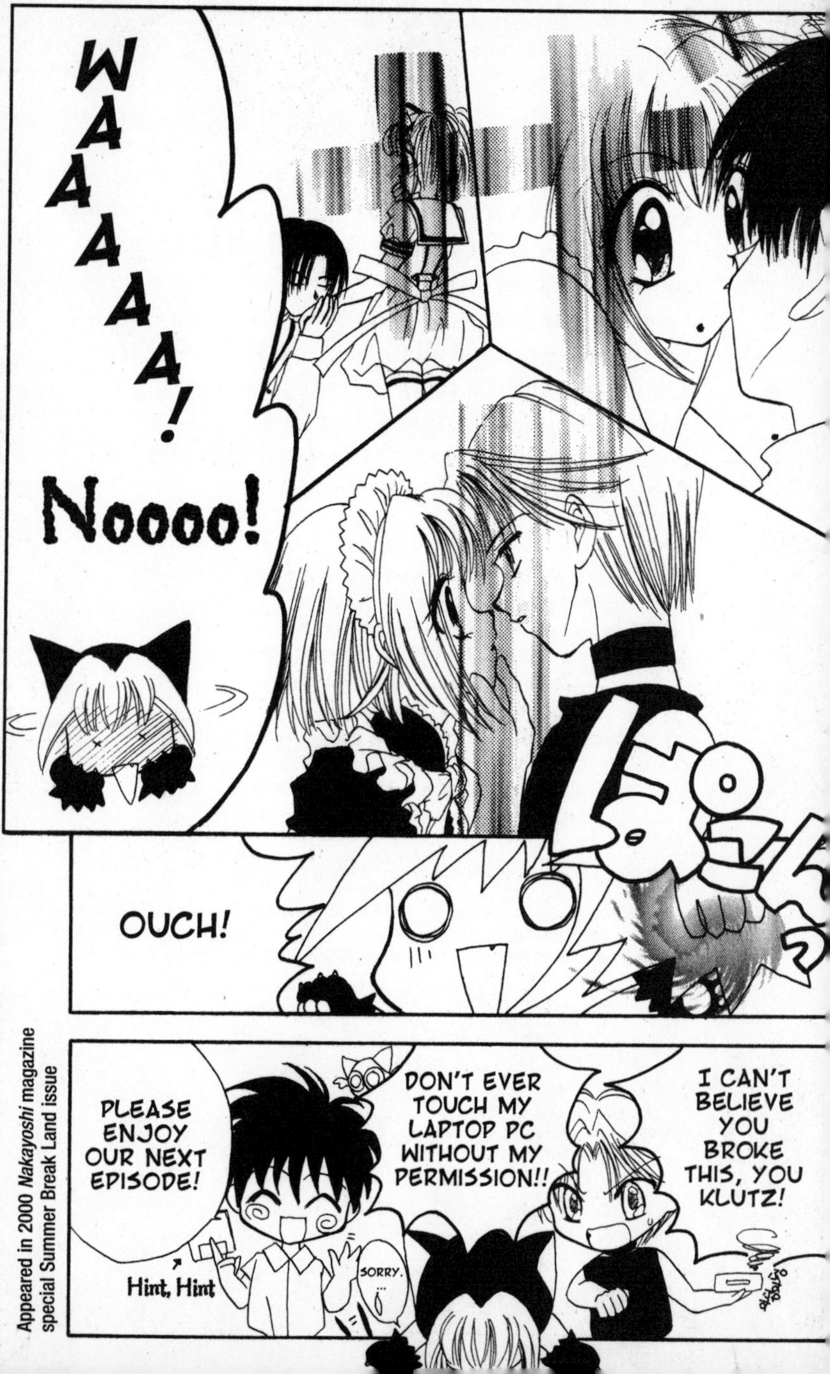
WAAAAA! Noooo!
OUCH!
I CAN'T BELIEVE YOU BROKE THIS, YOU KLUTZ!
DON'T EVER TOUCH MY LAPTOP PC WITHOUT MY PERMISSION!!
SORRY. ...
PLEASE ENJOY OUR NEXT EPISODE!
Hint, Hint

Appeared in 2000 *Nakayoshi* magazine special Summer Break Land issue

If you were suddenly injected with wildcat genes and asked to be a superhero, what would you do?

1. Just go along with it and fight the aliens—no questions asked.
2. Immediately believe this is your destiny, then dedicate your entire life to saving the planet.
3. Freak out over the situation, then spend every single waking moment worrying about all the bad things that could happen.
4. Outline the reasons that this new ability will enhance your future plans, then focus on your long-term goals.
5. Refuse to battle it out since it's so not your style, then just forget all about it and do your own thing.

If you chose...
1: You're the type of person who usually goes along with the crowd.
Learn to assert yourself and say no once in a while!
2: Make sure you have all the facts before making a decision.
Be careful not to jump into anything without thinking it through.
3: You need to lighten up, worrywart.
It's time to start thinking positive!
4: You're down-to-earth, but remember: It's okay to dream now and then.
Try not to be so practical all the time!
5: It's cool that you're so independent.
Just don't alienate the people around you.

Ichigo is type 1, Mint is 2, Lettuce is 3, Pudding* is 4, and Zakuro* is 5.

Which character matches your personality the most? Even though all these characters share the same circumstance, they are each on different paths. I believe that as long as you stay true to yourself, things will work out in the end. See you in episode 2!

*Pudding and Zakuro will be introduced in volume 2.

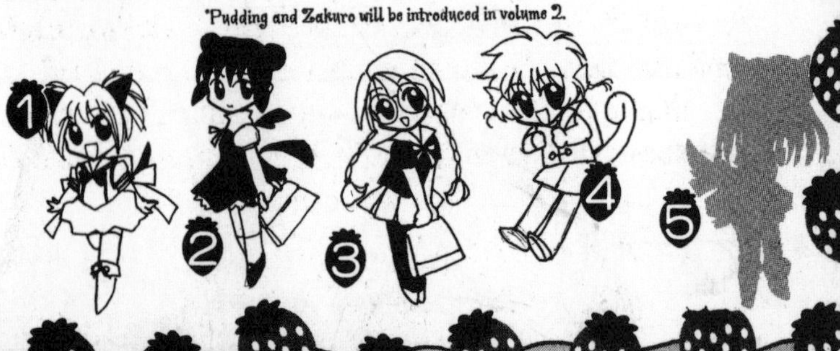
1
2
3
4
5

Before Tokyo Mew Mew was Created
by Reiko Yoshida

I first met Ms. Ikumi at a Chinese restaurant inside a metropolitan hotel. Since we were going to be eating Chinese food, she showed up in a cute Chinese dress. She is an adorable person in real life. She's also a generous type who would gladly share her dinner with you. During autograph signings, she would show up in cat ears and a tail. I thought she would be a really fun person to work with, and I became the story supervisor for this project.

Let me explain the creative process behind each "Mew Mew" volume. First, the basic plot of each volume is determined by me, along with two other editors. We turn that into a scenario (organizing stage directions with lines for each character). Then, we go over and edit our work, and once that's finalized, we present the scenario to Ms. Ikumi. At this point, she adds her own ideas into the scenario. The end result is an elegant first draft of the manuscript.

Who is this Character? Part 1

Is this a new member? The Dark Ichigo ? Ha! No, no, it's neither. This is one of the first characters I presented to the editors when a new series was being considered, so she is very special. At that time, the editors were asking me if I would be interested in a horror series. I thought that might be fun, but I always wanted a character with cat ears, even before my debut. I thought I might give that a shot and presented this character. They really liked it, and started to build a story around this character instead of doing a horror piece. After suggestions like "draw another character" and "we should have five characters like this," it ended up being a Female Superhero series. That was not my original intention. I wanted to have a more dramatic character, so I had some reservations after Ichigo was finalized as the main character. However, I don't think a dramatic character would have been appropriate for Nakayoshi magazine. It's funny to think that without this character, Tokyo Mew Mew would not exist today.

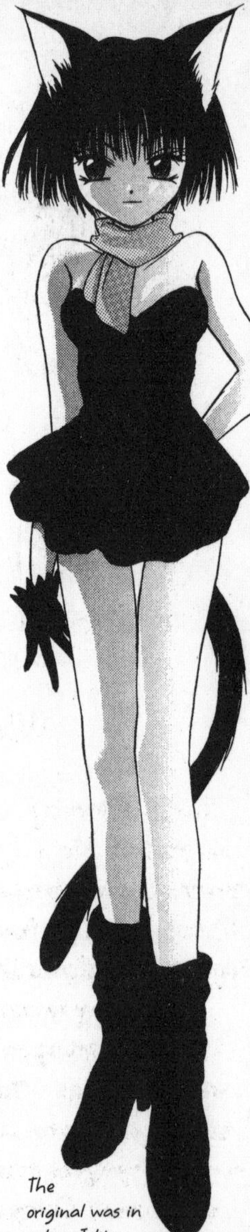

The original was in color. I like colors. Her scarf and eyes are pink, and the rest is black.

Who is this Character? Part 2

This is a drawing I came up with after the editors wanted to see more characters. Her colors are similar to Lettuce's—kind of a nice grassy green. I wanted her personality to be like Ijimi in a certain manga series. She was one of my favorite characters. This character disappeared during the design finalization of the five characters in this series. She was one of my favorites. One day, I want a mouse character!

I started working on these characters almost two years ago. At first, I wasn't even sure if this project was going to get approved, but the project was given a scenario writer and designers, and Tokyo Mew Mew became a very large project, indeed. It was featured on the cover, and its first page was in color. Every episode had a color page, and various tie-ins and marketing products were created for this series. I was really surprised. Even commercials were made for Tokyo Mew Mew!

I KNOW IT'S SUDDEN, BUT HERE IS MIA IKUMI'S PHOTO SHOOT REPORT!

I was given Ichigo's costume that was used in the commercial, and I was thrilled. But as a result, I ended up having to do a photo shoot wearing the costume.

I thought I'd write a bit about the time when I was featured in a manga newspaper...

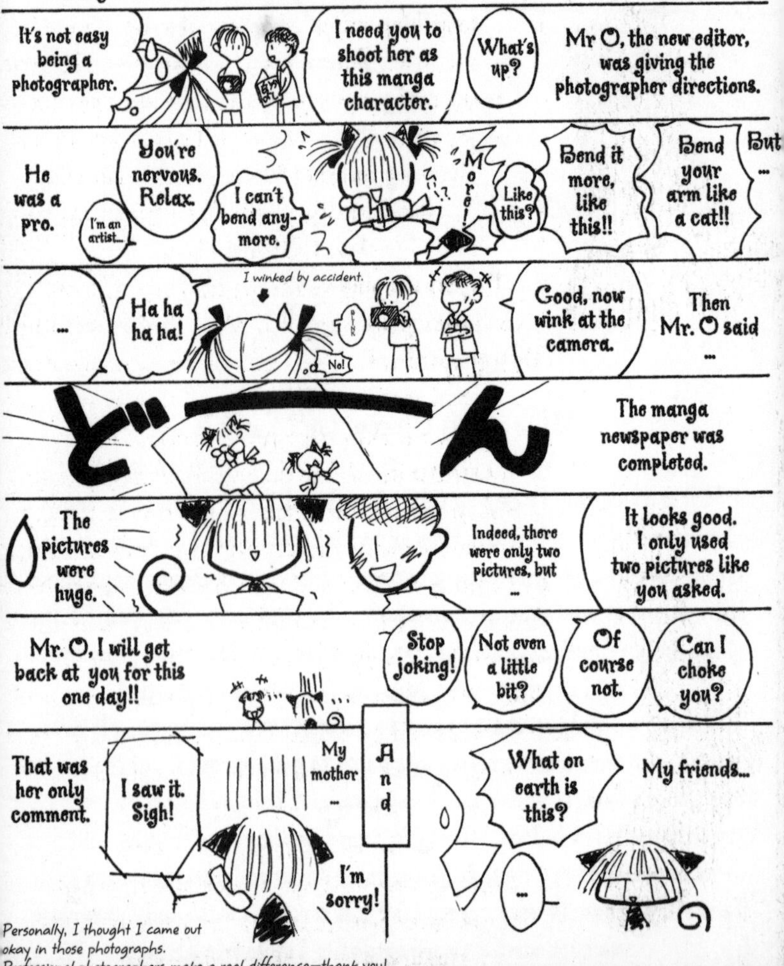

Mr O, the new editor, was giving the photographer directions.
What's up?
I need you to shoot her as this manga character.
It's not easy being a photographer.
But ...
Bend your arm like a cat!!
Bend it more, like this!!
Like this?
More!
I can't bend any-more.
You're nervous. Relax.
I'm an artist...
He was a pro.
Then Mr. O said ...
Good, now wink at the camera.
I winked by accident.
No!
Ha ha ha ha!
...
The manga newspaper was completed.
どーん
It looks good. I only used two pictures like you asked.
Indeed, there were only two pictures, but ...
The pictures were huge.
Can I choke you?
Of course not.
Not even a little bit?
Stop joking!
Mr. O, I will get back at you for this one day!!
My friends...
What on earth is this?
...
And
My mother ...
I'm sorry!
I saw it. Sigh!
That was her only comment.

Personally, I thought I came out okay in those photographs.
Professional photographers make a real difference—thank you!

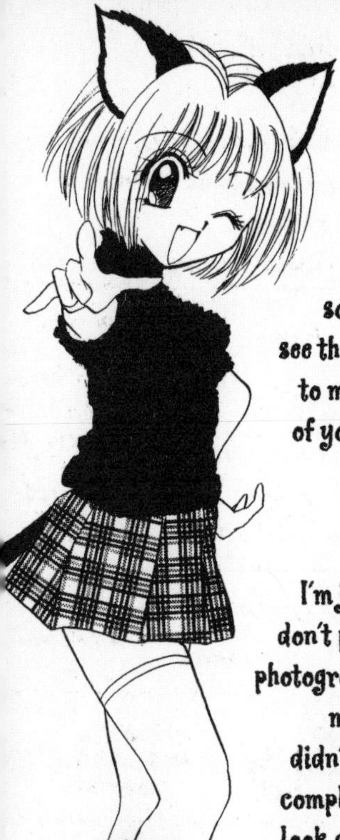
Drawing of me

I show up at a lot of events wearing my kitty ears. I'm just happy as long as you enjoy it in some way. People who saw my article in the newspaper said, "It was cool to see something different!" People who didn't see it said, "I'm glad I didn't have to see something weird." For fans who say, "I want to see that weird manga artist," please be sure to come to my autograph signings. (I hope there are many of you who feel this way!) I will be waiting for you, looking just like the character to the left. Incidentally, I looked like this at my last signing in Nara.

I'm just warning you to not take any pictures. I don't photograph very well at all. In fact, I've never photographed well. People occasionally write me fan mail that says, "The picture I took of you didn't come out quite right." I think a lot of those complaints are due to the fact that I simply do not look good in photos. Those photos may be good at keeping evil spirits away, though—in the same way gargoyles are. This year, I got tons of pictures taken with my cat ears. I don't get my picture taken in my personal life. (In the last few years, I'm in maybe ten photos.) It's just strange to think people all over Japan have my picture. I love doing signings, though. I get to meet my fans, and they serve yummy food at the signings, too. Yay!

I would like to do one again soon.

Anyway, thank you for coming to my signings. See you later! Special thanks to my friend, Ruka Hoshino, who made my kitty ears!

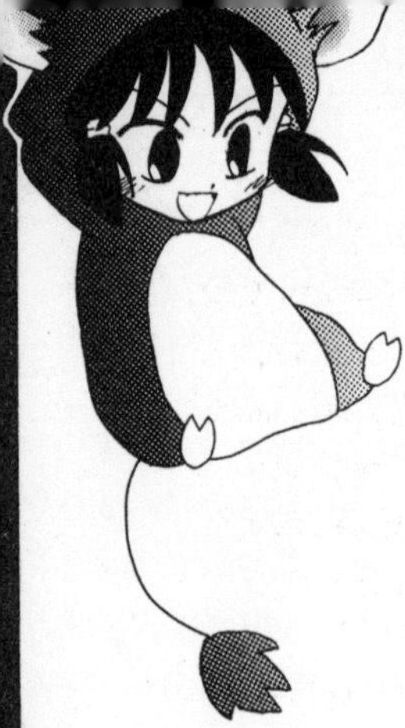

Last but not least, I'd like to thank everyone who was involved in this project, everyone who read this work,
and everyone who gave me support.
Thank you very,
very much.
To my favorite person: I am alive today because of you. Really.

Mia Ikumi

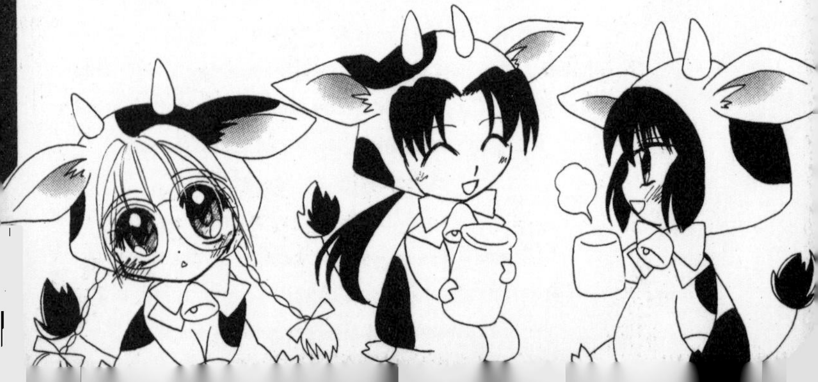

Afterward

I baked a chocolate cake earlier today. After I started this project, I didn't have a lot of free time, so I hadn't baked in a long time. This is the first time in a few years since I've baked anything. Maybe it's because it's been so long, but I was really happy to be baking again. I thought I wouldn't have the opportunity to bake when I moved out on my own, so I got rid of my baking stuff. However, every time I went shopping, I couldn't help but look at pastry-making tools. A long time ago, I remember baking over ten Christmas cakes and forcing them on my friends. I think my passion for baking pastries has come back full force. When I first started as a manga artist, I didn't have time to do much else. However, as I've become used to the work, I find myself having the time for other things. That's a good thing. I like people to enjoy my pastries and artwork. I want people to have fun reading my manga. I'm just really happy to be able to be in a field where I can bring enjoyment into other people's lives.

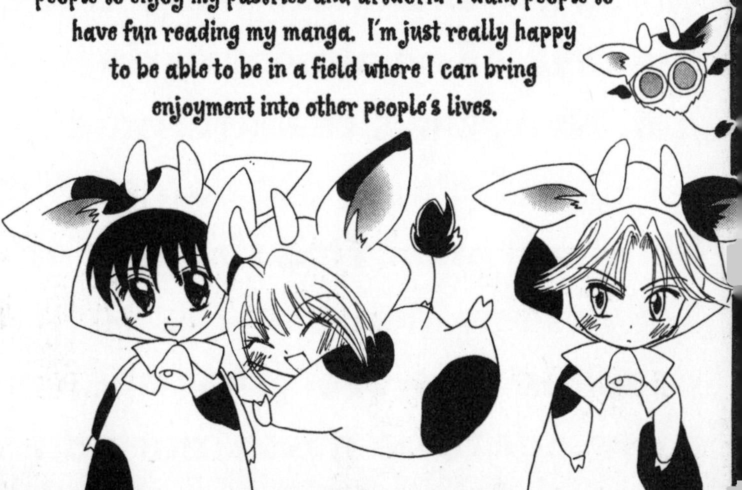

COMING SOON...

VOLUME TWO

Ichigo was just another normal seventh grader—until she was involved in an odd incident in which her DNA was merged with the DNA of an almost extinct wild-cat. Now, she's transformed into a crime-fighting cat named Mew Mew and must find the rest of the Tokyo Mew Mew crew as soon as possible. However, that mission turns out to be much more difficult than she ever imagined!

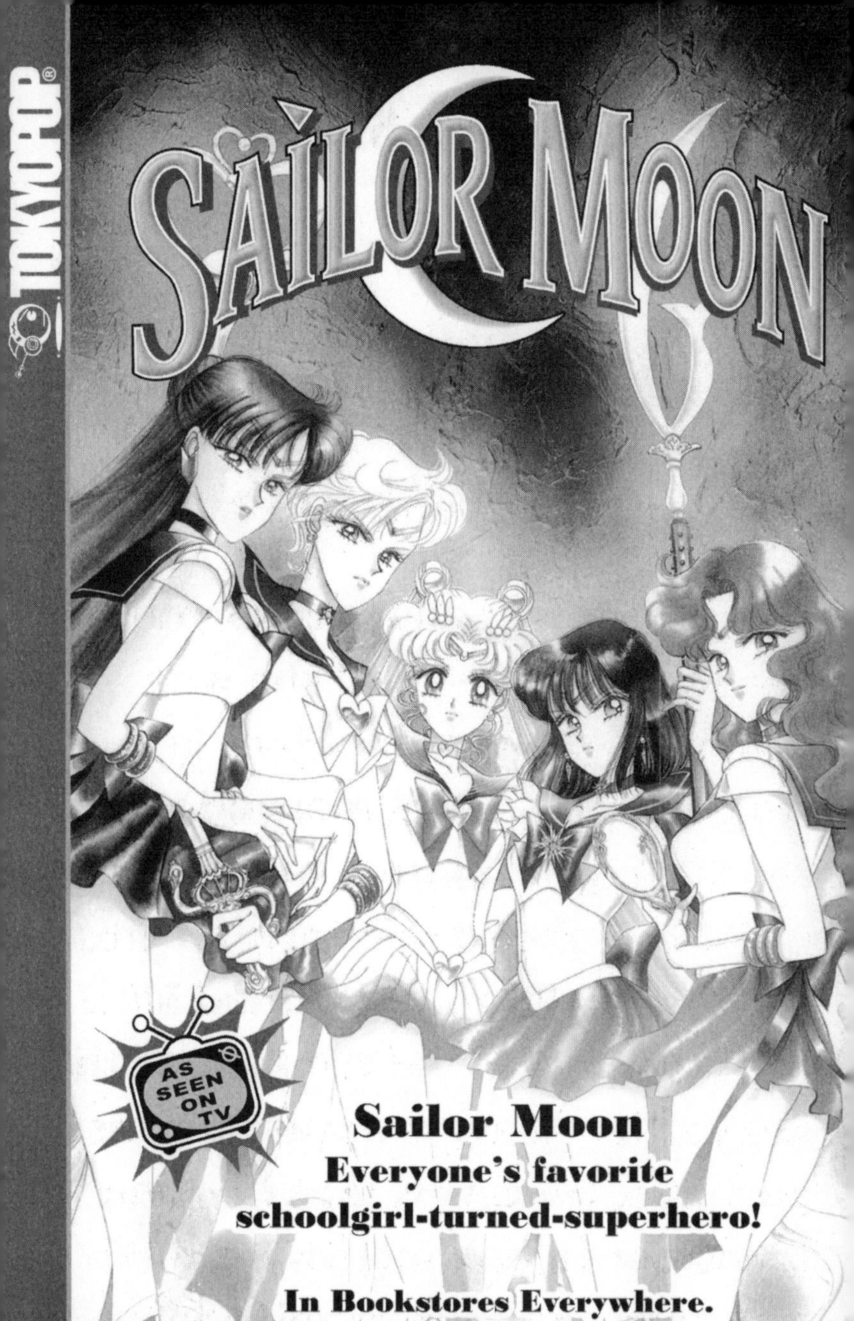
TOKYOPOP®
SAILOR MOON
AS SEEN ON TV
Sailor Moon
Everyone's favorite
schoolgirl-turned-superhero!
In Bookstores Everywhere.

Corrector Yui
TOKYOPOP®
It's 2020: Computers rule!
Evil viruses infect.
Yui's superhero daydreams have suddenly come true.
Wait! Don't I get a cute sidekick?
A techno-fantasy series filled with fun, light-hearted action from TOKYOPOP®.
Corrector Yui Manga Available NOW

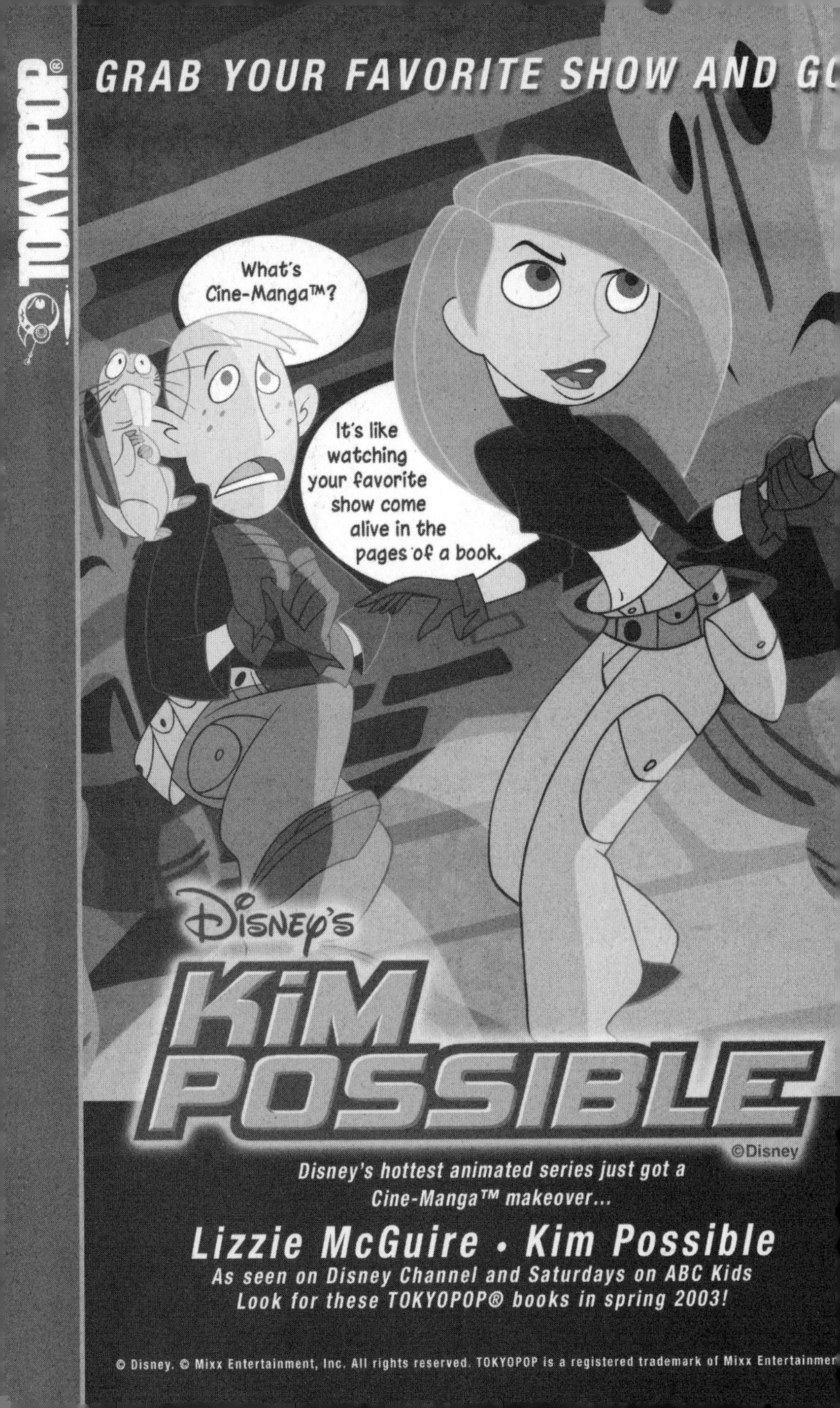
TOKYOPOP
GRAB YOUR FAVORITE SHOW AND GO
What's Cine-Manga™?
It's like watching your favorite show come alive in the pages of a book.
Disney's
Kim Possible
©Disney
Disney's hottest animated series just got a Cine-Manga™ makeover...
Lizzie McGuire • Kim Possible
As seen on Disney Channel and Saturdays on ABC Kids
Look for these TOKYOPOP® books in spring 2003!
© Disney. © Mixx Entertainment, Inc. All rights reserved. TOKYOPOP is a registered trademark of Mixx Entertainmer

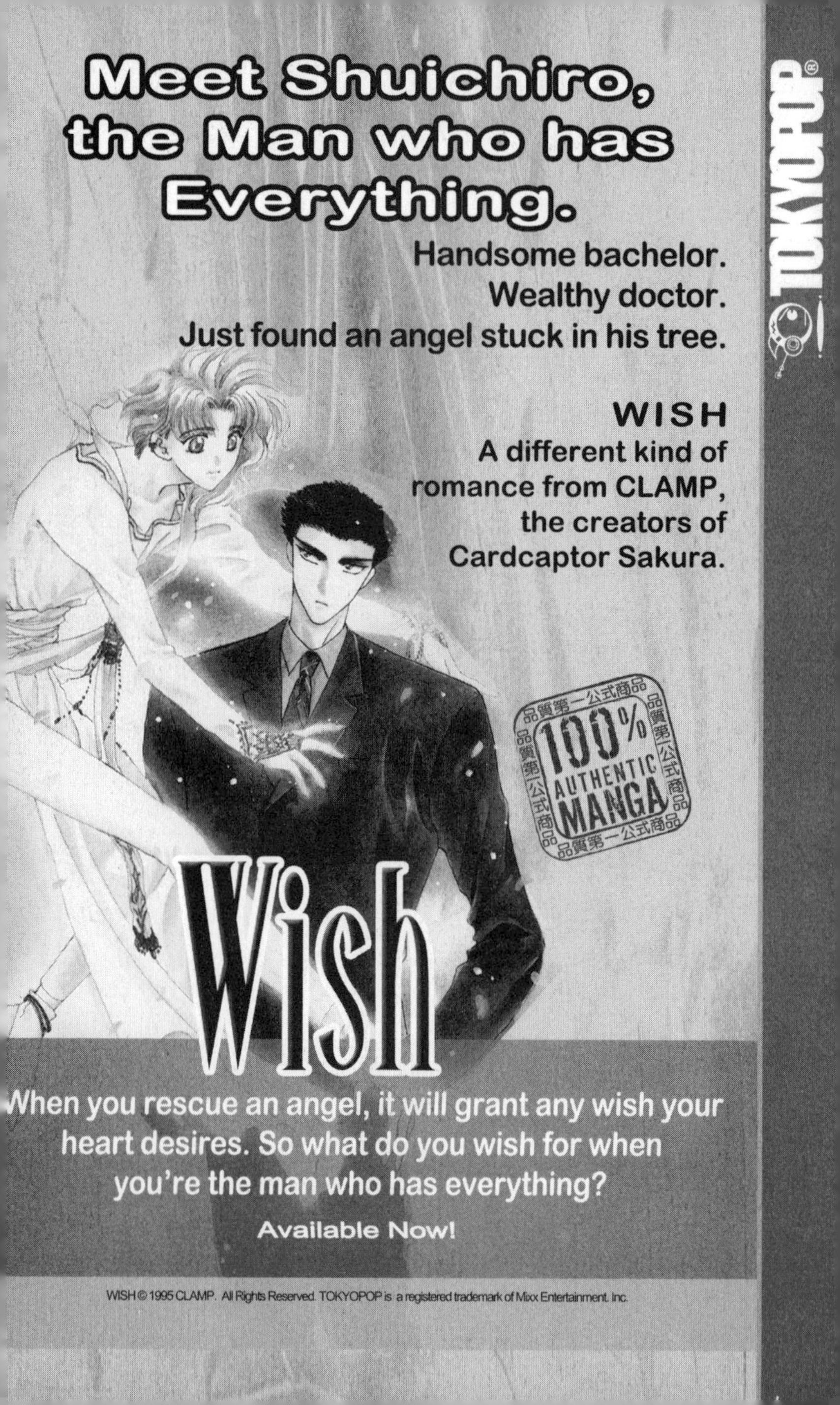
Meet Shuichiro, the Man who has Everything.
Handsome bachelor.
Wealthy doctor.
Just found an angel stuck in his tree.
WISH
A different kind of romance from CLAMP, the creators of Cardcaptor Sakura.
品質第一公式商品
100% AUTHENTIC MANGA
Wish
When you rescue an angel, it will grant any wish your heart desires. So what do you wish for when you're the man who has everything?
Available Now!
WISH © 1995 CLAMP. All Rights Reserved. TOKYOPOP is a registered trademark of Mixx Entertainment, Inc.
TOKYOPOP®

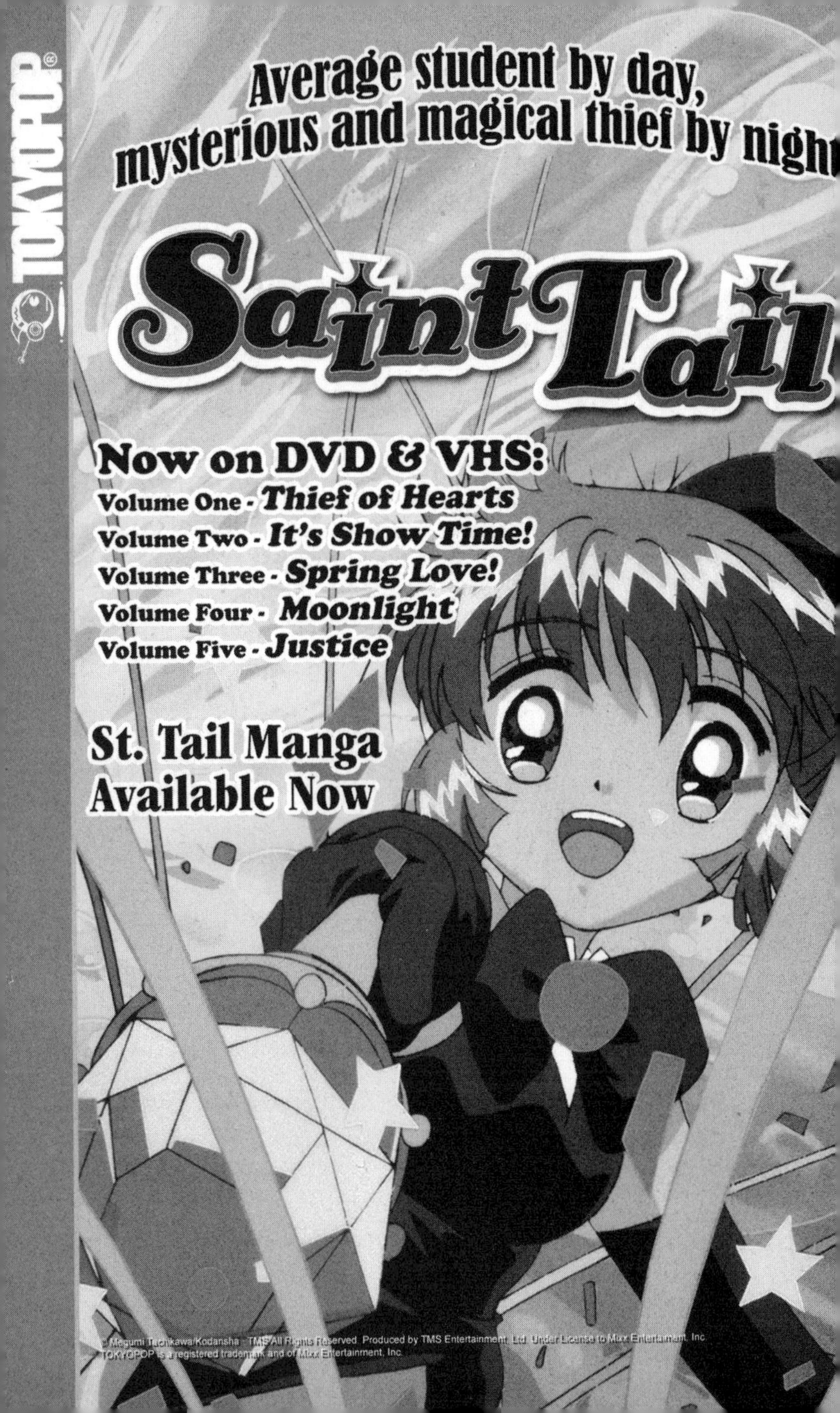
TOKYOPOP
Average student by day, mysterious and magical thief by night
Saint Tail
Now on DVD & VHS:
Volume One - Thief of Hearts
Volume Two - It's Show Time!
Volume Three - Spring Love!
Volume Four - Moonlight
Volume Five - Justice
St. Tail Manga Available Now
© Megumi Tachikawa/Kodansha · TMS All Rights Reserved. Produced by TMS Entertainment, Ltd. Under License to Mixx Entertainment, Inc.
TOKYOPOP is a registered trademark and of Mixx Entertainment, Inc.

STOP!

This is the back of the book.
You wouldn't want to spoil a great ending!

This book is printed "manga-style," in the authentic Japanese right-to-left format. Since none of the artwork has been flipped or altered, readers get to experience the story just as the creator intended. You've been asking for it, so TOKYOPOP® delivered: authentic, hot-off-the-press, and far more fun!

DIRECTIONS

If this is your first time reading manga-style, here's a quick guide to help you understand how it works.

It's easy... just start in the top right panel and follow the numbers. Have fun, and look for more 100% authentic manga from TOKYOPOP®!

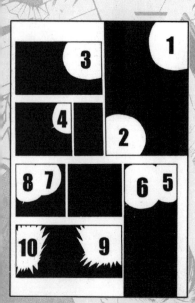